Human Resource Strategy

A BEHAVIORAL PERSPECTIVE FOR THE GENERAL MANAGER

George F. Dreher
Indiana University

Thomas W. Dougherty
University of Missouri

McGraw-Hill Irwin

Boston   Burr Ridge, IL   Dubuque, IA   Madison, WI   New York
San Francisco   St. Louis   Bangkok   Bogotá   Caracas   Kuala Lumpur
Lisbon   London   Madrid   Mexico City   Milan   Montreal   New Delhi
Santiago   Seoul   Singapore   Sydney   Taipei   Toronto

McGraw-Hill Higher Education ✎

A Division of The McGraw-Hill Companies

HUMAN RESOURCE STRATEGY

A Behavioral Perspective for the General Manager

Published by McGraw-Hill/Irwin, an imprint of The McGraw-Hill Companies, Inc. 1221 Avenue of the Americas, New York, NY 10020. Copyright © 2002, by The McGraw-Hill Companies, Inc. All rights reserved. No part of this publication may be reproduced or distributed in any form or by any means, or stored in a database or retrieval system, without the prior written consent of The McGraw-Hill Companies, Inc., including, but not limited to, in any network or other electronic storage or transmission, or broadcast for distance learning.

Some ancillaries, including electronic and print components, may not be available to customers outside the United States.

This book is printed on acid-free paper.

3 4 5 6 7 8 9 0 DOC/DOC 0 9 8 7 6 5

ISBN: 0256211892

Publisher: *John Biernat*
Sponsoring editor: *John Weimeister*
Senior developmental editor: *Laura Hurst Spell*
Marketing manager: *Ellen Cleary*
Project manager: *Karen J. Nelson*
Production supervisor: *Susanne Riedell*
Designer: *Pam Verros*
Cover image: © *Wonderfile / Digital Vision*
Supplement coordinator: *Betty Hadala*
New media: *Barb Block*
Compositor: *GAC / Indianapolis*
Typeface: *10 / 12 New Century Schoolbook*
Printer: *R. R. Donnelley & Sons Company*

Library of Congress Cataloging-in-Publication Data

Dreher, George F.
 Human resource strategy: a behavioral perspective for the general
manager / George F. Dreher, Thomas W. Dougherty.
  p. cm.
 Includes index.
 ISBN 0-256-21189-2
 1. Personnel management. I. Dougherty, Thomas W. II. Title

HF5549+
658.3—dc21

00-066438

www.mhhe.com

To our mothers
Retha O'Brien Dougherty
and
Shirlie Dreher

Preface

This book presents the knowledge appropriate for a first course in human resource management (HRM) for students of general management—individuals who are or will be assessing, designing/purchasing, delivering, and evaluating management systems for their own organizations or the business units of the companies for which they work. Management systems are the interrelated procedures, practices, and processes needed to accomplish specified goals and objectives in a firm.

Virtually all businesses, at one level or another, are comprised of subsystems that are intended to (a) improve and develop products and services, (b) procure materials, (c) produce and deliver products and services, and (d) market and sell products and services. In addition to these main business functions, support systems exist to provide control and to supply the human and financial assets needed to bring a business organization to life. Human resource management, finance, budgeting, accounting, engineering, and public relations systems must be integrated into the fabric of the business.

Effective general managers must work across, and strive to continuously improve, business subsystems. This book is based on the proposition that all aspiring general managers will benefit by studying and being able to critically evaluate all business subsystems, including systems that relate to the effective utilization of people. This particular combination of knowledge and skills is just as central to the effectiveness of business leaders and managers as knowledge-skill sets that relate to managing financial assets, technology, production processes, or even the strategic position of the firm.

This book is organized around the concept of an integrated HRM system, comprised of multiple managerial activities, designed to influence a set of critical employee behaviors. It differs from other HRM texts, which focus on the traditional human resource (HR) functions. That is, detailed and method-oriented chapters about HR planning, compensation and reward practices, staffing procedures, and training and development activities are not presented in the typical fashion. Instead, we use some basic theories and models that help managers explain and predict key employee behaviors to provide insights into how to translate theory into practice via the establishment of integrated HR systems. In fact, the illustrations comprising Part IV of the book, "Designing Human Resource Systems for Specific Business Situations," are all organized using a common format. Each addresses a unique set of managerial objectives for a particular type of company and the associated employee roles and behaviors that will be needed to meet these objectives. Then we develop an HR system that simultaneously considers how recruitment, selection, reward practices, and developmental activities all play a role in enabling a manager to achieve desired business results. Thus, the essence of the book is at the level of the integrated HR system. While we do present four chapters in Part II that reflect a functional orientation, these chapters are not intended to develop these topics in the traditional way. As noted below, they are at the level of "what the general manager needs to know."

We have already previewed Part IV of the book. Next we summarize each of the four parts of the text.

PART I: UNDERSTANDING BEHAVIOR IN ORGANIZATIONS: BASIC THEORETICAL ORIENTATIONS

Many of you have already completed courses in applied psychology, industrial/organizational psychology, or organizational behavior. The two chapters comprising Part I review some key concepts that underpin the understanding of behavior in work settings. Chapter 1 develops the argument that one important factor that separates high-performing companies from their more mediocre counterparts is the quality of their HR systems. The chapter outlines the roles general managers must play to improve HR system quality and also sets the stage for the rest of the book by explaining the framework used in subsequent chapters.

Chapter 2 reviews the processes that explain work behaviors. We believe that highly effective general managers are above average in their ability to explain and predict the behaviors of others. This competency is useful in a variety of ways. Effective general managers need to be able to make accurate predictions about the behaviors of subordinates, peers, and superiors. They also need to be able to predict how changes in HR system components will affect and influence the behaviors of organization members. A clear understanding of the determinants of behavior will enhance the accuracy of predictions. There is no appropriate way to separate the study of organizational behavior from the general manager's role in designing and evaluating a company's HRM practices. Thus, Chapter 2 reviews what we see as essential concepts from the discipline of organizational behavior—concepts that make clear how the attributes of work settings and the attributes of people interact to explain why people behave as they do when confronted with the demands of the workplace. Knowledge of these concepts will help managers make informed decisions about the design, delivery, and evaluation of HR systems.

PART II: HUMAN RESOURCE SYSTEMS: WHAT THE GENERAL MANAGER SHOULD KNOW

The five chapters that comprise Part II build on the organizational behavior theme established in Part I. First, the ways firms can differ with respect to managing people are explored. What are the possibilities? What choices, at the level of HRM issues, do general managers have? By selecting the options that have the best chance of influencing employee behavior in the desired direction, general managers have a powerful point of leadership leverage. Chapter 3 defines the possibilities and how choices about HR system characteristics relate to employee behavior.

As previously noted, the next four chapters in this section review what the general manager needs to know about the functional areas of HR. We were reluctant to move down the path of a functional treatment of the field of HR, but we believe that by focusing on the essence of what the general manager should know about these functional areas we have stayed true to the organizing principle of the book. These chapters should enrich the basic treatment of the possibilities, as presented in Chapter 3, and should help people interested in general management better understand the issues and choices confronting the HR specialist. To better prepare general managers to work with and evaluate the products and services provided by HR-oriented professionals, we believe this level of functional treatment is appropriate and needed.

PART III: ALIGNING HUMAN RESOURCE SYSTEMS WITH BUSINESS STRATEGY

Now that we have covered the basic components of an HR system, it is time to apply all of this information. Chapter 8 discusses the emerging field of strategic HRM and the relationships between people-management practices and firm performance. It addresses an important question: How should managers approach the issue of aligning business and HR strategy? We believe the framework presented in Chapter 1 represents the approach one needs to take, but we want to make the reader aware of existing controversies and roadblocks to achieving this goal. Chapter 8 also presents a general treatment of the cost-benefit analysis as applied to HRM. Here we introduce you to a way to estimate the financial return associated with investments in HR system improvements. Next, Chapter 9 expands on the importance of systems thinking by developing the argument that the difficulty of copying a competitor's full range of HR practices makes HR system design a source of sustained competitive advantage.

Just as effective HR systems must be internally congruent and aligned with business objectives, effective HR systems must be very sensitive to the changing nature of the firm's labor markets and legal environments. Chapter 10 describes the domestic and international labor markets that must be understood when making decisions about managing human resources. The objective is to make it clear that great variability exists both within and outside of a company's home region and country. This variability can have a profound impact on selecting preferred HRM options. Chapter 11 plays a corresponding role in relation to a firm's legal environment.

PART IV: DESIGNING HUMAN RESOURCE SYSTEMS FOR SPECIFIC BUSINESS SITUATIONS

Once a manager has considered the firm's business strategy, the corresponding behaviors required to bring the strategy to life, and existing legal and labor market opportunities and constraints, the time is right for making HRM decisions. In this part of the book we describe five unique business settings and then we prescribe a set of interrelated HRM practices that "fit" each setting. The settings are developed by considering actual business situations and then making realistic adjustments (e.g., introducing market factors that allow for a unique or interesting challenge); thus we think of these illustrations as company composites. The various business settings, which provide a wide range of examples, are (*a*) the consideration of customer service representatives in a company that distributes audio CDs directly to customers, (*b*) a focus on a manufacturing plant that builds diesel truck engines, (*c*) a review of the sales force of a financial services firm, (*d*) the project-development teams responsible for writing prime-time television programs, and (*e*) the business environment surrounding marketing managers in Asia. These settings were selected to illustrate a full range of HR systems. The selected business settings call for very different HRM prescriptions. Indeed, we believe that they illustrate very nicely a central premise of this book: **the proper mix of HRM practices depends on how work processes are organized and the unique environmental circumstances surrounding a given firm.** These illustrations provide five rounds of analysis. Each models a process we believe you should follow when making judgments about the quality of existing HR systems or proposed improvements that come from internal HR staff professionals or the growing legions of HR change-management consultants.

OBJECTIVES

After completing this book, you should be better able to describe the domain of HRM practices available to contemporary organizations; analyze business situations and choose HRM options that fit your organizations' business goals, culture, and environmental circumstances; recognize when a set of

HRM practices is likely to affect key classes of employee behaviors in dysfunctional ways; evaluate the quality of HRM practices and services from a cost-benefit and legal perspective; and intelligently interact with, use, and assist HR staff specialists and HR consultants who attempt to support your business objectives. This is all designed to make you a better and more informed consumer of the services provided by staff professionals in your current or future companies and by the consulting firms working in the area of change management and HRM. As you become a more informed consumer you also will become a manager who has the capability to introduce the changes needed to continuously improve the management systems that influence behavior at work. We believe that your success as a manager and business leader in contemporary organizations will largely be a function of your ability to compete for, retain, and properly manage talented employees.

ACKNOWLEDGMENTS

We would like to thank the following individuals, who provided valuable feedback regarding the manuscript for the book: Herschel N. Chait, Indiana State University; Lucretia Coleman, Georgia College and State University; Teresa Joyce Covin, Kennesaw State University; Ann Cowden, California State University, Sacramento; Angelo DeNisi, Texas A&M University; Satish P. Deshpande, Western Michigan University; Cynthia V. Fukami, University of Denver; Bob Gatewood, University of Georgia; John Kohl, University of Nevada, Las Vegas; Thomas Lee, University of Washington; Nicholas Mathys, DePaul University; Gordon A. Morse, George Mason University; Brian Murray, University of New Hampshire; Peter Richardson, Southwest Missouri State University; M. Susan Taylor, University of Maryland; Stuart Youngblood, Texas Christian University.

Contents

PART III
Aligning Human Resource Systems
with Business Strategy   163

Part I

Understanding Behavior in Organizations

BASIC THEORETICAL ORIENTATIONS

1

The Effective Management of People

AN INTRODUCTION AND POINT OF VIEW

General managers must be able to recognize and implement superior human resource management (HRM) systems. In this chapter you will

- See why effective HRM systems are now more important than ever before.
- Understand how human resource systems provide a unique source of competitive advantage.
- Learn how a proper mix of HRM practices for a particular job class depends on the way that work processes are organized as well as the firm's unique environmental circumstances.
- See why HRM systems should be targeted at particular employee behaviors such as task performance or decisions to accept job offers.
- Become acquainted with how managers' selection of an integrated set of HRM practices can follow a systematic process.
- Understand why implementing integrated human resource systems places general managers in the role of "change agent."

Your success as a manager and business leader will largely depend on your ability to improve business results through people. The most well thought-out business strategy will be executed effectively only when people are committed to achieving your organization's goals and when they possess the right set of skills demanded by the ever-changing marketplace. General managers are now charged with ensuring that their organizations continuously improve business results. Under constant pressure to improve results and stay competitive, contemporary companies must seek ways to become more efficient, productive, flexible, and innovative. This often means creating lean organizational structures that ask fewer and fewer people to do more and more. Leaner organizational structures, coupled with tight labor markets in many key occupational specialties, means that each employee carries more responsibility than in the past and is therefore of greater value to the employing organization.[1] Thus, designing and implementing superior human resource management (HRM) systems is now more important than ever before.

This first section of the chapter summarizes the ideas presented by four leading management authors who provide compelling arguments about the importance of HRM to firm performance and business competitiveness. This summary is followed by a discussion of how theorists develop their prescriptions and insights and the research process that underpins sound management theory. The chapter then presents our approach to reviewing HRM systems and making judgments about system quality. We also argue that you not only must be able to recognize opportunities to improve HRM systems; you must be able to orchestrate needed change. You must develop the change management skills that the best management consultants bring to their complex assignments. Thus, the chapter concludes with a review of what you must do to meet the need for speedy and sustained change.

HUMAN RESOURCE SYSTEMS AND FIRM PERFORMANCE

As you are undoubtedly aware, there currently exists a large and profitable industry comprised of high-powered consulting firms, management gurus, business school professors, and an assortment of motivational speakers—an industry providing prescriptions about how to rescue and renovate contemporary companies. Known as the **management theory industry** (MTI),[2] it has had a profound effect on businesses and on the people who either have lost their jobs during organizational restructuring and downsizing or had their jobs irrevocably altered. One problem you will constantly encounter in general managerial roles is that the MTI does not provide prescriptions of equal quality. You must be able to separate the charlatans from the management theorists who base their ideas on sound behavioral science research. You must become an informed consumer of the management literature. We open the chapter with a review of three ideas about organizational performance—ideas from four highly regarded organizational scholars.

Organizational Capability

The traditional way to think about gaining competitive advantage has been to focus on a company's financial, strategic, and technological capabilities.[3] Dave Ulrich and Dale Lake argue, however, that for contemporary businesses these traditional means of gaining competitive advantage must "be supplemented by **organizational capability**—the firm's ability to manage people to gain competitive advantage." In addition to competing merely on price through financial capability, or product quality and innovation, high-performing companies engage in an explicit competition for the most capable employees. This competition goes beyond simply hiring the best people. Organizational capability relates to hiring and retaining competent employees and "developing those competencies through effective human resource practices."[4]

As many organizational scholars now point out, it is organizational capability (because of the multiple factors that must come together in an integrated way), not financial capability or technological sophistication, that is most difficult for competitors to replicate. As will be developed in much more detail in Chapter 8, for a resource to provide a source of sustained competitive advantage to a firm, four conditions must hold. One of these conditions is that the resource be **inimitable**. Because high-quality human resource (HR) systems work as a set of highly integrated practices, it is very difficult for competitors to copy them.

Organizing for Success

Top-performing companies pay a great deal of attention to a number of common motivational factors, or needs. Robert Waterman—who wrote the landmark book *In Search of Excellence* with Tom Peters—argues that top-performing companies provide employees with

- Something to believe in.
- A feeling of control.
- Job challenge.
- The opportunity to engage in lifelong learning.
- Recognition for achievements.

According to Waterman, "what makes the best firms the best cannot be attributed to such things as technology, a bright idea, a masterly strategy, the use of a tool, or the lavish following of guidelines laid out in a book like *In Search of Excellence*. . . . [The best firms] are better organized to meet the needs of their *people*, so that they attract better people than their competitors do and their people are more greatly motivated to do a superior job, whatever it is they do."[5] Obviously, the important concept of motivation underpins many of Waterman's observations. As we will see, putting together a management system that simultaneously meets this set of needs is complex and difficult to replicate.

Competitive Advantage through the Effective Management of People

A third major contribution, offered by Jeffrey Pfeffer, holds that what distinguishes the most successful firms in our economy from all the others "is that for their sustained advantage, they rely not on technology, patents, or strategic position, but on how they manage their workforce."[6] Suppose, asks Pfeffer, that in 1972 you had been asked to pick the five companies that would provide the greatest return to stockholders over the 20-year period ending in 1992. Most informed readers would have likely picked established companies in industries with strong barriers to entry, low supplier and buyer bargaining power, and little threat of product or service substitutability. Within these industries, the conventional wisdom also would have been to select firms with the largest market shares and the associated cost benefits of economies of scale. As Pfeffer points out, however, the top five firms for this 20-year period consistently failed to meet the test of conventional wisdom. They were, in reverse order of return to shareholders, Plenum Publishing, Circuit City, Tyson Foods, Wal-Mart, and Southwest Airlines. These companies were in industries characterized by competition and economic loss, few barriers to entry, little in the way of proprietary knowledge or technology, and a high potential for product and service substitutability. Also, in 1972, none of these firms enjoyed the status of market-share leader.

Pfeffer enumerates 13 management practices that seem to distinguish these and other high-achieving firms from their lower-performing counterparts. We will describe only seven of these principles. These seven are particularly interesting because they can be implemented in ways that make them fit the unique business environments companies must face. Thus, they support the idea that sound HRM practices can be central to firm performance and also are compatible with the general premise of this book: The proper mix of HRM practices depends on how work processes are organized and on the unique environmental circumstances surrounding a given firm. Because we will refer again to some of Pfeffer's management pratices, we occasionally go beyond simple description. We, at time, comment on how a practice might be considered within the context of this book.

Selectivity in Recruiting

Hiring the right people means more than just securing employees who possess the knowledge, skills, and abilities required to perform a particular job; these people must also be able to acquire new knowledge and skills as jobs and environments change. In addition, employees must find that the work is satisfying and that the overall organizational climate and reward structure meets their needs. While Pfeffer simply argues that top-performing companies devote considerable resources and energy to creating high-quality selection systems,[7] we believe that the actual properties of the selection systems must vary as circumstances change. Top-performing companies have, in fact, established a particular core competency: They are better than their competitors at recruiting and retaining top talent. This core competency is particularly important when labor-market shortages develop and result in a "war for talent."[8]

Incentive Pay

If employees are expected to behave in extraordinary ways and add value to the firm, sharing that gain with employees meets most definitions of workplace justice and fairness. Some form of performance-contingent pay is required if employees are expected to be persistent in their efforts to add value to the firm.[9] If employees believe that their contributions are instrumental in enhancing firm performance and increasing profitability, they will want to share in the benefits.

This concept, however, does not tell us very much about the form of performance-contingent pay that will work in any given situation. Whether or not the payoff rule is at the individual, group, or organizational level is a question we return to in subsequent chapters of this book. There will be times when it is appropriate to share overall company profits with all employees, and there will be times when the payoff rule should be at the level of individual-employee contribution. We believe the key is to link rewards to the particular behaviors required of employees and to make sure that all relevant behaviors—for example, dependability, quality and quantity of output, the generation of new ideas about improving work processes, or cooperation—are encouraged and supported.

Employee Ownership

Employees can partake in the ownership of their company by holding shares of the company's stock. By making employees shareholders, the company reduces the natural conflict between capital and labor. What better way to align the interests of shareholders and employees than to turn employees into shareholders? This puts the performance-pay contingency at the organizational level. As will be developed in later chapters, we see this as one of many possible ways to link pay to performance.

Training and Skill Development

High-performing firms display a greater commitment to training and skill development than their lower-performing counterparts.[10] This practice, a core HRM activity, is related to other ideas about the need for continuous improvement and development over time. We note, however, that knowledge and skill acquisition will not lead to improved firm performance unless employees are allowed and encouraged to use job-related knowledge and skills when performing their jobs. Thus, firms must take care to select people with the ability and willingness to learn and develop, and they must establish reward practices that encourage employees to participate in training activities. However, in our view, the actual form and type of training will vary according to the firm's business environment.

Cross-Utilization and Cross-Training

Another take on the training and development orientation is driven by the need to be flexible and able to utilize employees even during times of production slowdowns. When people are able to perform multiple jobs, or are "multiskilled," they represent a reserve of talent and are more likely to appreciate how their work and output levels affect the work of other employees in jobs related to their own. We suspect that there will be times when multiskilling is important—and times when it is not.

Symbolic Egalitarianism

If the goal is to increase communication between and across organizational levels, a case can be made for reducing the salience of official subdivisions and job grades. Firms attempting to signal that all employees are equal with regard to their opportunity to suggest ways for improving operations often remove what they consider to be signs of inequality. These may include executive dining rooms, special parking privileges, or uniforms that distinguish between employees of different rank. While removing symbols of inequality may affect communication patterns in organizations, we believe the next practice more directly addresses inequality and stratification in firms by focusing on reducing pay differences.

Wage Compression

The relative pay differences between people at various organizational levels can have profound effects on employee perceptions of fairness and equity.[11] These perceptions, in turn, can affect a wide variety of employee attitudes and behaviors. Current theory and empirical evidence suggest that if the goal is to increase the level of cooperation and team-oriented behavior displayed by employees, pay differences between jobs should be de-emphasized. Note that this concerns pay distinctions at the level of the job, not at the level of the individual. That is, incentive pay (a pay rule that can provide more or less money as a function of employee job performance and contribution) is distinguished from pay hierarchy compression.

Our position, however, will stress that the key to establishing a formula for wage compression is to carefully consider the primary objectives to be served by the practice. If the primary objectives are to reduce interpersonal competition and enhance cooperation, a more compressed pay distribution will likely be appropriate. This may not be the case, however, if the primary objective is to attract and retain employees at the highest organizational levels or to motivate employees to seek promotions.

SOME WAYS OF LEARNING ABOUT
EFFECTIVE HRM PRACTICES

How a company manages its workforce, in large part, determines whether it will be able to establish and sustain a competitive advantage over other companies. We have reviewed the ideas of four influential authors who each reach the same conclusion about the importance of sound HRM practices, even though they use different methods and arguments in formulating their opinions. Before moving on to preview the decision-making approach that we advocate in the design and evaluation of HR systems, we want to say more about how knowledge is gained in this area of management. What is the "literature" from which researchers like Ulrich, Lake, Waterman, and Pfeffer draw their conclusions? Why should you depend on the conclusions reached in a book of this type? To familiarize you with the type of information used to formulate managerial prescriptions, we will briefly comment on two basic ways of learning about effective HRM.

Behavioral Research and
Targeted Employee Behaviors

Most of what we currently know about sound HRM practice is based on over 70 years of research in the behavioral sciences, that is, research with a focus on the behavior of individuals in work settings. The outcome, or dependent, variables addressed in this research are classes of employee behaviors.

These include observable behaviors, such as attendance or task performance, or the outcomes associated with certain cognitive processes, such as decisions to accept job offers or perceptions of equitable treatment. Behaviors like being dependable and attending work regularly and on time, generating new ideas about improving work processes, deciding to accept a job offer with one company while rejecting the offers from others, performing task assignments rapidly and without error, providing co-workers with support and encouragement, and serving as a sponsor and mentor to a new employee are examples of the types of behaviors that have interested researchers.

The research most related to the topics covered in this book often examines the links between HRM practices and one or more set of targeted behaviors. For example, there is a large and well-developed literature addressing the degree to which various selection procedures (e.g., selection interviews, cognitive ability tests, work sample tests, personality tests, letters of reference) prove useful in predicting the work behaviors of job candidates who have been hired and given the chance to make a contribution to the hiring organization.[12]

Other HRM research topics relate to understanding how changes to reward and compensation practices affect employee behaviors and perceptions of fairness. This research addresses traditional topics[13] as well as recent developments, such as the shift to more reliance on the use of variable pay policies.[14] There also is a growing empirical literature devoted to executive compensation.[15] Following the other so-called functional areas of HRM, we find well-developed literatures addressing topics in the areas of training and development[16] and management development.[17]

In short, a great deal is known about how various HRM practices affect key classes of employee behavior, and it is from these literatures that prescriptions are formed. The logic of using the knowledge gained from the behavioral sciences is based, however, on one more critical assumption. For changes in HRM practice to have a positive impact on firm performance, the marginal return associated with "improved" practice must exceed the marginal cost. Not only must a change in HRM practice affect employee behavior in the desired direction, it must also do so at a cost that adds value to the firm.[18]

Research at the Business Unit or Organizational Level

Research at the business unit or organizational level of analysis represents an approach that differs markedly from the more traditional research agenda. Instead of focusing on how separate HRM practices affect targeted employee behaviors, this approach considers the effects of entire HRM systems—integrated sets of activities that can cut across more than one functional area—on organization-level performance outcomes. This literature is still in its infancy, but important research projects are beginning to be reported. A few examples will illustrate this approach and provide some interesting data for your consideration.

The first illustration represents a true study at the level of an entire HR system (the second two are somewhat more limited on the systems dimension). The study examined the effects of HR system variation on the performance of steel minimills.[19] Distinguishing between "commitment" and "control" HR systems, the researcher reasoned that plants with commitment-oriented HR systems would have better manufacturing performance than those with control-oriented systems. A control-oriented system is one primarily concerned with reducing direct labor costs. It works to simplify and narrow tasks so that employees with little training and experience will be able to perform prescribed duties. This leads to lower training costs and lower wages. The commitment-oriented HR system, in comparison, works to decentralize managerial decision making. It sets up formal participation mechanisms and reward and training practices designed to develop committed employees who can be trusted to take, on their own, constructive steps to enhance organizational performance. While training costs and wages can be higher for the commitment-oriented system, the increased motivation and improved problem-solving skills associated with such a system are thought to be critical in facilities using the advanced manufacturing technology found in minimills.

The first illustrative study was based on data collected from 30 U.S. steel minimills. Human resource managers at each plant provided information on their respective HRM practices and also reported on their mills' labor efficiency, scrap rate, and employee turnover. Efficiency was defined in terms of the number of labor hours required to produce one ton of steel. A number of control variables were used, including the age, size, union status, and business strategy of each plant. The study concluded that the mills with commitment-oriented systems had higher productivity (efficiency), lower scrap rates, and lower turnover rates than those with control-oriented systems. While this study needs to be viewed with some caution because it is possible that other uncontrolled factors may have influenced its findings, it represents an excellent example of the type of research design that will likely be used with increasing frequency in the future.

A second illustration uses a firm's stock price as an indicator of performance at the organizational level.[20] The researchers reasoned that announcements of U.S. Department of Labor awards for exemplary diversity programs would be associated with positive stock returns and that announcements of damage awards from settlements of discrimination lawsuits would be associated with negative stock returns. On the basis of data from 34 firms that had won the U.S. Department of Labor's Exemplary Voluntary Efforts Award and 35 firms that had been cited in *The Wall Street Journal Index* or the Dow Jones News Retrieval Service for being found guilty of employment discrimination, the stock return predictions were confirmed. Here, of course, multiple HRM practices and managerial decisions were responsible for either receiving an award or losing a discrimination case. Thus, HRM practices that reflect a commitment to the fair and equitable management of diverse labor markets may be able to influence firm performance as reflected in stock prices.

Finally, our third illustration is an organization-level study[21] that directly tests the management practice that deals with wage compression, discussed on page 8. Recall that the earlier principle suggested that interclass pay equity is likely to be related to firm performance; that is, too much pay differentiation between lower-level employees and managers and top-level managers can result in perceptions of inequity that can interfere with achieving overall organizational goals. Using concepts from equity theory[22] and relative deprivation theory,[23] the authors of this third illustrative study reasoned that large pay differentials would reduce commitment to managerial goals and lower employee effort and cooperation. These reduced levels of employee motivation and cohesiveness would, in turn, have a negative impact on product quality.

To empirically test their predictions, the researchers used data collected from 102 business units in 41 corporations. The business units in their sample had headquarters in North America (74) and Europe (28). Data for each business unit were collected from the unit's general manager and from managers representing a variety of functional areas. The dependent (outcome) variable in the study was a rating of product quality. The independent (causal) variables in the study included two measures of interclass pay equity. The first (hourly pay equity) measured the pay of hourly employees relative to the pay of the top three levels of management. The second (lower-level exempt pay equity) was a measure of the pay differential between the bottom three levels of exempt employees and the top three levels of management. After controlling for such things as union representation, number of employees, technological complexity, and relative market share, the results supported the authors' predictions. The more egalitarian the pay system, the higher the rating of the business unit's product quality.

These, then, represent some illustrations of how researchers learn about the relationships between HRM practices and organizational-level outcomes like productivity, stock valuation, and product quality. This research agenda directly gets at the essential issues addressed in this text and complements the well-developed research literatures that come from the behavioral sciences. We will draw on both of these research approaches throughout this book.

HRM SYSTEM DESIGN AND EVALUATION: THE PROCESS

Throughout Part IV of this book, we will be designing HR systems that seem appropriate for a particular situation. You will be asked, in multiple chapters, to consider integrated HR systems that fit a company and its unique set of circumstances. You will be asked to consider the options from a menu of possibilities. To preview this approach, we present a brief illustration of the process we will follow in later chapters.

The process, represented in Figure 1–1, will lead to making informed decisions about putting together HR systems that will work for your company and about the need to improve an existing HRM process. We begin by

FIGURE 1–1. HRM system design

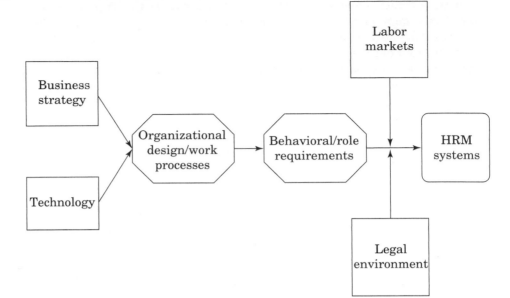

carefully considering the business strategies and manufacturing/service technologies that characterize your business or area of responsibility. These attributes of your business environment will dictate, in large part, how work needs to be organized and structured. How work processes are ordered, in turn, will lead to a determination of the key employee behaviors that will be required to successfully accomplish your business objectives. Only by focusing on these specific roles and behavioral requirements—and utilizing your knowledge about what determines and maintains these key behaviors—is it possible to begin to make informed decisions about the design of an appropriate HR system.

As shown in Figure 1–1, these decisions come directly out of the analysis of the behavioral requirements of the job. Of course, after considering the behavioral requirements of your situation, informed decisions about the HR system must take the conditions of the labor market and relevant labor/employment laws and regulations into account. Finally, while not explicitly diagrammed in the figure, the costs associated with implementing and maintaining the HR system must be compared to the likely returns. To be useful, the rate of return associated with investing in an HR system must meet or exceed the rate of return of other investment options.

To illustrate this process we ask that you consider a particular company: Compaq Computer Corporation. During the mid-1990s, Compaq was the world's top shipper of personal computers (PCs), shipping more than Dell, IBM, Apple, NEC, Packard Bell, and Hewlett-Packard.[24] Although by the late 1990s Compaq found itself in a fierce competition with Dell for market-share leadership, considering Compaq's high level of performance during the mid-1990s is very instructive. Like with most business successes, high performance can be attributed to a company's ability to implement a well-thought-out business strategy, the first component in Figure 1–1. In large part, how Compaq managed its people was central to implementing its business plan.

Historically, Compaq pursued an aggressive market-share strategy.[25] Its objective was to become the world leader in producing personal computers—to become number one in market share. At the business-strategy level, the approach was to continuously reduce manufacturing costs while maintaining high product quality. The goal was to systematically increase the number of PCs produced per square foot of factory floor and the number of machines produced per worker. Increases in production volume would also enable the company to negotiate for price concessions on key components like disk drives, further reducing costs and increasing demand for finished PCs. In the summer of 1996, Compaq modified this strategy and unveiled a plan to segment the PC market by building computers all along the price continuum.[26] As you will see, building machines across many price levels—and being able to quickly produce them at the points of greatest customer demand—relates to a second dimension of the model, technology.

At the level of technology, Compaq needed to use state-of-the-art manufacturing techniques; but it also needed to move toward the ability to build machines to customer order rather than relying on a system to forecast customer demand. The available technology for making such forecasts in this industry is notorious for its inaccuracy. By being able to adjust production schedules to take advantage of changing customer preferences, the company also would be able to reduce costs in other important ways related to inventory control (as chip prices fall, maintaining inventories of higher-priced chips is very damaging to margins[27]), handling, freight, and the processing of unsold and returned goods. Of course, underestimating customer demand for certain products also leads to other serious and negative consequences. Orders that cannot be filled often lead a customer to a competitor, and in the PC business initial customer purchases lead to company loyalty and subsequent purchases. Thus, a customer may be lost for good.

One of the key reasons Compaq was able to implement its revised business strategy was its experience with three-person "assembly cells."[28] The three-person cells represent the third component displayed in Figure 1–1. Three-person cells, compared to traditional assembly lines, fit Compaq's business strategy and available technology. Thus, the design of work processes follows the systematic review of organizational context.

As shown in Figure 1–2, workers in the three-person assembly teams, unlike traditional assembly-line workers, performed multiple tasks. Each team assembled an entire computer. One person on the team prepared the subassemblies (e.g., the disk drive and motherboard); a second team member installed the components into the computer's external case; and the third member of the team conducted tests of the circuits and electronics. The work cell takes up less space; moreover, the fewer the number of people touching each part, the higher the quality. On an assembly line, a problem can slow down the work of everyone. A problem in a cell affects only that group's production.

FIGURE 1–2. Three-person assembly cell

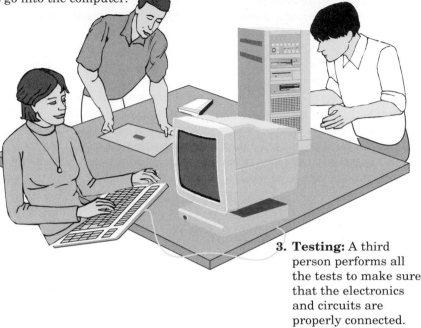

1. Subassembly: One person prepares all of the subassemblies, like the disk drive and motherboard, that go into the computer.

2. Assembly: A second person installs the components into the computer's external case.

3. Testing: A third person performs all the tests to make sure that the electronics and circuits are properly connected.

Source: Adapted from D. P. Levin, "Compaq Storms the PC Heights from Its Factory Floor," *New York Times,* November 13, 1994, p. C5.

It also would have been possible to multiskill this process even further by training each team member to be able to do the tasks of the other two members. This would have further enriched the jobs of each member and created a higher degree of flexibility. In addition to the actual assembly process, it would be possible to assign teams additional tasks. For example, given the focus on cost cutting and production efficiency, teams could be charged with continuously improving the way machines are assembled. This would require monitoring for quality, determining the causes for quality variability, and proposing and evaluating changes in the assembly process. It also would be possible to give the teams primary responsibility for hiring, training, and disciplining team members.

Now that work processes have been considered, it is time to move on to the next component of the process shown in Figure 1–1. We are now ready to specify the key employee behaviors required in a setting like the one created at Compaq. Not only would successful Compaq employees need to be proficient and dedicated assemblers, they would need to participate in extensive training opportunities, train newcomers, participate in the total quality management (TQM) process, attend work on a regular and on-time basis, and stay with the company for a sufficiently long period of time for the training and development costs to be "repaid."

Compaq employees would need a particular knowledge, skill, and ability profile. First, these employees would need to be able to learn a wide variety of tasks as the situation underwent change over time. Multiskilling requires that employees have the ability to learn and the willingness to participate in an ongoing training process. In addition to learning ability, these employees would need basic skills that would allow them to read technical manuals and follow complex instructions. They also would require basic mathematical and computational skills, along with an appropriate degree of manual dexterity and proficiency with hand tools and testing equipment.

Finally, in addition to the ability and willingness to perform duties associated with the assembly process, these employees would need skills that allow them to be effective team members. Oral and written communication skills, the ability to work with and train others, and a willingness to be good organizational citizens would be required in this type of team environment.

These behavioral, knowledge, skill, and ability requirements, along with knowledge about the values, interests, and perceptions related to the three-person assembly-cell concept, would need to be carefully considered when designing Compaq's HR system. By applying your theoretical understanding of what drives the required behaviors and your knowledge of what the research literature says about best practices, it should be possible to make informed decisions about HR system design. The remainder of this book should help you translate your knowledge about the behaviors that will be required in a particular situation into effective HR systems.

When you have completed this book, we suggest that you revisit the Compaq Computer illustration. At that time you will be ready to specify how this company should have staffed (after taking its labor market and legal environment into account) its manufacturing facilities, trained and developed its employees, and rewarded and encouraged employee behaviors that would be required for business success. Of course, your specifications will be at the level of an interrelated and congruent set of practices. We agree with Elliott Jaques that one clear sign of a dysfunctional organization is the "fragmentation of HR work into separate compartments—a bit of compensation here, a bit of selection there, training in this department, staff development in that, and leadership and organization development the business of everyone and no-one."[29]

THE GENERAL MANAGER AS AN AGENT OF CHANGE

So far we have focused on the general manager's role in identifying HR systems in need of modification and improvement. General managers must also be able to select the good from the bad when considering the products and services provided by HR-oriented consulting firms; but they also must bring about needed change. That is, successful managers are skilled at managing change. Implementing changes in existing HR systems, however, can be very challenging.

One of the earliest models of the change process was the one presented by Lewin.[30] His model proposed that for change to take place, the change agent must create an imbalance between the forces for change and the forces for the status quo that favors the forces for change. Moreover, this change in the balance should be created in a way that minimizes conflict and maximizes cooperation. Building on this model and providing a summary of the advice that comes from the change-management literature, Cummings and Worley proposed a five-step process that should lead to effective change management.[31] These steps are

- Motivating change.
- Creating a vision.
- Developing political support.
- Managing the transition.
- Sustaining momentum.

We will use this framework to suggest an approach to successfully guiding an organization through a process to modify an HR system.

Motivating Change

People must come to believe that change is necessary and must commit to abandoning the status quo for an uncertain future.[32] Changing HRM practices represents a large challenge because many current organization members have been successful, and satisfied, under the previous system. Convincing people to change something that has historically worked for them requires special skill. Current organization members need to understand that existing HRM practices that were useful in the past may no longer fit the new realities of the organization. Making the case that the changing business environment, and resulting change in business strategy and technology, necessitates the redesign of work processes is the first step. If the nature of work has or is about to change, a case can be made for the need to change components of the HR system (as shown in Figure 1–1). But motivation has to do with beliefs about the future (see Chapter 2). People need to be shown that changes to HRM practices will ultimately work to their advantage. They need to believe that they will be effective in the work roles called for in the new organization and that being effective in these roles will lead to desired outcomes.

In addition to changing beliefs about the future, some good ways to overcome resistance to change include (1) providing extensive communication about the overall structure of the new HR system, and (2) encouraging people who will be affected by the changes to participate in the redesign effort. For example, if there is a need to move from individually oriented pay incentives to more of a team-based payoff rule, prospective team members could provide guidance on how the new plan will operate in practice. Or current employees could be called on to help design new selection procedures needed to identify highly effective new team members.

Creating a Vision

This is a continuation of the previous step. Creating a vision of the future requires showing individuals and groups how they will fit into that future.

This might focus on specifying how proposed changes to HRM practices will lead to desirable organizational outcomes—outcomes that work not only to improve firm performance but also to improve the individual's chances of being successful in contemporary labor markets (e.g., a future where individuals will have developed new and demanded skills).

Developing Political Support

To initiate and guide change that relates to HRM will require a careful assessment of stakeholders who must work with you to turn your vision into reality. Proposed changes will not only affect operating employees and their managers; they will have a profound effect on your company's HR professionals. You will need their support and guidance. It is important to view HR systems as line systems rather than as mechanisms of control. HR cannot be perceived merely as an external regulator if line managers are to embrace and use these systems to improve business results. The quality of an HR system also depends on the technical expertise that resides in the HR community. Thus, you must persuade the HR professionals in your company that proposed changes will have positive benefits for them.

Managing the Transition

Bear in mind that modifying HR systems requires careful planning and attention to coordination. For example, changes to a compensation plan must be executed with precision. People must be paid, parameters for pay adjustments must be in place, and accounting systems must be ready for the changeover. Systemwide change must be almost instantaneous in some instances. Thus, new measurement systems must be carefully piloted and employees trained in how to use new HRM practices. The most well designed performance management system will not prove useful until all those who must make performance judgments are trained in the nuances of the plan. You must implement new recruiting and hiring practices systemwide, or you run the risk of being charged with biased, inconsistent patterns of decision making. While HR professionals will manage many of these implementation issues, general managers need to provide the incentives that will encourage all interested parties to pay attention to detail. Changing an aspect of an HR system requires the same precision called for when changing a complex manufacturing process or accounting system. And someone needs to be accountable for managing the transition.

Sustaining Momentum

Finally, the Cummings and Worley model provides several suggestions for sustaining momentum in order to stabilize the modified process or, for our purposes, HR practice. These include (1) providing resources for change, (2) building a support system for the agents of change, (3) developing related competencies and skills among those charged with administering and using the modified process, and (4) reinforcing new behaviors called for by the changed environment. All four recommendations are important, but the last two are particularly relevant to attempts at improving HRM practices. Once a modified practice becomes operational, the users need the knowledge, skill, and motivation required to sustain the improvement. Just as someone needs to be accountable for managing the transition, once a system is up and running, system users need to have the knowledge and motivation to make the system run over time. For example, a high-quality career planning and succession management system will not be sustained unless those devoting time and energy to making it work are rewarded for their efforts. Developing subordinates is hard, time-consuming work. Reasonable people will devote time and energy to what they are explicitly accountable for, ignoring things that are not explicitly measured and reinforced. Business leaders need to be accountable for managing people, just as they are accountable for managing financial assets or meeting production and sales targets.

CONCLUSION

In the next chapter we review and discuss some basic theoretical frameworks that should prove useful when attempting to understand and predict behavior in work settings. Remember, being able to predict the behaviors of others and being skillful at diagnosing the causes of problem behaviors are important competencies if you are to succeed in leading and motivating others.

This first chapter has set the stage for this discussion and for more in-depth treatments of issues related to the management of people. In your ultimate role as a general manager, you must be able to systematically improve a wide variety of business processes, including processes that relate to the behaviors of employees. To become effective in your organizational improvement efforts, you must become skillful in diagnosis, intervention, and program management. Successful general managers, in addition to possessing technical expertise and other basic managerial skills, really must become **organization development** specialists. A careful reading of this book will improve the odds that you will become skillful at identifying HR systems in need of improvement and setting in motion activities that will accomplish your objectives.

CONTINUOUS LEARNING: SOME NEXT STEPS

To follow future developments that relate to the topics developed in this chapter, you need access to timely information sources. We suggest you try these next steps, which can enrich your general knowledge of strategic human resources and change management.

- The Society for Human Resource Management (SHRM) is a professional association for HR and change-management professionals and consultants. Go to the SHRM web page (www.shrm.org) and explore the many services and information sources that are available on line. Prepare a report that characterizes how SHRM and its associated online services can be of use to the general manager.

- The *McKinsey Quarterly* is the online journal of one of the leading strategic management consulting firms in the world. Go to the McKinsey and Company web page (www.mckinsey.com) and learn about this consulting firm and its services. Then explore the information about the *McKinsey Quarterly*. Articles that most directly relate to this chapter are categorized under the label "Organization." A few recent articles we encourage you to read and discuss include, "The Talent–Growth Dynamic," "How Executives Grow," "The War for Talent," and "The CEO as Chief Performance Officer." Finally, review recent issues of this journal and develop a reading list that focuses on the change-management process.
- Go on line and conduct a general search to identify other consulting firms that provide HR and change-management services. The SHRM home page would likely be a good place to initiate such a search.
- Finally, identify an HR executive or consultant in a company that you know, and ask this individual if he or she would be willing to meet with you. During a scheduled meeting, explore the primary challenges this person, as a professional, currently faces and what he or she believes to be the primary challenges the profession will face in the next five years.

ENDNOTES

1. E. L. Gubman, *The Talent Solution* (New York: McGraw-Hill, 1998), chap. 9.
2. The MTI is cogently reviewed and critiqued by J. Micklethwait and A. Wooldridge, *The Witch Doctors: Making Sense of the Management Gurus* (New York: Random House, 1996).
3. D. Ulrich and D. Lake, *Organizational Capability* (New York: John Wiley & Sons, 1990); see also D. Ulrich and D. Lake, "Organizational Capability: Creating Competitive Advantage," *Academy of Management Executive* 5 (1991), pp. 77–92.
4. Ulrich and Lake, "Organizational Capability: Creating Competitive Advantage," p. 77.
5. R. H. Waterman, *What America Does Right: Learning from Companies That Put People First* (New York: W.W. Norton & Company, 1994), p. 17.
6. J. Pfeffer, "Producing Sustainable Competitive Advantage through the Effective Management of People," *Academy of Management Executive* 9 (1995), pp. 55–69. This section also draws heavily from J. Pfeffer, *Competitive Advantage through People* (Boston: Harvard Business School Press, 1994); and J. Pfeffer and J. F. Veiga, "Putting People First for Organizational Success," *Academy of Management Executive* 13 (1999), pp. 37–48.
7. Pfeffer, "Producing Sustainable Competitive Advantage."
8. E. G. Chambers, M. Foulon, H. Handfield-Jones, S. M. Hankin, and E. G. Michaels, "The War for Talent," *McKinsey Quarterly* 3 (1998), pp. 44–57.
9. Pfeffer, "Producing Sustainable Competitive Advantage."
10. Ibid.
11. Ibid.
12. Thorough reviews of the historical literature can be found in E. E. Ghiselli, "The Validity of Aptitude Tests in Personnel Selection," *Personnel Psychology* 26 (1973), pp. 461–78; J. J. Asher and J. A. Sciarrino, "Realistic Work Sample Tests: A Review," *Personnel Psychology* 27 (1974), pp. 519–33; and G. F. Dreher and P. R. Sackett, *Perspectives on Employee Staffing and Selection: Readings and Commentary* (Homewood, IL: Irwin, 1983). More contemporary reviews can be found in R. D. Gatewood and H. S. Feild, *Human Resource Selection* (Orlando, FL:

Dryden Press, 1998); H. G. Heneman and R. L. Heneman, *Staffing Organizations* (Middleton, WI: Mendota House, 1994); and N. Schmitt and W. C. Borman, *Personnel Selection in Organizations* (San Francisco: Jossey-Bass, 1993).

13. G. T. Milkovich and J. Newman, *Compensation* (New York: Irwin/McGraw-Hill, 1999).

14. B. Gerhart, H. B. Minkoff, and R. N. Olsen, "Employee Compensation: Theory, Practice, and Evidence." In G. R. Ferris, S. D. Rosen, and D. T. Barnum (eds.), *Handbook of Human Resource Management* (Cambridge, MA: Blackwell Publishers, 1995), pp. 528–47.

15. L. R. Gomez-Mejia, G. Paulin, and A. Grabke, "Executive Compensation: Research and Practical Implications." In G. R. Ferris, S. D. Rosen, and D. T. Barnum (eds.), *Handbook of Human Resource Management* (Cambridge, MA: Blackwell Publishers, 1995), pp. 548–69.

16. I. L. Goldstein, *Training in Organizations* (Monterey, CA: Brooks/Cole, 1990); K. N. Wexley and G. P. Latham, *Developing and Training Human Resources in Organizations* (New York: HarperCollins Publishers, 1991); and R. A. Noe, *Employee Training and Development* (New York: Irwin/McGraw-Hill, 1999).

17. T. T. Baldwin and T. E. Lawson, "Management Development in a New Business Reality." In G. R. Ferris, S. D. Sherman, and D. T. Barnum (eds.), *Handbook of Human Resource Management* (Cambridge, MA: Blackwell Publishers, 1995), pp. 511–27.

18. W. F. Cascio, *Costing Human Resources: The Financial Impact of Behavior in Organizations* (Boston: PWS-Kent Publishing Company, 1991).

19. J. B. Arthur, "Effects of Human Resource Systems on Manufacturing Performance and Turnover," *Academy of Management Journal* 37 (1994), pp. 670–87.

20. P. Wright, S. P. Ferris, J. S. Hiller, and M. Kroll, "Competitiveness through Management of Diversity: Effects on Stock Price Valuation," *Academy of Management Journal* 38 (1995), pp. 272–87.

21. D. M. Cowherd and D. I. Levine, "Product Quality and Pay Equity between Lower-Level Employees and Top Management: An Investigation of Distributive Justice Theory," *Administrative Science Quarterly* 37 (1992), pp. 302–20.

22. J. S. Adams, "Inequity in Social Exchange." In L. Berkowitz (ed.), *Advances in Experimental Social Psychology* 2 (New York: Academic Press, 1965), pp. 26–99; and G. C. Homans, *Social Behavior: Its Elementary Forms* (New York: Harcourt, Brace, Jovanovich, 1974).

23. J. Martin, "Relative Deprivation: A Theory of Distributive Injustice in an Era of Shrinking Resources." In L. L. Cummings and B. M. Staw (eds.), *Research in Organizational Behavior* 3 (Greenwich, CT: JAI Press, 1981), pp. 53–107; and F. Crosby, "Relative Deprivation in Organizational Settings." In B. M. Staw and L. L. Cummings (eds.), *Research in Organizational Behavior* 6 (Greenwich, CT: JAI Press, 1984), pp. 51–93.

24. J. Carlton, "Compaq Maintains Hold on PC Market as Hewlett Closes in on Packard Bell," *The Wall Street Journal*, August 8, 1995, p. A2.

25. D. P. Levin, "Compaq Storms the PC Heights from Its Factory Floor," *The New York Times*, November 13, 1994, p. C5.

26. K. Blumenthal, "Compaq Is Segmenting the Home-Computer Market," *The Wall Street Journal*, July 16, 1996, p. A3.

27. The number of times companies like Compaq could turn inventory each month was directly related to competitiveness. New technology caused the value of a completed PC to drop by as much as 1 percent per week; see E. Ramstad and R. Narisetti, "Compaq Stumbles Amid New Pressures on PCs," *The Wall Street Journal,* March 9, 1998, pp. B1, B4. This meant that companies that could move

inventories quickly had large pricing advantages over those that turned inventory more slowly.

28. Levin, "Compaq Storms the PC Heights."
29. E. Jaques, *Requisite Organization: The CEO's Guide to Creative Structure and Leadership* (Arlington, VA: Cason Hall & Co, 1989), p. 8.
30. K. Lewin, *Field Theory in Social Science* (New York: Harper and Row, 1951).
31. T. G. Cummings and C. G. Worley, *Organization Development and Change* (St. Paul, MN: West Publishing Company, 1993).
32. W. L. French and C. H. Bell, *Organizational Development: Behavioral Science Interventions for Organization Improvement* (Upper Saddle River, NJ: Prentice Hall, 1999).

2

Some Basic Theory about Ability, Motivation, and Opportunity

To design HR systems that promote key employee behaviors, you need an understanding of basic concepts of ability, motivation, and opportunity. In this chapter you will

- Learn about the distinctions between employee ability, motivation, and opportunity, and why these distinctions are important.
- Become acquainted with some particular aptitudes, competencies (abilities), and personal traits likely to play major roles in employee effectiveness.
- Understand how managers can use the expectancy theory to diagnose motivation problems and motivate employees to improve performance, attendance, and other behaviors.
- See how the concepts of distributive justice (equity theory) and procedural justice can help you to understand certain employee behaviors and enhance employee performance and satisfaction.

We illustrate the key concepts of this chapter—*ability, motivation,* and *opportunity*—with a description of a human resource problem witnessed by one of the authors. A number of years ago a Fortune 100 firm decided to create a state-of-the-art word processing center. The new center was designed to provide accurate, timely service to headquarters employees who submitted word processing work to be keyed at this centralized facility. Management had great success in achieving the goal of staffing the center with highly competent people. Partly because of the excellent pay and benefits, the firm was able to hire mostly college graduates, many with degrees in English, for positions that involved preparing documents at the center.

Management was proud of the new center and delighted to have attracted such well-educated people. But after a few months, an onslaught of personnel problems puzzled and frustrated management. The center began to suffer increasing employee absence rates, which were significantly higher than those elsewhere in the firm. Turnover accelerated at an alarming level. Most surprising of all, sloppy work and poor customer service increasingly drew complaints from internal clients. What was the problem here? Why were such seemingly qualified personnel displaying such poor performance? Managers of the center soon arrived at the idea that *employee training* could rectify these problems. They decided to set up extensive training for employees to instruct them in the details and expectations of their work tasks, with the intention of improving the quality of their work.

However, some wise heads among the firm's human resource specialists quickly surmised that training would not be an effective solution. They understood that training is a good solution for performance problems that stem from employees' lack of *ability*, sometimes termed "can't do problems" (see Chapter 6). But these well-educated, highly able staffers exhibited *motivation* problems, sometimes termed "won't do problems." Motivation refers to an employee's *willingness to exert effort toward a goal*. These employees had plenty of ability but were not motivated by the rewards available in their jobs, which, although fairly well-paying, were routine and mundane. In other words, they were not willing to exert high levels of effort. During the hiring process, not enough attention had been paid to the needs and the rewards sought by these types of applicants. These employees also had little *opportunity* to challenge themselves in their work and to advance to higher positions within the firm. Effectively diagnosing and suggesting solutions for problems such as those at the word processing center begins with an understanding of the concepts of ability, motivation, and opportunity.

This chapter presents some basic theory related to ability, motivation, and opportunity. This theory is valuable for general managers because it provides basic tools for diagnosing practical HRM problems and also for generating and evaluating concrete solutions. We argued in Chapter 1 that HR systems should be designed to support key behavioral and role requirements. Thus, for managers to allocate their human resource expenditures efficiently, they need to be able to determine the likely causes of employee behavior. To determine the appropriateness of HRM program changes it is critical for managers to first consider how the change will affect employee behavior. Moreover, managers can enhance their effectiveness by establishing a systematic framework for determining **how** and **why** an HR-system adjustment will influence behavior. This chapter provides such a framework. After completing this chapter, you should be better able to diagnose behavioral problems in your organizations and be able to reason how and why a change to an HR system will modify behavior. The how and why focus will enable you to specify the **processes** that account for change.

This chapter sets the stage for other chapters by focusing on three key factors that explain employees' behavior: ability, motivation, and opportunity. In developing this general framework for understanding employee behavior, we explicitly address what often has been ignored in the management literature. Most models of employee behavior emphasize that behavior is a function of employee *motivation* and *ability* to perform. A simple way of distinguishing these two concepts is "will do" (motivation) and "can do" (ability). But another of our primary objectives in this chapter is to consider ability and motivation along with a third major determinant of employee behavior—a dimension we term *opportunity*.

THE GENERAL FRAMEWORK

Management studies historically have emphasized the dimensions of ability and motivation; few have developed full models that take into account all three of the critical determinants of behavior.[1] In this type of general framework, as seen in Figure 2–1, employee behavior is influenced by a variety of factors. This figure states that organizational environments and individual characteristics must be simultaneously taken into account in attempts to predict, explain, or modify employee behavior. Throughout this book we encourage you to consider how and why a change to an HR system influences one or more of the key dimensions accounting for behavior (i.e., ability, motivation, and opportunity).

In a more particular way, the figure shows that given a pattern of person-centered attributes, the individual will be influenced by the task demands and reward system from the organization and assigned job. Job performance (or any desired behavior) will likely be most effective when the person's **temperament**, **preferences**, and **expectations** are congruent with the organization's reward system. This is essentially a form of person–job matching that influences motivation to perform. For example, employees who possess high levels of "need for achievement" (a concept we

FIGURE 2–1. A general model of employee behavior

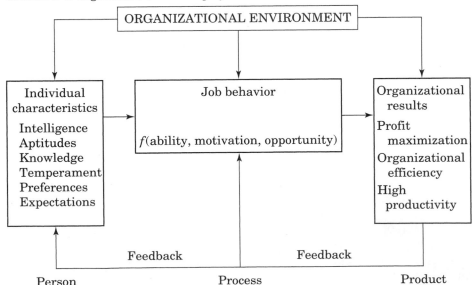

Source: From J. P. Campbell, M. D. Dunnette, E. E. Lawler, and K. E. Weick, *Managerial Behavior, Performance, and Effectiveness* (New York: McGraw-Hill, 1970). Reprinted with permission of the McGraw-Hill Companies.

will discuss shortly) would be especially well-matched to the use of bonuses, commissions, or other pay strategies that link rewards directly to the level of one's individual productivity.

However, at least two additional ingredients are necessary before motivation ("will do") is translated into accomplishment and career success. First, certain job knowledge, skills, and aptitudes—**KSAs**—all part of what we call "ability," must be present. The KSAs also must be accompanied by the **opportunity** to perform. For example, opportunity to perform may be enhanced by a number of situational factors, including (1) sufficient information to do the job, (2) tools, equipment, materials, or supplies needed to do the job, (3) the help of co-workers in accomplishing the job, (4) the time needed to do the job, and (5) a physical environment which fosters job performance by regulating such factors as excessive heat, cold, or noise.[2]

Finally, Figure 2–1 makes the important point that desired job behavior translates into positive outcomes at the level of the *firm* (e.g., profits, productivity, and growth) only under certain conditions. An HRM practice may influence employee behavior, but organizational results depend on the value of the behavior change in relation to the costs associated with the practice. The administrative and labor costs associated with a particular HRM practice may be too high to justify its continued use (a topic we return to in Chapter 8).

We next consider the building blocks of models designed to explain employee behavior, stressing behavior as a function of ability, motivation, and opportunity. We begin by considering the ability to perform.

THE APTITUDE–ABILITY DISTINCTION

Definitions of human capacities give rise to considerable overlap, confusion, and unnecessary complexity. To avoid this, we follow one generally accepted orientation and make the distinction between *aptitudes* and *abilities*.[3]

The distinction between an aptitude and an ability is rather subtle. An *aptitude* is a relatively stable attribute that indicates a person's general pattern of performance. "Relatively stable" means that these attributes are difficult to modify through training—they might be termed "sticky" attributes. After they are acquired in a person's developmental years, they tend to remain rather stable throughout a person's life.[4] Thus, some people possess high levels of mechanical aptitude, musical aptitude, or managerial aptitude. These aptitudes represent *potential to develop specific abilities*.

Abilities develop as a result of specialized *training* and the possession of prerequisite aptitudes: A person may possess certain aptitudes which, when nurtured through training, will lead to a set of acquired abilities. As a result of training, people with mechanical, musical, or managerial aptitudes might become skilled mechanics, accomplished violinists, or competent practicing managers.

Although these definitions may seem arbitrary, the distinction is important from an HRM perspective. Certain HRM practices are designed to identify people with *aptitude* and to then develop these individuals through training and education. Other HRM practices identify people with an *ability,* that is, people who are *currently ready* to perform job duties with minimal training and orientation. Some firms hire at entry level, based on applicants' aptitudes and attempts to "grow their own" workforce. Other firms tend to hire new employees at higher levels, based on the applicants' current ability.

Aptitudes

We will consider aptitudes to be of two general types: cognitive and motor. The following are examples frequently classified as **cognitive aptitudes:**[5]

Spatial Aptitude. This is the ability to visualize objects in space and to perceive their properties and spatial relations with other objects if changed in position.

Perceptual Speed. This is the ability to perceive visual details (similarities and differences) quickly and accurately.

Rote Memory. This is the aptitude for recalling paired words, lists of numbers, and so forth.

Verbal Comprehension. This refers to understanding the meaning of words and their relations to each other, as in anagram games.

Inductive Reasoning. This is the aptitude for discovering a rule or principle and applying it to solving a problem.

Numerical Aptitude. This focuses on a facility for numerical reasoning (e.g., to be speedy and accurate in making numerical calculations).

Relatively stable motor and physical skills also have been identified. Fleishman concluded that there are 11 independent motor skills that are appropriately classified as aptitudes.[6] These include such motor skills as manual dexterity, arm–hand steadiness, finger dexterity, reaction time, and multiple-level coordination.

Abilities for the Twenty-First Century: Some Illustrations

The word *competencies* is increasingly being used to reflect abilities, considered somewhat broadly. Many writers have argued that the competencies needed to be effective—defined as being able to acquire and maintain a high-paying job—in the twenty-first century will be the competencies required to provide *symbolic-analytic services.*[7] Reich distinguishes three types of jobs:[8]

1. *Routine production services* are the repetitive services and their associated tasks that characterize low- and middle-level supervisory, blue-collar production, and clerical work.
2. *In-person services* also entail simple and repetitive tasks, but they are performed in person with the consumer (hairdressers, flight attendants, security guards, and residential real estate agents).

3. *Symbolic-analytic services* are characterized by the problem-identifying, problem-solving, and brokering activities performed by a wide range of occupations (lawyers, research engineers and scientists, software engineers, investment bankers, and public relations executives).

Because of the growth of symbolic analyst work, we discuss in detail two competencies from this area. The following working definitions of each illustrate the level of detail that is required when creating what is now regularly termed a "competency model" or a "competency profile." The competencies selected are likely to be central to effectiveness in a wide range of symbolic analyzer roles. Although a variety of competencies generally appear in competency models (e.g., oral communication and presentation skills, technical knowledge, stress tolerance, planning and execution skills), the two reviewed here relate to effectiveness at the highest organizational levels. Like their more basic counterparts, they illustrate what we mean when discussing the *competency to perform* in specified work roles. They develop over time as a result of specialized training and education and the possession of prerequisite aptitudes.

Complex Problem Solving/Long Time Horizon Decision Making

This dimension is based on the theoretical work of Elliott Jaques.[9] It is about the ability to take into account multiple sources of information and to use this information to make informed decisions about how actions today will influence events in the future. This dimension measures the individual's ability to (1) plan and carry out initiatives that extend into the future, (2) forecast trends and circumstances that will influence the business or technical environment of the future, and (3) make sense out of complex and rapidly changing business environments. The further into the future the individual can plan and bring plans to conclusion, the higher the level of development along this dimension.

Interpersonal/Intrapersonal Intelligence

"*Interpersonal* intelligence is the ability to understand other people: what motivates them, how they work, how to work cooperatively with them."[10] It entails understanding the causes and predictors of behavior, developing insights into the motives and causes that underlie the behavior of others, seeing patterns or trends in others' behavior, and using this information to predict and prepare for how others will respond to critical situations. *Intrapersonal* intelligence is a related ability, but turned inward. It is the ability to form an accurate model of oneself and to use that model to function in life.

MOTIVATION: WILLINGNESS TO EXERT EFFORT

As illustrated in Figure 2–1, effective performance is a function of *ability*, *motivation*, and *opportunity*. Some level of all three of these factors must be present for an individual to achieve desired results. Motivation—the *willingness* to exert effort in a particular way—is an extremely important factor in understanding or predicting employee behavior. It is a factor that often responds to changes in HR systems, particularly reward systems. Given the centrality of motivation for employee behavior, we devote the latter part of this chapter to some well-known "process" models of motivation and use this section only to highlight another aspect of the *motivation* dimension. Here we comment on the role played by some well-known personal attributes and traits in accounting for key behaviors.

We use the term **personality** to refer to a person's tendency to act in a consistent way when confronted by similar situations. People seem to display an individual style that characterizes how they will behave in a particular setting. The consistency of behavior that seems to differentiate one person from another is central to the concept of personality.[11] In this section we simply illustrate a few possibilities.

McClelland's Learned Needs. McClelland, working alone and with Burnham, proposed a theory of motivation that focuses on learned needs.[12] Three of these are the need for achievement (*n* Ach), the need for affiliation (*n* Aff), and the need for power (*n* Power). High **n Ach** is a characteristic of people who desire accomplishment. These individuals seek situations in which it is possible to take personal responsibility and get personal credit for a successful outcome. They attempt to achieve success through their own efforts and abilities, prefer tasks of intermediate levels of difficulty and risk, and seek situations that provide knowledge of results within a reasonable time. Individuals with high **n Power** seek to control their environments and influence the behavior of others, while **n Aff** is associated with the need to develop friendships and to be sociable and caring of others. McClelland views power motivation as an essential attribute for explaining managerial effectiveness in large corporations. A strong need for affiliation, however, may interfere with effective managerial performance. Perhaps the greatest attention has been paid to the need for achievement. There is evidence that *n* Ach is related to being successful in a variety of work roles but is most often associated with entrepreneurial (versus managerial) success.

Gough's Work Orientation. Work orientation is characterized by high personal work standards.[13] Regardless of task type, high work-oriented people are described as industrious, conscientious, responsible, and persevering. The concept resembles what has historically been termed the Protestant work ethic.

Miner's Managerial Motivation. Miner's research suggests that this attribute is a stable, multidimensional personal trait that relates to managerial role performance.[14] Individuals with high managerial motivation strive to engage in competitive activities, to behave in an active and aggressive manner, to influence others, and to seek highly visible and distinctive positions.

While these attributes all relate to important workplace behaviors, they display some degree of overlap with each other and taken separately do not represent a complete picture of the person. A recent development has been the realization that most methods of classifying individual differences in social behavior are based on five broad themes or dimensions of personality. These dimensions have been labeled the **big five.**[15] This five-factor classification system is briefly described as follows:[16]

Extraversion. This factor addresses the degree to which the person requires attention from others and social interaction. It distinguishes people who are quiet, reserved, and shy from people who are typically talkative, assertive, and interpersonally active.

Agreeableness. Here the focus is on whether the person needs pleasant and harmonious relations with others. People who require a high degree of pleasantness are typically seen as interpersonally perceptive, tactful, and socially sensitive. Their counterparts may appear to be cold, unfriendly, fault finding, and direct in their approach to others.

Conscientiousness. This factor addresses the degree to which a person is willing to comply with conventional rules and standards. Highly conscientious people are described as being organized, thorough, and careful planners. A high degree of conscientiousness may also signal that a person is somewhat inflexible and resistant to change.

Emotional Stability. This factor characterizes the degree to which the person experiences the world as threatening and beyond his or her control. It distinguishes people who are described as tense, anxious, and nervous from those who are typically stable, calm, and content.

Openness to Experience. This factor characterizes the degree to which the person needs change, variety, and intellectual stimulation. People needing environmental change and stimulation are seen by others to be imaginative, inventive, easily bored, and inattentive to detail.

For now, we end the discussion of the concept of *motivation.* Much of what has been discussed so far in this section relates to needs and interests. We return to the concept of motivation in more depth in the latter part of the chapter. As previously noted, this is a treatment of "process" models of motivation. Interests and needs play an important role in these models. We now turn our attention to the final basic determinant of performance and effectiveness—**opportunity**.

OPPORTUNITY

We reported earlier that employee behavior and effectiveness are influenced by **ability**, **motivation**, and **opportunity.**[17] Opportunity is quite distinct from ability and motivation: It is a kind of constraining or enabling force beyond one's control. We see this construct as a *set of interrelated factors that provide organizational members with the opportunity to* **acquire** *and* **display** *attributes related to role competence and effectiveness.*[18] Some of the factors we have in mind are outlined in Table 2–1. These ideas draw on the work of Peters and O'Connor (1980) and their thinking about the situational constraints that affect work outcomes.[19] We also draw from the literature on

TABLE 2–1. The Opportunity to Acquire and Display Attributes Related to Role Competence and Effectiveness

Opportunity to Acquire	Opportunity to Display
Access to information needed to complete assigned tasks (e.g., receiving information from peers, supervisors, and subordinates regarding such things as customer preferences, company rules and policies, and technical specifications and updates)	Being provided with the tools, equipment, supplies, and machinery needed to complete assigned tasks
Access to information about organizational cultures and reward systems (e.g., forming a mentoring relationship and learning about the likes, dislikes, and personal beliefs of powerful decision makers)	Being provided with the staff support and help from co-workers needed to complete assigned tasks
Access to formal training and development opportunities (e.g., being selected to participate in "executive" MBA program; forming a formal career development plan with assistance from immediate manager)	Being provided with the budgetary support required to accomplish objectives (e.g., funding to hire consultants and temporary support staff, funding to travel and to communicate electronically)
Access to information through technology (e.g., being supplied with computer technology and software needed to access the Internet and to run interactive educational software)	Having the time available to engage in critical work activities
Being designated a "high-potential" employee and receiving the associated training and development opportunities	Having performance record reviewed by a talent-pool committee
Being provided with the opportunity to learn about the entire organization via systematic job rotation experiences	Being given challenging and visible assignments early in a career
Having access to a senior-level role model	Being able to display talent as a member of a special task force or project team

sponsorship and mentorship in organizations, which suggests that employees with impressive ability and motivation may be constrained in their level of achievement and career success by a lack of opportunity.[20]

To illustrate the concept of opportunity, consider the early careers of two equally qualified and motivated graduates of masters of business administration (MBA) programs. Sharon and Susan both had liberal arts undergraduate degrees, completed MBA programs at the age of 27, and took positions as management trainees for regional retailers. Both had been married at the age of 23, received Graduate Management Admissions Test

(GMAT) scores exceeding 600, and had completed their undergraduate programs with 3.80 grade point averages (GPAs). Sharon was admitted and enrolled in a regional MBA program (she was unwilling to enroll in an MBA program greater than 50 miles from her husband's place of employment). Susan was admitted to an MBA program that *Business Week* rated as one of the three best programs in the United States (she and her husband relocated to the Chicago area so that Susan could attend this prestigious program). Sharon and Susan were both capable and self-motivated students and in their respective MBA programs developed equally in terms of their knowledge of accounting, marketing, and finance.

Upon receiving their MBA degrees, both women took positions with the same large corporation and pursued careers in the consumer products division of the company. Both devoted approximately 60 hours weekly to their professional careers and both were dedicated and committed to the success of their employing organization. Both women joined this company during the same month and year and both had completed MBA programs, yet their careers progressed in very different ways. Sharon was placed on the staff of a regional marketing manager and took on assignments that essentially meant that she became very knowledgeable about the development and marketing of a single product line. She performed at a high level and within two years was promoted to a midlevel marketing position within the southeast region.

Within the first three months of her employment, the company sent Susan to the offices of a well-known consulting firm to participate in a "managerial assessment center." Assessment centers consist of a variety of individual and group-oriented situational exercises in which relatively high-level managers observe and rate the performance of lower-level members of their firm. The use of assessment centers for the selection of managers and the identification of long-range managerial potential has been well documented since the 1960s.[21] At the end of this experience, Susan was placed in the company's High Potential Targeted Careers (HPTC) program. As a member of HPTC, Susan obtained a variety of developmental opportunities not available to her early career peers. For example, a planned sequence of cross-functional project team assignments allowed Susan to learn about a wide range of business issues and come into contact with managers and executives throughout the company. In fact, HPTC participants met twice a year with the officers of the company and participants were assigned to a designated managerial adviser, a manager two levels above the participant who is available for confidential consultation and advice-giving to the junior colleague.

Five years after joining the company, Sharon and Susan arrived at very different places. Sharon is considered to be a solid-performing individual contributor. Susan is considered to be a person with senior-management potential. Susan is about to take her first assignment as a project leader in the company's rapidly growing Asian market. The likelihood that Sharon will move beyond being a midlevel individual contributor is slight; she may not even survive the frequent rounds of organizational downsizing and restructuring that are typical in this industry. Susan has made the select list of junior managers who are designated to replace their more senior colleagues. Much of the difference between the career prospects of these two women can be explained in terms of differential opportunity structures that were in place within the first few post-MBA years. Here, reasonably equal levels of talent and motivation led to very different levels of contribution and achievement.

Opportunity, as defined by the type of MBA program attended and subsequent early career experiences, can make a major difference in career outcomes. However, individual circumstances and personal career objectives should guide choices about where to attend graduate school. For some individuals, opportunity might be maximized by attending a small, relatively little known school of business.[22]

Equal Opportunity and Career Systems

Since the passing of the Civil Rights Act of 1964, considerable time, effort, litigation, and financial resources have been devoted to creating "equal opportunity" for members of what is now a very diverse labor market. Many equal employment opportunity (EEO) laws have been enacted during this period (some will be summarized and discussed in Chapter 11). But beyond removing artificial (and biased) barriers to employment opportunities, firms can use high-quality *career management and assessment systems* to enhance equal opportunity for all employees. We conclude this part of the chapter with a description of these systems and a discussion of how they promote equal opportunity. The goal is to further characterize the types of HRM practices that relate to opportunity.

Career Systems and Equal Opportunity

Even with a variety of critical factors held constant, women and nonwhite men in U.S. labor markets face barriers to career advancement. Typically they report receiving less compensation than their white male counterparts and are less likely to achieve senior-management status,[23] apparently in part because they lack access to powerful senior mentors (usually white males). These senior mentors are most likely to provide mentoring to those who are similar to themselves—other white males. Relationships with white male mentors provide greater career returns to protégés (e.g., compensation) than do relationships with other mentors.[24] But in firms with a variety of career management and assessment systems, *all* employees, including women and minority group members, have access to opportunities to enhance their careers and attain outcomes such as senior-management status and the accompanying compensation. Individuals in these firms should be on a more even footing with their white male counterparts with respect to the opportunity to **acquire** and **display** core organizational competencies: They will be more likely to have opportunities that are equivalent to the opportunities provided white males.

Career management programs in organizations have been discussed comprehensively elsewhere.[25] We draw from these sources and provide some additional viewpoints next. The goal here is to highlight some components of high-quality career systems that can provide additional opportunity for all employees.

Succession planning would likely represent a key component of any good-quality career system. Teams of managers meet on a regular basis to identify individuals as replacements for current managers. As part of the process of identifying replacements for key positions, these managers discuss, on an individual basis, their junior colleagues' records, including their skills, experience, strengths, weaknesses, and future development needs. The key here is that *all* candidates—not just those with mentors or those who have already been identified as being potential high-level employees—are discussed during the succession planning meeting.

The **skill inventory** is a tool that facilitates the identification of junior managers who are ready for new and challenging roles. In computerized skills inventories, each manager's education, work experiences, competencies, and career interests are described and updated so that more senior decision makers have ready access to this information. Thus, senior managers can learn about individuals with whom they have had no direct or personal contact.

Through systematic **job rotation** programs, managers gain both a companywide perspective and the opportunity to display talent to senior managers. For example, by undertaking a variety of short-term positions in different divisions of the organization, a new employee can meet and become known to a number of higher level managers. Job rotation also exposes a newcomer to subcultures and alternative positions throughout the organization.

Assessment centers, as previously discussed, provide the opportunity to display talent to "assessors"—frequently higher level managers within the firm. In addition, assessment centers can help participants acquire new skills. In a coaching and developmental context, for example, the detailed information on the strengths and weaknesses of each assessee's performance that appears in assessment center reports can open up a significant developmental opportunity for the assessee.

Succession planning, skills inventories, job rotation, and the use of managerial assessment centers illustrate components of HR systems that can provide opportunity to all employees. They have a special role to play in promoting equal opportunity for employees who have been traditionally disadvantaged in U.S. labor markets. We hope this brief discussion of these formal career systems enhances our use of the term *opportunity*. Other components of high-quality career systems also are listed in Table 2–2.[26]

TWO MOTIVATION MODELS: EXPECTANCY THEORY AND EQUITY THEORY

As explained earlier in this chapter, "willingness" to perform key behaviors is an important determinant of behavior. That is, employees must be "motivated" if they are to perform behaviors such as high task performance, job

TABLE 2–2. Career Systems Enhancing Opportunities for Managers and Professionals

Succession planning	Assessment centers
Skill inventories	Competency ratings
Job rotation	Expanded performance feedback
Special task forces	Designated managerial advisers
Career pathing	Project teams
Career development workshops	

seeking, attendance, or cooperation with others. Most of us, for example, have personal experience with co-workers who had impressive abilities but who performed poorly because they were unwilling to exert effort toward performance goals. Indeed, motivational differences among employees can account for huge differences in their relative productivity.[27] Thus, an understanding of key theories or "models" of employee motivation can equip managers with tools which are essential for managing people.

We conclude this chapter with an overview of two models of motivation which we believe are especially valuable for managers: expectancy theory and organizational justice (distributive and procedural justice). Managers can use these two theories both in *diagnosing* motivational problems and also in identifying *strategies* for increasing employees' motivation to perform key behaviors. In our discussion of the expectancy and organizational justice models, we also provide a variety of examples of how managers can use these models to promote key employee behaviors.

Expectancy Theory

A conceptual basis for the expectancy theory is sometimes called "subjective expected utility" (SEU) theory. This theory has a long history in the study of human motivation and decision making in economics and psychology.[28] The SEU and expectancy theory approaches assume that people are cognitive information processers and decision makers. More specifically, this approach assumes that employees are largely rational decision makers, who set or accept goals for themselves. They also assess the likelihood that they can achieve various goals and the likelihood that they will receive rewards or punishments from achieving their goals.[29] We are *not* saying that employees have full knowledge of all possible behaviors and outcomes, or that they are perfectly rational decision makers who "optimize" their decisions (some economists might disagree with us). We do assume that employee **perceptions** are the critical elements in motivation, as opposed to "objective reality," and that two employees working in the same setting can have very different perceptions relevant to motivation.

In a sense, expectancy theory provides a shorthand way to capture the personal life history of an employee. That is to say that the best way to make a prediction about a person's willingness to perform some behavior would be to observe that person over the course of his or her life. We would observe the person's level of success or failure in attempting to accomplish goals, and we would note the rewards and punishments experienced by the person for various actions and the relative preferences the person developed for various rewards. Obviously, we do not have these long-term opportunities to observe employees' histories. But the expectancy theory directs us to determine employees' *current* views or perceptions about the odds of achieving certain goals and relative preferences for different rewards or "outcomes" in their work. Expectancy theory provides us with a "current summary" of these kinds of employee perceptions resulting from the personal life experience of the employee.

To appreciate the usefulness of expectancy theory for managers, we must also acknowledge that most behavioral science theories are not completely correct or completely wrong. Scholars do perform multitudes of research studies subjecting theories to empirical scrutiny, and they engage in debates about the validity of various theories. The theory has been subjected to such scrutiny and debates and has survived quite well.[30] The more important concern for this book, however, is the heuristic value of expectancy theory for identifying the *key* variables for managers' attention in promoting certain employee behaviors and solving human resource problems. Thus, we use the expectancy theory as a practical problem-solving tool.

Expectancy, Instrumentality, and Valence

The expectancy (or VIE) theory posits three key employee perceptions that determine an employee's willingness to direct effort toward performing some behavior, or achieving some goal (e.g., high performance). One perception is labeled *expectancy*, which is an employee's perception of the **likelihood** of performing the behavior if he or she tries. The employee, for example, is making the assessment "If I try to achieve excellent performance, what's the likelihood that I actually will achieve it?" An employee who believes that there is a low probability that she could achieve high performance **if she tried** would thus have a low expectancy perception. Since expectancy is a key determinant of motivation, a low expectancy perception ("I'm not so sure I could achieve it") would contribute to low employee motivation for performance.

The second key perception is labeled *instrumentality*. This is an employee's perception of the extent to which a particular "outcome," either positive or negative, is **linked** to performing the behavior. The employee, for example, might consider "If I do perform the behavior (e.g., excellent performance), what's the likelihood that I'll get a salary increase?" or "What's the likelihood that achieving excellent performance will lead to a promotion?" The employee typically assesses the instrumentality or linkage between performing the behavior (performance) and an entire set of individual outcomes. To summarize, the employee perceives a set of distinct outcomes as individually linked to the performing of the behavior. Each of these potential linkages has some level of certainty or probability in the employee's perception. It is also important to note that a strong instrumentality means that *if* one performs the behavior, the outcome results, and if that behavior is not performed, **no outcome** is likely to result. Since instrumentality is a key perception, employees' overall level of motivation is higher the more they see performing the behavior as having many strong linkages to desirable outcomes.

The third key perception is *valence*, which is the level of **attractiveness** or **desirability** of an outcome to the employee. Some of the outcomes which employees see as linked to a behavior have positive valence or desirability (e.g., salary increases, promotions) while other outcomes may have negative valence (e.g., more work responsibility, more stress).

The expectancy model has even been put into an equation, which illustrates the relationship among the three key perceptions:

$$\text{Motivation for a behavior} = E \times [\Sigma\ (I \times V)]$$

where E = expectancy
I = instrumentality
V = valence

This equation illustrates that one perceives *an* expectancy for performing the behavior, but also perceives instrumentalities and valences for a *number* of positively or negatively valent outcomes—thus the summation sign. The sum of (instrumentality × valence) products across the entire set of outcomes is thus an important component of our motivation formula. In addition, the "multiplicative" nature of the model (note the multiplication signs in the formula) means that *if any major component of the motivation model (e.g., expectancy) is zero, then there can be **no** motivation to perform the behavior*.

To summarize, using the expectancy theory, an employee's level of motivation to perform a particular behavior is determined by perceptions of

1. The **expectancy**, or the likelihood that the employee can perform the behavior.
2. The **instrumentality** for (or strength of the linkage of the behavior with) a number of outcomes.
3. The **valence**, or attractiveness (positive or negative) of those outcomes.

We emphasize that the expectancy approach can be used to explain one's motivation to perform *any* behavior, including such diverse work behaviors as attendance, turnover, job performance, cooperation with others, mentoring others, and early retirement.

Applying the Expectancy Approach to Motivating Employees

Let's consider again one of the typically most important target behaviors for human resource management: job performance. An employee's motivation for the behavior of high job performance could suffer for a number of reasons. First, the employee could have a **low-expectancy** perception, thinking that she would not be likely to achieve high performance if she tried. (She may benefit from some training or coaching, issues we will take up later.) Second, the employee may perceive **weak instrumentalities** for valent outcomes: She does not see much connection between achieving high performance and the obtaining of valuable outcomes. She does not see how *whether or not* she is a high performer makes much difference for obtaining salary increases, promotions, bonuses, or even praise and recognition. This is another source of low motivation. Third, the employee may actually be **demotivated,** or avoid the goal of high performance, if she sees that negatively valent outcomes tend to be linked to achieving high performance (e.g., fatigue, more responsibility). Thus, if managers wish to promote a target behavior such as high performance, their efforts may fail because of lack of employee motivation. The source of the lack of motivation could be (1) low expectancy for performing the behavior, or (2) a lack of high instrumentalities for (or connections to) outcomes, or (3) a lack of outcomes with high enough positive valence, or (4) *all* of these problems.

Clearly, one goal of managers is to create a work environment in which employees are confident that they can achieve important behaviors if they try and perceive that many positively valued outcomes will result if they perform these behaviors—outcomes which are *not* likely to result if the behavior is not performed.

Human Resource Practices that Promote Expectancy, Instrumentality, and Valence

Example 1. Enhancing Performance Motivation. Managers can put into place practices that encourage employee motivation to perform important behaviors. Table 2–3 illustrates some practices that could be implemented to encourage employee motivation for high task performance. Keep in mind that a similar set of practices could be suggested to encourage motivation to seek a position with the organization, motivation to stay with the firm, or motivation to perform any other target behavior.

First, we could focus on practices to enhance **expectancies** for high task performance. Here we are interested in activities that will enhance employee perceptions that if they try, they will able to achieve high performance. Thus, "confidence-boosting" activities such as providing coaching for performance, mentoring of employees, giving systematic performance feedback, providing the necessary tools and resources, and providing job-related training programs could all enhance employee expectancies for high performance. Similarly, effective employee selection can also enhance the expectancy component of motivation, because new hires are well-matched to the requirements of their jobs and thus should feel confident that they can perform. As you can see from Table 2–3, the set of HR practices that enhance expectancy perceptions tends to be staffing and development activities.

Next, we consider HR practices to enhance **instrumentalities** for high task performance. Here our efforts primarily relate to various types of contingent reward systems. In fact, one could argue that virtually all of the various financial reward systems in use today are designed to directly enhance employee instrumentality perceptions for job performance. One could also argue that of the three components of motivation, instrumentalities are the employee perceptions most easily and directly influenced by human resource practices.[31] Thus, bonuses for reaching performance goals, commissions for sales personnel, merit salary adjustments, recognition programs

TABLE 2–3. Human Resource Practices that Enhance Motivation for Job Performance

Enhancing Expectancy	Enhancing Instrumentality	Enhancing Valence
Coaching	Merit pay	Add outcomes with positive valence
Mentoring	Bonus plans	
Goal setting	Commissions	
Performance feedback	Supervisor praise for performance	
Tools and resources	Teammate praise for performance	
Selection for person–organization fit		
Training and development		

for high performance, and even supervisory or teammate praise are practices which can create a direct connection—and thus an instrumentality perception—between achieving high performance and obtaining (presumably) valuable outcomes.

The research literature of HRM reports many examples of HR programs that created performance–outcome instrumentality perceptions to increase employee motivation. In one rather novel study, for example, unionized employees of the Weyerhaeuser Corporation, in the forest products industry, were given financial incentives based on individual performance.[32] These employees were originally paid an hourly wage ($5/hour) to trap mountain beaver, which destroy young trees. In the incentive program trappers were awarded $1 for each beaver trapped, for a period of four weeks. Then they were switched to a new reward schedule, in which they received $4 after trapping a beaver *and* correctly guessing the color of one of four marbles prior to drawing it from a bag. In another group of trappers the order of reward schedules was reversed. Thus, under both reward strategies an instrumentality perception was created in which level of performance (number of beavers trapped) was linked to level of outcomes (financial rewards). Results indicated that under both schedules employee productivity increased and company costs decreased.

Finally, what can managers do to enhance employee **valence** perceptions for outcomes provided by the organization? Keep in mind that the attractiveness of outcomes is an individual perception stemming from an employee's basic need structure. It follows that managers cannot expect to change or enhance individual employee valences for particular outcomes. Managers can, however, ask employees. Asking employees, either personally or through formal communications (e.g., surveys), can help managers to identify the outcomes most valued by employees. Not surprisingly, it seems that financial rewards have high valence for most employees. Many other

TABLE 2–4. Human Resource Practices that Enhance Attendance Motivation

Enhancing Expectancy	Enhancing Instrumentality	Enhancing Valence
Flexible schedules	Attendance bonuses	Add valent outcomes
Van pools	Earned time off for attendance	
Child care programs	Recognition programs for attendance	
Telecommuting options	Supervisory praise	
	Progressive discipline for nonattendance	

outcomes, however, can be effective in motivating behavior (and much less expensive).

It also follows that managers can increase the overall valence of the set of outcomes linked to a behavior (e.g., performance) by **adding more valuable outcomes** to the set of outcomes already linked to the behavior. That is, a larger set of valuable outcomes, say, a variety of financial and nonfinancial rewards, produces more overall valence for the behavior compared to a smaller set of outcomes.

Example 2. Enhancing Attendance Motivation. Table 2–4 illustrates some practices that could be put in place to encourage employee motivation for faithful attendance at work.

First, to improve **expectancies** for attendance, we are interested in activities enhancing employees' perceptions that if they try, they will be able to faithfully attend work. Programs such as van pools, flexible work schedules, employer child care centers or other child care assistance, and even homework arrangements (telecommuting) can enhance employees' expectancies for attending work. Note that these programs would improve employee ability to get to work—which would result in higher expectancies for attending and thus more overall motivation to attend.

Programs to enhance **instrumentalities** for attendance focus on identifying various types of *behavior–reward linkages* for attendance or *behavior–punishment linkages* for absence. Financial bonuses, earned time off, recognition programs for excellent attendance, and supervisory praise could all be linked to attendance. Of course, each of these outcomes would likely have a positive valence for employees. Similarly, progressive discipline programs can be successful as punishment (negatively valent outcomes) linked to a lack of attendance.

To enhance the overall level of **valence** for outcomes linked to attendance, we could ask employees to help us identify outcomes they value which could be linked to attendance behavior. Identifying additional valued outcomes to link to attendance, of course, would raise the overall level of valence for attendance behavior.

The research literature of human resource management includes a number of empirical demonstrations of HR programs which have motivated increased employee attendance. In one field study, for example, a lottery-style reward was linked to the attendance behavior of blue-collar workers in an industrial plant. Workers who had achieved a week of perfect attendance were allowed to participate in a lottery. At the end of each week a cash prize was awarded to the lottery winner. This program created a clear attendance–outcome connection (instrumentality) for a valuable outcome. The program resulted in a significant increase in attendance over the course of a number of weeks.[33]

Expectancy Theory and Human Resource Systems

From the perspective of integrated HR systems we should also consider how *changes* in some aspect of an HR system might affect employee perceptions of expectancy, instrumentality, and valence. Managers often overlook the "side effects" of a change in one HR practice on other important employee perceptions and behaviors. Consider an organization's decision to change from **seniority-based salary increases** to a **merit salary system**. This change may have been made to be more cost conscious or efficient, to try to raise employee productivity, or even to follow the lead of other firms in implementing a popular management fad. Expectancy theory yields valuable insight into exactly how this new program should affect employee motivation.

First, consider expectancy. A merit pay system should have *no* effect on employees' perceptions about their probability of high performance if they try. Next, consider instrumentality. A major change has taken place in that "years of service" is no longer the basis for pay increases. Effective merit pay creates a strong connection (instrumentality) between the employees' level of performance and the subsequent size of their salary increase—an instrumentality which did not previously exist. This salary increase is also likely to have high valence, assuming it is of a noticeable magnitude. Thus, because of a new instrumentality for a valuable reward, the shift to a merit pay system should result in substantial increases in employee motivation for high performance.

This example illustrates how managers can use expectancy concepts to diagnose HR problems and recommend solutions. The expectancy theory also assists managers in understanding how changes in HR practices could have side effects on other behaviors in a way that was not anticipated. Next we turn to another motivational concept that also has tremendous practical value for managing human resource systems—organizational justice, including distributive justice (equity theory) and procedural justice.

Organizational Justice: Equity Theory

The concept of organizational justice includes both distributive justice and procedural justice. The equity theory, a well-known theory of distributive justice, is especially valuable for diagnosing problems and suggesting solutions to motivational problems. This theory will receive most of our attention in this section.

Equity theory focuses on the idea that an employee, as a member of a work organization, is willing to exert effort to achieve (or to restore) a perception of fairness or justice. Equity theory is concerned with *distributive justice,* which means the level of rewards that are distributed to employees are perceived as just. Another type of justice, *procedural justice,* will be discussed later in this chapter. Equity theory, similar to expectancy theory, considers employee **perceptions** (versus objective reality) to be critical to one's motivation for achieving fairness.

Embedded in equity theory are two key concepts: **social exchange** and **social comparison.**[34] Social exchange is the notion that people often see themselves as involved in exchange relationships with other parties, such as other individuals, groups, or organizations. Social comparison refers to people's tendency to compare themselves to others in terms of their exchanges and their treatment.

Inputs, Outcomes, Person, Other

Exchange relationships could include a variety of business or personal relationships in which both parties contribute something to the relationship—in a sense, the two parties exchange resources. In the workplace, employees participate in exchange relationships with their employers. Both parties contribute and each expects the other party to contribute to the exchange. Using equity theory terminology, **inputs** include whatever an employee believes that he or she brings to the exchange relationship (e.g., effort, loyalty), and **outcomes** are whatever the employee perceives that he or she receives in return (e.g., pay, promotions). Table 2–5 lists inputs and outcomes that employees might see as being relevant to their exchange relationship with the organization. The perceived **ratio** of one's inputs to the outcomes received is an important part of this theory.[35]

But the outcome-to-input ratio an employee perceives is also viewed in reference to the outcome-to-input ratio for some **other.** This comparison "other" is typically a peer co-worker but could be a subordinate, an employee

TABLE 2–5. Inputs and Outcomes in Equity Theory

Perceived Inputs	Perceived Outcomes
Effort	Salary
Productivity	Benefits
Education	Job challenge
Training	Promotions
Experience	Status symbols
Loyalty	Pleasant working conditions
Age	Travel allowance

of another firm in a similar job, a supervisor, or even oneself in a previous job.[36] Thus, one's perception of equity can be summarized as follows:

Person		Other	Perception
$\dfrac{\text{Outcomes}}{\text{Inputs}}$	$=$	$\dfrac{\text{Outcomes}}{\text{Inputs}}$	Equity
$\dfrac{\text{Outcomes}}{\text{Inputs}}$	$\lessgtr$	$\dfrac{\text{Outcomes}}{\text{Inputs}}$	Inequity

If the employee ("person") feels that the ratio of outcomes to inputs is equivalent to that of the "other," then the employee will perceive equity, or a feeling of fairness. However, if **person** feels that this ratio is lower (or higher) than that of **other**, then person will perceive inequity, which could be described as a kind of psychological tension—which the employee will be motivated to resolve. The larger the perceived gap between the two ratios, the greater the perception of inequity and thus psychological tension.

Note that it is one's **ratio** of outcomes to inputs compared to the other which is important in equity theory. For example, just because an employee perceives that a co-worker earns more in salary does not mean that the employee will perceive inequity. If the co-worker is also viewed as contributing additional inputs (e.g., education, experience) to go with the higher salary, then the relative outcome-to-input ratios could be seen as equivalent.

Employees' Strategies for Dealing with Perceived Inequity

How do employees resolve the psychological tension that results from perceptions of inequity? They might use several different ways to restore equity.[37] Suppose that person A feels that she is underpaid in relation to her co-workers. She might try to restore equity by working on one of the four components in the two ratios:

1. She may increase her own outcomes by, for example, asking for a raise.
2. She may decrease her own inputs by, for example, becoming less productive.
3. She may decrease the other's outcomes by, for example, persuading their managers to alter other's pay.
4. She may increase other's inputs by, for example, pressuring him or her to work harder.

What if the four components cannot be altered and the magnitude of under-reward inequity perceived by person B is substantial? Then person B would have to choose another course of action:

1. He might alter or distort his perceptions of the situation so the inequity is diminished or eliminated. He might say, for example, "Maybe my effort and performance haven't really been that exceptional," thus altering the perceptions of his inputs in a downward direction. Alternatively, he might say, "I guess my co-worker really has done an outstanding job," thus altering the perception of the other's inputs in an upward direction.

2. He might choose a different comparison other, someone for whom the comparison does not produce inequity perceptions.
3. He might "leave the field" by quitting or obtaining a transfer, in order to get out of the inequity situation.

As just illustrated, employees have a variety of strategies to use in dealing with the tension produced by perceptions of inequity. We expect that some of these strategies are more likely to be used than others.[38] First, employees are more likely to maximize the amount of positive outcomes obtained and to minimize big increases in their inputs. Second, employees are likely to resist large changes in important inputs or outcomes. Third, employees are more likely to change their views of *other* people than their views of themselves. Finally, "leaving the field," or quitting, is a last resort, and one of the least likely strategies.

Implications of Equity Theory for Managing Human Resources

What are the implications of equity theory for managers? First, managers must acknowledge that employees pay close attention to the exchanges that they and others make with the organization. Next, managers must determine how to produce a work environment in which the majority of employees perceive equity. Clearly, employees often perceive situations (e.g., inputs and outcomes) quite differently from management. Managers must strive not to provide all employees with the same level of rewards, but to create a **culture of consistency**. That is, managers must strive to apply HR policies, programs, rules, and rewards in a way that will produce employee perceptions of consistency, and thus equity. For example, policies about distribution of outcomes such as starting salaries, salary increases, benefits, promotions, or training opportunities must be administered with unwavering consistency. Clear and open communication of the policies for distribution of rewards would certainly be a part of this culture of consistency.

Human Resource Management Practices and Equity Theory

Example. Family-Friendly Programs. Again, let's consider the introduction of a new HR policy and the policy's impact on employees from the equity perspective. Suppose that an organization decided to put into place a new set of "family-friendly" programs. These programs, such as child care facilities, special parental leave provisions, and home-work arrangements, are seen as helping employees to balance their work with their personal lives. Expectancy theory suggests that we have provided new, highly valuable outcomes which are linked to (are instrumental for) membership in the organization. Thus, we have increased motivation for membership in our organization—at least for some people.

The equity theory, however, suggests some potential problems. We would expect employees with families to view these new family-friendly programs as additional **outcomes** provided in the exchange relationship. But what about the employees with no children? They may consider these new programs to be irrelevant and useless to them. They would perceive new outcomes provided only to their **comparison others,** placing them in a state of perceived inequity. In fact, a recent study of employee reactions to parental leave provisions suggests that some employees do have these negative perceptions.[39] Management may expect to hear some grumbling about the unfairness of the new programs and requests to spend the organization's resources on programs more valuable to all employees. Childless employees may try to resolve this perceived inequity using a variety of strategies discussed earlier in this chapter, including applying pressure to eliminate these programs in the organization and attempting to get additional outcomes which *they* find valuable.

Thus, the equity theory, similar to expectancy theory, provides a valuable way to assess the impact of changes in HR systems on employees and their motivation for important behaviors.

PROCEDURAL JUSTICE AND ITS IMPLICATIONS

Equity theory is about distributive justice, or the employees' perception of the fairness of the amount of outcomes received. *Procedural* justice is also an important employee perception. Procedural justice refers to employee perceptions of the fairness of **policies** and **procedures** used in determining outcome distributions. Perceptions of procedural justice or injustice can also have a significant influence on perceptions of the fairness of outcome distributions.[40] For example, employees are more willing to accept low pay if they believe that pay was determined **fairly**—that is, if fair procedures were followed to determine pay.

Perceptions of procedural justice are relevant to a wide variety of phenomena in organizations and to many other aspects of society. Fair procedures communicate a regard for employee dignity and self-respect. In general, procedures granting employees some **control** over the process of outcome attainment are seen as more "procedurally" fair.[41] Thus, human resource decisions involving reward allocations, such as pay decisions, are more likely to be seen as fair if employees are given a "voice" in the process. Table 2–6 illustrates some practices which can enhance the perceived procedural justice of performance appraisal and compensation programs.

CONCLUSION

We now have a basic framework for understanding the determinants of employee behavior. Just as we reviewed certain components of HR systems that can affect the opportunity dimension, we encourage you to begin thinking about how staffing, compensation, and development practices can influence employees' ability and motivation to perform on the job. Later chapters will develop the theme that reward and compensation practices are uniquely suited to affect the motivation dimension, while staffing and

TABLE 2–6. Human Resource Practices that Enhance Procedural Justice

Performance Appraisal	Compensation
Inform employees of performance standards in advance	Use employee involvement in setting up pay programs
Include opportunities to express feelings and viewpoints during appraisal sessions	Provide appeals procedures
	Provide clear communications of pay policies and decisions
Have supervisors keep diaries for accurate measurement of employee behavior	
Include employee self-ratings of performance	
Provide appeals procedures	

development practices tend to primarily influence the abilities required to be an effective performer. However, staffing practices can influence motivation levels within work groups and training and development practices can be used to increase the motivation to perform in a variety of ways.

The point of this chapter is that effective managers and HR professionals are able to diagnose the primary factors that account for important employee behaviors. One way to begin to develop this skill is to study employee behavior from the perspective of ability, motivation, and opportunity. Any time a change in an HR system is proposed, you should understand how the change is likely to affect each of these three dimensions. All HRM practices influence processes that change behavior. Effective managers have developed insights into the linkages between managerial practice and these key processes. In fact, some companies consider the capacity to predict and understand employee behavior a central requirement for an effective senior executive.[42] Earlier in this chapter we labeled this attribute "interpersonal/intrapersonal intelligence."

CONTINUOUS LEARNING: SOME NEXT STEPS

This chapter has had a theoretical/conceptual orientation. To make this material come to life we suggest that you actively seek out new information and attempt to translate some of this theory into practice. Try some of these next steps—we think you will find them useful.

- In this chapter there was extensive coverage of expectancy theory. Using the key concepts of expectancy, instrumentality, and valence perceptions, develop a questionnaire that could be used to measure employee motivation to perform assigned tasks. That is, develop a series of self-report questions that address employee perceptions about each of the three key components of this theory. In addition to devising a way to measure each component of the theory, devise a way to take all of this information simultaneously into account so that an overall motivation score for each respondent can be calculated. Repeat this process and design similar data collection tools for measuring employee motivation to (1) attend work on a regular basis, (2) exert effort during an assigned training program, and (3) seek promotion to a higher level job.

- A leading HR-oriented consulting firm is Personnel Decisions International (PDI). Go to this firm's web page (www.personneldecisions.com) and review the types of services offered. Note those services that provide clients with measurement tools for (1) analyzing positions in terms of required competencies and KSAs, and (2) strategic job modeling. Then conduct a general web search and identify five or six other consulting firms that compete with PDI by providing similar services and products. After these other firms have been identified, compare each firm's web-based services in terms of "user friendliness" and usefulness.

- Return to the home page for the Society for Human Resource Management (www.shrm.org) and then go to "SHRMSTORE." Here you will find a variety of useful services and products. Take a look at the section called "New Books." Review this section and create a reference list of books explicitly addressing employee motivation, values, and interests.

ENDNOTES

1. J. P. Campbell, M. D. Dunnette, E. E. Lawler, and K. E. Weick, *Managerial Behavior, Performance, and Effectiveness.* (New York: McGraw-Hill, 1970); H. P. Dachler and W. H. Mobley, "Construct Validation of an Instrumentality–Expectancy–Task–Goal Model of Work Motivation: Some Theoretical Boundary Conditions," *Journal of Applied Psychology Monograph* 58 (1973), pp. 397–418; and N. R. F. Maier, *Psychology in Industry* (Boston: Houghton Mifflin, 1955).

2. L. H. Peters and E. J. O'Connor, "Situational Constraints and Work Outcomes: The Influence of a Frequently Overlooked Construct," *Academy of Management Review* 5 (1980), pp. 391–97.

3. M. D. Dunnette, "Basic Attributes of Individuals in Relation to Behavior in Organizations." In M. D. Dunnette (ed.), *Handbook of Industrial and Organizational Psychology* (Chicago: Rand McNally, 1976).

4. L. G. Humphreys, "Commentary: The *g* Factor in Employment," *Journal of Vocational Behavior* 29 (1986), p. 443.

5. Dunnette, "Basic Attributes of Individuals."

6. E. A. Fleishman, "The Description and Prediction of Perceptual Motor Skill Learning." In R. Glaser (ed.), *Training Research and Education* (Pittsburgh: University of Pittsburgh Press, 1962).

7. J. Hage and C. H. Powers, *Post-industrial Lives: Roles and Relationships in the 21st Century* (Newbury Park, CA: Sage Publications, 1992); and R. B. Reich, *The Work of Nations* (New York: Random House, 1991).

8. Reich, *The Work of Nations.*

9. E. Jaques, *Requisite Organization* (Arlington, VA: Cason Hall & Co, 1996).

10. H. Gardner, *Multiple Intelligences: The Theory in Practice* (New York: Basic Books, 1993).

11. H. G. Gough, "Personality and Personality Assessment." In M. D. Dunnette (ed.), *Handbook of Industrial and Organizational Psychology* (Chicago: Rand McNally, 1976).

12. D. C. McClelland, *The Achievement Motive* (New York: Appleton-Century-Crofts, 1953); and D. C. McClelland and D. Burnham, "Power Is the Great Motivator," *Harvard Business Review,* March–April 1976, pp. 100–111.

13. H. G. Gough, "A Work Orientation Scale for the California Psychological Inventory," *Journal of Applied Psychology* 70 (1985), pp. 505–13.

14. J. B. Miner, "Twenty Years of Research on Role-Motivation Theory of Managerial Effectiveness," *Personnel Psychology* 31 (1978), pp. 739–60.

15. M. R. Barrick, and M. K. Mount, "The Big Five Personality Dimensions and Job Performance: A Meta-analysis," *Personnel Psychology* 44 (1991), pp. 1–26.

16. R. Hogan and J. Hogan, *Hogan Personality Inventory Manual* (Tulsa, OK: Hogan Assessment Systems, 1995).

17. Campbell et al., *Managerial Behavior.*

18. M. Blumberg and C. D. Pringle, "The Missing Opportunity in Organizational Research: Some Implications for a Theory of Work Performance," *Academy of Management Review* 7 (1982), pp. 560–69.

19. Peters and O'Connor, "Situational Constraints and Work Outcomes."

20. See K. E. Kram, *Mentoring at Work: Developmental Relationships in Organizational Life* (Glenview, IL: Scott, Foresman, 1985); M. London and S. A. Stumpf, *Managing Careers* (Reading, MA: Addison-Wesley, 1982); and M. W. McCall, M. M. Lombardo, and A. M. Morrison, *The Lessons of Experience: How Successful Executives Develop on the Job* (New York: Lexington Books, 1988).

21. D. W. Bray and D. L. Grant, "The Assessment Center in the Measurement of Potential for Business Management," *Psychological Monographs* 80, no. 17, whole no. 625 (1966); and B. B. Gaugler, D. B. Rosenthal, G. C. Thornton III, and C. Benton, "Meta-analysis of Assessment Center Validity," *Journal of Applied Psychology* 72 (1987), pp. 493–511.

22. H. Lancaster, "Making Your M.B.A. from a Small School Grab Some Attention," *The Wall Street Journal,* January 28, 1997, p. B1; and H. Lancaster, "Readers Revisit How to Pick M.B.A. School," *The Wall Street Journal,* February 11, 1997, p. B1.

23. M. M. Marini, "Sex Differences in Earnings in the United States." In W. R. Scott and J. Blake (eds.), *Annual Review of Sociology* 15 (Palo Alto, CA: Annual Reviews, 1989), pp. 343–80; A. M. Morrison and M. A. Von Glinow, "Women and Minorities in Management," *American Psychologist* 45 (1990), pp. 200–208; and L. K. Stroh, J. M. Brett, and A. H. Reilly, "All the Right Stuff: A Comparison of Female and Male Managers' Career Progression," *Journal of Applied Psychology* 77 (1992), pp. 251–60.

24. G. F. Dreher and T. H. Cox, "Race, Gender, and Opportunity: A Study of Compensation Attainment and the Establishment of Mentoring Relationships," *Journal of Applied Psychology* 81 (1996), pp. 297–308.

25. T. G. Gutteridge, "Organizational Career Development Systems: The State of the Practice." In D. T. Hall and Associates (eds.), *Career Development in Organizations* (San Francisco: Jossey-Bass, 1986), pp. 50–94; R. A. Noe, J. R. Hollenbeck, B. Gerhart, and P. M. Wright, *Human Resource Management: Gaining a Competitive Advantage* (Burr Ridge, IL: Irwin, 1994); and London and Stumpf, *Managing Careers.*

26. G. F. Dreher and T. W. Dougherty, "Substitutes for Career Mentoring: Promoting Equal Opportunity through Career Management and Assessment Systems (CMAS)," *Journal of Vocational Behavior* 51 (1997), pp. 110–24.

27. E. E. Lawler, *Motivation in Work Organizations* (Monterey, CA: Brooks/Cole, 1973).

28. Ibid.; and V. H. Vroom, *Work and Motivation* (New York: John Wiley & Sons, 1964).

29. Lawler, *Motivation in Work Organizations.*

30. J. B. Miner, *Theories of Organizational Behavior* (Hinsdale, IL: Dryden Press, 1980).

31. Lawler, *Motivation in Work Organizations.*

32. G. P. Latham and D. L. Dossett, "Designing Incentive Plans for Unionized Employees: A Comparison of Continuous and Variable Ratio Reinforcement Schedules," *Personnel Psychology* 31 (1978), pp. 47–61.

33. E. Pedalino and V. U. Gamboa, "Behavior Modification and Absenteeism: Intervention in One Industrial Setting," *Journal of Applied Psychology* 59 (1974), pp. 694–98.

34. J. S. Adams, "Toward an Understanding of Inequity," *Journal of Abnormal and Social Psychology* 67 (1963), pp. 422–36; J. S. Adams, "Inequity in Social Exchange." In L. Berkowitz (ed.), *Advances in Experimental Social Psychology* 2 (New York: Academic Press, 1965), pp. 267–99.

35. J. Greenberg, "Organizational Justice: Yesterday, Today, and Tomorrow," *Journal of Management* 16 (1990), pp. 399–432.

36. R. D. Pritchard, "Equity Theory: A Review and Critique," *Organizational Behavior and Human Performance* 4 (1969), pp. 75–94.

37. R. B. Vecchio, *Organizational Behavior* (Fort Worth: Dryden Press, 1995).

38. Adams, "Inequity in Social Exchange."

39. S. L. Grover, "Predicting the Perceived Fairness of Parental Leave Policies," *Journal of Applied Psychology* 76 (1991), pp. 247–55.

40. R. Folger and M. Konovsky, "Effects of Procedural and Distributive Justice on Reactions to Pay Raise Decisions," *Academy of Management Journal* 32 (1989), pp. 115–30; and Greenberg, "Organizational Justice."

41. J. Greenberg and R. Folger, "Procedural Justice, Participation, and the Fair Process Effect in Groups and Organizations." In P. B. Paulus (ed.), *Basic Group Processes* (New York: Springer-Verlag, 1983), pp. 235–56.

42. G. F. Dreher and D. W. Kendall, "Organizational Staffing." In G. R. Ferris, S. D. Rosen, and D. T. Barnum (eds.), *Handbook of Human Resource Management* (Cambridge, MA: Blackwell, 1995).

Part II Human Resource Systems

WHAT THE GENERAL MANAGER SHOULD KNOW

3

Staffing, Reward, and Development Systems

A LOOK AT THE POSSIBILITIES

As a general manager you should be aware of the many possibilities that exist when evaluating, designing, and implementing HR systems. In this chapter you will

- Be introduced to the concept of a *domain statement* of HRM practices.
- Learn how 19 specific dimensions of HRM practices in our domain statement reflect attributes of a firm's reward system, staffing system, training and development system, and performance management system.
- See that managers must make informed decisions about the set of HRM practices that will maximize the firm's key employee behaviors for a job class.
- Become acquainted with an illustration of how you could select from the menu of 19 HRM practices if your firm's business objectives required a focus on *Total Quality Management (TQM)-oriented behaviors.*

W̄e are now ready to examine HRM practices in detail. This chapter suggests there is a domain of practices that can be linked to the behavioral requirements of a job. It initiates a process of helping you understand the many possibilities inherent in the design and implementation of HR systems. This chapter also is about managerial discretion—about making choices that should relate to firm performance and organizational effectiveness. While we begin Part II with this chapter about a decision-making framework, the next four chapters (4–7) view HRM practices in greater detail. At first glance, these chapters may appear to be like chapters in more traditional HRM textbooks, which represent the functions of HRM. But these four chapters focus on the essential concepts needed by *general managers.* Overall, this book is about strategic HRM, but you need some grounding in functional HRM to begin to think strategically.

When observing management practices and styles across companies, it quickly becomes clear to almost all observers that large differences in HRM practices are common, even when industry and job class are held constant. Also, as noted in Chapter 1, many observers believe that this variation accounts for much of the observed difference in firm performance. Waterman, for example, states that what makes top performing companies different is that they "are better able to meet the needs of their people."[1] What Waterman is talking about is being able to attract, develop, and retain top quality employees and being able to motivate these individuals to perform in extraordinary ways.

This variation in HRM practices can exist for virtually all job classes, even when the nature of work is very similar across firms. For example, Williams and Dreher found that commercial banks used widely disparate methods in selecting, training, and paying tellers.[2] Within a single company, practices also can change dramatically over time. Dreher and Kendall provided a clear example of this when describing the Associated Group (as of late 1993, a $3.3 billion company in the insurance, health and property brokerage, and financial services business).[3] This company's strategic restructuring included very large-scale adjustments to HR systems. For example, in 1987, the company's approach to compensation (across most hierarchical levels) was to provide highly competitive base pay, very generous benefits, and little pay at risk (some incentive pay limited to a small group of managers and executives). By 1993, most employees were part of an incentive plan and large proportions of pay were at risk for higher level managers and executives. More recently, even the "individual contributor" level (entry level) was targeted for a 10 percent pay-at-risk component. Top-level executives (corporate staff officers and operating company CEOs) have not received annual base salary increases since 1987, instead receiving additional compensation from incentive opportunities.

This chapter emphasizes the concept of a **domain statement** and how managers can make informed decisions about selecting from this domain. While we build on earlier work, we offer our version of a domain statement—a version that is particularly concerned with the linkages between desired employee behaviors and associated HRM practices.

The use of this approach was pioneered by Schuler and Jackson.[4] Their ground-breaking work made explicit connections among competitive strategies (e.g., innovation, quality enhancement, and cost reduction), needed role behaviors, and a typology of HRM practices. We, of course, are using this same approach throughout this text. As developed in Chapter 1 (see Figure 1–1), business strategy and existing technology lead to certain optimal ways to organize work processes. Once work processes have been clarified, key employee behaviors can be specified. Once we know the desired behaviors, informed selections can be made from what Schuler and Jackson call a **human resource–management–practice** menu.

Our menu, or what we call a domain statement, includes 19 dimensions or categories within which HRM practices can be classified. It is within these dimensions that firms can vary their approach to managing human resources. Each dimension provides managers with choices. The 19 dimensions are organized within four categories as listed in Table 3–1.

TABLE 3-1. Domain Statement Menu 53

CHAPTER THREE
Staffing,
Reward, and
Development
Systems

REWARD SYSTEM ATTRIBUTES

1. Pay level
2. Pay at risk
3. Performance-contingent pay
4. Internal versus external job pricing

5. Skill-based pay
6. Seniority-based pay
7. Benefit system flexibility
8. Benefit level

STAFFING SYSTEM ATTRIBUTES

9. Career system orientation
10. Potential versus achievement orientation

11. Organizational fit
12. Exit orientation

ATTRIBUTES OF THE TRAINING AND DEVELOPMENT SYSTEM

13. Skill orientation
14. Training-method orientation
15. Career pathing

16. Succession planning
17. Skill inventories

ATTRIBUTES OF THE PERFORMANCE MEASUREMENT SYSTEM

18. Measurement type

19. Measurement source

DEFINING THE DIMENSIONS
OF HRM PRACTICE VARIATION

The remainder of this chapter defines (and illustrates by using) the 19 dimensions of our domain statement. We provide a general description of each dimension and also suggest that the reader learn about these dimensions in a direct and interactive way. This more interactive approach will require firsthand data collection. The appendix at the end of the chapter reproduces an **HRM Practices Survey.** We suggest that you use the survey to learn about the HRM practices currently in place at a particular company. You might ask a company representative to complete the survey, or complete the survey yourself based on a position you recently held or continue to hold, or you might use the survey as an interview guide as you discuss HRM practices in a targeted firm. Gathering this information should help clarify the distinctions made in the chapter and enrich (and at times complicate) the definitions themselves. Also, we remind you that a more detailed treatment of HRM practices is presented in Chapters 4–7, where we highlight what the general manager should know about the key functional areas of HRM.

We now turn to the description of the HRM domain statement. Each dimension addresses choices managers need to make when considering how to best use human talent to maximize the return to the many stakeholders of the company.

Pay System Attributes

Pay Level

One basic pay policy decision managers have discretion over is whether to pay at (**meet**), below (**lag**), or above (**lead**) the market—where the market is defined as the average pay level offered by companies competing for employees with similar skill profiles. Although this decision is related to the more general question of **external** competitiveness versus **internal** equity (see dimension 4), we think decisions about pay level deserve a unique dimension in our domain statement. Milkovich and Newman define pay level as "the average of the array of rates paid by an employer."[5] Thus, this concept captures an overall pay policy (perhaps a companywide pay policy) and it is possible for an employer to focus on internal equity and still set average pay rates at or above the so-called market average.

Being a pay-level leader should enable an employer to attract and retain employees possessing critical skill profiles. Based on the principles of **equity theory** (see Chapter 2), being a pay-level leader also might encourage cooperative and organizational citizenship behaviors because the perception of overcompensation may lead to the display of extraordinary role behaviors as a way to establish balance.

Following a lag policy is a typical method of controlling labor costs. A company whose corporate strategy or past financial performance leads to a decision to follow a lag-the-market policy will have to make other adjustments if it hopes to compete for the most desirable job candidates. Some employers successfully negotiate this difficult position by (1) providing other desirable outcomes to employees (e.g., rapid career advancement, exceptional training opportunities) or (2) finding some other way to encourage very high levels of individual effort (e.g., put a great deal of pay at risk).

Pay at Risk

The concept of pay at risk is associated with traditional job-based pay plans, but it emphasizes some rule for linking performance to a supplementary payment—typically, a lump-sum payment in the form of cash or company stock. More pay is "at risk" when the job-based component of total pay is reduced and the supplementary component is increased.[6] The issue surrounding this dimension of our domain statement is **how much** pay is at risk. The rule for linking performance and pay is the focus of the next dimension. That is, when at least some pay is at risk, there needs to be a decision about the **form** of the performance–pay linkage.

Performance-Contingent Pay

Making pay (or other valued job outcomes) contingent on performance should enhance instrumentality perceptions and employee motivation (see Chapter 2 and the discussion of VIE theory). The performance-contingent rule can be at the individual, group, or organizational level. When at the level of the individual, performance-contingent pay can take many forms. For example, individuals working in sales often receive a significant portion of their pay as "commission" income. Since commissions are directly tied to sales, employees' motivation should be enhanced because pay levels rise and fall in line with revenues. These plans can become highly elaborate and specific to a unique set of circumstances.[7]

Individual-level bonus plans can be used in a wide variety of settings. One very informative article characterizing an individual-level bonus plan applied to workers of a paper products firm found the appropriate time to use this form of pay at risk is when

1. Individuals perform independent tasks (individual performance does not depend on the performance level of someone else).
2. Job performance can be measured in a complete and objective way (all important aspects of the job can be captured in the plan).
3. Performance can be measured at a reasonable cost.[8]

Other variations to the pay-at-risk theme alter the measure of performance and the size of the performance unit.[9] Profit sharing and gain sharing are two such variations. Profit sharing has a long history of use and relates payoffs to company or business unit profitability.[10] Gain sharing also has a long history and focuses not on business unit profit but on work unit success in reducing labor costs.[11] With gain-sharing plans, work teams or units must first devise ways to improve work processes, thereby reducing labor costs. Some proportion of the cost savings is then returned to the work group.[12]

Before leaving the area of performance-contingent pay, we need to consider the special case of "merit" pay plans. Merit plans are commonly used as a way to link job performance to pay. This is typically accomplished by making annual adjustments to base pay on the basis of rated performance (as reflected in an annual performance review or appraisal). There is, of course, a large literature devoted to the performance appraisal process[13] and to procedures used to make these annual adjustments to base pay. Whereas we consider merit pay plans (at the level of the individual) to be a form of performance-contingent pay, we do not consider merit plans to be a form of pay at risk. True pay-at-risk plans create a sense of uncertainty for the participant. For pay-at-risk plans, total annual compensation varies as a function of individual, group, or business-unit performance. At the beginning of a new bonus or profit-sharing cycle, participants will experience uncertainty about what their total compensation for the coming year will be. In these plans, it is possible for total compensation to increase, remain about the same, or **decline** from one year to the next.

In the typical merit plan, participants do not experience the same degree of uncertainty. Since annual merit increases are added to base pay, total annual compensation is very unlikely to decrease. Also, merit adjustments often reflect factors other than performance. The factor most commonly considered is the individual's pay rate relative to the midpoint of the individual's pay range.[14] As employees begin to reach the upper limits of the pay range in which their job is located, the frequency and size of pay increases must be controlled. If the position within the pay range is not taken into account, it is difficult to retain the integrity of the entire pay hierarchy because pay for top performers can exceed the maximum rate allowed for their job. If a top performer cannot be promoted into the next higher job grade, merit plans can lose their ability to provide sufficient incentives for many key contributors.

Internal versus External Job Pricing

A focus on external equity, or external job pricing, is a focus on what other companies pay employees in similar job classifications. External competitiveness is concerned with relative pay rates among (not within) organizations.[15] Employers emphasize external equity by conducting or purchasing wage and salary surveys and setting pay rates to reflect what the competition is paying (after taking into account their pay-level policy). With an internal equity focus, the goal is to create within-firm fairness based on a job's contribution to organizational objectives. The primary way to estimate a job's internal or relative worth to any given employer is to conduct a job evaluation. Job evaluation techniques attempt to provide a way to determine the relative worth of jobs inside an organization by measuring what are called "compensable factors." Note that job worth (holding type of work constant) can vary among organizations, depending on how central the job is to the overall mission of the organization.[16]

A particular company may well have unique reasons to internally value a given job at a level that is well above or well below what a so-called market comparison suggests is appropriate. The issue addressed in this dimension of our domain statement has to do with what a firm does when confronted with an internal versus external discrepancy. When an internal evaluation of a job's worth does not agree with an external evaluation, what will the firm emphasize?

Skill-Based Pay

This dimension asks whether a company provides what is called "skill-based" pay, a form of pay that is not job-based, as is traditionally the case in compensation systems. Skill-based pay plans assign pay differentials based on differences in skills possessed by workers, not the type of job a worker might be performing at a given time.[17] For example, on a given day in a manufacturing facility, two workers who are both operating a drill press could receive different rates of pay. The difference would be the result of skill differences between the employees. If one worker could perform only drill press operations while the other is qualified to operate the drill press, lathe, and automated painting equipment, the organization would pay a differential to the worker who has the capacity to perform multiple tasks. These plans, designed to encourage workers to acquire training and skills, should provide the employer with increased flexibility to address changing customer demands.

Skill-based pay can reward employees for acquiring either a "breadth" or "depth" of skills. Although we often consider skill-based pay to be a relatively new and innovative approach to compensation, Mahoney correctly points out that these plans have been around for a long time.[18] For example, the longstanding distinction in crafts of apprentice, journeyman, and master recognizes differences in skill level (breadth of skill level), even though the journeyman and master may perform essentially the same tasks over long periods of time. This concept also relates to the practice of paying teachers on the basis of educational level. For example, two math teachers, both teaching first-year algebra, will often receive different rates of pay because one possesses an undergraduate degree and the other a graduate degree (more depth). The graduate degree, of course, is assumed to add skills that relate to the mission of the school. Skill-based pay is now finding increased application in the service sector and among managerial/professional employees.[19]

Seniority-Based Pay

Seniority, defined as the length of service in an employment unit, can be used as a basis for allocating many organizational outcomes (e.g., wages, promotions), including the right to continue as an employee (i.e., seniority can serve as a criterion when making layoff decisions). Unions in the United States have long supported seniority-based decision rules, as shown by the prevalence of explicit seniority clauses in collective bargaining agreements.[20] Union officials typically argue that seniority rules promote stability and perceptions of fairness in organizations. They also argue that because more senior workers are protected from layoffs and receive higher wages and benefits than newcomers, they will be more likely to stay with an employer (thereby gaining the advantages that go along with experience) and will provide on-the-job training to new employees (who will not be direct competitors for wages and promotions).

The value of seniority rules remains a point of controversy because they may (1) work to disadvantage highly productive newcomers and (2) lead some of the most productive workers to seek employment in companies where pay and promotions are directly linked to performance and contribution.[21] We encourage readers to develop an expectancy theory–based argument for or against seniority rules. Under certain circumstances, however, it does make good sense to use seniority-based rules. For example, seniority makes sense when (1) the goal is to promote a high degree of company loyalty and commitment, (2) there is a need to encourage cooperative and team-oriented behavior, including the willingness to provide on-the-job training, and (3) the situation requires extensive learning of company-specific knowledge and skills.

Benefit System Flexibility

This dimension assesses whether an employer offers a flexible benefit, or cafeteria, plan, defined as one that permits "employees to select benefits they want from a package of employer-sponsored coverages, including plans that offer a choice between cash compensation and benefits."[22] This dimension measures the degree to which the company's discretionary benefit options (e.g., life insurance, medical insurance, and paid days off) are offered to full-time employees in a fixed versus flexible way.

In practice, flexible benefit options can help employers control costs, but they are primarily used when employees disagree on what is most important. If there is a lot of diversity with regard to the values (valence perceptions) associated with receiving different benefit options, a flexible plan can provide a better fit between what is available and what employees want or need. Moreover, since they require employees to make regular decisions or to choose among the alternative options, the process of reviewing and evaluating options should make the value of each more salient to the decision maker.

Benefit Level

Companies can vary not only in the flexibility of their benefit programs, but also in their expenditure levels. While the cost of employee benefits in the United States has reached almost staggering proportions,[23] what is particularly interesting is the observed variability in benefit expenditures across firms and industries. For example, the average percentage of payroll expenditures devoted to benefits among companies in the retail sales industry (30 percent) is far lower than that devoted to benefits in the chemical industry (45 percent).[24] In analyzing this dimension (very much like the **pay-level** dimension), consider whether a company tends to lag, mcct, or lead the market with respect to the resources devoted to employee benefits. Note that when examining this issue, the analysis is almost always at the job class or organizational level (i.e., benefits are rarely distributed on the basis of individual performance or contribution).

Attributes of the Staffing System

Career System Orientation

This attribute of the staffing system is concerned with the typical sources of talent for a company. Termed a "supply flow," this dimension is "measured by the openness of the career system to the external labor market at other than entry level."[25] Some companies focus on internal labor markets, drawing from the external labor market only for entry-level assignments, and then follow a "promotion-from-within" policy. Others hire as needed, across organizational levels, from the external labor market. The difference in approach seems to be a function of the firm's strategic focus and the employee behaviors required to implement the desired strategy.[26]

Hiring at the top is one interesting area within which to consider this dimension. In many countries, such as Germany and Japan, CEOs are promoted almost exclusively from within.[27] In the United States, studies from the 1970s to the early 1990s reflect a steady increase in the proportion of outside hires. The number of new CEOs who had been with their companies for less than three years is estimated to have grown by nearly 50 percent during this 20-year period.[28] Thus, variation on this dimension is likely to be a result of many factors, many of which are changing over time.

Potential versus Achievement Orientation

Another interesting way to characterize a staffing system (or perhaps the term "career system" is best applied here) is to use the framework originally proposed by Turner and subsequently refined by Rosenbaum.[29]

Rosenbaum considered staffing, career, and succession systems in terms of what he called sponsored versus contest mobility norms. The **sponsored-mobility approach** stresses the early identification of talent. Firms following this norm attempt to benefit from the efficiencies of specialized training and socialization by providing high-potential candidates with challenging assignments and other opportunities believed to be conducive to employee development. Often, promotional opportunities are curtailed for persons not assigned to these so-called fast-track programs. The focus is on identifying job candidates who have the potential to learn and develop—not candidates who necessarily possess a current level of knowledge or skill.

At the other extreme, firms following a form of **contest mobility** focus on identifying individuals with proven achievement records. Recognizing that potential is more difficult to identify than is proven achievement or performance, these firms attempt to minimize selection error and emphasize the identification of individuals who currently possess the knowledge, skills, and abilities required to perform required tasks. The contest-oriented company is attempting to maximize its ability to make rapid adjustments to business needs by avoiding time-consuming training of high-potential candidates, thus it is more likely than a sponsored-mobility firm to seek talent from any source, including the external labor market.

Organizational Fit

Some companies seek "right types" or candidates who will "fit" the company's culture and who are similar to current incumbents. At the managerial level this might take the form of seeking candidates who are similar to the company's current leadership.

While many forces can operate to move a company toward ever higher levels of workforce homogeneity,[30] some firms explicitly seek "non–right types" in an attempt to effect organization change and to take advantage of workforce diversity.[31] It is this distinction between organizational cultures that promote homogeneity and those that promote diversity that characterizes this dimension.

Exit Orientation

Here we consider the level of job security the company attempts to provide employees. Some companies attempt to promote stability and loyalty by creating a high degree of job security. Other companies systematically manage the turnover process by continually downsizing and restructuring. These companies aggressively work to retain only those employees who are top performers or who possess a critical set of skills and abilities. This dimension relates to the "employment security" prescription, one of Pfeffer's 13 prescribed management practices discussed in Chapter 1. Pfeffer argues that some degree of security is required if employees are expected to suggest ways of improving operations or if they are expected to help train other employees.

Attributes of the Training and Development System

As you will learn in Chapter 6, high-quality training and development in organizations is based on systematic thinking about

- Assessing training needs
- Designing training solutions
- Deploying these solutions
- Evaluating the results of these initiatives

Here we want to highlight some dimensions along which firms can differ with respect to their general approach to training. This is in keeping with the decision-making theme of this chapter. As you will see when you read Chapter 6, along each of these dimensions many more detailed issues must be resolved about the content and method of training.

Skill-Orientation

Does the company's orientation to training tend to focus on functional and technical skills, or does the orientation emphasize the development of skills that might generalize to a variety of situations? Generalizable skills include such things as communication and conflict resolution skills, problem-solving and analysis skills, and skills that relate to how to improve business processes. Variation on this dimension also is characterized by the difference between firms that do and do not attempt to create "multiskilled" and cross-functionally trained employees.

Training-Method Orientation

Here we are concerned with the traditional distinction between emphasizing "on-site training methods" and "off-site training methods."[32] Does the company approach training from a coaching, on-the-job, apprenticeship, job rotation, and project team assignment basis, or is there an emphasis on the use of formal training centers and programs (e.g., the corporate campus, teleconferencing, computer assisted and programmed instruction)?

Although we think this distinction is useful, we note that technological advances are working to blur and complicate this dimension. As an illustration, one of the authors recently worked with a corporate training staff charged with providing technical skills training on a worldwide basis. In addition to training employees, the corporate training staff needed to train customers in the use and maintenance of the company's highly sophisticated products. The approach taken was to produce self-contained, CD-ROM–based training modules that could be sent to work sites around the world. The training took place on-site, often as a "just-in-time" intervention, but used a formal training package or module.

Career Pathing

Does the company offer clearly defined career paths and formal advice on career planning and development or is the career management process very informal and dependent on self-initiated mentoring relationships? Some firms extensively use job posting systems and career development workshops; others do not. A heavy emphasis on career pathing and associated career development activities will often include the use of HR information systems (see dimension 17, **skill inventories**). These systems characterize employees in terms of career interests, training and development experiences, and measures of current and future capability. Formal career paths help employees identify the knowledge, skill, and ability requirements for higher level jobs. This information can direct individuals as they create training and development plans to help them achieve their career goals.

Succession Planning

Does the company have an effective (and formal) succession planning program in place? In an effective succession planning process, teams of managers typically meet on a regular basis to identify early career managers as replacements for current managers in key positions. As part of the process of identifying replacements, these managers discuss their junior colleagues on an individual basis, considering each person's skills, experiences, strengths, weaknesses, and future developmental needs.

Skill Inventories

In today's business environment, skill inventories are becoming more commonplace because the technology needed to create and update such systems is now readily available. Computerized skill inventories are essentially spreadsheet files. The rows of the spreadsheet list each included employee, and the columns list variables that represent a variety of HR issues. Typically, the variables include employee education level and type, information about past work experiences and assignments, performance appraisal data, information about career objectives and preferences for assignments and geographical placement, and the like. When a position within an organization becomes available, a list of individuals possessing the required competencies, experiences, and preferences can be generated.

These data sets can be very useful when reviewing the overall level of over- or understaffing that may exist in a particular business unit. These data also relate to the previous dimension: They become an essential tool in the succession planning process.

Attributes of the Performance Measurement System

Performance measures include an almost astonishing array of types, forms, and purposes served.[33] Hundreds of different types of rating formats have been proposed and tested, and it is possible to make judgments about operating results, employee behaviors, or person-centered attributes like personality dimensions. In addition, measurement can be at the individual, work team, or organizational level, and the rating strategy can be comparative (individuals are compared to the average performance level of their peer group) or absolute (comparisons are not in relation to other performers, but to some reasonably objective external standard).

In addition to type and form variation, measurement systems can be used for many different purposes, with, of course, some being more usefully applied to particular organizational problems than others. Purposes range from the identification of training needs, to providing feedback to help improve a work process, to making layoff decisions, to allocating bonus funds. Thus, if we cross performance measurement type with the purpose to be served by the measurement system, we are left with many possibilities.

Instead of focusing on all of these possibilities (many of which will receive more attention in Chapter 7), we choose to address what we see to be two fundamental ways of distinguishing among firms.

Measurement Type

By measurement type, we are thinking about results- versus process-oriented measurement practices. Some performance measurement systems focus on the outcomes or products of work (or the time taken to complete tasks). Other systems tend to focus more on **how** the work gets done.

Results-oriented measurement systems count the outcomes of work (e.g., number of units produced, dollar sales value per month) or the time taken to complete assignments (e.g., number of hours taken to rebuild an automatic transmission). These systems tend to be used to allocate scarce resources like money or promotions. **Process-oriented** systems rate the way work is completed (e.g., the salesperson greets the customer within the first three minutes the customer is in the store, the maintenance mechanic uses the proper tools for a particular operation). Typically, process-oriented systems provide employees with feedback about work with the intent of improving performance (via process improvements).

Measurement Source

The final dimension of our domain statement has to do with a concern for the source of measurement data. The traditional approach is unidirectional and hierarchical. Performance measurement is directed from superior to subordinate: Managers rate supervisors, supervisors rate hourly employees, and so on. But some organizations now consider performance measurement from a multidirectional perspective, characterized by the 360-degree appraisal, with feedback being received from subordinates, peers, superiors, and customers.

Figure 3–1 presents a very interesting illustration of a multidirectional approach (and an illustration of how firms put pay at risk; see dimensions 2 and 3). Here, the top 200 Sears, Roebuck and Company executives receive long-term bonuses if a performance index that takes into account (1) the company's overall financial performance, (2) customer satisfaction, and (3) employee satisfaction, reaches a predetermined level.[34] This is "pay at risk." If executives do not reach their performance targets, there is no bonus.

A PRACTICE-BY-BEHAVIOR MATRIX

This chapter has illustrated some general dimensions along which HRM practices can vary (more detailed illustrations follow in the next four chapters), but remember that this chapter is really about a decision-making framework. The objective is to increase the probability that desired behaviors take place in work settings by selecting from many alternatives. Table 3–2 is a general approach to HRM decision making that reinforces this objective.

The rows of Table 3–2 represent the 19 dimensions of HRM practice reviewed in this chapter. The entries in the left-hand column of the table present the possibilities and those on the right the practices that would be prescribed to accomplish the stated behavioral objectives. For each required type of behavior, a new column could be added to the table. For this illustration of the decision-making process, assume that a company's business objective requires an HR system that encourages a high degree of TQM-oriented behaviors. That is, imagine a manufacturing company that needs to create a highly flexible assembly process that continually improves over time. In this section, this class of employee behavior is briefly discussed and

FIGURE 3–1. Multidirectional performance measurement and pay at risk

63

CHAPTER THREE
*Staffing,
Reward, and
Development
Systems*

Pay for performance

Sears has devised an innovative compensation plan that bases 200 top executives' long-term bonuses equally on customer satisfaction, employee satisfaction and financial performance.

How the three-part plan works:

FINANCIAL PERFORMANCE

First the company's financial performance is taken into account. If it meets or exceeds expectations, customer satisfaction and employee satisfaction indexes are considered. The value of any long-term bonus is then based equally on outcomes in all three areas.

....

CUSTOMER SATISFACTION

Cash register issues receipt asking customer to participate in a phone survey . . .

Customer phone survey results are fed into an econometric model in a computer . . .

Computer derives a customer satisfaction index.

1/3

....

EMPLOYEE SATISFACTION

Employees fill out job satisfaction survey . . .

Survey results are fed into an econometric model in a computer . . .

Computer derives an employee satisfaction index.

1/3

1/3

LONG-TERM BONUS

Improvements in index numbers and company performance can mean bigger payouts; likewise, disappointing numbers can mean smaller bonuses, or none at all.

Source: S. Chandler, "Sears's System of Rewards Has Ups and Downs," *Chicago Tribune,* February 15, 1998.

the likely consequences of a few HRM decisions are highlighted. This discussion introduces a process that will be more thoroughly described in terms of situation-specific choices in Part IV.

The behavioral requirements for the company outlined in Table 3–2 are needed to be effective in a TQM-oriented manufacturing facility. These are

TABLE 3–2. HRM Practices Needed to Encourage TQM-Oriented Behaviors among Assemblers in a Manufacturing Facility

Variable	Action Taken
PAY LEVEL	
Lag	
Meet	Meet
Lead	
PAY AT RISK	
None	
Moderate	Moderate to extensive
Extensive	
PERFORMANCE-CONTINGENT PAY	
Individual	
Team	Team
Organization	
JOB PRICING	
Internal equity	Internal
External equity	
SKILL-BASED PAY	
Yes	Yes
No	
SENIORITY-BASED PAY	
Yes	
No	No
BENEFIT SYSTEM FLEXIBILITY	
Yes	Depends on degree of labor market diversity
No	
BENEFIT LEVEL	
Lag	
Meet	Meet
Lead	
CAREER SYSTEM ORIENTATION	
Internal	Internal
External	

(Continued)

behaviors and related skills that allow the employee to participate in the process of monitoring outcomes and work processes, determining the "root" causes of quality problems, and identifying and implementing solutions to these identified problems. In essence, employees are charged with improving work processes over time.[35] In addition to assembling the company's products, these employees gather data about quality and production efficiency. They summarize these data, looking for areas that can be improved and the factors that explain quality variation. They often work as teams,

TABLE 3–2. *(Concluded)* 65

CHAPTER THREE
*Staffing,
Reward, and
Development
Systems*

Variable	Action Taken
CANDIDATE PREFERENCE Potential Achievement	Potential
ORGANIZATIONAL FIT Right types Diversity	Right types emphasized for certain work values; but background diversity needed for the generation of new ideas
EXIT ORIENTATION Security Managed turnover	Security
SKILL ORIENTATION Technical General	General, but will depend on career stage
TRAINING-METHOD ORIENTATION Informal/on-the-job Formal/classroom	Informal and formal
CAREER PATHING Yes No	No
SUCCESSION PLANNING Yes No	No
SKILL INVENTORIES Yes No	Yes
MEASUREMENT TYPE Results Process	Results and process
MEASUREMENT SOURCE Traditional 360 degree	360 degree

meeting to review their findings, brainstorming to formulate plans to improve how products are made, trying out their ideas for improvement, and evaluating the results of their change efforts.

To illustrate our approach, a few of the choices displayed in Table 3–2 will be discussed. For those choices not discussed, the appropriate practices are indicated in the table, but it is up to you to consider the rationale behind each choice. After completing the remainder of this book, we suggest that you return to this section and critique our choices.

First, we consider some dimensions related to pay. Our decision about **pay level** is to meet the market. Anything less would interfere with the company's ability to compete in the labor market for individuals possessing the needed skills to work in this type of setting. However, note that the **pay-at-risk** dimension shows that moderate to extensive levels of pay should be put at risk and that the type of **performance-contingent pay** should be at the level of the work team. An internally integrated approach to pay would encourage teams to seek quality and productivity solutions. When they succeed, they would share in the monetary gains that follow. If a team can find a way to reduce manufacturing costs, the team would receive a portion of the cost savings (a gain-sharing approach to compensation). Because it is possible, when the team contributes to enhanced productivity, for team members to make well above a market wage, setting base pay at the lead-the-market level would be unnecessary.

Moving to some staffing dimensions, we would argue that the **career system** should be internal and that **candidate preference** be directed at finding employees with the potential to learn and adapt to new situations. These prescriptions come about because TQM-oriented employees will be improving this company's manufacturing processes over time. Thus, a great deal of company-specific knowledge and skill will be passed on to newcomers. Employees must be encouraged to stay because they understand the nuances of these improved systems. External job candidates with specific skill sets are not as important as finding newcomers with the potential to learn and adjust to a flexible manufacturing process. We also show the **organizational fit** dimension with some preference for diversity. This preference for diversity is at the entry level. People who have diverse backgrounds but who share the potential to learn should be useful when attempting to solve novel problems.

Finally, we show that devoting resources to **training** is essential in a TQM environment and that performance **measurement** needs to be wide in scope and be at both the results and process levels. Both informal and formal training would need to occur. Early, employees would need to receive formal training in the principles of TQM and the interpersonal skills required to be an effective team member. But this is the type of environment in which employees must continuously help and coach their teammates. Also, TQM companies devote considerable resources to performance feedback. These data are used to help employees improve their effectiveness. Measuring results gives the company a yardstick to determine whether objectives are being met—but performance data are also needed to help people improve and develop over time. The reward and performance measurement systems need to encourage a lot of cooperation and coaching among team members.

To summarize, then, the rows displayed in Table 3–2 represent the beginning of a domain statement. After identifying the behaviors that are most likely to be related to the stated business objectives, managers should make informed choices, selecting the options that maximize their behavioral objectives (and, as will be developed in Chapters 8 and 9, selecting options that meet our standards of system congruence and cost effectiveness).

CONCLUSION

This, then, should give you a fuller appreciation for how firms can manage human resources to create variation both across functions and operating units within the same firm and across firms. This chapter is not meant to be a final statement about what is possible, but primarily an illustration of how diverse HRM practices can be among and within firms. We also see these dimensions as being some of the key or essential dimensions that theory and empirical evidence suggest are fundamentally related to firm performance. In later chapters of this book, as we prescribe HRM systems for particular companies and situations, we will be returning to the themes presented here.

In addition to simply reading this chapter, we want to encourage you to use the appendix. The best way to understand the distinctions presented here is to experience them firsthand. Use the **HRM Practices Survey** as a guide in gathering information about real operating companies or recalling experiences you have had in previous positions. Also, use the survey as another way to define the 19 dimensions of our HRM domain statement.

Finally, use the next four chapters to learn more about the detailed choices functional HRM specialists are confronted with. These chapters were specifically designed to give you, as a general manager, the knowledge needed to interact with this important group of professionals.

CONTINUOUS LEARNING: SOME NEXT STEPS

To more fully appreciate the range and richness of HR practices and strategies we encourage you to complete the next three steps in what should become a process of continuous learning. The first step can be initiated immediately; the second will require active data collection on your part; and the third will follow naturally from the first two.

- Using any web browser, conduct a general search using the key words "Human Resource Management Journals." You will return a long list of related journal titles. Review the entries and take a look at the table of contents for journals that interest you. Try to identify two or three journals that seem worthy of further review and use these sources to expand your knowledge of the "menu" of possible HR practices. For example, the *International Journal of Human Resource Management* is a very good source of information about how HR practices vary across cultural borders. Develop a reading program to learn more about the possibilities—or the ways HR systems are designed to take into account the unique circumstances of a business environment.
- Complete the HRM Practices Survey that is presented in the appendix. Using your network of business and professional associates, identify two or three individuals who work in very different occupations and industries. Interview these individuals, using the survey as an interview guide. In addition to describing the HRM practices associated with the positions of each of these individuals, ask about practices that were not covered by the 19 dimensions presented in the

survey. One useful way to conduct the interviews is to identify HRM practices that were not covered that seem to be unique, setting the company apart from its competitors, and ask about them.

- Finally, as your knowledge base grows, consider modifying the 19-dimension "menu" presented here. Add new dimensions, consolidate dimensions, and delete dimensions as you see fit.

ENDNOTES

1. R. H. Waterman, *What America Does Right: Learning from Companies That Put People First* (New York: W. W. Norton & Company, 1994), p. 17.
2. M. L. Williams and G. F. Dreher, "Compensation System Attributes and Applicant Pool Characteristics," *Academy of Management Journal* 35 (1992), pp. 571–95.
3. G. F. Dreher and D. W. Kendall, "Organizational Staffing." In G. R. Ferris, S. D. Rosen, and D. T. Barnum (eds.), *Handbook of Human Resources* (Oxford, UK: Blackwell Publications, 1995).
4. R. S. Schuler and S. E. Jackson, "Linking Competitive Strategies with Human Resource Management Practices," *Academy of Management Executive* 3 (1987), pp. 207–19.
5. G. T. Milkovich and J. M. Newman. *Compensation* (New York: Irwin/McGraw-Hill, 1999) is perhaps the most widely read and respected compensation text (a text devoted solely to compensation system design and administration) currently available. Almost without exception, most HRM professionals who have completed a masters degree during the last 10 years have been exposed to this work. Therefore, being knowledgeable about concepts from Milkovich and Newman should prove helpful when you need to understand and communicate with these professionals in your company or similarly trained external consultants. For more detailed treatments of any compensation issues, we highly recommend Milkovich and Newman. (Quote is from p. 185.)
6. T. A. Mahoney, "Multiple Pay Contingencies: Strategic Design of Compensation," *Human Resource Management* 28 (1989), pp. 337–47.
7. For example, see J. K. Moynahan, *The Sales Compensation Handbook* (New York: Amacom, 1991); and J. Tallitsch and J. K. Moynahan, "Fine Tuning Sales Compensation Programs," *Compensation and Benefits Review,* March–April 1994, pp. 34–37.
8. G. P. Latham and D. L. Dossett, "Designing Incentive Plans for Unionized Employees: A Comparison of Continuous and Variable Ratio Reinforcement Schedules," *Personnel Psychology* 31 (1978), pp. 47–62.
9. Mahoney, "Multiple Pay Contingencies."
10. C. O'Dell and J. McAdams, "The Revolution in Employee Rewards," *Management Review,* March 1987, pp. 68–73.
11. See Milkovich and Newman, *Compensation,* pp. 334–41, for an excellent set of illustrations characterizing the Rucker and Scanlon approaches to gain sharing.
12. E. E. Lawler, *Pay and Organization Development* (Reading, MA: Addison-Wesley, 1981).
13. For example, H. J. Bernardin and R. W. Beatty, *Performance Appraisal: Assessing Human Behavior at Work* (Belmont, CA: Wadsworth, 1984); and R. L. Cardy and D. H. Dobbins, *Performance Appraisal: Alternative Perspectives* (Cincinnati: Southwestern Publishing, 1994).
14. Milkovich and Newman, *Compensation,* pp. 365–67.
15. Ibid., p. 185.

16. The literature devoted to the methodology of job evaluation is lengthy, complex, and controversial. For a good overview, we suggest Milkovich and Newman, *Compensation,* Chapter 5. For studies and reviews of the measurement properties of job evaluation systems, see D. P. Schwab, "Job Evaluation and Pay Setting: Concepts and Practices." In E. R. Livernash (ed.), *Comparable Worth: Issues and Alternatives* (Washington, DC: Equal Employment Advisory Council, 1980), pp. 49–78; R. D. Arvey, "Sex Bias in Job Evaluation Procedures," *Personnel Psychology* 39 (1986), pp. 315–35; R. J. Snelgar, "The Comparability of Job Evaluation Methods," *Personnel Psychology* 36 (1983), pp. 371–80; and C. H. Lawshe and P. C. Farbo, "Studies in Job Evaluation: 8. The Reliability of an Abbreviated Job Evaluation System," *Journal of Applied Psychology* 33 (1949), pp. 158–66.

17. E. E. Lawler and G. E. Ledford, "Skill-Based Pay: A Concept That's Catching On," *Personnel,* September 1985, pp. 30–37; and F. Luthans and M. L. Fox, "Update on Skill-Based Pay," *Personnel*, March 1989, pp. 26–31.

18. Mahoney, "Multiple Pay Contingencies."

19. J. R. Schuster and P. K. Zingheim, *The New Pay: Linking Employee and Organizational Performance* (New York: Lexington Books, 1992).

20. R. B. Freeman and J. L. Medoff, *What Do Unions Do?* (New York: Basic Books, 1984).

21. Ibid., pp. 133–35.

22. R. M. McCaffery, *Employee Benefit Programs: A Total Compensation Perspective* (Boston: PWS-Kent Publishing Company, 1992), p. 190.

23. Currently, the average percentage of payroll costs devoted to benefits exceeds 40 percent (U.S. Chamber of Commerce, *Employee Benefits, 1993* [Washington, DC: Author, 1994]), with companies like General Motors reporting that it now pays more to provide employees with medical benefits than it does for steel.

24. Ibid.

25. J. A. Sonnenfeld and M. A. Peiperl, "Staffing Policy as a Strategic Response: A Typology of Career Systems," *Academy of Management Review* 13 (1988), p. 590.

26. J. D. Olian and S. L. Rynes, "Organizational Staffing: Integrating Practice with Strategy," *Industrial Relations* 23 (1984), pp. 170–83.

27. R. H. Frank and P. J. Cook, *The Winner-Take-All Society* (New York: Free Press, 1995), p. 71.

28. Ibid.

29. R. Turner, "Sponsored and Contest Mobility and the School System," *American Sociological Review* 25 (1960), pp. 855–67; and J. E. Rosenbaum, *Career Mobility in a Corporate Hierarchy* (New York: Academic Press, 1984).

30. B. Schneider, "An Interactionist Perspective on Organizational Effectiveness." In K. S. Cameron and D. A. Whetton (eds.), *Organizational Effectiveness: A Comparison of Multiple Models* (Orlando, FL: Academic Press, 1983).

31. T. Cox, *Cultural Diversity in Organizations: Theory, Research and Practice* (San Francisco: Berret-Koehler Publishers, 1994).

32. K. N. Wexley and G. P. Latham, *Developing and Training Human Resources in Organizations* (New York: HarperCollins Publishers, 1991).

33. Bernardin and Beatty, *Performance Appraisal.*

34. S. Chandler, "Sears's System of Rewards Has Ups and Downs," *Chicago Tribune,* February 15, 1998, pp. C1, C6.

35. W. E. Deming, *The New Economics for Industry, Government, Education* (Cambridge, MA: Massachusetts Institute of Technology Center for Advanced Engineering Study, 1994); and H. V. Roberts and B. F. Sergesketter, *Quality Is Personal: A Foundation for Total Quality Management* (New York: Free Press, 1993).

APPENDIX: HRM PRACTICES SURVEY

Instructions

This survey is designed to describe the HRM practices that are associated with the job class of interest within a particular company or organization. A job class should be considered in the fullest sense. That is, consider the jobs that comprise a class of related positions. This often will be at the level of a job progression within a defined organizational unit (e.g., functional area or department).

The methods used to gather these data can vary, depending on the situation and objectives to be served by collecting this information. At times, job incumbents and their immediate managers (subject matter experts, SMEs) can be asked to complete the survey. Other situations will require that the information be gathered by conducting interviews with SMEs. When conducting interviews, consider the survey to be a structured interview guide.

Before addressing the specific questions to follow, use the space provided below to describe the context surrounding the job class of interest. Here, the description is at the level of the entire organization or company. Use the following categories to organize the description:

Industry of employing organization

Size of employing organization (number of employees)

Positions (use position titles) that are the focus of analysis

Pay/Reward System Attributes

In this section of the survey you are to make judgments about the organization's orientation to pay and benefits. Each area of inquiry requires either a rating (e.g., a low to high level of some attribute) or a discrete judgment about the presence or absence of a practice.

1. Pay Level. How does this company price *jobs* with respect to the "market" pay level (the average pay level for similar jobs among competing companies)? Circle the level shown below that best characterizes this company's relative pay rates.

1	2	3	4	5
The company tends to *lag* competitive market pay level		The company strives to *meet* the average competitive pay level		The company strives to be a pay *leader*

2. Pay at Risk. What percentage of direct pay (on average) does this company put "at risk" for this class of jobs/positions? Pay at risk refers to the use of commission income, lump-sum bonuses, profit sharing and gain sharing, and other forms of direct supplemental income. It does *not* refer to traditional "merit" pay plans, or any plan for which annual increases become part of base pay. Circle the level shown below that best characterizes the degree to which this company puts pay at risk for the designated jobs.

1	2	3	4	5
No pay at risk; an hourly or monthly rate is used to determine pay amount		Moderate degree of risk; pay can vary between 30% and 60% as a function of individual, group, or organizational performance		Extensive degree of risk; pay can vary by 90% or more as a function of individual, group, or organizational performance

3. Performance-Contingent Pay. Consider any form of performance-contingent pay that may exist for these positions. Review the options described below and mark the alternative that best characterizes the company's pay policy (mark only one alternative).

1	2	3	4
Performance-contingent pay is based on individual contribution and performance	Performance-contingent pay is based on group or work-team contribution and performance	Performance-contingent pay is based on overall organization or business unit performance	Does not apply; no pay is contingent on performance

4. Internal versus External Job Pricing. When considering how this company prices jobs, which description below best characterizes pay policy (mark only one alternative)?

1	2	3
Internal equity focus: the goal is to create within-firm fairness based on a job's contribution to organizational objectives (job evaluation is the primary tool used to price jobs)	The company strives to *balance* the internal and external perspective	External equity focus: the goal is to price jobs in relation to what the competition is paying (extensive use of market surveys to price jobs)

5. Skill-Based Pay. Are individuals who work in the designated jobs paid a premium based on the number of *skills* they have mastered or are qualified to perform?

1	2
Yes	No

6. Seniority-Based Pay. Do individuals who perform these jobs receive a premium based on the number of years of service with the company or the number of years of service in a particular position?

1	2
Yes	No

7. Benefit System Flexibility. Consider the degree to which the company's discretionary benefit options (such things as life insurance, medical insurance, and paid days off) are offered to full-time employees in a fixed versus flexible way. Circle the value that best characterizes the level of flexibility.

1	2	3	4	5
Common benefit package offered to all full-time employees		A moderate amount of flexibility		Full benefit flexibility designed to take individual employee needs into account

8. Benefit Level. When considering the overall level of benefits provided, how does this company compare to other companies competing in the same labor market?

1	2	3	4	5
Company tends to *lag* the competition		Company strives to *meet* the "market"		Company strives to be a benefit level market *leader*

Staffing System Attributes

In this section of the survey you are to make judgments about the organization's orientation to staffing. Each area of inquiry requires either a rating (e.g., a low to high level of some attribute) or a discrete judgment about the presence or absence of a practice.

9. Career System Orientation. Consider the typical sources of talent for jobs/positions within the company. Circle the level that best reflects the degree of "external" orientation present in this situation.

1	2	3	4	5
Internal focus: employees typically are hired at the entry level and the company then pursues a promotion-from-within policy		Company will hire externally if necessary but tends to give first preference to current employees		External focus: employees (for positions at various organizational levels) are regularly hired from external sources

10. Potential versus Achievement Orientation. Consider the options described below and mark the alternative that best characterizes the company's approach to staffing the positions being considered here (mark only one alternative).

1	2
Company prefers to identify candidates with high "future potential" and provide resources and development opportunities to prepare these individuals for promotions and advancement	Company prefers to identify candidates with proven achievement records and tends to hire and promote individuals who possess the current capability to perform the target job

11. Organizational Fit. Consider the options described below and mark the alternative that *best* characterizes the company's approach to staffing the positions being considered here (mark only one alternative).

1	2
Company seeks "right types": the concern is to identify candidates who will "fit" the company's culture, who are similar to current incumbents (or, for management positions, candidates who are similar to the company's current leadership)	Company seeks a diverse, heterogeneous workforce and occasionally will purposely seek a "wrong type"

12. Exit Orientation. Here you are to rate the level of job security the company attempts to provide employees. Identify a level on the scale below that best characterizes this company.

1	2	3	4	5
Company promotes stability and loyalty by creating a high degree of job security				Company systematically manages the turnover process by downsizing and restructuring, aggressively attempting to retain only top performers

Attributes of the Training and Career Development System

In this section of the survey you are to make judgments about the organization's orientation to training and development. Listed below are five areas that address a particular training issue. Within each of these areas select the *one* description that *best* characterizes this organization's approach to training (select only one alternative per area).

13. Skill Orientation

1	2
Training focus tends to be on narrow functional or technical skills	Training focus tends to be on general problem-solving or interpersonal skills

14. Training-Method Orientation

1	2
Company tends to use informal, on-the-job training and coaching	Company tends to use formal "classroom" training and instruction

15. Career Pathing

1	2
Little information and advice is available regarding likely career paths, opportunities, or requirements needed for advancement	Clearly defined career paths and developmental opportunities are available to help employees prepare for promotional opportunities

16. Succession Planning

1	2
Succession planning is best characterized as very informal, often taking place as the need arises because of an unexpected departure or rapid and unplanned growth	The organization has a formal succession planning process in place (characterized by a set of procedures that lead to the regular evaluation of employee readiness for advancement)

17. Skill Inventories

1	2
No formal skill inventory is in place and being used in this organization	An information system (typically a computerized database) is in place to "inventory" the knowledge, skills, abilities, developmental experiences, and career interests of employees

Attributes of the Performance Measurement System

For the following question, describe the performance measurement approach associated with the positions being considered here.

18. Measurement Type. Consider the options described below and mark the alternative that *best* characterizes the company's approach to measuring and monitoring employee performance (mark only one alternative).

1	2
Most performance measurement systems are "results" oriented; that is, the outcomes of work or the time taken to complete work are emphasized	Most performance measurement systems are at the level of "process," or how the work gets done

19. Measurement Source. Consider the options described below and mark the alternative that *best* characterizes the company's approach to performance measurement (mark only one alternative).

1	2
Performance measurement is directed from superior to subordinate (i.e., managers rate supervisors, supervisors rate hourly employees)	Performance measurement is multidirectional (i.e., it is 360-degree measurement, with feedback being received from superiors, subordinates, peers, and customers)

4

Reward and Compensation Systems

Most managers regularly grapple with the complex challenges presented in rewarding and compensating employees. A theme of this book is that a firm should align its HRM practices with its business strategy by rewarding key employee behaviors. In this chapter you will

- Understand how competitive pay levels affect the firm and its employees as well as the firm's rationale for meeting, lagging, or leading the market in setting pay levels.
- Learn about alternative approaches for maintaining an internally consistent pay structure, including "job-based" and "skill/competency-based" structures.
- Become acquainted with the process by which external competitiveness and internal consistency are brought together to form the pay structure and create pay grades.
- Examine some key approaches for performance-contingent pay and pay at risk.
- See how flexible employee benefits and overall benefit levels can help maintain a high-quality workforce.

America's fat cats are getting fatter," according to the title of a recent article in *The New Yorker* magazine.[1] The article begins by reporting that "J. P. Morgan, seldom portrayed as a radical, maintained that no corporate chieftain should earn more than twenty times what his workers were paid. Things have changed since Morgan's day." The article goes on to claim that by 1990, CEOs took in about 85 times as much as factory workers. "Still, the rewards that senior executives enjoyed . . . were mere hors d'oeuvres compared with what was to come." The article reports a study finding that between 1990 and 1998 the annual compensation of CEOs at large firms rose from $1.8 million to $10.6 million—an increase of almost 500 percent. The author goes on to assert that, in the past year, "big-league CEOs" pocketed, on the average, 419 times the earnings of a typical production worker. These top executives' huge compensation increases, we are told, come in the form of stock grants and options packages.

The author of this article points out that "in theory at least, these remuneration schemes can perform useful economic functions," such as rewarding executives for acting in the interests of shareholders, allowing companies to recruit talented executives, and rewarding outstanding performance. The article concludes, however, that the payment of stock options to executives has, in fact, "degenerated into a boondoggle that robs shareholders and taxpayers while rewarding cronyism and mediocrity."

Similar magazine, newspaper, and television reports about the rising tide of executive compensation often promote a particular point of view, represent some identifiable bias, or at least include assertions that can be debated. But they also highlight some of the key issues that managers must understand in maintaining effective compensation and reward systems. Managers' decisions about compensation and reward systems are intended to fulfill some of the objectives mentioned in the article cited above. For example, we expect our pay systems to help us attract high-quality employees to our firms, help us retain our valuable contributors, and help us maintain positive morale among our employees. We even expect our pay systems to enhance our employees' motivation, and therefore their productivity.

We cannot claim that after reading this chapter you will possess a precise knowledge of why some top executives earn 400 times the pay of a production worker. The myriad reasons for these findings are often quite a mystery, even to compensation experts. But insight into the major components of a total compensation system and the key decisions managers must make might provide at least some understanding of why a top executive, a rock star, or a professional athlete makes so much more than a secretary, a production worker, or even a professor. For example, managers must consider both the external competitiveness of their firms' pay levels compared to other firms and the internal consistency and fairness of the pay for various jobs within the firm. And in determining how to reward the contributions of individual employees, managers must consider how various performance-contingent pay practices, including executive stock options, might enhance employee motivation.

This chapter focuses on what general managers need to know about compensation systems—systems that relate to how employees are given pay and benefits based on factors such as the jobs they hold, or their skills, their performance, or even their seniority. A definition of compensation for our purposes is "all forms of financial returns and tangible services and benefits employees receive as part of an employment relationship."[2]

The themes presented in Chapter 3 are our starting point for this chapter. We elaborate as to what general managers need to know about aligning a company's reward and compensation systems with its business strategy, deciding on appropriate levels of pay compared to competitors, and establishing a systematic and fair way to set pay ranges for various job classes within the company. We also delineate managers' options for placing at risk some portion of employees' pay and for linking pay to employee performance, skill, or seniority. Finally, we discuss what managers should know about delivering employee benefits, including both the level of benefits compared to competitors and the amount of flexibility offered to employees in choosing benefits.

Since our intention is to provide general managers with knowledge of key issues in maintaining effective compensation systems, we do not analyze compensation systems in depth or describe pay and benefit options in detail. The reader who intends to work as a human resource specialist can consult a number of excellent resources for thorough coverage of these reward and pay system issues.[3] Managers should be aware of the possibilities for employee rewards and compensation and then be able to select an integrated set of compensation practices that fit the unique circumstances of job classes in their companies. This knowledge will also assist them in working with both internal HR compensation specialists and outside consultants.

ALIGNING REWARD AND COMPENSATION SYSTEMS WITH THE FIRM'S BUSINESS STRATEGY

A review of the model of an HR system presented in Figure 1–1 will suggest how the firm's business strategy could be translated into a compensation system that is congruent with that strategy. Our model asserts that the firm's *business strategy,* along with its *technology,* determines the organization's *design* and *work processes*. These work processes call for a particular set of *behavioral/role requirements* for employees. Managers must design HR systems that promote these behaviors, while also taking into account contextual factors affecting the firm, especially labor markets and the legal environment.

For example, a particular firm's strategic priorities may include an emphasis on total quality management, including the forming of partnerships with customers and suppliers. This strategic approach would also require a partnership orientation of the firm toward its employees, including a focus on employee behaviors of teamwork, cooperation, and team efforts toward continuous improvement of systems.[4] When faced with choosing a menu of options for the total human resource system (as described in Chapter 3), managers would want to choose options that promote these employee behaviors. One part of this firm's compensation system would likely be group-based variable pay, including a moderate amount of pay at risk, with the pay at risk based on the teams' improvement of systems as shown by quality measures. The pay system can be a powerful mechanism for encouraging and supporting a variety of alternative employee behaviors, such as individual goal achievement, or teamwork, cooperation, and quality improvement.

As we discuss in Chapter 8, human resource systems have a direct effect on the firm's bottom line. Not surprisingly, general managers' decisions about a number of facets of the compensation system can play a major role in determining the firm's performance. Some of the specific outcomes of an effective total compensation system include

- The ability to attract and retain outstanding employees.
- The maintenance of employees' perceptions of fairness and therefore overall employee satisfaction.
- The enhancement of individual and group motivation for high performance.

This enhanced performance can pertain to high-quality products and services, customer satisfaction, and cost containment. An effective set of choices about compensation systems is also a major component of the firm's compliance with federal and state laws and regulations that focus on pay.

We hope that after reading this chapter you will have a good understanding of the relevant issues and the rationale behind managers' choices of a set of integrated practices in the area of compensation.

PAY LEVEL: MAINTAINING EXTERNAL COMPETITIVENESS IN COMPENSATION

One basic pay policy decision managers must make is whether to pay at (**meet**), below (**lag**), or above (**lead**) the market. The market is defined as the average pay level offered by companies competing for employees with similar skill profiles. Managers typically consider the pay of other employers in the area or industry. The company's financial situation, labor costs, expected profits, and union pressures are also sometimes relevant.

The pay policy decision can have a major impact on the quality of a company's workforce—and therefore on company performance. Table 4–1 shows the probable effects of alternative pay-level policies.

Rationale for Meet, Lag, and Lead Pay Strategies

One option is to **meet** the pay rates of competitors—the most common pay-level policy. Managers have three reasons to justify the policy to meet the market:

1. Employee dissatisfaction would result from failure to match competitors' pay rates.

TABLE 4–1. Effects of Pay-Level Policies

Pay Level Policy	Compensation Objective			
	Attracting Employees	Retaining Employees	Controlling Labor Costs	Enhancing Employee Satisfaction
Lead market	+	+	?	+
Meet market	=	=	=	=
Lag market	−	?	+	−

2. The firm's ability to attract employees would be limited by lower pay rates.
3. Managers feel somehow obligated to pay prevailing rates.[5]

Because there are so many forms of compensation and many ways to survey competitors' rates and compute the statistics, maintaining a policy of meeting the market can at best be an approximation.

A second option available to managers is to **lag** the market, meaning to pay lower than prevailing pay rates. Not surprisingly, a lag policy may hinder a company's ability to attract and retain employees. Following a lag policy is typically a way to control labor costs. If a company's corporate strategy or past financial performance leads to a decision to follow a lag-the-market policy, the company will have to make other adjustments to compete for the most desirable job candidates. Surely, this can be a difficult position for the company. But some employers are successful because (1) they provide other desirable outcomes to employees, such as advancement and training opportunities, or (2) they find some other way to encourage high levels of individual effort, such as creating performance–reward connections by putting large amounts of pay at risk.

Following a **lead** policy should provide a number of positive outcomes for the company:

1. The ability to attract the cream of the crop from the labor market.
2. High levels of employee satisfaction.
3. The ability to retain outstanding employees.

Offering higher-than-market pay may also help the company to offset undesirable features of the work, such as lack of advancement opportunities, poor working conditions, or undesirable geographic locations.

Managers should also be aware that they have the option of adopting different pay-level policies for different **job classes.** For example, a company may be a pay leader for job classes requiring critical skills, meet the market for most other job classes, and lag the market for a few job classes readily filled by the local labor market. Managers may also decide to use different pay-level policies for different **components** of pay. Consider a company that has decided that, to generate more sales, it is important to stimulate high levels of motivation for its sales force. To accomplish this, the company's managers may decide to offer above-average levels of incentive pay along with base pay that slightly lags the market.

Use of Pay Surveys for Comparative Market Data

To implement and monitor a company's compliance with its pay-level policy (meet, lag, or lead), managers use pay surveys. These surveys may be conducted by the company's HR specialists or by consulting firms. Sometimes industry consortia or trade associations conduct pay surveys for the members. The U.S. Bureau of Labor Statistics (BLS) also publishes pay information on a variety of occupations for different geographic areas in the country. The BLS provides wage and benefit data by occupation in particular regions in COMP 2000, a new survey. The BLS also publishes the Employment Cost Index (ECI), which reports changes in compensation costs.

81

CHAPTER FOUR
Reward and
Compensation
Systems

Managers typically find that the various kinds of market data from the BLS are quite general. They are useful as an overall check on how well the company is complying with its pay-level policies, but usually not specific enough to be used alone.

Methods of Collecting Data

Whether performed in-house or by a consulting firm, some fairly standard issues and decisions arise in gathering pay survey data. However, firms exhibit wide diversity in the specifics of how the data are gathered, analyzed, and presented. One decision is the selection of jobs for surveying. Surveys typically do not cover all the jobs in a firm, but focus on a particular job family such as secretarial/clerical jobs or technical/engineering jobs.

In gathering survey data not all jobs in the job family are included. Instead, the survey uses a smaller set of **benchmark jobs:** jobs that are well-known across companies, have relatively stable job content, and have current pay rates that are considered to be acceptable. These prototypical jobs are taken as reference points in using market pay data for a compensation system. In addition, this set of jobs covers the entire pay range.[6]

The pay survey data can be collected in a variety of ways. The HR specialists or the consultants conducting the survey can conduct interviews in person or over the phone or mail out questionnaires. Of course, it is important that the persons from the companies providing the data can be trusted to be knowledgeable and accurate. A survey questionnaire would include a listing of benchmark jobs, a **job description** for each, and spaces for the respondent to provide information about the total compensation for each corresponding job in the respondent's company.

Types of Data Collected in Pay Surveys

A variety of information is gathered on pay surveys. Three basic types of data are

1. **Organization data.**
2. Information about the **total compensation system.**
3. Specific **pay data on each incumbent** in the jobs under study.

Survey data are typically summarized in reports to management illustrating the pay for a particular job in each organization in terms of the minimum, maximum, and midpoint of the organization's pay ranges. The report may also include the *actual* average pay rate for employees in that job in each organization.

It is important to acquire information about the **total compensation package** for the benchmark jobs in each surveyed company. This is necessary for an accurate judgment about how a firm's compensation matches up to that of other firms. A company's base pay, for example, may be slightly below the market. Before managers draw any conclusion about the need to raise base pay, however, they would want to look at the total compensation package. When bonuses and incentives are added it may become clear that the firm's pay package is in fact *above* the market. Thus, pay surveys should collect information about bonuses, long- and short-term incentives, cost of living adjustments, shift differentials, uniforms, subsidized parking and cafeterias, and other kinds of benefits and services provided to employees.

To summarize, managers must decide on an external competitiveness pay policy: whether to meet, lead, or lag market pay levels for a particular job class. Pay surveys are a tool for implementing and maintaining this pay-level policy. Because of a variety of limitations of pay survey data, pay surveys are usually not relied on exclusively for setting specific pay rates but are used as a general guide for setting and monitoring levels of pay. For determining specific pay rates, techniques such as job evaluation are necessary, as we will explain in the next section.

PAY STRUCTURE: MAINTAINING INTERNAL CONSISTENCY IN JOB PRICING

The pricing of individual jobs or job families within the firm is another key decision-making issue. In setting the pay for individual jobs, **internal consistency** in the relative pay of different jobs within the firm must be maintained. It is important to design a pay structure that is fair to employees, that is tied in to the work performed, and that directs employees' key behaviors as desired by the firm.

The overall pay structure also includes decisions about

- The number of pay grades or levels.
- How much pay differential exists between and within pay levels.
- The criteria used for determining pay differentials.

The ultimate success of a company's pay structure depends on how well the structure supports key employee behaviors and, possibly most important, the level of *employee acceptance* of the pay structure. The level of employee acceptance is critical for maintaining the firm's ability to attract and retain valuable employees.

Establishing an Internally Consistent Pay Structure Using Job Evaluation

Establishing a pay structure means deciding on the relative pay for different jobs within the firm. Thus, most pay structures can be labeled **job-based** pay: The employee's pay is primarily based on the particular job. Some firms have begun to change their pay systems toward **skill-** or **competency-based pay**. In these new systems, employees are given pay increases as they acquire additional skills or competencies, not as they move to a job in a higher pay range. We will discuss the skill/competency approach to pay later in this chapter.

Given that most pay systems continue to be job-based, we believe that general managers need a basic understanding of this approach to setting up pay structures. The developing and refining of pay structures can become very complicated, involving technical issues that we do not cover here. Instead, we provide an overview of the key issues general managers need to be aware of in working with HR specialists or consultants.

It is possible for managers to determine the relative pay for various jobs using a simple **unilateral** approach—*setting up the pay structure by "top-manager edict."* Small and medium sized organizations that are not unionized frequently use this approach.[7] The manager simply uses his or her judgment to arrive at the relative value to the firm of various jobs, and then sets the pay. The owner of a small auto service station might use this approach in setting the pay of those whose job is to pump gas, those who operate the road service truck, and the station's mechanic-in-residence (the highest paid, of course). We would expect the owner to be able to set fair pay differentials that would be accepted by the employees holding the various jobs.

In recent years there appears to be an increase in firms setting pay ranges for their jobs using **market pricing**—*determining pay ranges based directly on rates paid in the external market.* These firms deemphasize any kind of internal assessment of jobs to achieve internal consistency in pay. Instead, the market (e.g., average pay from a pay survey) determines the pricing of jobs within the firm. It is not hard to think of drawbacks to a strict market pricing approach:

1. The firm is basically letting competitors determine its pay structure.
2. It is unlikely that the firm's business strategy or key behavioral requirements would be aligned with an externally determined pay structure.
3. Base pay rates are usually not the totality of a compensation package.
4. The accuracy of market survey data are often questionable.[8]

If you consider the HRM model we use in this book, it might make sense to emphasize market pricing in some specific circumstances. For example, consider a high-tech firm competing for professional employees in volatile and active labor markets. The firm is growing rapidly while experiencing high rates of turnover, thus needing to regularly fill vacancies from the outside. The firm might decide that the critical importance of attracting professionals from the outside would mandate staying very close to the market in pricing jobs within the firm.

In the vast majority of medium sized and larger firms, the pay structure is developed using **job evaluation**—*a systematic technique for determining the relative worth or value of jobs to the firm in order to establish pay differentials.* Using systematic approaches such as job evaluation is important for pricing jobs in a way that is seen as fair and acceptable by employees.

A number of techniques of job evaluation are used in establishing an internally consistent pay structure. Whatever the technique used, the process often involves forming a job evaluation task force, assisted by HR specialists or consultants. The task force usually is evaluating (or reevaluating) a particular family of jobs in the firm, such as the secretarial/clerical jobs or the managerial jobs. The task force also obtains an up-to-date **job description** for each job, consisting of a detailed summary of the specific tasks and employee requirements (e.g., education, experience) for each job. These job descriptions assist the evaluators in assessing job content and the relative value of various jobs. If the available job descriptions are not accurate, it may be necessary to perform a detailed study of the firm's jobs—a *job analysis*—to update the descriptions.

We believe that general managers do not need exposure to all of the variety of job evaluation techniques available, so we provide only a brief overview. One job evaluation technique is to simply **rank** the jobs to be evaluated on the basis of their relative value. This technique, while easy to perform and easy to explain to employees, has the drawback of being somewhat crude and imprecise; it may not be easy to *defend* to employees. On the other hand, probably the most popular job evaluation technique is the **point method,** or point-factor method, of job evaluation, so we will consider it in some detail.

The Point Method of Job Evaluation

In the point method approach, **compensable factors**—qualities such as level of skill, responsibility, or required working conditions—are determined as a basis for valuing the entire set of jobs for pay purposes. Compensable factors should relate to the actual work performed; be linked to the strategy, culture, and values of the firm; and be easy to communicate and acceptable to employees.[9] The use of 3 to 5 compensable factors is adequate for developing a sound pay structure, although some firms have used as many as 20 or more.

Determining an appropriate set of compensable factors for evaluating a family of jobs is part of an overall process of generating a **job evaluation manual** for use in the actual assigning of points to jobs by the task force. The entire job evaluation manual would include

1. The *compensable factors* and their definitions.
2. A *factor degree scale* for each compensable factor, which reflects the differing degrees or amounts of each factor required for a job (e.g., how much responsibility on a 5-point scale does this job require?).
3. *Weights* assigned to each compensable factor, reflecting a judgment of the relative importance of each factor for determining the pay of various jobs in the firm.

Table 4–2 illustrates some key aspects of a point method of job evaluation. It reproduces a page from a job evaluation manual that includes a set of compensable factors, their definitions, and weights. A separate factor degree scale would be created for each of the compensable factors.

With a job evaluation manual and job descriptions in hand, the work of the job evaluation task force consists of rating each job factor-by-factor on the factor degree scales. Usually the members of the task force do this individually, and then meet as a group to arrive at a decision on the final ratings of each job on each factor. Using the system in the job evaluation manual, the points for each job can simply be added to arrive at a point total for each job.

TABLE 4–2. Job-Based Pay: Example of Compensable Factors and Weights in a Point System of Job Evaluation

Factor	Weight
Supervision received: Involves the amount and type of supervision received.	45
Physical demand: This factor measures and compares application, endurance, fatigue, and strength under normal or abnormal conditions. Relates to expenditure of physical exertion inherent in a job to be performed at a normal pace. Consideration must be given to muscular exertion required for material handling, use of tools, and operation of machines. Also, consider weights when the job requires pushing, pulling, or lifting: frequency of weight handling, speed, and time required to complete a job are important. Consider bodily motions and positions (sitting, bending, standing, kneeling) required in a day's work.	60
Working conditions: Involves general working conditions, variety of disagreeable factors present, and the degree and extent of exposure to such disagreeable factors. Consider such things as cold, dampness, darkness, dirt, dust, fumes, grease, glare, heat, noise, oil, use of coolants, vibration, and so on.	80
Experience and training: The time required by the worker to learn how to do the job, or the experience necessary to perform the job competently. Produced work would be of a quantity and quality to justify continuous employment. Avoid confusing experience with formal schooling (education).	100
Complexity of duties: Involves the amount of judgment, initiative, mental ability, knowledge, and independence from supervision necessary to perform the job.	75
Contact with others: Involves frequency, importance, and diversity of contacts with other people in the performance of the job.	90
Responsibility for equipment and/or tools: Measures the degree of responsibility placed on the worker to prevent loss of or damage to equipment and/or tools.	100

Source: A. N. Nash and S. J. Carroll, *The Management of Compensation* (Monterey, CA: Brooks/Cole, 1975), p. 118.

From Job Evaluation to an Internally Consistent Job Structure

Once the job evaluation task force has generated a point total for each job, the jobs can be ordered on the basis of their point totals. This ordering, or ranking, of jobs to reflect their relative worth or value to the company is known as the **job structure**. For example, in a job structure for a family of managerial jobs we might see that the job of senior vice president is ranked above vice president, which in turn is ranked above division director. Thus, the job structure is the direct output of the job evaluation process.

CREATING A PAY STRUCTURE: BLENDING EXTERNAL COMPETITIVENESS AND INTERNAL CONSISTENCY

The final pay structure brings together market pay rates and the firm's internally consistent job structure. Getting from a job structure to the pay structure involves a series of steps:

1. **Market pay rates and the job structure are brought together in the form of a market pay line.** Figure 4–1 illustrates such a line (labeled "pay policy line" for reasons we will soon explain). A y axis representing market pay rates (from pay surveys) and an x axis representing the job structure (e.g., the array of point totals for the jobs) are drawn, and market pay rates for a small number of benchmark jobs are plotted. A line (e.g., a least-squares regression line) is run through these plotted points—the market pay line.

2. **The market pay line can be adjusted up or down to maintain a lead or a lag pay-level policy.** This adjusted line is often called the **pay policy line.**[10] Of course, if the firm's pay-level policy is to meet the market, the pay policy line is the same as the market pay line. Note that Figure 4–1 illustrates a line that is both the market pay line and the pay policy line.

3. **Pay grades are created around the pay policy line.** Most firms' pay structures use pay grades, which group different jobs that are

FIGURE 4–1. Pay structure with pay policy line and pay grades

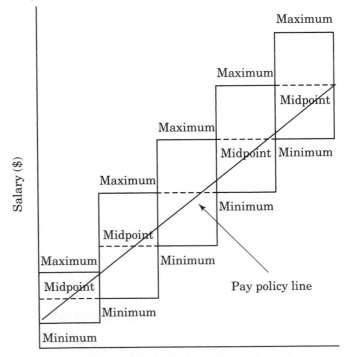

Salary ($)

Jobs (ordered by job evaluation points)

considered to be the same for pay purposes. Jobs that have a similar number of evaluation points, even if quite different in content, are positioned in the same pay grade. This means that the minimum and the maximum pay for these jobs will be the same. Figure 4–1 also illustrates a pay structure with a series of pay grades. The pay grades are created around the pay policy line with the policy line passing through the midpoint of each grade. Each pay grade has a minimum, a midpoint, and a maximum that applies to every job within that pay grade. These pay grades need to have enough spread from the minimum to the maximum to allow jobholders to receive base pay increases while still remaining within the same pay grade. Thus, each pay grade is broad enough that the pay ranges for adjacent grades overlap, often by as much as 50 percent.

In recent years firms have tended to use fewer pay grades. Indeed, firms that may have had 20 or more pay grades for managerial–professional jobs are likely to have reduced the number of grades down to 10 or even fewer. Many firms use the term **broadbanding** to describe the movement toward a small number of *"fat" pay grades*. These new bands contain a large number of jobs that are treated the same in terms of salary minimums, midpoints, and maximums. Four or five traditional pay grades may be combined into a single band. The movement toward fewer grades and broadbanding supports a new emphasis on combining jobs, cross-training employees, seeking increased flexibility in moving employees across jobs, and a movement toward lateral (versus vertical) promotions, teamwork, and deemphasizing individual employees' jobs.

In spite of this trend, a firm may still wish to reinforce employee behaviors such as individual performance and to support the possibility of successive vertical promotions for employees. If so, then a more traditional hierarchical pay structure may be advisable, with a fairly large number of separate pay grades. A hierarchical structure emphasizes measuring distinctions among individual employees' contributions; it provides the opportunity for employees to be regularly rewarded with promotions to higher level pay grades.

The next issue for managers to consider is how employees should be given pay increments. On what basis should employees progress through their pay ranges? Firms may decide to reward employee loyalty and encourage tenure with the firm by basing pay increases on seniority. Alternatively, managers may decide to provide pay increments based on job performance. We take up these issues in the next sections of this chapter in our discussion of pay at risk, performance-based pay, and pay for other employee contributions.

PERFORMANCE-CONTINGENT PAY AND PAY AT RISK

Most managers understand that pay can be a powerful tool for enhancing employee motivation. To put it more precisely, pay and other rewards can stimulate employee *effort* toward reaching key goals—such as high performance. Consider again our Chapter 2 discussion of the expectancy model of motivation, and the key concepts of *expectancy, instrumentality,* and *valence.* We can enhance employee motivation for performance by fostering employees' perceptions that there are strong connections (instrumentalities) between performance and the receipt of valuable (highly valent) outcomes. Of course, employees also need to perceive that if they try, they will be able to achieve high performance (expectancy).

Thus, the key to the use of performance-contingent rewards is creating in the minds of employees this instrumentality connection: High performance leads to valuable rewards. There are a number of alternative approaches for creating this performance–reward connection. First, keep in mind that pay is one of a variety of rewards that can be linked to performance. Other rewards include status and recognition, challenging work, promotions to higher level jobs, opportunities for skill development, and benefits. Second, pay can be used to motivate through a variety of particular mechanisms, which we will consider shortly.

In recent years, firms have begun to more frequently choose pay-for-performance mechanisms that put **pay at risk.** Pay at risk is a type of variable pay that can be contrasted with the more traditional **add-on pay.** Add-on pay is a system in which the firm pays employees base pay and then shares gains (from increased profits or reduced costs) with employees. If the firm reduces base pay by a certain amount (e.g., 5 percent) and offers variable pay for performance improvement, then the former fixed base pay becomes at-risk pay.[11] This approach to performance-contingent pay shifts some of the risk of doing business from the firms to the employees. In pay-at-risk plans, total annual compensation varies as a function of individual, group, or business-unit performance. This approach increases employees' level of uncertainty about the total amount of pay they will receive. It is possible for total compensation to increase, remain about the same, or decline from one year to the next. We often find that making pay contingent on performance also puts some pay at risk. We next provide an overview of some of the mechanisms for linking pay to performance.

Merit Pay

In the typical merit plan employees' performance is evaluated using some type of rating scale, and their base pay is adjusted upward based on the level of their individual performance. Since base pay is not adjusted downward, merit plans involve little pay risk compared to other types of performance-contingent plans. Likewise, under merit plans the performance–pay connection is not as strong as under other types of performance-contingent plans (e.g., incentives) in which pay can increase *or* decrease.

In addition, the size of merit adjustments often reflects factors in the pay structure other than performance. The factor most commonly considered, in addition to performance, is the level of an employee's base pay *relative to the midpoint of the job's pay range.* Employees whose base pay is *below* the midpoint of the pay range are allowed to receive a higher pay increment for a given level of performance than employees located above the midpoint. This reflects the need to control the frequency and size of pay increases as employees begin to reach the upper limits of their pay range. If the position within the pay range is not taken into account, the integrity of the entire pay hierarchy is jeopardized because pay for top performers can exceed the maximum rate allowed for their job. Merit plans maintain their ability to provide sufficient incentives for many key contributors only if top performers can be promoted into the next higher pay grade.

When using this extremely popular motivational tool, managers should be aware of possible pitfalls or problems. Merit pay will lose its motivational power if the performance appraisal system is seen as unfair or inaccurate (see Chapter 7). Merit pay, like any individual-oriented pay-for-performance mechanism, may also inhibit cooperation and instead foster competition among work group members. In addition, because of the use of subjective performance evaluations, some argue that merit pay can harm employees' self-esteem, perceptions of equity, and even their "intrinsic" interest and motivation in their work.[12]

Lump-Sum Bonuses

Lump-sum bonuses are increasingly being used as a substitute for merit pay. These financial bonuses are granted to individual employees after they are judged by the firm to have reached their performance goals. The bonuses are not added into employees' base pay; thus there is more risk to employees since they must re-earn this extra pay year after year. Using lump-sum bonuses allows the firm to better control wage costs, since the bonuses are not added to base salaries and are not necessarily paid in subsequent years.

Individual Incentives/Commissions

Individual incentives and commissions are increments to an individual's pay tied directly to the employee's extra output, such as piece rate pay for production workers or sales commissions. Thus, the measure of performance is more objective than under merit adjustments and lump-sum bonuses. Incentives and commissions can place significant amounts of pay at risk if they are the only element of pay. However, often they are an add-on to base pay. But base pay may be set at a low rate, thus making performance output or sales a critical determinant of one's overall pay.

Stock Options: Long-Term Incentives for Executives

As we reported at the beginning of this chapter, in recent years the seemingly extravagant levels of top executive pay have produced headlines in the business press.[13] The graph in Figure 4–2 illustrates the tremendous rising tide of CEO pay during the decade of the 1990s. Unfortunately, as you can see from the production worker pay curve for the same period, the rising tide of the decade's economic boom did not lift all boats.

FIGURE 4–2. Executive pay and stock options

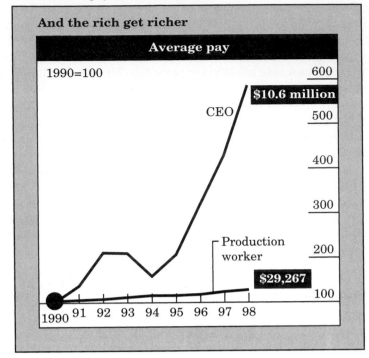

Cashing in

Company	Chief Executive	Gain on Exercising Options 1998, $ in millions
Travelers Group	Sanford I. Weill	220.2
Intel	Andrew S. Grove	49.0
Monsanto	Robert B. Shapiro	46.7
Morgan Stanley	Phillip J. Purcell	36.4
H. J. Heinz	Anthony J. F. O'Reilly	34.8
General Electric	Jack Welch	31.8
American Express	Harvey Golub	27.1
Bristol-Myers Squibb	Charles A. Heimhold	25.3
AlliedSignal	Lawrence Bossidy	23.1
Wells Fargo	Paul Hazen	20.2

Source: The Economist, September 11, 1999; August 7, 1999. Reprinted with permission. Further reproduction prohibited. www.economist.com

The use of an individual long-term incentive known as *stock options* for top executives is a major reason for this upward spiral of compensation.

Long-term incentives in 2000 account for 35 percent of total executive compensation, which is an increase from 28 percent in one decade.[14] Under a stock option plan executives are allowed to purchase shares of the company's stock at a stipulated price. As the company's stock prices rise, they can exercise their options—that is, buy the much higher priced stock at the initial grant price. The idea here is that executives are rewarded for their performance, that is, their contributions to the firm's long-term profitability. Although rewarding these contributions by executives seems desirable, we acknowledge that this can be a complex and controversial issue. For example, other stakeholders, say, employees, may not fare well under a system where executives are motivated to get their firms' stock price as high as possible. The table in Figure 4–2 lists the gains several top executives experienced in 1998 from exercising options.

These stock option incentives have generated considerable controversy: Are they doing what they were designed to do? Are they really motivating executives to do their best for the shareholders?[15] If the stock market rises for *all* firms, the payout to executives may be attributed more to the general health of the economy than to any specifics of executive performance. Some have suggested that a better approach is to require executives to "beat the overall market" or to hit specific performance targets.

Group Incentives: Gain Sharing

As opposed to the kinds of individual performance-contingent pay mechanisms just discussed, group-oriented plans can motivate employee behaviors such as cooperation and teamwork. Gain-sharing plans are unitwide bonus systems based on performance in comparison to some cost index (e.g., labor costs). Work teams or units must first devise ways to improve work processes, thereby reducing labor costs. Some proportion of the cost savings is then returned to the work group.[16] For example, in a medium sized manufacturing plant, if overall labor costs are below a particular target, the gains are shared with all the employees according to a single formula. Thus, some pay is at risk, although performance standards such as labor costs are somewhat under the employees' control. Some particular gain-sharing plans are Scanlon plans, Rucker plans, and Improshare.[17]

Group Incentives: Profit Sharing

Profit sharing involves an add-on to pay, linked to division or total company profits as compared to some predetermined goal. Because profits can be influenced by many factors beyond employees' control, such as the overall economic climate, profit sharing is riskier than gain sharing. Profit-sharing rewards can be paid in cash, deferred into a retirement fund, or administered in a combined plan, with features of both. Profit sharing is a basic part of the compensation program for more than 150,000 American businesses. However, a major problem, from a motivational standpoint, is that once profit sharing has been incorporated into the compensation system, it can become institutionalized as a permanent, unchanging fixture of the workplace. It may then have little motivational impact as far as improvement in work performance. From a motivational standpoint, use of monthly or bimonthly bonus payments in a profit-sharing plan is most desirable.[18]

PAY FOR OTHER EMPLOYEE CONTRIBUTIONS

So far our overview of compensation and rewards has focused on the use of "job-based" pay structures and performance-based reward systems. Managers should understand, however, that not all pay structures are strictly job-based, and not all pay increments are based on performance.

Paying for Skills or Competencies

The use of skill-based pay is an innovation that appears to have picked up much steam during the 1990s. Remember that in a job-based pay structure, an employee's pay range is typically based on (1) consideration of the market rate for the job, and (2) the evaluation of the job's worth or value compared to others within the firm. The majority of firms still use some kind of job-based pay.

But firms can also pay employees for their possession of particular **skills, knowledge,** or **competencies.** We should first acknowledge that paying employees more for the acquisition of knowledge is not a particularly new idea. In the field of education, for example, it has been common practice for many years to provide base salary increments to teachers who have acquired more depth of knowledge in their field, as evidenced by their obtaining advanced degrees.

In new applications of this concept, employees are not rewarded for advancing into higher level jobs or "growing" their jobs, but instead for increasing their skills. Skill-based pay helps to focus the firm's culture on personal growth and development and encourages a workforce in which employees can perform multiple tasks. In general, skill-based pay seems to fit in companies that want a flexible, relatively permanent workforce focused on learning, growth, and development. Many plant startups use this approach, as do firms moving toward "high-involvement" management methods.[19]

Between 1987 and 1993 the percentage of Fortune 100 companies using some form of skill-based pay increased from 40 percent to 60 percent.[20] Most of these systems appear to be focused on manufacturing workers who receive an hourly pay rate and employees in routine, high-volume service jobs, such as financial services and insurance operations. In these types of jobs, it is relatively easy to determine the needed skills for high performance and to train and certify employees for these skills. As employees learn new skills and are certified in these skills, their base pay levels are increased. Not surprisingly, the specification of skills, skill blocks, and certification procedures can potentially generate as much administrative complexity and "bureaucracy" as any other human resource program. Figure 4–3 illustrates a skill-based pay structure for technicians.

FIGURE 4–3. Skill-based pay: example of a skill-based pay structure for technicians

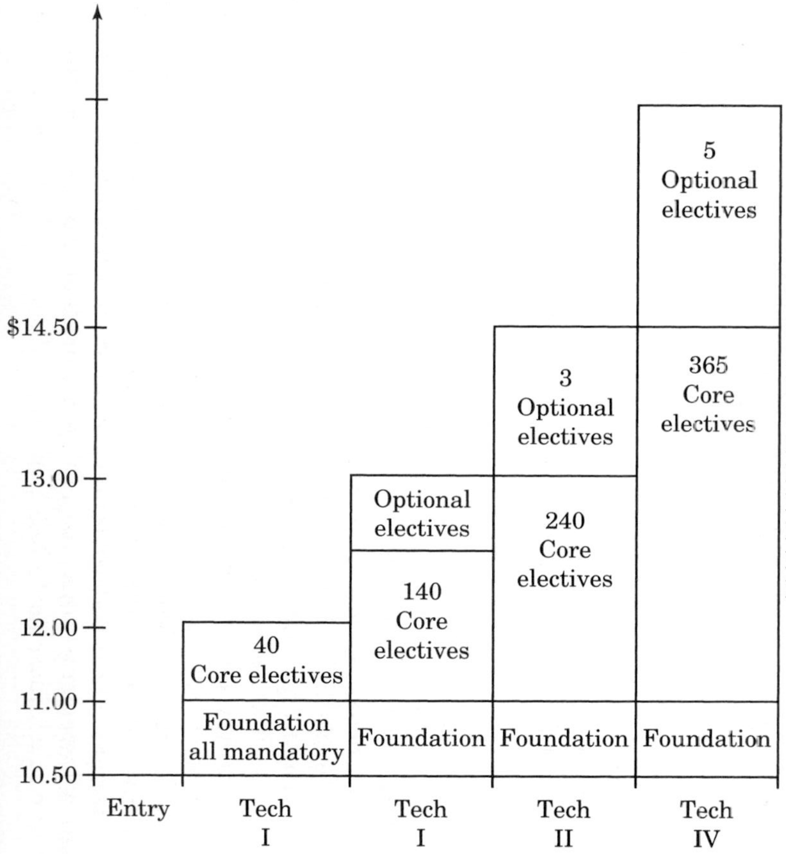

Foundations

Quality course
Shop floor control
Materials handling
Hazardous materials video
Safety workshop
Orientation workshop

Core Electives

Skills	Points	Skills	Points
Longeron Fabrication	10	Leak Check/Patch Weld	5
Panel Fabrication	15	Final Acceptance Test	10
Shell Fabrication	15	Welding Inspection	15
End Casting Welding	20	Flame Spraying	15
Finishing—Paint	20	Assembly Inspection	5
Finishing—Ablative/Autoclave	20	Safe % Arm Assembly	15
Finishing—Surface Prep	10	MK 13 Machining	25
MK 13 Assembly	15	MK 14 Machining	25
MK 14 Assembly	15	Tool Set Up	10
Finishing Inspection	5	NCI Inspection	30
Machining Inspection	20	Degrease	10
Pad Welding	15	Guide Rail Assembly	5
		Receiving Inspection	5

Optional Electives

Maintenance	Career Development
Logistics—JIT	Group Decision Making
Plant First Aid	Public Relations
Geometric Tolerancing	Group Facilitator
Computer-Lotus	Training
Computer-dBASE III	Group Problem Solving
Computer-Word Processing	Administration
Assessment Center	Plant Security
Consensus Building	

	Entry Tech I	Tech I	Tech II	Tech IV
$14.50				5 Optional electives
				365 Core electives
13.00			3 Optional electives	
			240 Core electives	
12.00		Optional electives		
		140 Core electives		
11.00	40 Core electives	Foundation	Foundation	Foundation
10.50	Foundation all mandatory			

Source: G. T. Milkovich and J. M. Newman, *Compensation,* 6th ed. (New York: Irwin/McGraw-Hill, 1999), p. 150. Reprinted with permission of the McGraw-Hill Companies.

Many firms have also explored what they label "competency-based pay" for managers and professionals. Although there is no agreed-on definition, one representative definition of a competency is "demonstrable characteristics of the person, including knowledge, skills, and behaviors, that enable performance."[21]

Example. Competency-Based Pay for Managers. One unit of Monsanto, a large U.S.-based chemical company, identified a set of broad competencies for its managers.[22] Taking account of the company's strategic objectives and direction, these competencies included adaptability, communication, creativity, customer focus, problem solving, expertise, relationships, results orientation, team orientation, and understanding the business (see Figure 4–4). Each manager selected two competencies per year as part of a personal development plan, oriented toward building on a strength or improving a weakness. The development of these competencies took place mostly on the job, and included an action plan, coaching and support from three to five assessors, and self-assessment. At the end of the year, the employee's manager assessed the extent of competency development and rated on a scale the level of the employee's progress. This rating was the basis for the size of the employee's salary increase.

Paying managers and professionals for their knowledge and skills promotes the objectives for manufacturing and service workers noted earlier but also presents new challenges. Identifying sets of "competencies" is not as straightforward as specifying "skill blocks" needed to produce tangible products or services.[23] But the proponents of skill- or competency-based pay also point out that this concept fits the strategic management focus on the "core competencies" of the firm—factors that provide the firm with competitive advantage.

Whether for skilled manufacturing workers or managers, various forms of skill-based pay are here to stay. There are a number of potential advantages compared to the traditional job-based pay. But there are also many challenges for general managers who attempt to understand the appropriate use and implementation of these new forms of pay.

Seniority-Based Pay

We briefly mention the possibility that seniority, defined as the length of service in an employment unit, can be used as a basis for allocating many rewards, including wages, promotions, and the right to continue as an employee in the face of a downsizing program. Unions in the United States traditionally have supported seniority-based decisions, which can be readily seen in collective bargaining agreements.

However, for *any* employees, seniority-based rewards might be appropriate for the particular circumstances surrounding a job class in a firm. Consider our discussion of the use of pay grades and the criteria for moving employees through their pay grades (e.g., seniority, performance). Clearly, the trend in HRM is to focus on performance as the basis for providing base salary increments—merit pay. But some firms provide predetermined, automatic salary increments based on length of service. And as we mentioned in

Firm Identifies Broad Competencies

- Adaptability
- Communication
- Creativity
- Customer focus
- Problem solving
- Expertise
- Relationships
- Results orientation
- Team orientation
- Understanding the business

Manager's Annual Development Plan

- Two competencies selected for attention
- Manager generates specific plan

Coaching and Support

- On the job
- From 3–5 assessors
- Self-assessment

End-of-Year Assessment

- Supervisor rates progress on competencies
- Salary increment determined

Chapter 3, seniority makes sense as a basis for rewards when (1) the goal is to promote a high degree of company loyalty and commitment, (2) there is a need to encourage cooperative and team-oriented behavior, and (3) the situation requires extensive learning of company-specific knowledge and skills.

EMPLOYEE BENEFITS: FLEXIBILITY AND LEVELS

A significant portion of a firm's total compensation package consists of employee benefits, which are often viewed as a type of "indirect compensation" as opposed to direct payment for time worked. Most managers are aware of the huge increase in benefit costs over several decades. These costs have risen from around 25 percent of total payroll costs in 1959 to over 40 percent by the mid-1990s.[24]

A firm's total benefit package can include "nonfinancial" rewards also. Consider the benefits of Volvo factory employees in Sweden: the use of a gym, swimming pool, badminton/tennis courts, an outdoor track, and tanning beds.[25] Benefits even included a hot-water pool, where workers went for physical therapy sessions after a taxing day on the assembly line. Imagine the workers' anxiety on learning that their new owner was Ford Motor Company. The $600,000 per year recreation center raised the issue for Ford of "perk parity" with Ford workers elsewhere. In fact, the extra Swedish benefits might make good HRM sense—they are highly valued by employees because they compensate for the extremely high taxes in that country.

Compensation elements such as the following are frequently defined as benefits:

1. Legally required payments (e.g., Social Security, worker's compensation.
2. Private pension and welfare plans (e.g., retirement income, health and life insurance).
3. Pay for time not worked (e.g., vacation, sick leave, rest/lunch periods).
4. Premium pay (e.g., overtime, shift differentials).
5. Miscellaneous benefits (e.g., education assistance, child care).[26]

We do not address all the issues involved in benefits administration, largely because we believe that general managers do not need such detailed knowledge. Benefits administration has become a highly specialized field; managers regularly call on benefits experts in the HR department for assistance with specific problems. Here we call attention to a few key issues and decisions for managers to assess in their own organizations: benefit system flexibility and the role of overall benefit levels in maintaining a high-quality workforce.

Since the 1970s firms have increasingly offered employees flexibility in choosing their benefits, using terms such as "cafeteria" or "smorgasbord" benefits. A flexible benefit plan has been defined as one that permits "employees to select benefits they want from a package of employer-sponsored coverages, including plans that offer a choice between cash compensation and benefits."[27] The advantages of flexible benefits include offering employees some choice, controlling benefit costs, and remaining competitive in attracting and retaining employees.

Managers need to decide whether benefits should be offered in a fixed or flexible way, based on assessment of their particular circumstances. If the workforce is highly diverse, there are likely to be widely varying preferences ("valences") for benefits; then a flexible plan would be best. Flexible benefits would provide a better fit between what individual employees desire and what is available. Flexible benefits also require employees to focus more attention on understanding and making choices about benefits. Thus, they would be expected to *value* their benefits more highly.

The second benefits issue pertains to the overall *level* of benefits compared to competitors in the labor markets. This issue is similar to the issue of external competitiveness in pay levels discussed earlier in this chapter. As we mentioned in Chapter 3, there is quite a bit of variability in benefit expenditures in firms and industries. Thus, as a manager you must decide whether your company should meet, lead, or lag the market in terms of overall benefits for a job class or organizational level. This decision may be critical for your ability to attract, retain, and maintain the morale of your workforce.

CONCLUSION

In this chapter we have looked at concepts, decisions, and techniques relevant to maintaining effective compensation and reward programs. Our goal was to assist general managers in making key decisions about compensation. These decisions begin with identifying key employee behaviors for aligning compensation with the firm's business strategy. Managers must then make decisions about the appropriate levels of pay compared to other firms (external competitiveness) and develop a systematic approach to determining a pay structure for jobs within the firm (internal consistency).

Another key aspect of compensation management is deciding how to reward employees for their individual contributions in a way that best fits the unique circumstances of the firm. A variety of individual and group-based pay-for-performance strategies may be used to stimulate increased employee motivation and productivity. In setting up pay-for-performance programs, managers are increasingly considering the use of pay at risk to align employees' effort with the strategic goals of the firm. A new emphasis on identifying and paying employees for enhancing their knowledge, skills, and competencies offers additional possibilities for moving the workforce and the organization toward accomplishing critical goals.

We hope this chapter has informed the general manager about some of the key issues involved in making decisions about the wide variety of options available in managing compensation and rewards.

CONTINUOUS LEARNING: SOME NEXT STEPS

As you have learned throughout this chapter, the process of establishing wage, salary, and benefit plans depends heavily on the availability of high-quality data. Try these next steps to seek out data using the power of the

Internet, or to learn about some compensation-oriented consulting firms, firms that your future companies will often use as a source of information and expertise.

- Two well-known compensation-oriented consulting firms are Hewitt Associates (www.hewitt.com) and Towers Perrin (www.towersperrin.com). Go to these websites and review the services provided by each firm. In what ways do the firms offer similar services and in what way does each attempt to distinguish itself? Do the firms offer benefits-oriented consulting services, executive compensation services, and integrated organization effectiveness services?
- The job evaluation process is very technical and often requires the use of sophisticated consulting services. Go to the home page of the American Compensation Association (www.acaonline.org) and search the site for information about consulting firms that are providing job evaluation services.
- As discussed in this chapter, organization-level compensation plans such as employee stock ownership plans (ESOPs), employee stock options, and other forms of employee ownership are becoming increasingly popular. Review the home page of the National Center of Employee Ownership (www.nceo.org), and locate and explore links to other Internet resources that address this important topic.
- Explore online sources of information about salary data and regional as well as international living costs. Two good places to start are (dir.yahoo.com/business and economy/employment and work/salary information) and (www.homefair.com). Compare the cities that interest you (e.g., San Francisco, Hong Kong, Tucson, and Indianapolis) in terms of housing costs. How might a company address very high housing costs when attempting to recruit recent college graduates? How would you go about adjusting a company's salary structure to take into account regional living cost differences? What type of related services would you expect from high-quality consulting firms?

ENDNOTES

1. J. Cassidy, "Wall Street Follies: A New Study Shows America's Fat Cats Are Getting Fatter," *The New Yorker,* September 13, 1999, p. 32.
2. G. T. Milkovich and J. M. Newman, *Compensation,* 6th ed. (New York: Irwin/McGraw-Hill, 1999), p. 6.
3. For example, L. R. Gomez-Mejia and D. B. Balkin, *Compensation, Organizational Strategy, and Firm Performance* (Cincinnati: South-Western, 1992); R. I. Henderson, *Compensation Management in a Knowledge-Based World* (Upper Saddle River, NJ: Prentice Hall, 2000); and Milkovich and Newman, *Compensation.*
4. P. K. Zingheim and J. R. Schuster, "Linking Quality and Pay," *HRMagazine* 37, no. 12 (1992), pp. 55–59.
5. Milkovich and Newman, *Compensation.*
6. Ibid.
7. A. N. Nash and S. J. Carroll, *The Management of Compensation* (Monterey, CA: Brooks/Cole, 1975), pp. 104–5.
8. Henderson, *Compensation Management,* pp. 214–15.
9. Milkovich and Newman, *Compensation.*
10. Ibid.
11. J. R. Schuster and P. K. Zingheim, *The New Pay: Linking Employee and Organizational Performance* (New York: Lexington Books, 1992).

12. R. L. Heneman, *Merit Pay: Linking Pay Increases to Performance Ratings* (Reading, MA: Addison-Wesley, 1992).

13. For example, "Cutting the Cookie," *The Economist,* September 11, 1999, p. 26.

14. Milkovich and Newman, *Compensation,* p. 461.

15. "Share and Share Unalike," *The Economist,* August 7, 1999, pp. 18–20.

16. E. E. Lawler, *Pay and Organization Development* (Reading, MA: Addison-Wesley, 1981).

17. For illustrations of these plans, see Milkovich and Newman, *Compensation,* pp. 311–17.

18. Henderson, *Compensation Management.*

19. E. E. Lawler, "The New Pay: A Strategic Approach," *Compensation and Benefits Review,* July–August 1995, pp. 14–22.

20. G. E. Ledford, "Paying for the Skills, Knowledge, and Competencies of Knowledge Workers," *Compensation and Benefits Review,* July–August 1995, pp. 55–62.

21. Ibid., p. 56.

22. J. R. Schuster, "The New Pay: Competency Pay and Variable Pay." Presented to the Human Resource Association of Central Missouri, Compensation and Benefits Network of Greater St. Louis, and Kansas City Compensation and Benefits Association, Columbia, Missouri, October 12, 1995.

23. Ledford, "Paying for the Skills, Knowledge, and Competencies."

24. U.S. Chamber of Commerce, *Employee Benefits, 1993* (Washington, DC: Author, 1994).

25. "Detroit Meets a 'Worker Paradise'," *The Wall Street Journal,* March 3, 1999, pp. B1, B4.

26. R. M. McCaffery, *Employee Benefit Programs: A Total Compensation Perspective,* 2nd ed. (Boston: PWS-Kent, 1992).

27. Ibid., p. 190.

5

Staffing Systems

As a general manager you need to know a high-quality staffing system when you see one. Effective staffing goes beyond hiring new employees. Staffing involves attraction, selection, and retention of these key organizational assets. In this chapter you will

- See how effective staffing systems depend on the firm's business strategy.
- Become acquainted with some key practices in selecting employees based on their *achievement* or on their *potential*.
- Learn that to select and retain motivated employees, you must identify people who fit your firm's unique culture.
- See how employee turnover, which produces both costs and benefits, can be effectively managed during stable times and periods of organizational restructuring.

In September 1997 the Toyota Motor Corporation decided to build a new manufacturing facility in Princeton, a community not far from Evansville, in the southwestern corner of Indiana. Although the region's unemployment rate was one of the lowest in the United States, the Japanese auto maker had to use the town's sports stadium to take in the initial wave of 30,000 applicants—which grew to 55,000—for the 1,300 positions needed to build its Tundra pickup truck. In 1998 Toyota announced that it would expand plant capacity in order to build a new sports-utility vehicle—an expansion that would require another 1,000 production workers.[1]

Toyota purposely created a situation that encouraged thousands of workers to apply because Toyota wanted to hire only a blue-collar elite— employees who would thrive under the Toyota management system. Although the unemployment rate was at its lowest level since 1970, the offer of $19 an hour after completion of a 24-month "grow-in" period attracted a staggering number of applicants. Moreover, Toyota's wage and benefit package, which was well above the level being offered in the local labor market, created great controversy and resentment among other local employers in this Indiana town.[2] Thus, Toyota purposely used hiring standards that required extensive HR involvement.

Staffing this assembly plant represents one of the general manager's most important areas of responsibility. As general manager, your role is to identify and oversee the HR professionals (in-house staff or consulting firm) charged with recruiting, selecting, and retaining these valuable assets. You will need to know a high-quality staffing system when you see one. You will need to be in a position to demand and recognize the highest quality staffing solutions currently available.

But the staffing function goes beyond hiring new employees. Staffing decisions create many opportunities for the general manager to contribute to the company. There are times, too, when the general manager must respond to a variety of very public crises. For example, managers at Coca-Cola were confronted with a race-bias suit alleging disparities between white and black employees in terms of pay, promotions, performance evaluations, and dismissals.[3] Coca-Cola's staffing practices are at the center of this controversy.

This chapter focuses on what general managers need to know about the staffing function—a function that relates to the attraction, selection, and retention of key organizational assets. It is about the entry, internal movement up to high leadership levels, and retention of what many companies consider their most important resource—people. This chapter develops the themes introduced in Chapter 3 by presenting more information about what general managers need to know about

- Aligning a company's career systems with its business strategy.
- Selecting for potential versus achievement.
- Addressing questions of organizational fit and employee motivation.
- Managing the exit process.

As was the case in the previous chapter, this is not an in-depth analysis of the staffing function of the type needed for individuals aspiring to be HR professionals. Many excellent writers have reviewed organizational practice and the research literature devoted to staffing techniques and procedures.[4] Instead, we want to inform general managers about what constitutes sound staffing practices and about what to demand and expect from a company's HR staff specialists and from consulting firms providing staffing services.

CAREER SYSTEM ORIENTATION: RECOGNIZING STAFFING SYSTEMS THAT FIT THE FIRM'S BUSINESS STRATEGY

To begin your analysis of a company's general approach to staffing, we suggest a review that focuses on the links between business strategy and various staffing decisions. Recall from Chapter 1 that these links come about because different strategies call for different employee behaviors. For example, a firm concerned with efficiency and operations improvement often will create an internally oriented staffing system. These firms value employee retention and cooperation; they seek employees who will stay with the firm for the extended periods of time needed to acquire the company-specific knowledge that has been generated to improve production efficiency.

Employees must work together because they often find themselves on quality-oriented teams charged with improving products or services.

When considering the internal versus external staffing orientation, consider focus and balance, not whether to be internal or external.[5] The *internally oriented* firm tends to assess, review, summarize, and make estimates about its internal labor market. Likely activities, processes, and measurement systems that signal an internal orientation include

1. The preparation and maintenance of detailed position descriptions and/or explicit competency profiles specific to key job classes.
2. Human resources information systems that inventory the knowledge, skill, and ability (KSA) profiles of existing employees.
3. The analysis and establishment of formal career paths.
4. Analyses designed to detect KSA deficiencies among existing employees.
5. Analyses designed to detect future staffing needs by focusing on the internal supply and demand for labor (e.g., the calculation and use of turnover and retirement rate estimates to predict future supply).

The *externally oriented* company tends to pay more attention to the size, quality, and stability of the external labor market. The goal is to monitor the external labor market so that when a need develops, the firm can take advantage of existing opportunities. Likely processes and activities that signal an external orientation include

1. Monitoring enrollment and curricular trends developing at colleges and universities that supply managerial and technical graduates.
2. Monitoring research on the values, needs, and skill levels of individuals comprising various regional and international labor markets.
3. Using executive recruitment firms to learn about the availability of promising job candidates.
4. Questioning—perhaps subtly—newly hired employees for information about employment opportunities in competing companies.

Two Frameworks for Integrating Staffing Practice with Strategy

Two very useful frameworks for considering your firm's career system orientation that have appeared in the research literature underlie this chapter. Both approaches require you to explicitly characterize your company's business strategy and way of doing business and then make judgments about whether existing staffing practices appear to be aligned with your strategic orientation. Both perspectives utilize the writing of Miles and Snow, whose topology of firm types appears throughout this book.[6] We take this opportunity to initiate our treatment of the topic, then return to the two frameworks.

The first step uses the Miles and Snow framework to identify your firm's primary way of competing. There are three firm types:

Defender Firms. Defenders tend to focus on improving production efficiency in relatively stable product markets. These firms attempt to beat the competition by producing goods or providing services at lower cost and with higher quality than their counterparts. Their objective is to get better and better at whatever it is they currently do. A good example of such a firm would be a producer of a commodity such as oil, gas, or aluminum.

Prospector Firms. Prospectors attempt to be the first to market with new products and services. These firms rely on innovation, flexibility, and speed. They exploit new market and product opportunities. Companies like Lucent Technologies and 3Com are good examples of prospectors. Among other things, these companies are competing by attempting to be the first to market with technological solutions for emerging Internet businesses and services. 3Com's annual report makes it clear that one of the company's principal strategies is to "drive innovation." Research-oriented pharmaceutical companies like Eli Lilly and Pfizer also are representative of prospector firms. On the other hand Mylan Laboratories, which produces generic drugs, is more like a defender firm—very concerned about competing on price, not innovation.

Analyzer Firms. Analyzers are hybrid firms that closely monitor their more innovative competitors for new ideas and then quickly move to develop efficient production methods for those ideas that appear to be the most promising. Companies like IBM were at the forefront of designing personal computers, but it was companies like Dell and Compaq that devised efficient ways to produce and distribute these products to their customers. While IBM has lost its leadership role in the area of personal computer (PC) innovation, it continues to display its prospectorlike qualities in other ways. For example, IBM recently announced that it plans to build a supercomputer that will work at a speed 500 times faster than the two fastest supercomputers operating at this time. "If successful, the IBM project would not only be a breakthrough in cutting-edge computing, but also help supply fundamental insights into the basic physics and chemistry of biology."[7]

Now that we have established the definitions of firm types, we can examine the two frameworks. We begin with the classical theoretical perspective of Olian and Rynes.[8] This was perhaps the first comprehensive statement about the connections between human resource management and organizational type. This connection also characterizes the subsequent treatment of this topic presented by Sonnenfeld and Peiperl.[9] Both frameworks convincingly argue that staffing practices must reflect a company's strategic orientation. Each provides arguments for and illustrations of staffing practices that are appropriate for the three strategic types. In both cases the strategic type is linked to staffing practice through the roles or behavioral requirements needed to make the strategy come to life. The selection criteria, recruitment methods, and selection techniques are among the critical choices for the general manager. Table 5–1 is a compilation of these ideas. As a general manager, your focus should be on whether or not your firm's overall approach to staffing is aligned with its primary business strategy.

TABLE 5–1. Business Strategy and Selected Staffing System Dimension Attributes

OLLIAN AND RYNES'S STRATEGIC STAFFING PRACTICES

Defender Firms	Analyzer Firms	Prospector Firms
Successful defender organizations are likely to meet most of their key staffing needs by pursuing an internal labor-market orientation	These firms will use a mixture of recruitment methods, including cross-divisional and cross-product transfers	Successful prospector organizations are likely to meet most of their key staffing needs by pursuing an external labor-market orientation
The key knowledge, skills, and abilities sought after by defender organizations will tend to be concentrated in the areas of production and finance	The key knowledge, skills, and abilities sought by analyzers will tend to be in applied research, marketing, and production	The key knowledge, skills, and abilities sought after by prospector organizations will tend to be concentrated in the areas of marketing and basic research
Because defender organizations hire individuals into low-level positions and then provide planned upward mobility, selection criteria give minor weight to past achievements and major weight to future aptitude or potential	More like defenders in stable areas of the business; more like prospectors in the change-oriented sectors	Prospector firms, because they hire directly into upper-level positions, will focus on selection criteria that demonstrate proven achievement in desired knowledge, skills, and ability
Selection criteria are likely to emphasize a relatively narrow range of specialized skills because defender organizations are often highly specialized along functional lines	Like prospectors, analyzers require a wider range of aptitudes and abilities for adapting to their more rapid production of service shifts	Because they must quickly adapt to much more rapidly changing technical and business environments, prospector firms will require a wider or more general range of aptitudes and abilities
Individuals with high needs for security and structure and low tolerances for change and ambiguity will be relatively better suited for employment with defender organizations than prospector organizations	More like defenders in stable areas of the business; more like prospectors in the change-oriented sectors	Individuals who are independent and creative and who have a preference for risk taking are likely to be better matched to prospector firms than to defender organizations
Defender organizations are likely to use selection devices that assess applicants' future aptitudes and potential (e.g., cognitive ability tests or graduation from highly selective universities and colleges)	More like defenders in stable areas of the business; more like prospectors in the change-oriented sectors	Prospectors are more likely to use selection techniques that emphasize applicants' work histories or techniques that directly measure current skill and ability levels (e.g., work samples or managerial simulations)

Sonnenfeld and Peiperl's Career System

The career system priority for defender firms is the retention of organization members who have acquired firm-specific knowledge and skills	The career system priority here is the development of firm-specific functional specialists	The career system priority for prospectors is the recruitment of celebrity and specialist talent to address innovation as needed
Defenders emphasize early career entry (through a limited number of portal positions) and organizational exit at retirement	For analyzers there is exclusive entry at early career and exit at retirement	Entry at multiple career stages and exit resulting from either poor individual performance or the pull of external opportunities
Loyalty, length of service, and age grading (i.e., advancement at planned life stages) drive movement within the defender	An internal tournament drives advancement through the position hierarchy	Internal and external contest for advancement

Source: Compiled from J. D. Olian and S. L. Rynes, "Organizational Staffing: Integrating Practice with Strategy," *Industrial Relations* 23 (1984), pp. 170–83, and J. A. Sonnenfeld and M. A. Peiperl, "Staffing Policy as a Strategic Response: A Typology of Career Systems," *Academy of Management Review* 13 (1988), pp. 588–600.

POTENTIAL VERSUS ACHIEVEMENT ORIENTATION

The general manager must first understand how a firm's business strategy informs decisions about (1) where and how to recruit talent, and (2) the importance of various selection criteria such as the appropriate aptitude, knowledge, skill, and interest profiles for key positions. Next the general manager needs to be aware of what is likely to work when implementing a staffing plan—that is, what does and what does not work when making selection decisions. Fortunately, a great deal of research is now available to assist in making these distinctions.[10] This section gets at the essence of this interesting research.

Recognizing High-Quality Practices When Selecting for Achievement

In devising useful solutions to organizational staffing issues, industrial/ organizational psychologists have been very successful in identifying individuals possessing the knowledge, skill, and position-specific ability to succeed on the job. Historically, measures of current achievement provided by state-of-the-art assessment tools have been successfully used to predict subsequent job performance. But assessment tools—ranging from work sample tests to structured situational interviews to certain types of managerial assessment centers to structured job tryouts—have shown useful levels of predictive power in only one context: finding employees *currently possessing* the skill profile needed for the immediate assignment to an operational job.

For this selection issue the general manager needs to know that high-quality solutions are available and should demand the best in current practice. To give you a better feel for what is available, some illustrations are presented.

Work Sample Tests

In a classic research paper, Campion described how he devised and evaluated a set of work sample tests to be used in identifying maintenance mechanics in a coffee processing plant.[11] This company wanted to hire additional journeyman-level mechanics. That is, new hires would be expected to immediately join the current group of mechanics, after only a brief orientation to the particular facility. They needed to already possess the critical knowledge and skills required to perform the job. Instead of relying on nothing more than a review of past educational and employment histories, the company wanted to test directly (through behavioral samples) the knowledge and skill level of each applicant. Campion went about the process of designing miniature and representative samples of the actual job. Multiple work sample tests allowed for the observation of applicants as they actually repaired mechanical systems in a controlled and simulated environment. These tests asked candidates to do such things as disassemble and then reassemble a transmission, install a bushing, and repair a system of pulleys.

Campion then evaluated the usefulness of this approach by studying the degree to which scores on these graded work sample tests correlated with subsequent ratings of actual job performance. The correlations were in the 0.4 to 0.5 range and when compared to other selection techniques were judged to be superior. Campion's research still represents a state-of-the-art design strategy—one that professionals can replicate (across many different occupational specialties) in contemporary organizations.

Structured Situational Interviews

Interviews are perhaps the most frequently used selection tools, and yet there is a very large research literature showing that the typical unstructured, informal employment interview is not a very accurate predictor of subsequent job performance.[12] The solution is to use either a situational interview format[13] or a structured interview that reviews past experiences and accomplishments.

Interviews of the situational type ask the same questions of all candidates for a particular job and make the candidates describe what they would do if confronted with a particular job challenge. The questions are all job-related—they address issues that regularly must be confronted by job incumbents—and formal scoring guides are used to evaluate the quality of candidate answers. Structured interviews typically address candidates' work and educational histories, but they do this using standardized job-related questions and scoring guides.

To maximize selection system accuracy and to reduce the legal liability that surrounds the use of potentially discriminatory employment practices (as discussed in Chapter 11), general managers should insist that all employment interviewing be conducted using the basic principles outlined by the advocates of structured or situational interviews. This is now a technology that all HR professionals should be well aware of and is a technology that can be purchased from many HR-oriented consulting firms.

Managerial Assessment Centers

A managerial assessment center represents a technology that applies the principles of work sample testing to the world of managerial and professional work. Job candidates are put through a standardized, often lengthy assessment experience in which they are presented with simulated managerial and professional problems or assignments they must address as they would if given the chance in a real organization. Assessment centers are characterized by methods designed to measure multiple dimensions (competencies) using multiple assessment exercises. Behavioral dimensions typically measured in assessment centers are shown in Table 5–2.

These dimensions are assessed by observing the behavior of assessees as they complete exercises like

1. The managerial in-basket: Items typically found in a manager's in-basket must be analyzed and resolved.
2. The leaderless group discussion: A hypothetical group of managers must reach a business decision or allocate a scarce organizational resource.
3. A case analysis: A series of business decisions must be made taking account of an organization's history and environment.

TABLE 5–2. Behavioral Dimensions Frequently Measured in Assessment Centers

Dimension	Definition
Oral communication	Effectively expressing oneself in individual or group situations (includes gestures and nonverbal communications)
Planning and organizing	Establishing a course of action for self or others to accomplish a specific goal; planning proper assignments of personnel and appropriate allocation of resources
Delegation	Utilizing subordinates effectively; allocating decision making and other responsibilities to the appropriate subordinates
Control	Establishing procedures to monitor or regulate the processes, tasks, or activities of subordinates and job activities and responsibilities; taking action to monitor the results of delegated assignments or projects
Decisiveness	Expressing a readiness to make decisions, render judgments, take action, or commit oneself
Initiative	Actively attempting to influence events to achieve goals; showing self-starting actions rather than passive acceptance; taking action to achieve goals beyond those called for; originating action
Tolerance for stress	Maintaining a stable performance under pressure or opposition
Adaptability	Maintaining effectiveness in varying environments, with various tasks, responsibilities, or people
Tenacity	Staying with a position or plan of action until the desired objective is achieved or is no longer reasonably attainable

Source: G. Thornton and W. Byham, *Assessment Centers and Managerial Performance* (New York: Academic Press, 1982).

4. The role-play exercise: A manager must interact with another manager, customer, or subordinate and solve a problem or attempt to influence the other individual's behavior in a meaningful way.

The most well known research on the assessment center method comes from AT&T.[14] In a series of carefully conducted studies, the accuracy of assessor ratings for predicting job performance and hierarchical position was demonstrated. Thus, as is the case for the appropriate use of standard work sample tests, a good case can be made for using the assessment center methodology when identifying competent managerial and professional talent.

Thus far, the methods we have reviewed all attempt to directly sample candidates' behaviors and then use these real-time samples to infer the existence of required job competencies. There are less direct ways of making inferences about the existence of key job competencies. For example, a careful review of a résumé or of a letter of reference may help learn about past behavior and performance; this information can then be used to make predictions about how a person will behave in a new situation. Caution, however, must be exercised when relying on secondhand information of this type. Reviews of the past rely on the willingness and ability of others to accurately portray the candidate's performance in situations similar to the new target job. A lot can go wrong when relying on this type of information. For example, when listing people who are willing to serve as a reference, job candidates may only pick individuals who are likely to write very favorable letters.

Clearly, the technology now exists to accurately assess current knowledge, skill, and ability levels using a direct sampling approach. The general manager should demand that only high-quality assessment techniques of the situational interview, work sample, or assessment center variety be used in their organizations.

Recognizing High-Quality Practices When Selecting for Potential

In the previous section, devoted to recognizing high-quality practices for estimating *achievement,* the focus was on the technology of behavior sampling in simulated environments. The task of estimating the *potential* to be effective at some time far into the future is a much more difficult problem. Here we must often rely on "signs," or indicators of underlying processes or aptitudes (e.g., learning ability) when making these types of predictions.[15]

After reviewing two standard ways of estimating potential, we will recommend what we think organizations should do to improve the likelihood of making accurate staffing decisions when confronted with the need to select for potential rather than achievement. Note that hundreds of published tests are available, covering a wide range of physical (e.g., manual dexterity) and cognitive (e.g., learning ability, creativity) attributes.

Cognitive Ability Tests

The use of paper-and-pencil cognitive ability tests in employment settings has a long and controversial history in the United States.[16] These tests come in many forms, but typically they all ask test takers to perform tasks that are rarely performed on the job. For example, one popular test is the Miller Analogies Test,[17] an instrument with 100 items using a verbal analogies format—even though very few people work verbal analogy problems when doing their assigned jobs. Or consider the Thurstone Test of Mental Alertness. The test publisher describes this as a test that can help "measure an individual's ability to learn new skills quickly, adjust to new situations, understand complex or subtle relationships and be flexible in thinking."[18]

This test includes a quantitative section with arithmetic reasoning items and number-series problems. It also contains a verbal section with items consisting of same–opposite word meanings and definitions.

Tests of this type do not measure actual work behaviors—that is, they are not work samples. They purport to measure underlying cognitive processes—signs—that should signal the potential to learn and the ability to be successful later in a career. Overall, these types of tests have been shown to be useful predictors of important employee behaviors and can contribute to making the workforce more productive.[19] The general manager needs to know, however, that the appropriate and constructive use of these types of tools requires that highly trained testing specialists and professionals be consulted before testing-based hiring practices are implemented.

Educational Attainment and Elite Colleges and Universities

Perhaps one of the most frequently used strategies for identifying individuals who are presumed to possess potential for advancement is to recruit at elite colleges and universities. In the world of managerial and professional employment it is not uncommon for employers to recruit for their "high-potential" programs only from a small number of highly ranked schools, believed to do an excellent job of recruiting and selecting top students. A good example of this has been the demand for graduates of elite MBA programs. As early as 1994, the median starting pay for graduates of Harvard's and Stanford's MBA programs reached $100,000.[20] Demand was clearly outstripping supply.

The problem here is that what often is considered to be the application of state-of-the-art, high-quality selection procedures at elite colleges and universities is little more than the application of a simple process that has not undergone major change in many years.[21] For example, most graduate schools of business have for many years relied on very simple and low cost procedures for making initial screening decisions. They have emphasized the use of two selection tools, combining undergraduate grade-point average and Graduate Management Admission Test scores in some way to screen applicants. This method has been found to be moderately accurate in predicting GPA in a graduate program[22] but typically does not predict success in postgraduation careers.[23] Thus, we encourage general managers to learn about the selection practices used at the schools from which so-called high-potentials are recruited and then make informed judgments about the adequacy of this particular recruitment strategy.

A Recommendation

Unfortunately, little progress has been made recently to improve the technology available for estimating managerial and executive potential. Such estimates about early career managers and professionals are likely to entail considerable measurement error. We recommend, when attempting to estimate managerial potential, that thorough early career performance reviews (based on performance in challenging early career assignments) be used to supplement the very early career signals of potential that have been discussed in this section. In our view, the combination of challenging early career assignments and high-quality performance measurement (see Chapter 7) represents a more costly but more accurate and appropriate way to make judgments about potential.

ORGANIZATIONAL FIT AND SYSTEMS FOR ADDRESSING EMPLOYEE MOTIVATION

Identifying job candidates who possess not only the ability to be top performers but also the motivation to work hard and the desire to stay at a company represents another difficult challenge. Both the motivation to perform and the motivation to stay are determined by a complex interaction between the outcomes associated with each type of behavior and the individual's unique mix of interests and values (see Chapter 2). In times of tight labor markets, a firm's ability to retain top talent becomes a critical factor in organizational success. Thus, managing the turnover process and identifying job candidates who will likely find their work situation highly motivating represent important managerial challenges. Both are discussed as we consider managing for motivation.

Systems for Selecting Motivated Employees

Finding and retaining motivated employees is often about identifying individuals who "fit" your company's unique culture and who find the outcomes associated with high performance to their liking (see Chapter 2). Thus, managing motivation would seem to require a full understanding of both the organization's culture—the mix of role requirements and the rewards and penalties associated with various ways of behaving—and the values, interests, and needs of individuals. It is not just about understanding organizational and individual attributes, it is about understanding how the two sets of attributes interact. While both sets of attributes require careful attention, treatment of motivation must not focus on the individual at the expense of a thorough examination of organizational attributes and how they interact with the individual. The tendency to ignore this is mirrored by the existence of a large and well-developed literature about the personality dimensions of individuals and how to measure these dimensions—but no equivalent treatment of the organizational and cultural context surrounding these individuals.[24]

Because much of what we know about selecting for motivation is based on the use of personality assessment as a selection tool, we turn to this subject next.

Personality Assessment

While there are multiple ways of estimating what are referred to as personality traits, most of what is known about using personality estimates to predict workplace behaviors comes from the application of self-report, paper-and-pencil assessment. This is a technique that asks job candidates to complete self-report personality inventories that cover the elements of multiple dimensions of personality. One of the first things that can go wrong when using this form of assessment is that the items on these inventories can be rather transparent; that is, test takers will infer that certain correct responses reflect what is needed in a specified job, so candidates in need of a job may respond in ways that they believe will help them receive job offers. For example, consider the following items, which resemble those used in two widely used inventories. For each item the job candidate is to reflect on how the item relates to his or her likely personal response tendencies.

1. I rarely attend social functions, preferring to stay away when I can.
    a. Yes.
    b. Uncertain.
    c. False.
2. I have real problems with my self-confidence.
    a. Agree.
    b. Disagree.
3. It would be more interesting to take a position in a business:
    a. Where there is a lot of customer interaction.
    b. In between.
    c. Where I work on accounts and records.
4. It is clear to me when I am boring people.
    a. Agree.
    b. Disagree.

For items of this type, it is likely that job candidates who were inclined to would be able to "fake" correct responses for specified occupations—for example, applicants for sales positions might be hard-pressed to admit discomfort at being around people, lack of self-confidence, and inability to perceive how others are feeling. In addition to the problem of faking, personality assessment tools estimate only the attributes of the job candidate. These tools do not simultaneously assess the culture or organizational outcomes associated with a target job. Thus, personality assessment tools estimate only half of the motivation framework.

Given the conceptual problems associated with this form of assessment, it is instructive to briefly review what is currently known about how well paper-and-pencil personality tests predict important work behaviors. Barrick and Mount thoroughly investigated the relationships between the personality dimensions known as the "Big Five" and multiple job performance criteria, statistically summarizing the results of the empirical studies that existed at the time of their review.[25] The labels applied to these five dimensions were **extraversion/introversion, emotional stability, agreeableness, conscientiousness,** and **openness to experience**. For each label certain traits are frequently associated with either high or low scores:

Extraversion: sociable, gregarious, assertive, talkative, and active (high scores).

Emotional stability: anxious, depressed, angry, embarrassed, emotional, worried, and insecure (low scores).

Agreeableness: courteous, flexible, trusting, good-natured, cooperative, forgiving, soft-hearted, and tolerant (high scores).

Conscientiousness: careful, thorough, responsible, organized, and dependable (high scores).

Openness to experience: imaginative, cultured, curious, original, and broad-minded (high scores).

In reviewing the literature, Barrick and Mount found that the estimated true correlations between the various dimensions of personality and various job performance criteria never exceeded 0.30 and were typically less than 0.15. Only the **conscientiousness** dimension consistently correlated with the three performance criteria at greater than the 0.20 level (with a mean correlation across all criteria of 0.22). The mean estimated correlations for **extraversion, emotional stability, agreeableness,** and **openness to experience** were 0.13, 0.08, 0.07, and 0.04, respectively.

These correlations are not high and suggest that even under the best of circumstances, personality assessment will contribute only a small amount of unique predictive power to most selection situations. We also note that the results from the Barrick and Mount review were similar when the validity of personality testing was estimated for employee turnover or tenure with an employer. The estimated correlations with this criterion variable ranged from a low of 0.00 for **agreeableness** to a high of 0.12 for **conscientiousness**. This high of 0.12 is in the positive direction, however, suggesting that people displaying a lot of conscientiousness are more likely to change jobs than those with lower scores on this dimension. The lesson here seems to be that personality assessment of the type just described needs to be used only under the direction of a selection specialist. To maximize the usefulness of this approach, this specialist needs to be very well acquainted with the organizational culture and work requirements of the employing organization. Perhaps with detailed information about the setting along with information about job candidates' personality profiles, some type of matching can take place that will prove helpful when predicting a candidate's motivation levels.

We think a better approach, however, currently exists for addressing the issue of employee motivation. This approach explicitly attempts to measure both organizational and job candidate attributes and then focuses on conducting a "motivational fit analysis." This approach is summarized next.

Profile Matching and Structured Selection Interviews

Well-researched theories of motivation lead us to advocate the use of what might be termed *motivational fit analysis* when making assessments about job candidates' motivation levels. Consultants and internal HR professionals who are well versed in the emerging technology of candidate–position profile matching should be helpful in this area.

Development Dimensions International (DDI) is one consulting firm that has developed a full assessment system based on the principles of profile matching. This system pays as much attention to describing the outcomes associated with particular work roles as it does to assessing the values and interests of individuals. The first step is to collect information about 21 motivational facets that may be associated with specified work roles. Facets like the following are rank ordered to form the first part of the assessment:

Interaction: the opportunity to work with others (as team members, customers, suppliers, etc.).

Task variety: the opportunity to work on several tasks or projects.

Creativity: the opportunity to devise your own unique approaches to performing tasks and solving problems.

Promotion opportunities: the opportunity to assume roles of greater responsibility and status.

Coaching others: the opportunity to foster others' job-related development.

Commission: the opportunity to work under a pay structure that offers the possibility of more income along with the risk of less income based on performance.

Once the motivational facets of the position are thoroughly understood, the DDI system provides a way to develop structured interview questions that review a candidate's preferences and interests. Alternatively, DDI has developed a questionnaire that asks candidates to describe the attributes of their ideal job. Finally, DDI provides a scoring technique that takes information about the job and candidate simultaneously into account and leads to an assessment of motivational fit.

We believe that systems of this type, based on sound theories of employee motivation (e.g., expectancy theory), hold the greatest promise of solving the problem of assessing employee motivation. General managers should be suspicious of related HR practices that do not explicitly take these concepts of fit into account.

Organizational Fit and Retaining Top Performers

When attempting to identify individuals who will be motivated to perform at high levels, the goal is to find a match between the work outcomes that candidates want and value and the work outcomes that an employer is able to associate with superior job performance. In this section we focus on another type of matching or fit analysis. Here the issue is employee retention. At its most basic level, employees are more likely to stay with firms that provide them with what they value.[26] Here the match is between staying and getting what is desired. In the performance model, the match was between high performance and getting what is desired.

General managers must monitor and control employee turnover—but the key is to manage turnover, not simply reduce it to a very low level. To effectively manage the flow of employees into, through, and out of an organization, the quality of newcomers must be compared to the quality of existing employees. Over time the goal is to improve overall workforce quality at a cost that results in a net benefit to the firm. Therefore, the general manager must simultaneously consider the costs and benefits of turnover. Thus, while managing turnover does involve selecting newcomers who have value profiles that match the company's culture and reward system, this management process is more complex than one might initially believe it to be. The costs of turnover must be balanced with the potential benefits of turnover and with the costs associated with reducing a turnover rate.

The Costs and Benefits of Turnover

Turnover is costly because replacements must be recruited, selected, and trained. A high voluntary turnover rate also can disrupt the social and communication patterns among stayers and increase stayer workloads and stress levels. But certain benefits also can be associated with turnover. For example, newcomers might perform at higher levels than leavers and might bring to the firm an infusion of new ideas about strategy, technology, and customer preferences. In fact, recall from the discussion in Chapter 3 that there will be times when firms would be advised to seek out people who **do not fit** the current corporate culture. Too much fit over time can lead to complacency and an inability to respond to change.

While the costs and benefits of turnover must be balanced, a third dimension to this problem also must be considered. Changes in HR systems designed to reduce turnover can have major cost consequences of their own. To reduce turnover, employers may choose to increase wages, redesign jobs, or modify selection systems to better identify individuals who will not resign. These costs of retention must be compared to the overall costs of turnover to properly manage a firm's turnover rate. One useful managerial guide is to consider what is termed the optimal turnover rate.

The Optimal Turnover Rate

The concept of an optimal turnover rate, described by Abelson and Baysinger as "the rate that minimizes the sum of the costs of turnover plus the costs associated with reducing it,"[27] is illustrated in Figure 5–1. The costs associated with the separation and replacement of employees—turnover costs—are labeled TC. The costs associated with programs to retain employees—retention costs—are labeled RC. As firms spend more on programs to retain employees, turnover rates are decreased, as are turnover costs. At high rates of turnover, retention costs are likely to be low, whereas turnover costs are likely to be high. At low rates of turnover, retention costs are likely to be high, whereas turnover costs are likely to be low. The optimal rate of turnover occurs at the point where total turnover costs (TC + RC) are at their lowest level.

The point is basic: Employees should be allowed to leave if the cost to retain exceeds the cost to replace. Be careful to note, however, that turnover costs ultimately reflect the performance and contribution levels provided by those choosing to leave. Thus, all resignations are not equal—the cost of turnover depends on who chooses to leave. Retaining top performers should be the goal—so long as this can be achieved at a reasonable cost (i.e., reasonable retention costs).

FIGURE 5–1. Optimal organizational turnover

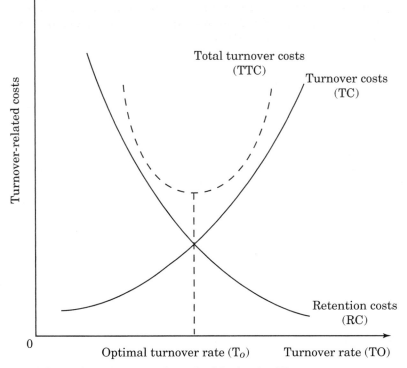

Source: M. A. Abelson and D. B. Baysinger, "Optimal and Dysfunctional Turnover:
Toward an Organizational Level Model," *Academy of Management Review* 9 (1984), p. 333.

EXIT ORIENTATION AND MANAGING THE RESTRUCTURING PROCESS

The final staffing dimension described in Chapter 3, exit orientation, is addressed here by considering the process of merging corporate cultures. A company may have many reasons to restructure and downsize, but the merger and acquisition process drives much of this activity. The rate of mergers and corporate acquisitions accelerated during the last half of the 1990s, fueled by the competitive pressures of the global economy. Staffing issues dominate this process, as we will illustrate by examining one of the largest industrial mergers of all time.

Example. Merging Corporate Cultures: The Case of BP Amoco. While some companies have been able to continue to provide a degree of security for their employees, for most companies the decade of the 1990s was characterized by a relentless process of organizational restructuring and downsizing. This process was largely driven by the need to increase efficiency and cut costs. No longer do firms downsize only during difficult times—now the restructuring process is becoming an ongoing corporate activity. One of the largest organizational restructuring initiatives ever attempted took place when British Petroleum (BP) merged with U.S.–based Amoco to become one of the world's largest integrated energy companies, BP Amoco. Late in 1999, BP Amoco was in the process of growing even larger as it pursued the acquisition of another U.S.–based petroleum company, the Atlantic Richfield Company (ARCO).[28]

The scope of this merger and some consequences during the first year of operation are seen in Tables 5–3 and 5–4. This was clearly one of the largest corporate mergers ever attempted. Of particular interest here is the scope of the downsizing and the targeted cost savings associated with the merger. The company anticipated a reduction in the workforce of 6,000 employees by year-end 1999 and was committed to a $2 billion improvement in pretax earnings by the end of 2000. As of November 1999, the company was well ahead of these targets.[29]

The HRM implications associated with a merger of this scope are many. Recall from Chapter 1 that change management consists of a series of integrated activities. For instance, the need for the change and the vision for the

---

TABLE 5–3. The Scope of BP Amoco

One of the largest industrial mergers (as of November 1999)

Largest producer of oil and gas in the United States; **15 billion barrels** of oil in reserve; daily production of **3 million barrels**

Target to add **$2 billion extra to pretax earnings** by end of 2000; anticipated ARCO acquisition to improve earnings

One of the three largest integrated energy companies in the world; operations in **100 countries on six continents**

Customers can call on fueling services at more than **800 ports and 600 airports**

Outside North America a worldwide network of 11,500 service stations exists; in the United States, 15,000 service stations exist; the successful addition of ARCO will bring the total to **28,000 service stations** in the United States

Each day **10 million customers** are serviced worldwide

Source: C. Cridland, class presentation, November 22, 1999.

TABLE 5–4. BP Amoco—The Merger as of November 1999

Reduction in force twice the forecast

  Target was 6,000 vs. anticipated 14,500 by year-end 1999

Full $2 billion in synergies to be captured by year-end 1999

  Committed to $4 billion in three years

ARCO acquisition—pending approval of U.S. Federal Trade Commission

The stock is up 90%

Source: C. Cridland, class presentation, November 22, 1999.

new company must be thoroughly communicated to all employees. Next, the organizational structures and work processes need to be specified for the new, merged organization. Then, the new enterprise needs to be staffed. This is a complex process whereby early retirement and severance packages are typically used in conjunction with targeted layoffs to identify and retain the individuals who will be needed to take the new organization forward.[30] Related to these staffing issues is the need to provide career support for displaced employees. Finally, compensation, benefit, and training systems must be integrated and deployed in a way that will contribute to new organizational objectives.

While this all has a strategic and planning quality to it, there also are enormous challenges that must be met at the level of relationships between people. Maintaining employee morale when the actions taken by management seem to suggest that people are expendable requires extraordinary leadership skill.[31] The evidence is clear that some firms manage these types of transitions better than others. These management practices, many of which relate to decisions about staffing, are manifested in firm performance.[32]

CONCLUSION

In this chapter we introduced some basic information and concepts that relate to staffing organizations. We focused on helping general managers make better judgments about the quality of their organizations' staffing and selection systems. This summary of critical decision points ranged from a consideration of staffing practice–business strategy alignment, to a review of what is known about the usefulness of various selection techniques, to a realization that staffing decisions are central to effectively managing large-scale organization restructuring activities. We conclude by noting that as companies restructure and become more and more efficient, there is a clear tendency for each employee to carry far more responsibility for the sales, assets, and ultimately, the value of the company than before the restructuring. Thus, every decision to hire, promote, or lay off has more impact on business results now than in the past. As asset-to-employee, sales-to-employee, and equity-to-employee ratios grow—as they have dramatically done since the mid-1970s—each employee, and the associated staffing decision regarding that employee, has become more important than ever before.[33]

CONTINUOUS LEARNING: SOME NEXT STEPS

One of the most interesting developments in the area of employee staffing and selection is the use of the Internet by employers and employees (or job applicants) alike. The first next step provides a few starting places for a preview of what is now available. The second asks that you learn about consulting firms that provide staffing and selection services to corporate clients.

- The Internet now provides sites for the posting of job openings and for the posting of applicant information (e.g., résumés). Review sites www.yahoo.com/business/employment and www.ajb.dni.us and conduct an Internet-based search to learn about either a position you have always been interested in but have been afraid to pursue (i.e., something that would represent a totally new career path) or a traditional position for you, but in a distant city that you have always imagined to be a great place to live.

- One of the first consulting firms to provide corporate clients with assessment-center technology (simulation/work sample exercises for managerial and professional positions) is now known as Development Dimensions International (DDI). Go to this consulting firm's website (www.ddiworld.com) and learn about its products and services. What is "Targeted Selection"? What other products and services are provided by this firm?

   Now conduct a search to identify other consulting firms that sell selection-system products and services. In addition to finding competitors that sell assessment-center exercises and related services, try to find firms that sell personality and "integrity" tests. Can these tests be taken on line? If you were going to attempt to establish a web-based staffing and selection consulting business, what types of services and products would you provide? Why are the products and services you intend to provide well suited for an Internet-based application?

ENDNOTES

1. T. Aeppel, "Scaling the Ladder: Toyota Plant Roils the Hiring Hierarchy of an Indiana Town," *The Wall Street Journal*, April 6, 1999, pp. A1, A8.
2. Ibid.
3. N. Deogun, "A Race-Bias Suit Tests Coke: Can the Real Thing Do the Right Thing?" *The Wall Street Journal*, May 18, 1999, pp. B1, B4.
4. For example, see R. D. Gatewood and H. S. Feild, *Human Resource Selection* (Orlando, FL: Dryden Press, 1998); H. G. Heneman and R. L. Heneman, *Staffing Organizations* (Middleton, WI: Mendota House, 1994); and N. Schmitt and W. C. Borman, *Personnel Selection in Organizations* (San Francisco: Jossey-Bass, 1993).
5. G. F. Dreher and D. W. Kendall, "Organizational Staffing." In G. R. Ferris, S. D. Rosen, and D. T. Barnum (eds.), *Handbook of Human Resource Management*, pp. 460-461 (Oxford, UK: Blackwell Publications, 1996).
6. R. E. Miles and C. C. Snow, *Organizational Strategy, Structure, and Process* (New York: McGraw-Hill, 1978).
7. S. Lohr, "I.B.M. Plans a Supercomputer that Works at the Speed of Life," *The New York Times*, December 6, 1999, pp. C1, C6.
8. J. D. Olian and S. L. Rynes, "Organizational Staffing: Integrating Practice with Strategy," *Industrial Relations* 23 (1984), pp. 170–83.
9. J. A. Sonnenfeld and M. A. Peiperl, "Staffing Policy as a Strategic Response: A Typology of Career Systems," *Academy of Management Review* 13 (1988), pp. 588–600.
10. For a thorough, research-based treatment of this literature, see Gatewood and Feild, *Human Resource Selection*.
11. For a thorough description of the procedures used, see J. E. Campion, "Work Sampling for Personnel Selection," *Journal of Applied Psychology* 56 (1972), pp. 40–44.

12. L. Ulrich and D. Trumbo, "The Selection Interview since 1949," *Psychological Bulletin* 63 (1965), pp. 100–16; and M. A. McDaniel, D. L. Whetzel, F. L. Schmidt, and S. D. Maurer, "The Validity of Employment Interviews: A Comprehensive Review and Meta-analysis," *Journal of Applied Psychology* 79 (1994), pp. 599–616.

13. For a detailed description of how to develop this type of interview, see G. P. Latham, L. M. Saari, E. D. Pursell, and M. A. Campion, "The Situational Interview," *Journal of Applied Psychology* 65 (1980), pp. 422–27.

14. D. W. Bray, R. J. Campbell, and D. L. Grant, *The Formative Years in Business* (New York: Huntington, 1979).

15. P. Wernimont and J. Campbell popularized the distinction between signs and samples in the selection process in "Signs, Samples, and Criteria," *Journal of Applied Psychology* 52 (1968), pp. 372–76.

16. D. C. McClelland, "Testing for Competence Rather Than for Intelligence," *American Psychologist,* January 1973, pp. 1–14; and F. L. Schmidt and J. E. Hunter, "Employment Testing: Old Theories and New Research Findings," *American Psychologist* 36 (1981), pp. 1128–37.

17. O. K. Buros (ed.), *The Eighth Mental Measurements Yearbook* 1 (Highland Park, NJ: Gryphon Press, 1978), pp. 274–75.

18. SRA, *SRA Human Resource Assessment Catalog for Business and Industry* (Rosemont, IL: London House, 1998), p. 58.

19. M. L. Tenopyr, "The Realities of Employment Testing," *American Psychologist* 36 (1981), pp. 1120–27; and F. L. Schmidt, J. E. Hunter, R. C. McKenzie, and T. W. Muldrow, "Impact of Personnel Programs on Workplace Productivity," *Personnel Psychology* 35 (1982), pp. 333–48.

20. J. Micklethwait and A. Woolridge, *The Witch Doctors* (New York: Random House, 1996); and J. Kotter, *The New Rules: How to Succeed in Today's Post-corporate World* (New York: Free Press, 1995).

21. R. M. Dawes, "Graduate Admission Variables and Future Success," *Science* 187 (1975), pp. 721–23; and W. W. Willingham, "Predicting Success in Graduate Education," *Science* 183 (1974), pp. 273–78.

22. G. F. Dreher and K. C. Ryan, "Prior Work Experience and Academic Achievement among First-Year MBA Students," *Research in Higher Education* 41 (2000), pp. 505–24.

23. R. J. Sternberg and W. M. Williams, "Does the Graduate Record Examination Predict Meaningful Success in the Graduate Training of Psychologists? A Case Study," *American Psychologist* 52 (1997), pp. 630–41.

24. M. R. Barrick and M. K. Mount, "The Big Five Personality Dimensions and Job Performance: A Meta-analysis," *Personnel Psychology* 44 (1991), pp. 1–26, provide extensive references.

25. Ibid.

26. W. H. Mobley, H. H. Griffeth, H. H. Hand, and B. M. Meglino, "Review and Conceptual Analysis of the Employee Turnover Process," *Psychological Bulletin* 86 (1979), pp. 493–522.

27. M. A. Abelson and B. D. Baysinger, "Optimal and Dysfunctional Turnover: Toward an Organizational Level Model," *Academy of Management Review* 9 (1984), p. 333.

28. S. Liesman and J. R. Wilke, "BP Amoco to Sell Assets to Satisfy Alaska's Concerns," *The Wall Street Journal*, November 4, 1999, p. A14.

29. C. Cridland, personal communication, November 22, 1999.

30. N. Labib and S. H. Applebaum, "Strategic Downsizing: The Human Resource Perspective," *Human Resource Planning*, Fall 1993, p. 243.

31. C. R. Leana and D. C. Feldman, "When Mergers Force Layoffs: Some Lessons about Managing the Human Resource Problems," *Human Resource Planning* 12 (1989), pp. 123–40.

32. W. F. Cascio, "Downsizing: What Do We Know? What Have We Learned?" *Academy of Management Executive* 7 (1993), pp. 95–104.

33. E. L. Gubman, *The Talent Solution: Aligning Strategy and People to Achieve Extraordinary Results* (New York: McGraw-Hill, 1998).

6

Employee and Career Development Systems

Managers of firms that perform well need to be familiar with key aspects of systems that help employees to acquire knowledge, skills, and abilities relevant to their work. These managers also must be able to recognize when a training system is likely to be effective. In this chapter you will

- See the value of adopting a systematic approach to employee training and development.
- Learn about the key components of the (1) assessment phase, (2) training and development phase, and (3) evaluation phase of a systematic approach.
- See how to determine when the conditions are right for implementing training and development initiatives in your organization.
- Understand the value of promoting career and personal development opportunities for employees, and the role of succession planning in these efforts.

In the opening chapter of this book we reviewed the idea that high- and low-performing companies and organizations could be clearly distinguished by the presence or the absence of certain well-implemented management practices.[1] Jeffrey Pfeffer described one characteristic of many high-performing companies as the extensive use of training, a theme he later reemphasized by stating that "training is an essential component of high performance work systems because these systems rely on frontline employee skill and initiative to identify and resolve problems, to initiate changes in work methods, and to take responsibility for quality."[2]

Traditionally, training in organizations has been about the "systematic acquisition of skills, rules, concepts, or attitudes that results in improved performance in another environment."[3] That is, training, education, and development have been about processes designed to help employees acquire knowledge, skills, and other attributes needed to be effective in new and changing work settings. Unfortunately, general managers today must make sense out of much more than the very useful existing literature devoted to traditional training and development. They must now confront and understand a growing literature that not only addresses learning at the level of the individual, but also attempts to apply the concept of learning to the entire organization. For example, an issue for many management consultants in the mid-1990s was the notion that organizations, just like people, must learn—that is, they must become **learning organizations.**[4] Apparently, learning organizations do things "like hire teenagers to surf the World Wide Web to bring back new ideas."[5] The good news is that the processes and concepts that lead to high-quality systems for developing employees also underpin the notion of a learning organization. We begin our treatment of this topic by introducing a framework from the past that seems perfectly positioned to demystify the New Age thinking about how organizations—just like people—learn.

123

CHAPTER SIX
*Employee
and Career
Development
Systems*

A SYSTEMATIC APPROACH TO TRAINING

In the first of a series of classic books devoted to the training and development process in organizations, Goldstein introduced an instructional model that still informs and guides this area of management.[6] We believe that managers who use this model as a framework will be much more likely than their less systematic counterparts to reap appreciable returns when investing in employee development programs. Recent management literature is replete with books and articles about how to transform a company into a place where knowledge acquisition is encouraged and how to transform this knowledge into improved business processes,[7] but the basic concepts were already in place with the publication of Goldstein's first book.

The first thing general managers should know about training and development is that the success of their company's instructional programs is "dependent upon an approach that considers a number of interacting components."[8] After we present the original Goldstein framework, we will argue that this framework also can guide more general managerial decisions related to organizational renewal and learning.

GOLDSTEIN'S INSTRUCTIONAL SYSTEM

Figure 6–1 represents Goldstein's model of an instructional system. It is depicted as consisting of three phases, the **assessment phase,** the **training and development phase,** and the **evaluation phase.** The model is particularly useful when designing, selecting, and modifying a company's training initiatives over time. But the model also offers clues about a set of conditions that must be met before management should devote resources to developmental activities. After discussing the Goldstein model, we will review these conditions, providing the general manager with a set of guidelines that can be used to evaluate the appropriateness of investing in training.

FIGURE 6–1. Goldstein's instructional system.

Assessment Phase   Training and Development Phase   Evaluation Phase

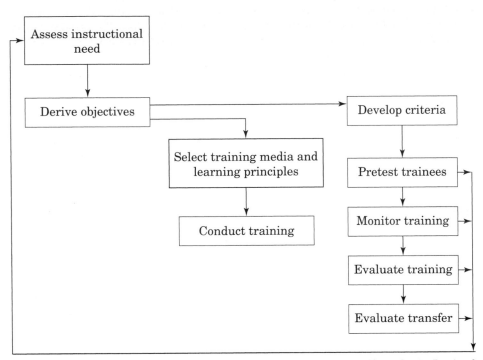

Source: From Training: Program Development and Evaluation, first edition, by I. Goldstein © 1974, Reprinted with permission of Wadsworth, an imprint of the Wadsworth Group, a division of Thompson Learning.

Assessment Phase

High-quality training and development systems are characterized by some form of systematic needs assessment. This type of analysis begins with an examination of the broader organizational and environmental context. It may be that training is not the preferred solution to a particular problem. Good training systems are capable of ruling out a particular training intervention if all the conditions supporting such an intervention are not met. For any training program to be useful, it needs to affect outcomes that are congruent with the firm's business and tactical strategies. It also must receive support from high-level decision makers and must make good conceptual sense given the organization's environment.

Consider companies that face very turbulent environments, perhaps through frequent scientific discoveries, technical innovations, or changes in labor- and product-market conditions. Such companies confront perplexing alternatives. Change can signal that continuous training will be needed to keep employees up to date. However, when the rate of change is very fast, there may not be sufficient time to prepare current employees for the new challenges they must confront. At some point, the speed required to deploy people with the needed knowledge and skills may necessitate external hiring.

125

CHAPTER SIX
Employee
and Career
Development
Systems

Finally, many performance problems are not brought about by deficiencies in knowledge, skill, or ability. Factors such as poor organization and work design, low wages, and poor physical working conditions may be the leading contributors to the underutilization of talent.

Once it has been determined that training represents the appropriate solution to an organizational problem, the assessment process moves to identify discrepancies between the knowledge, skills, or competencies required in a targeted job and the knowledge, skills, or competencies possessed by current jobholders. Of course, this analysis can address future skill or knowledge requirements in an attempt to be ready for the realities of the organization and its environment at some future date. A variety of sources and inputs can be used in making this judgment about training needs. For example, employees can be asked to make self-evaluations about areas most in need of training. These assessments can also be made during formal training needs discussions as part of the career planning process. Or managers might request that existing data be summarized so that clues about training needs are forthcoming (e.g., data contained in performance appraisal or performance management systems can be summarized around ratings at the level of knowledge, skill, or ability dimensions).

Finally, Goldstein shows that training objectives need to be carefully defined during the assessment phase.[9] These objectives serve as standards or criteria against which the training program can be evaluated. One framework commonly used by training and development specialists to define various types or levels of training objectives or criteria is the framework proposed in 1974 by Kirkpatrick.[10] He argued that when evaluating the effectiveness of a training experience it is important to work at multiple levels. His framework is as follows:

1. **Reactions.** Reaction measures are based on what trainees thought of the training experience. That is, trainees' reports of satisfaction with training may not be directly related to whether or not any learning took place, but it probably is the case that when satisfaction is very low, high degrees of attention and subsequent learning are unlikely.

2. **Learning.** The focus here is on the learning of principles, facts, techniques, and attitudes that ideally should influence job-related behaviors.

3. **Behavior.** This is defined as the extent to which knowledge, skills, and abilities acquired during training generalize or transfer to actual work settings. The issue here is to set job performance objectives that are the target of the training initiative.

4. **Results.** Results-oriented objectives are formulated to address the consequences of employee behavior. Training objectives of this type could address such things as production costs, turnover rates, the number of grievances, or change in revenue.

The importance of Kirkpatrick's relatively simple framework should not be overlooked. There are many examples in the research literature showing that setting and measuring only level 1 or level 2 objectives can lead to mistakes in judging the value of a training or developmental program.

Reactions to the training experience may not be highly correlated with how much is actually learned, and even when learning takes place this new knowledge or skill may not be fully utilized when attempting to complete actual job duties. To the degree possible, managers should seek evaluative information at multiple Kirkpatrick levels.

Training and Development Phase

Two fundamental standards need to be met during this phase of the process before a training initiative is typically considered to be of high quality. First, high-quality training encompasses the knowledge, skill, and ability categories that (1) have been identified as being critical to successful job performance, and (2) are possessed at below-acceptable levels by a meaningful number of job incumbents. Thorough needs assessment is what is needed to help meet this standard.

Second, to be of high quality, the method or media used in the developmental program needs to be appropriate for the stated objective. Many different training options are available—but each is likely to be best suited for only a limited set of objectives. The key is to select the correct method for the stated purpose. To develop this point further, consider the following typology of training methods, as illustrated in Table 6–1.

Some training approaches could be categorized as *instructor centered*. That is, knowledge and information tend to flow from some type of expert to the learner. The learner often is a passive participant in the process. Reading a textbook and listening to a lecture or presentation are representative of instructor-centered approaches to learning. There is, of course, a time and place for attending a lecture or listening to an audiotape. These media are well suited for transferring and organizing facts and for interpreting facts and principles.

Other methods have been classified as *learner centered*. The learner here plays a more active and interactive role in learning or acquiring a needed skill. Any form of skills training that actively involves the learner fits this category. Active involvement includes such things as observing an expert perform a task and then trying or practicing the task under the watchful eye of the expert. After receiving round-one feedback, the learner then continues to practice and receives more feedback until an acceptable level of skill can be demonstrated. In fact, an entire class of training and development techniques has been devised based on Albert Bandura's principles of *behavior modeling*.[11]

Active participation also can be achieved in other ways. For instance, many MBA programs now select only applicants who have three to five years of work experience. When students are asked to draw on these past work experiences—perhaps sharing unique perspectives with other students—the learner is actively providing content and substance to the curriculum. Learner-centered instruction serves objectives very different from those of instructor-centered instruction.

Finally, other forms of training may focus on teams or groups as sources of the content of training or even to generate new knowledge. Baldwin,

TABLE 6–1. Some Illustrative Training Methods

Learning Outcomes	Dissemination of Knowledge (Instructor Centered)		Sharing of Knowledge (Learner Centered)		Creation of Knowledge (Learning-Team Centered)	
	Lecture	Audio/Video Presentations	On-the-Job Training	Simulations (Role Playing, Behavior Modeling)	Task Force Assignments	Collective Exploration
Information transfer	☑	☑				
Beliefs/attitudes	☑	☑				
Interpersonal skills				☑	☑	
Problem-solving skills			☑	☑	☑	
Creativity					☑	☑
Motor skills			☑	☑		
Self-insight				☑		
Problem-identification skills					☑	☑

Danielson, and Wiggenhorn described a training process at Motorola (devised in a corporate "university"—Motorola University) that was designed to help the company gather new information (and formulate new questions) about Latin America. Thirty managers spent a week each in Mexico City, São Paulo, Santiago, and Buenos Aires. They were given a rather ambiguous assignment: They were to immerse themselves as fully as possible in the local culture. They were then required to share their experiences and insights with others.[12] Training here had moved from a knowledge dissemination exercise to a knowledge generation exercise.

The training and development phase is all about making sound decisions when selecting (or developing) training methods that fit the training objective. As shown in Figure 6–1, it also is about delivering or implementing the training in a professional and high-quality manner.

Evaluation Phase

Finally, Goldstein's framework calls for the systematic evaluation of the program's effectiveness. The classic treatment of program evaluation and experimental design in the social and behavioral sciences is that of Campbell and Stanley,[13] and Goldstein draws heavily from this work. Campbell and Stanley propose that two primary issues—internal and external validity—be considered in evaluating whether a particular training or change initiative actually works.

Questions of *internal validity* address whether an observed change in behavior is attributable to a specified change-management practice (in this case a training program) or to some rival explanation. Campbell and Stanley identified a variety of factors that could account for a change in behavior over time: the natural maturation of employees, informal on-the-job training, individual attempts to meet a training need, and so on. When these factors and a formal training program are covariants, the evaluator can falsely conclude that the change was brought about by the training intervention. The ideal solution to this problem is to conduct a true experiment where employees are assigned randomly to either a training group or a control group that does not receive instruction. This can be difficult and costly to implement. Therefore, a variety of quasi-experimental research designs offer useful alternatives.

While true experiments are rare, we want to share one example from the research literature.[14] This study is unique because a commercial bank in Canada actually conducted a pretest–posttest experiment. Trainees were assigned to either an experimental group, where they received training, or to a control group, with no training. The subjects in the study were branch managers. The managers in the experimental condition participated in a leadership-effectiveness training program. A variety of pre- and posttraining measures were collected to see if the training resulted in performance improvements. For most measures there were clear improvements for the trained but not for the control-group managers. But there was one interesting exception. Among trained managers, an index measuring credit card sales declined after training. Of course, the existence of a control group

129

CHAPTER SIX
*Employee
and Career
Development
Systems*

allowed for an examination of credit card sales over the same time among the managers who had not completed the training. The finding was that for the control-group managers, the rate of decline over the time data were being collected was much more severe than it was for the managers who had completed the training. Something in the bank's business environment was apparently accounting for the decline in credit card sales. But the training was probably effective because it seemed to reduce the negative impact of this environmental factor. Without a research design of this type, the bank may have falsely concluded that the training program was not successful in effecting this type of important business outcome.

The problem of *external validity* is essentially a problem of generalizability. Once it is determined that training is responsible for the improvement in performance, we ask if this same form of training will work in other settings, with other trainees, and in future time periods. Often we are concerned with the transfer of learning to actual job settings. While it is possible to acquire skills in protected learning environments, it is sometimes difficult to use these new skills in a nonsupportive or stressful workplace.

Although true experimentation is the ideal, let us point out that there are likely to be instances when evidence of this type is not essential. For example, there are certain work roles that require extensive knowledge that can be acquired only through the experience provided by the employing firm (i.e., company-specific technical and operating information). It can be assumed that new employees do not possess this knowledge. Experimental procedures may be useful in evaluating the relative effects of alternative training techniques, but comparing posttraining performance to some standard is likely to provide sufficient evidence that the training program was successful.

A Review: When Are the Conditions Right for Training?

When is it appropriate to invest in employee training and development and when are such investments likely to produce disappointing returns? A careful review of Goldstein's framework provides many clues about how to answer this type of question. Think of this section as a virtual checklist. We suggest that training and development initiatives are not likely to produce desired results and are not likely to improve over time unless **all** of the following conditions are in place. If these conditions for training success are not present, either the proposed training should be abandoned or steps should be taken to remedy the deficiency.

Is There a Need for Training?

This may seem like a trick question, but all of us can remember times when we were sent off to a training experience that proved nearly useless for one or both of the following reasons:

1. We didn't need the training because we already possessed the target knowledge, skill, or ability (KSA) at an acceptable or appropriate level.

2. We lacked a specified KSA, were successfully trained, but later learned that the KSA was not relevant or related to being effective in our jobs (and not even likely to be relevant in the future).

It sounds simple, but don't send your employees off to training or supply expensive on-the-job developmental experiences if there is not a clear training need!

Are Employees Ready for Training?

Even if there is a training need, there is little likelihood that training will be effective if learners are not (1) motivated to learn and (2) prepared and ready to learn. As discussed in Chapter 2, motivation has to do with the belief that effort will lead to success (e.g., success in training), and the belief that this success (e.g., acquiring new knowledge and skill) will lead to valued outcomes (e.g., increased chances for a promotion or more labor-market mobility). If learners don't exert effort and work hard to master a new skill, they will not benefit from training at the level needed to make the investment worthwhile. Similarly, training effectiveness is not likely if learners are not prepared and if learners do not possess the prerequisite skills assumed to be present. Carefully selecting employees to attend training sessions and offering "jump-start" sessions before the actual training begins may help—but if learners are not ready, training investments are likely to be squandered.

Is There Method–Purpose Congruence?

The possible ways to help employees learn and develop are now vast. As previously discussed, methods can range from instructor centered to learner centered to methods that relate to the generation of new knowledge. In addition, a vast array of technologies can be utilized across these basic learning categories. In particular, technological innovation is quickly changing the training and development environment.[15] Information technology now makes it possible to provide various forms of "just-in-time" developmental experiences, and "distance learning" represents a way to bring people together, from an educational perspective, when they may be geographically separated by thousands of miles.

Weber provided an interesting example of technology rapidly transforming the delivery of training-program content in his description of Daimler-Chrysler's "Academy WebLink."[16] This training system uses the Web, but much of the course material is distributed on CD-ROM disks. To use the system, employees work at Internet-connected PCs and simultaneously draw on material from the Web and CD-ROMs. Such systems allow for frequent updating and can quickly distribute training content throughout the world. They also allow employees to complete the training just before they need it—that is, it is just in time.

When general managers make judgments about whether to invest in employee training, they need to carefully review the proposed methods, asking if they are the best way to meet the targeted training objectives. They also need to carefully review the organization's capability to deliver and implement the training in a professional and state-of-the-art manner. This review needs to also consider the possibility of outsourcing the developmental activity. Many organizations simply do not have the in-house capability to deliver high-quality training experiences. Making judgments about method–purpose congruence and training capability may require the help of training and development experts.

131

CHAPTER SIX
*Employee
and Career
Development
Systems*

Will the Training Generalize?

Goldstein sequenced components in his model to evaluate training effectiveness before evaluating "transfer," or generalizability.[17] In a way this makes sense: Why worry about transfer if nothing was learned in the first place? But we will leave the issue of evaluation to the last step because we are approaching this problem in a slightly different way—a way that should serve the general manager, not the training and development specialist. From this perspective, the problem of generalizability has to do with the question, Will newly acquired knowledge and skills be regularly used while performing the job? Will the display of these new KSAs be reinforced and supported by management, co-workers, and customers? For us, this and the previous three "conditions" must be present before it is appropriate to move ahead with training and development initiatives. The only caveat to this reasoning is that meeting these conditions may be unnecessary if the training opportunity is being provided not to help employees learn job-relevant KSAs, but as some type of incentive to persuade employees to stay with the company or to persuade job applicants to accept job offers.

Can Training Effectiveness Be Evaluated?

It may be that unless there is a way to evaluate training effectiveness at a reasonable cost, training should not be undertaken. This prescription is important because by generating evaluative data, the evaluation may provide clues that lead to ideas about how to improve training over time. However, the point we want to make here is that if the first four conditions discussed are met, the likelihood is very good that a holistic training program evaluation will reveal a positive return. If these contextual factors are in place, general managers should feel justified to pursue training opportunities.

CAREER AND PERSONAL DEVELOPMENT

In addition to helping people acquire job-related knowledge, skills, and abilities, employers have a stake in helping employees develop from a career and personal perspective.

Development as a Selection and Attraction Tool

Every two years *Fortune* magazine lists "The 100 Best Companies to Work For." Using multiple data sources, including answers to a human resources questionnaire designed by Hewitt Associates (an international compensation and benefits consulting firm), the *Fortune* 100 Best Companies list identifies companies that are regarded as great places to work. This designation represents a very important recruitment and retention tool for the recipients.

The list presented in the January 10, 2000, issue of *Fortune* shows that in addition to providing excellent job-related training, many of the 100 best provide extensive opportunities for personal growth and development. For instance:

- The Container Store, a small retailer of storage and home and office organization products, gives employees with 10 years of seniority a sabbatical leave.
- Timberland, the outdoor gear company, offers employees 40 hours of paid time a year for volunteer work.
- Lucent, the networking equipment company, provides a generous tuition reimbursement program: $7,000 a year for undergraduate study and $9,000 for graduate study.
- Tellabs, a Lucent competitor, also provides $7,000 per year in tuition reimbursement.
- Patagonia, the outdoor clothing-by-catalog company, provides paid time off so that employees can work for the nonprofit organization of their choice.

Many other companies on the *Fortune* list provide additional developmental opportunities, ranging from health club memberships with personal trainers to access to personal financial planners. In fact, in a related study conducted by Hewitt, 86 percent of the employers who provided matching funds for 401(k) plans also provided investment education to their employees.[18] This type of training and development can impact employee performance—but it also is designed to help companies compete in tight labor markets. Thus, it's really about attracting and keeping top talent.

Development as a Succession-Management Tool

Many companies in the United States are experiencing or are about to experience a shortage of top-level talent.[19] One of the contributors to this growing problem is the demographic makeup of the country: The raw number of management candidates is declining. Population estimates indicate a 15 percent drop will occur between 2000 and 2015 in the number of 35- to 44-year-olds—the group typically being groomed for senior management assignments. The second factor stems from today's highly competitive business environment: The greater leadership demands being placed on senior executives now than in the past is leaving a declining number of managers who have the capability to assume true executive roles. To meet this challenge, it is likely that more emphasis will need to be placed on growing internal talent. This means more of an emphasis on succession planning, the creation of high-potential talent pools, and the accelerated development of these high-potential employees.

In discussing what companies need to do to create effective succession-planning systems, Byham offered the following suggestions:[20]

133

CHAPTER SIX
*Employee
and Career
Development
Systems*

These systems rest on the premise that although everyone gets developed, only a select group qualify for accelerated development. Because this type of development is expensive and intense (e.g., it includes "stretch assignments," expert feedback and coaching, and special assignments), companies need valid tools for identifying people who will receive this talent-pool designation. Thus, rigorous assessment and better tools for estimating senior management potential will be required in the future.

At regular intervals (e.g., every six months) individuals in this talent pool need to be carefully reviewed relative to their career development needs, their personal interests and career plans, and the company's need for management talent. Thus, senior managers need to develop the skills required to be effective career developers. This includes the ability to help subordinates make informed estimates of their strengths, weaknesses, and career aspirations. It also will require extensive information about where in the organization advancement opportunities are likely to develop over time.

This talent-pool designation should not offer any presumption of upward mobility—staying in the pool and subsequent promotions need to be based on performance and achieved development. Thus, high-quality performance management and appraisal practices will be needed.

General managers need to be aware of what constitutes sound career management and assessment practices and need to know when these types of systems should be designed and implemented. In environments characterized by rapid change, fluid job assignments, and talent shortages at the top, many of Byham's ideas about creating "acceleration pools" would seem to make good conceptual sense. In other, more stable environments, simply providing information about available career paths, using information technology to create skill inventories (see dimension 17—Chapter 3), and letting all employees work with their managers to develop individual career plans may be all that is required.

SUMMARY

In Chapter 3, we discussed an approach or way of thinking about the design of effective HR systems. We saw that firms might vary in how they manage training and development systems along five dimensions: **skill orientation, training-method orientation, career pathing, succession planning,** and **skill inventories.** To summarize, we now relate these dimensions to the sound decision-making practices for considering investments in training and development systems discussed in this chapter.

Skill Orientation

In Chapter 3, we asked, Should a company's orientation to training focus on specific and narrow functional and technical skills, or should the orientation emphasize the development of skills that will generalize to a variety of situations? The answer to this general question will come out of what Goldstein called the "assessment phase" of a well-designed training and development system.[21] Taking into account all aspects of the business context, the assessment presents the key training needs for an organization, which will lead to a conclusion about "skill orientation."

For job classes that are in stable environments and for which incumbents must learn a great deal of company-specific knowledge, a training orientation that focuses on narrowly defined functional and technical skills might be in order. However, in a company that is encountering great technological change and having great difficulty predicting customer demand for its various products and services, a training needs analysis is likely to reveal that employees require additional training in generalizable skills that relate to problem identification and process improvement. Simply put, decisions about skill orientation are the outcomes that flow from the systematic assessment of training needs.

Training Method Orientation

Although firms can be characterized in terms of their typical *approach* to training, the training method selected should be most sensitive to the training *objective*. The distinction between "on-site" and "off-site" training makes clear the range of possibilities, but it doesn't highlight the almost unlimited number of choices that information technology now makes possible. For example, on-site apprenticeship training was almost always an experience that brought the "apprentice" and more knowledgeable "journeyman" together in the same on-site location. Now, using telecommunication equipment, the journeyman may monitor the progress of the apprentice from a distant location. On-site training may also occur with no person-to-person contact of any type. The training content may be delivered through files accessed from a CD-ROM drive.

For these reasons, "training-method orientation" should be thought of as a multidimensional concept—perhaps best summarized in Table 6–1. This table was presented to make a point about method–purpose congruence; it lists only a few illustrative possibilities. There are, of course, many additional possibilities that can be classified under the instructor-, learner-, and learning-team–centered labels. The general manager should expect that either internal HRM staff or external HR-oriented consultants can provide a clear and reasonable answer to the important question: Is this the most appropriate way to meet this training objective?

Career Pathing

Some companies are able and willing to provide a lot of detailed information about existing career options and paths, along with information about the knowledge, skills, and experiences needed to make career moves. Others choose to be more secretive, with this type of information only coming from relationships with mentors or from other members of a person's informal network of associates. Other firms are not able to provide this type of information because their environments are so fluid that almost as soon as information is gathered and presented, it becomes obsolete.

135

CHAPTER SIX
Employee
and Career
Development
Systems

Choices on this dimension need to take into account both the speed with which structures and role requirements change and the behavioral objectives that might be served by offering clearly defined career paths and the career-planning advice that makes this type of information interpretable.

Succession Planning

Succession planning in business represents both a training and development activity and a staffing activity. To be ready for future staffing needs, organizations must forecast both the demand for and supply of talent for key job assignments. When forecasting supply, these companies must go beyond simply analyzing raw internal person counts and age distributions. They must forecast not only how many people will be available at some future date, but also what knowledge, skill, and ability mix will be represented by these people. Thus, much of the work associated with succession planning is very much like the training needs assessment work represented in Goldstein's framework.

If future skill shortages are predicted, one of two remedies may be called for. Either the firm will need to accelerate training and development activities (in an effort to grow internal talent), or the firm will need to pursue a more aggressive external hiring strategy. As noted throughout this book, decisions about when to initiate a formal and complex succession planning process need to take into account many factors—ranging from business strategy, to labor market conditions, to issues about using technology in place of people.

Skills Inventories

Decisions about putting in place a computerized skills inventory really follow decisions about whether these data are needed to implement training needs analyses or succession planning systems. If training and development represents a central HR theme and the need for comprehensive succession planning is critical to business success in the future, developing and deploying a high-quality skills inventory probably makes good sense. Although gathering the input data is still very expensive and labor intense, excellent computer software is now available to make these inventories much more useful than ever before.

CONCLUSION

Early in this chapter we stated that general managers today must make sense out of much more than the very useful existing literature devoted to traditional training and development. They must now confront and understand a growing literature that not only addresses learning at the level of the individual, but also addresses learning at the level of the entire organization. The term "learning organization" is now commonly used in the management literature.

In conclusion, we suggest that the notion of a learning organization is not very different from the notion of a high-quality training and development system. Building on Goldstein's ideas from his classic book of 1974, we present Figure 6–2. In Figure 6–2*a,* the training process is shown as a form of individual change and development. In Figure 6–2*b,* the same general

FIGURE 6–2. (*a*) The training process as a form of individual learning and development; and (*b*) the renewal process as a form of organizational learning.

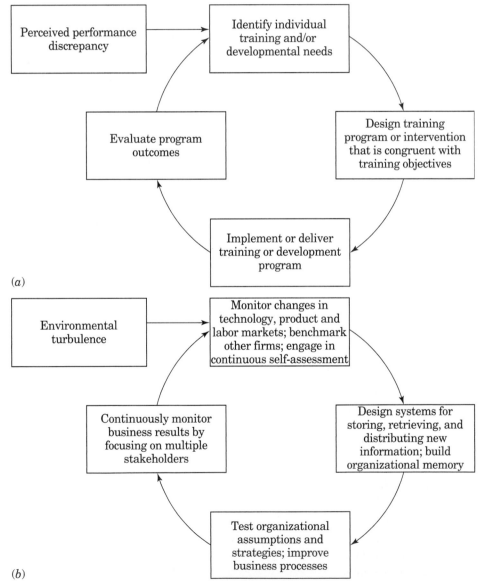

framework is used to depict the organizational change process as a form of organizational learning. General managers need to become skilled practitioners of both processes.

137

CHAPTER SIX
*Employee
and Career
Development
Systems*

CONTINUOUS LEARNING: SOME NEXT STEPS

For the first step we once again will be sending you to a web page to explore some training-related material that will be of interest to the general manager. The second step asks that you take a personal training and development step to better understand the processes discussed in this chapter.

- The American Society for Training and Development provides a very useful web page for learning about new training initiatives and to help you locate training and development–oriented consulting firms. Go to www.astd.org and review what these sources include.
- One good way to really appreciate the complexity of high-quality training systems is to conduct a personal training needs assessment and then suggest a training intervention to help you achieve your stated goal. We suggest the following. Systematically evaluate a current knowledge, skill, and ability (KSA) profile that relates to some important personal goal. Then select a KSA or set of KSAs that is an appropriate target for a training intervention. Next, analyze your readiness for training. Finally, suggest a training experience designed to remove any current deficiency. That is, (1) identify a personal performance objective (e.g., restoring a vintage automobile); (2) conduct an analysis of the activities you will need to complete to achieve your objective; (3) identify the KSAs required to perform these activities; (4) identify the KSAs you are in the greatest need of developing further; (5) propose the type of training that will be needed to help you achieve your goals; and (6) determine if you are motivated and have the ability to complete a training experience designed to alleviate any observed KSA deficiencies.

ENDNOTES

1. J. Pfeffer, *Competitive Advantage through People* (Boston: Harvard Business School Press, 1994); and J. Pfeffer, "Producing Sustainable Competitive Advantage through the Effective Management of People," *Academy of Management Executive* 9 (1995), pp. 55–69.
2. J. Pfeffer and J. F. Veiga, "Putting People First for Organizational Success," *Academy of Management Executive* 13 (1999), p. 43.
3. I. I. Goldstein, *Training: Program Development and Evaluation* (Belmont, CA: Wadsworth, 1974), p. 3.
4. For example, see G. Hamel and C. K. Prahalad, *Competing for the Future* (Boston: Harvard Business School Press, 1994); D. Leonard-Barton, *The Wellsprings of Knowledge* (Boston: Harvard Business School Press, 1995); and I. Nonaka and H. Takeuchi, *The Knowledge-Creating Company: How Japanese Companies Create the Dynamics of Innovation* (New York: Oxford University Press, 1994).
5. J. Micklethwait and A. Wooldridge, *The Witch Doctors: Making Sense of the Management Gurus* (New York: Random House, 1996), p. 127.
6. Goldstein, *Training*.

7. For a critique of this literature, see Micklethwait and Wooldridge, *The Witch Doctors,* pp. 119–40.
8. Goldstein, *Training.*
9. Ibid.
10. D. L. Kirkpatrick, "Techniques for Evaluating Training Programs," *Journal of the American Society of Training Directors* 13 (1974), pp. 3–9, 21–26.
11. A. Bandura, *Social Foundations of Thought and Action* (Englewood Cliffs, NJ: Prentice Hall, 1986).
12. T. T. Baldwin, C. Danielson, and W. Wiggenhorn, "The Evolution of Learning Strategies in Organizations: From Employee Development to Business Redefinition," *Academy of Management Executive* 11 (1997), pp. 47–58.
13. D. T. Campbell and J. C. Stanley, *Experimental and Quasi-Experimental Designs for Research* (Chicago: Rand McNally, 1963).
14. J. Barling, T. Weber, and E. K. Kelloway, "Effects of Transformational Leadership Training on Attitudinal and Financial Outcomes: A Field Experiment," *Journal of Applied Psychology* 81 (1996), pp. 827–32.
15. D. E. Leidner and S. L. Jarvenpaa, "The Use of Information Technology to Enhance Management School Education: A Theoretical View," *MIS Quarterly*, September 1995, pp. 265–91.
16. T. E. Weber, "The New Corporate Dress Code for Corporate Training: Slippers and Pajamas," *The Wall Street Journal*, January 31, 2000, p. B1.
17. Goldstein, *Training.*
18. "Two Tides Are Rising in Retirement Plans," *The New York Times*, January 30, 2000, p. B12.
19. W. C. Byham, "Bench Strength," *Across Board: The Conference Board Magazine*, February 2000, pp. 34–38.
20. Ibid.
21. Goldstein, *Training.*

7

Performance Management Systems

One of the most important—and most difficult—tasks faced by managers is the managing of employee performance. As a manager you must not only strive to accurately measure performance, but also work to orient employees to improve performance. In this chapter you will

- Learn about purposes and uses of measures of employee performance.
- See the value and the challenges of using results-oriented performance measures.
- Become acquainted with the major types of judgmental performance measures, including rating scales, employee comparisons, and 360 degree appraisal.
- Learn about some key principles for making performance appraisal as effective as possible.
- See that an overall performance management system includes a systematic set of integrated components.

If less than 10% of your customers judged a product effective and if seven out of 10 said they were more confused than enlightened by it, you would drop it, right? So, why don't more companies drop their annual job performance reviews?"[1] This question was asked in a *Wall Street Journal* article, "Annual Agony," which conveys a litany of employee and management grumbles about performance appraisal as practiced today. Almost every major survey of performance management finds that both employees and managers rate their firms' process as a "resounding failure." Examples are cited of firms that spend millions of dollars each year to overhaul their performance review systems—while providing a lucrative and rapidly expanding business for consulting firms. Specific grumbles include the view that performance appraisal is "just a ritual," requiring a quick update of last year's rating. It is also acknowledged that "most of us don't like to sit down and hear where we're lacking and where we need to improve," and that few firms provide any help to managers on how to conduct an effective conversation with an employee about performance. One survey even found that 98 percent of managers reported encountering some type of aggression after giving employees negative appraisals. But the *Journal* article also reports that few firms have eliminated their written performance evaluations. Managers and employees are under pressure from their legal and human resource staffs to continue conducting performance appraisals in order to combat "wrongful discharge lawsuits" from terminated employees.

In contrast to this bleak picture of performance appraisal, consider another recent article in the same publication concerning Jack Welch, chairman and chief executive of the General Electric Company (GE).[2] The focus is on Welch's commitment to careful evaluation of GE employees ("Raises and Praise or Out the Door"). Welch reports that his most important task, and the one he devotes more time to than any other, is motivating and assessing GE's employees. His practices include the grading of GE's 85,000 managers and professionals annually on a curve. Using an overall performance rating on a 5-point scale, Welch also reports that rewards, including stock options, are showered on the top performers. Welch argues that measuring performance and tying levels of performance to rewards is a key to motivating employees. When asked how he motivates the "average" performers, Welch answers: "By telling them they can get to be 2's and 1's, and telling them they are eligible for options. But only the best of them will get options."

Strangely enough, these articles both reflect commonly held views of performance management and its role in effective human resource management systems. Formal appraisal and management systems are a reality in almost all work organizations today. Their design and implementation typically are characterized as frustrating, complicated, contentious, and at the same time as strategic, linked to organizational effectiveness, and necessary for effectively managing people.

In this chapter we review some of the key issues and alternatives available to managers in the area of performance management. By "performance" we mean the extent to which an employee fulfills his or her job requirements. Performance appraisal and performance management involve identifying, measuring, revising, and developing human performance in organizations.[3] Nowadays most organizations of even medium size conduct some kind of systematic appraisal of the performance of each employee. The typical approach has a supervisor rating each employee on some kind of performance rating scale once each year. Increasingly, there is also a requirement that supervisors provide a one-to-one annual performance feedback/counseling session to each employee. In these sessions supervisors communicate the employee's numerical ratings and overall evaluation, discuss expectations for performance improvement, and suggest ways to enhance performance. The most progressive organizations go a step further by instituting a performance management system that includes a systematic sequence of components connected to employee development and the goals of the organization.

As the examples we used to introduce this topic illustrate, performance management is a complex process. As with all HRM practices, there is plenty of variability in how performance management is handled across organizations. In recent years organizations have introduced a number of new approaches. The serious student of performance management can consult a number of substantive books on this complicated topic.[4] As we repeatedly emphasize in this book, managers should be aware of the possibilities and then select an integrated set of performance management practices that are most appropriate for their unique circumstances.

ALIGNING PERFORMANCE MANAGEMENT SYSTEMS WITH THE FIRM'S STRATEGY: MEASURING WHAT MATTERS

In the HRM framework we presented in Chapter 1, we explained how a series of key factors contribute to the design of integrated HR systems for particular classes of jobs. In this framework (see Figure 1–1) we explain how the firm's overall business strategy and its technology determine the organizational design and work processes, which then translate into specific **role/behavioral requirements** for particular job classes. A key theme of this book is that managers must design integrated HR systems that promote these role/behavioral requirements, while taking into account contextual factors affecting the firm, especially labor markets and the legal environment.

We also acknowledge that a performance management system appropriate for a particular business unit should focus on adding value for the firm, as opposed to serving as a bureaucratic constraint emanating from the corporate level. Given that there may be tension in an organization between local needs for performance management and overall corporate needs, a "toolbox" approach to performance management may be the solution.[5] Both local and corporate representatives can design and maintain a performance management system. Local managers are offered a range of practices; they can select those practices that fit their unique circumstances. These performance practices may even be developed by employee work teams, using HRM professionals as consultants.

Following from our point of view and the conceptual framework used in this book, performance management systems are a key component of an overall HR system. Performance management systems involve the traditional task of measuring, as directly and accurately as possible, employees' level of performance of the key behavioral requirements for a job class. Performance management also includes providing one-to-one performance feedback, counseling, and coaching to enhance employees' motivation and competence for performing key behaviors. The technology, organizational design, and work processes may be such that work is performed and evaluated at the individual, group, or organizational level. Performance management systems should accommodate these various levels. However, in this chapter, as we examine issues and options in performance management we focus our illustrations on those systems geared toward *individual* employees. Individual-oriented performance appraisal and feedback is still the most frequently used approach, but keep in mind that these same performance issues and techniques can be applied to group-oriented work.

As we will discuss in Chapter 8, HR systems, including performance management, have a direct effect on a firm's bottom line. In Chapter 8 we also provide some detailed illustrations of how more effective HRM practices translate into enhanced financial returns. Not surprisingly, improvements in a firm's performance management system—through, for example, more accurate measurement and more effective feedback and counseling—can result in overall improvements in levels of employee performance, with the accompanying financial returns to the firm.

PURPOSES AND USES FOR MEASURES OF EMPLOYEE PERFORMANCE

Consistent with the *Wall Street Journal* report of "annual agony," in our own experience managers are rarely satisfied with their employee performance measures—whatever they may currently be. Organizations seem to generate new performance rating scales every few years, searching, if not for the Holy Grail, at least for some improvements over the last version. This is not too surprising, given the complexity of the measurement task and the multiple purposes and uses for employee performance data. It is not easy to find an overall measurement system that adequately fulfills all of these purposes. We note that in recent years the scholars of performance appraisal seem to have finally concluded that the question "Which performance measurement system is the best?" is not as important as "How can we ensure that our managers *understand* and are *thoroughly trained* in using our system?" We next briefly survey three key managerial uses of performance appraisal data and offer some comments about the relationship of total quality management (TQM) to performance appraisal.

Administrative Uses

In the eyes of managers, probably the most important purpose of performance appraisal is to make administrative decisions. Performance data are used in making decisions about employees, including promotions to higher level jobs, size of annual base salary adjustments, performance bonuses and commissions, lateral transfers, and terminations. In Chapter 4 we discussed the importance of performance measures for merit-based pay. It is essential that employees view their firms' performance measures, whether concrete, "results-oriented" measures or more subjective performance ratings, as credible. This credibility is crucial for maintaining employee morale, for justifying employment decisions to employees, and also for legal defense in the event of formal complaints or discrimination lawsuits.

A barrier to the accuracy and credibility of performance measures is posed by a number of rater errors, perceptual biases, and other sources of distortion in performance ratings. Some of these errors reflect everyday errors in our perceptions of others (displayed later in Table 7–1). Some credibility problems, however, reflect "political" distortions that creep into performance measures, because these measures are used for so many important decisions and employee rewards.[6] In any case, for an effective performance management system, managers at all levels must be willing to commit significant amounts of time on a regular basis.

Employee performance is "multidimensional" in that there are almost always multiple role and behavioral requirements for a job class. It follows that an employee is likely to be stronger on some dimensions (e.g., customer relations) than on others (e.g., product knowledge). For accurate measurement, providing detailed feedback to employees, and legal defensibility, performance measures should capture these multiple dimensions. Performance rating forms, for example, usually ask the rater to rate the employee on a number of dimensions of performance. Although these **multidimensional** measures are necessary, organizations also need an overall summary index for administrative decisions, called a **composite** measure of employee performance. This composite measure can then conveniently be used as input into the firm's salary increase system and for other administrative decisions about employees.

Feedback, Counseling, and Performance Improvement

In a performance management system, performance measures are also used as the basis for providing employees with feedback and counseling to improve their performance. As mentioned earlier, continuous performance improvement adds value to the organization. However, sitting down for a one-to-one performance feedback session with an employee is one of the toughest tasks for any manager. Managers often avoid these meetings, preferring instead to "casually" relate to employees the size of their salary increase, and not much else. But many employees expect detailed feedback and assistance in how to improve their work—and enhance their rewards. Scholars studying work stress have even determined that a *lack of* clear performance expectations and detailed performance feedback is a major source of stress for employees.[7]

Managers must be systematically trained in a variety of interaction skills needed for effective performance feedback and counseling. Many of the necessary skills are similar to those required of effective employment interviewers and of counselors. Later in this chapter we illustrate some specific steps for managers to follow in conducting performance appraisal and feedback sessions, in the context of an overview of the components of an overall performance management system.

Another important dimension of performance feedback sessions is the motivational potential for employees (as discussed in Chapter 2). These sessions serve as a vehicle for coaching employees in specific strategies for improving their performance. As a result, employees' *expectancy* perceptions for high performance should be enhanced. Supervisors can also clarify to employees the *connection* between performing key behaviors and receiving valuable rewards (*instrumentality* and *valence* perceptions). Thus, performance feedback sessions can enhance both an employee's expectancy and instrumentality perceptions—the key to motivating high performance.

Evaluation of Organizational Programs

A third major use of performance measures centers around the evaluation of organizational programs. Performance measures can serve as criteria for assessing the effectiveness of, or "validating," employee selection measures (see Chapter 5 on staffing systems), employee training programs, work-family programs, or any other intervention designed to improve employee productivity or organizational functioning. For example, a firm might collect employee performance measures *before* and again *after* a training program, as part of evaluating the success of that program. For research and program evaluation it is crucial that these performance measures be as accurate and bias-free as possible. Because political processes may distort employee performance evaluations, some researchers even insist on collecting special performance measures (e.g., special supervisor ratings) designed strictly for research purposes. These measures are likely to be more nearly bias-free than performance measures that managers know will be used for administrative decisions.

Performance Appraisal and Total Quality Management

Is the use of performance appraisal in conflict with an organization's adopting total quality management (TQM)? Masterson and Taylor have discussed this issue and offer the view that TQM and (what they label as) total performance management (TPM) can be *complementary* in advancing an organization's goals.[8] They cite a survey indicating that by the early 1990s, some 93 percent of manufacturing companies and 69 percent of service companies had implemented quality management practices. W. Edwards Deming, the celebrated guru of TQM, was critical of performance appraisal, labeling it one of the "seven deadly diseases" and an obstacle for TQM in organizations. At the same time, organizations have been reluctant to discard performance appraisal. Thus, managers have tried to make TQM's emphasis on team and system variables compatible with the needs of employees for individual recognition and development. And performance management systems do appear to contribute to an organization's effectiveness. Masterson and Taylor point out that many scholars agree that organizations can adopt performance appraisal and other HR systems to *support* rather than hinder TQM initiatives.

We cannot provide an in-depth discussion of all the issues here. But Masterson and Taylor assert that TQM and TPM can be used to complement each other because of two characteristics of these systems:

1. TQM focuses on systems and processes within organizations but ignores the individual—a potential source of quality improvement and competitive advantage.

2. TQM provides an overall quality vision for a firm but no specific set of mechanisms for achieving this vision, while TPM offers a valuable tool for developing and managing employees.

Thus, firms using both TQM and TPM can realize the benefits of an overriding quality vision along with some specific tools for working with employees to achieve that vision. For example, in TQM not all employees are capable of meeting the firm's quality standards. Managers, as coaches, can help employees achieve these objectives. Performance management provides training and methods for observing and recording employee performance (discussed later in this chapter). In addition, the developmental focus of performance management requires diagnosing performance problems and identifying actions to address performance weaknesses—thus facilitating continuous improvement for individual employees. We next discuss specific options for measuring employee performance.

MEASURING RESULTS: USE OF OBJECTIVE OUTCOME MEASURES

Measuring performance using "results"—objective, verifiable outcome measures—has strong intuitive appeal. As discussed in Chapter 3, results-oriented measurement systems count the outcomes of work. A variety of objective performance measures have been identified and used over the years for just about every occupational group. These include number of units produced, dollar sales value per month, and number of hours taken to rebuild an automatic transmission. But it is usually not practically feasible to use objective output measures as the *sole* measure of employee performance, for reasons we discuss shortly.

Examples of Use of Results-Oriented Performance Measures

Consider the familiar set of measures surrounding the performance of professional and college athletes. Many of us are regularly intrigued (or bored) by daily conversations about the latest points scored, bases stolen, rebounds gathered, or yards per carry of popular athletes. Presumably, these objective outcome data are also used for at least part of the assessment of athletes' performance and their value to their organizations. Another familiar example is the use of sales commissions as financial incentives for those selling all sorts of products, from real estate to college textbooks. An objective calculation of performance in terms of dollars of sales is included in determining commissions paid to salespersons.

Another popular form of results-oriented performance measure is the program of goal-setting and feedback known as *management by objectives* (*MBO*). This practice can be seen as an integrated organizational program for enhancing productivity—and also as a type of employee performance appraisal. In a typical MBO program employees negotiate with their supervisors a small number of concrete performance objectives for the upcoming time period. These objectives are recorded in terms of *explicit, measurable,* and *verifiable* criteria, each with specific time deadlines attached (see Figure 7–1). These objectives are also expected to reflect important activities for the employee's job and to be well-integrated with the strategy and objectives of the organization and work unit.

The term "MBO" has been around for decades.[9] But regardless of whether the MBO terminology is adopted, it appears that in the 1990s a

FIGURE 7–1. An MBO worksheet.

Sam Speedy		General Manager	Progress Reviews
Prepared by Manager	Date	Position Title	1st _____
			2nd _____
Harry Slow		Production	3rd _____
Reviewed by Supervisor	Date	Position Title	Date

Major Job Objectives	% Work Time	Measures of Results	Std. of Perf.	Results		Dates	
				Target	Actual	Target	Actual
1. Product Delivery (May be broken down by products)	25%	a. % of on-schedule delivery	94%	Increase to 98%		8/31	
		b. Number of customer complaints as a % of monthly purchase orders	4%	Decrease to 3%		9/30	
2. Product Quality (May be broken down by products)	30%	a. % of rejects per total monthly volume	6%	Decrease to 4%		7/31	
		b. Ratio of factory repair time to total production hours/month	7%	Decrease to 4%		9/31	
		c. Number of units service-free during warranty period	73%	Increase to 86%		10/31	
3. Operating Efficiency	25%	a. Cost per unit of output per month	$35.75 /unit	Reduce to $35.50/unit		2/1	
		b. Equipment utilization time as a % of monthly available hours	86%	Increase to 95%		11/15	
4. Other Key Objectives	20%						

Source: R. W. Beatty and C. E. Schneier, *Personnel Administration: An Experiential Skill-Building Approach,* Reprinted by permission of Prentice-Hall, Inc. Upper Saddle River, NJ.

growing number of firms implemented performance management systems based on concrete "goals," "objectives," "performance targets," or a variety of similar terms that reflect the major components of MBO. The employees' goals typically relate to business outcomes such as increasing market share, dollars of sales, productivity, or decreasing numbers of customer complaints or defective products produced. We can see the importance of these kinds of performance goals for the careers of corporate managers by noting the daily reports in the business press of the rise or demise of a corporate executive. These accounts typically attribute the executive's rise or demise to changes in the market share, sales, or productivity of the business unit.

Advantages and Disadvantages of Results-Oriented Measures

The intuitive appeal of a firm's use of results-oriented performance measures is based on objectivity or, to use a more technical term, the *reliability* of these types of measures. By reliability, we mean that these performance measures can be captured with a minimum of measurement error. This measurement accuracy contributes to the credibility of results-oriented measures in the perceptions of managers and employees. "Hard numbers," unlike "ratings," cannot be distorted by personality clashes, biased perceptions or stereotypes, or corporate politics. But there are also potential drawbacks to results-oriented measures.

One drawback is the possibility that these measures suffer from **contamination**. A performance measure is contaminated to the extent that the measure is influenced by factors *beyond the employee's control*. A professional football running back would surely cry foul if his performance—using "yards per carry"—was judged to have declined shortly after the team had traded away several outstanding members of the offensive line. Similarly, using "dollars of sales" may be unacceptable as the performance index for two sales reps if one works a large territory with high sales potential while the other covers a smaller territory with low potential. In each of these examples, the *measure used* to capture performance is highly contaminated by factors beyond the employee's control.

Contamination is a potential problem for all kinds of performance measures, but results-oriented measures are especially susceptible to this problem. It may be impossible to find good performance measures that do not have at least some level of contamination. Ultimately, this is a judgment call: If the measure appears to be "too contaminated," it probably should not be used for assessments of an individual employee's performance.

Another problem with reliance on results-oriented performance measures is the possibility of **deficiency**. Adequate measurement of employee performance must cover *all the important dimensions of job performance*. This requirement of job-relatedness is important for producing an effective and credible measure of performance and also for any legal defense of the performance measure. Certainly a university that monitors only "numbers of articles published" for each professor would be using a highly deficient measure of performance. Or consider a clothing store that assesses salesperson performance using one results-oriented measure: dollars of sales. This deficient measure ignores other aspects of a salesperson's job performance, such as customer relationships, maintaining merchandise, and recordkeeping. For most job classes, in order to minimize deficiency managers must supplement objective, results-oriented performance measures with additional measures such as rating scales.

Results-oriented measures also raise motivational concerns. Managers must realize that employees will focus their attention at work on tasks that are measured and rewarded. It follows that a kind of "side effect" of narrow, results-oriented performance measures is employee neglect of other important aspects of work. If dollars of sales is what a retailer measures, then dollars of sales is what will be produced—possibly to the detriment of everything else.

For some job classes it is also true that objective, results-oriented measures are simply not available. There may be no easy way to capture important aspects of employee work with objective output measures. This limitation is most likely for certain managerial and professional job classes, where critical aspects of performance are "cognitive" and thus not easy to observe or compute.

To summarize, results-oriented measures can be valuable in a performance management system. They have a number of advantages for performance measurement and for tie-ins to incentive pay strategies. They also have a number of limitations, so they usually need to be supplemented with judgmental, rating-oriented approaches. We next turn to a discussion of these judgmental approaches.

MEASURING "PROCESSES" AND THE USE OF HUMAN JUDGMENT

In contrast to results-oriented performance measurement systems, process-oriented systems rate the *way* work is completed. These types of systems usually involve the use of human judgment, requiring some type of performance rating or ranking, and can justifiably be considered "subjective." Rating scales are by far the most widely used method of performance measurement in organizations. Managers face a number of challenges in the use of ratings and rankings. These challenges include dealing with various kinds of perceptual errors that result when people form judgments and rate others on a scale. Table 7–1 lists some of the major "rater errors" that can occur when raters evaluate the performance of others. In the last section of this chapter we discuss strategies for minimizing errors and enhancing the overall quality of judgmental performance measures.

Rating Scales: Absolute Standards in Performance Appraisal

Probably the most frequently used approach for performance measurement is some form of **graphic rating scale**. A graphic rating scale contains a series of performance dimensions reflecting the work of a job class (e.g., quality of work, customer relations) and some kind of continuum, such as a scale of 1 to 7. The rater places a check or circles a number on the scale to describe the level of an employee's performance.

Figure 7–2 illustrates nine different scale configurations that could be used for a graphic scale to measure one performance dimension, quality of work. The dimensions of graphic rating scales are often fairly broad in scope (e.g., planning, relationships with co-workers), so that the scale can apply to large numbers of people and numerous job classes in the firm. However, these kinds of scales are also susceptible to most of the rater errors. For example, the scale allows a rater to rate an entire set of employees at the high end of the scale (leniency error). The scale also allows raters to rate everyone using the middle of the scale (central tendency error; see Table 7–1).

Although all configurations of graphic rating scales share potential weaknesses, some are clearly better than others. An effective rating scale should include rating dimensions that are directly linked to the job requirements in the particular organization. The scales must also thoroughly cover the domain of performance (not be "deficient"). But two important criteria

TABLE 7–1. Common Rater Errors in Performance Appraisal

Halo error: A rater's overall positive or negative impression of an individual employee leads to rating him or her the same across all rating dimensions.

Leniency error: Raters' tendency to rate all employees at the positive end of the scale (positive leniency) or at the low end of the scale (negative leniency).

Central tendency error: A rater's tendency to avoid making "extreme" judgments of employees (even when deserved) results in rating all employees in the middle part of a scale.

Recency error: Rater's tendency to allow *more recent* incidents (either effective or ineffective) of employee behavior to carry too much weight in evaluation of performance over an entire rating period.

First-impression error: Raters' tendency to let first impressions of employee performance carry too much weight in evaluation of performance over an entire rating period.

Similar-to-me error: Raters' tendency to be biased in performance evaluation toward those employees seen as *similar to the raters* themselves.

FIGURE 7–2.   Examples of graphic rating scales.

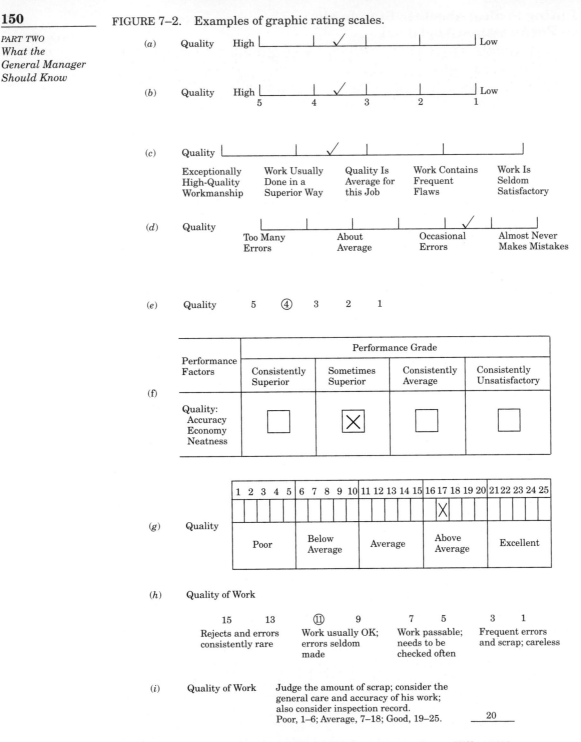

Source: R. M. Guion, *Personnel Testing* (New York: McGraw-Hill, 1965).

relating to performance dimensions and scale values must be considered in the actual construction of the scales.

Thoroughly defined performance dimensions is our first criterion. Referring to the example in Figure 7–2, the dimension definition for quality should spell out thoroughly and precisely which employee behaviors are included in this dimension and therefore should be considered in the rating. If all raters hold in their minds the *same* definition of quality of performance, the more accurate the overall performance appraisal system will be. Looking at the nine scale examples in Figure 7–2, all of which measure the quality dimension, we would choose scale *i* as the best in terms of dimension definition. This scale appears to provide the most thorough and precise definition of the quality dimension.

Precisely defined scale anchor points is the second important criterion for a graphic rating scale. Here we refer to the meaning of the numbers on the scale. What does it mean when an employee is rated "1" versus "3"? Again, every rater in our organization should share a common conception of the meaning of the scale anchor points. Once again viewing the graphic rating scale examples in Figure 7–2, we can see that several of the scales include anchors. We would choose scale *h* as having the most effective anchors, in that the scale *h* anchors are the most "behaviorally specific" and precise, spelling out the kinds of employee behaviors representing points on the scale. Perhaps the best overall graphic rating scale for measuring the quality dimension of performance would be a new scale incorporating the dimension definition from scale *i* and the anchors from scale *h*.

A variation on the basic graphic rating scale is the **behaviorally anchored rating scale (BARS)**. This is essentially a graphic rating scale custom-designed for a particular job class in the organization. Developing BARS involves working closely with groups of the raters themselves to determine a set of job-related performance dimensions. First, the dimensions are carefully defined by the managers. Next, scale anchors are established, using familiar language reflecting specific examples of effective and less effective job behaviors. These examples are placed as anchor points on the scale continuum, after considerable refinement. Thus, BARS are well-developed graphic rating scales tailor-made for a job class. They are somewhat time-consuming and costly to develop, but because of the developmental work they are strongly job related, and also considered to be useful for feedback and for employee training.

A final example of a rating scale is the **behavior observation scale (BOS)**, a more recent addition to the set of available performance rating scales.[10] Figure 7–3 illustrates part of a BOS developed for the job of waitperson in a small restaurant. Note that there are no "performance dimensions" per se. Instead, this scale includes a detailed listing of specific behaviors of a person holding the job. The rater marks a scale indicating his or her estimate of the percentage of time the employee performs this behavior. Such scales are obviously directly and thoroughly linked to job requirements. They are also excellent for feedback, in that supervisors can discuss performance in terms of specific employee behaviors observed or not observed on the job.

FIGURE 7–3.   Example of a behavior observation scale (BOS).

I. WAITER/WAITRESS

1. Comes to work on-time

    Almost never   1   2   3   4   5   Almost always

2. Uses the words "please" and "thank you" when talking to customers

    Almost never   1   2   3   4   5   Almost always

3. Uses the words "please" and "thank you" when talking to fellow employees

    Almost never   1   2   3   4   5   Almost always

4. Tries to remember the names of customers who come to Beazley's three or more times a week

    Almost never   1   2   3   4   5   Almost always

5. Keeps ashtrays clean

    Almost never   1   2   3   4   5   Almost always

6. Keeps counters clean, including creamer bottles and steel shelves

    Almost never   1   2   3   4   5   Almost always

7. Stops talking to a fellow employee as soon as a customer approaches the counter

    Almost never   1   2   3   4   5   Almost always

8. Answers the telephone within three rings regardless of how busy with customers

    Almost never   1   2   3   4   5   Almost always

9. Refuses to gossip about the personal lives of Beazley employees

    Almost never   1   2   3   4   5   Almost always

10. Passes rather than shoves food to customers

    Almost never   1   2   3   4   5   Almost always

11. Cleans the floor when it is dirty

    Almost never   1   2   3   4   5   Almost always

12. Asks customers if everything is satisfactory

    Almost never   1   2   3   4   5   Almost always

Source: G. P. Latham and K. N. Wexley, *Increasing Productivity through Performance Appraisal* (Reading, MA: Addison-Wesley, 1981).

Employee Comparison Approaches

153

CHAPTER SEVEN
Performance
Management
Systems

Graphic scales, BARS, and BOS can all be categorized as using "absolute standards" for assessing employee performance. Another option for judgmental performance measures is the explicit use of **employee comparisons**, which essentially involves *ranking* the employees against each other. For example, using a basic ranking approach, the supervisor of 10 employees would simply record who is the best performer, who is number 2, and so on. In contrast to the absolute standards of rating scales, rankings spread out the ratings. A ranking also avoids some of the rater errors because it is not possible for the ranker to give a high performance assessment to everyone (leniency) or to place everyone in the middle (central tendency). In fact, this spreading out of the performance ratings represents the major strength of ranking and illustrates how an overall ranking of an employee group can be useful for administrative decisions such as awarding promotions.

But note that ranking does not allow for detailed performance feedback for employees. An employee who is told that she is "number 5 out of 10 employees" would not be getting useful feedback for performance improvement. It is also hard to demonstrate that an overall ranking is directly tied to the role and behavioral requirements of employees. This weakens the legal defensibility of ranking.

We conclude that ranking can be useful, especially if managers need to spread out the employee ratings for administrative decisions. But the use of rankings illustrates the point that particular performance appraisal techniques tend to be more or less effective for particular purposes, such as feedback or administrative decisions. Rankings would almost always need to be combined with other types of performance measures to ensure an effective overall performance management system.

MEASUREMENT SCOPE IN PERFORMANCE APPRAISAL

In determining an overall performance management system, managers must make decisions about the *scope* of measurement, as pointed out in the discussion of the "possibilities" for HRM reward systems in Chapter 3. For example, a supervisor, peer, or customer might be asked to assess an employee's performance. But anyone who rates an employee should

1. Have the ability to regularly observe (or otherwise determine) the employee's job behavior.
2. Be familiar with the requirements of the employee's job.

As we mentioned in Chapter 3, the traditional approach to measurement scope is unidirectional and hierarchical. Employees are rated by their immediate supervisor. Thus, top executives rate managers, managers rate supervisors, and supervisors rate hourly employees. The rationale here is that the direct supervisor is the person who has the best opportunity to observe the target employee's performance. However, organizations are well aware that given the existence of rater errors, relying on the observation and judgment of just *one* rater is fraught with potential problems.

As a check and balance on a single supervisor's rating, many organizations have supplemented these ratings with additional ratings from others. Sometimes additional managers who have worked with an employee are asked to provide a rating. Sometimes *peer ratings* are used, in which colleagues rate each other. Peers possess unique knowledge of the job requirements and also have the ability to observe aspects of performance that are inaccessible to supervisors. In organizations that have reorganized into a team-oriented structure, for example, one's team members are valuable sources of performance appraisal. Peer ratings have also been especially useful for evaluating the performance of professionals, such as nurses, attorneys, and professors.

A recent appraisal trend includes the use of *self-ratings* of performance. Self-ratings are especially useful as part of a performance feedback/counseling discussion between a supervisor and employee.

360 Degree Appraisal

A recently popular innovation in performance management is the use of **360 degree appraisal**, which provides a multidirectional measurement scope for employee performance. Thus, an employee might receive feedback from several sources, including

- Downward feedback from the supervisor.
- Upward feedback from subordinates.
- Lateral feedback from peers.
- "Inward feedback" from oneself.
- Customer feedback from both internal and external customers.[11]

Figure 7–4 is an example of a customer appraisal form that could be used in a 360 degree feedback system.

The focus of 360 degree assessment is typically *developmental*—feedback and performance improvement—as opposed to *evaluative*—allocating rewards or promotions. This focus on development versus evaluation stems from the potential for unhealthy political processes involving subordinates or customers to subvert honest, accurate feedback about performance.[12] The 360 degree approach has become popular for a variety of reasons. With the reduction in layers of management, individual managers now have increased numbers of employees reporting to them, making it difficult to thoroughly observe and assess each person. In addition, the traditional hierarchical evaluation is often incongruent with organizations that emphasize teamwork and high employee involvement.[13]

As is true for all performance assessments, 360 degree feedback should be congruent with the organization's strategy and should measure important target behaviors. As one recent article relayed this point: "What gets measured (and rewarded) drives behavior. Even when 360 degree feedback ratings are used strictly for developmental purposes, individuals will tend to modify behaviors in ways to receive more positive ratings. Therefore, it is extremely important that 360 degree surveys reflect those behaviors that the organization values most highly. Care should also be taken to ensure

FIGURE 7–4.   360° feedback customer appraisal form.

MANAGEMENT SERVICES
COMMENT CARD

Name:

This survey asks your opinion about specific aspects of the products and services you received. Your individual responses will remain confidential and will be compiled with those of other customers to improve customer service. Please use the following scale to indicate the extent to which you agree with the statement. Circle one response for each item.

  1 = Strongly Disagree
  2 = Disagree
  3 = Neutral
  4 = Agree
  5 = Strongly Agree
  ? = Unsure

If you feel unable to adequately rate a specific item, please leave it blank.

QUALITY

I had to wait an unreasonable amount of time for my requests to be met . . . . 1 2 3 4 5 ?

The products I have received have met my expectations . . . . . . 1 2 3 4 5 ?

My requests were met on or before the agreed upon deadline . . . . 1 2 3 4 5 ?

The products I have received have generally been error free . 1 2 3 4 5 ?

SERVICE/ATTITUDE

When serving me, this person:

Was helpful . . . . 1 2 3 4 5 ?

Was cooperative in meeting my requests. 1 2 3 4 5 ?

Communicated with me to understand my expectations for products . . . . 1 2 3 4 5 ?

Was uncooperative when I asked for revisions/additional information . . . . 1 2 3 4 5 ?

Told me when my requests would be filled . . . . 1 2 3 4 5 ?

When necessary, sufficiently explained to me why my expectations could not be met . . . . 1 2 3 4 5 ?

Kept me informed about the status of my request . . . . 1 2 3 4 5 ?

CUSTOMER SATISFACTION

How would you rate your overall level of satisfaction with the *service* you have received?

  1 = Very Dissatisfied
  2 = Dissatisfied
  3 = Neutral
  4 = Satisfied
  5 = Very Satisfied

What specifically could be done to make you more satisfied with the *service*?

_____

_____

_____

How would you rate your overall level of satisfaction with the *products* you have received?

  1 = Very Dissatisfied
  2 = Dissatisfied
  3 = Neutral
  4 = Satisfied
  5 = Very Satisfied

What specifically could be done to make you more satisfied with the *products*?

_____

_____

_____

Source: From Performance Appraisal Alternatives Perspectives, 1st edition, by R. L. Cardy and G. Dobbins © 1994. Reprinted with permission of South-Western College Publishing, a division of Thomson Learning. Fax 800-730-2215.

that behaviors measured are closely tied to the accomplishment of the organization's goals."[14]

IMPROVING THE QUALITY OF PERFORMANCE MEASURES

As we mentioned at the beginning of this chapter, performance measurement and management is a complicated endeavor with multiple objectives. There is no such thing as the "ideal" performance management system. The general managers in your firm should be able to make effective choices pertaining to key performance management issues. The choices, of course, may vary considerably across managers of different units within your firm. You should expect the managers who report to you to have made a set of conscious choices in creating the performance management system used with their employees. They should be accountable for explaining how these choices make sense for their particular set of circumstances. Indeed, your performance evaluation of the managers who report to you should be in part based on the effectiveness of the performance management systems they have implemented.

We offer a few general principles for making appraisals as accurate and effective as possible. Of course, a first principle that applies to all HRM activities is that performance appraisal should be congruent with the organization's strategies and circumstances as well as relevant for the work of the particular job classes involved. Beyond this, we make several recommendations.

Results-Oriented versus Process-Oriented Measures

We have argued that both results-oriented and process-oriented measures can be appropriate for a class of jobs. Results-oriented measures, such as objective output measures, are particularly useful for tying rewards to performance in various bonus and incentive plans, as discussed in Chapter 4. Process-oriented—that is, judgmental—measures are useful for merit salary adjustments and for feedback and performance counseling. However, remember that even though a firm may choose to emphasize results-oriented measures, these measures typically do not cover all the important dimensions of an employee's job performance. Therefore, to avoid deficiency in measuring performance, results-oriented measures usually need to be supplemented with some process measures, such as rating scales.

Improving Raters' Appraisal of Employee Performance

As we have noted, the most frequently used measures of performance involve human judgment, most typically in the form of performance rating scales. We offer three strategies for improving the quality of these judgments. These recommendations emphasize *orientation* and *training* of the raters.

Pay Attention to Rating Scale Construction

Performance appraisal experts no longer believe that we will find the perfect rating scale that accurately measures performance and is resistant to all rater errors. But in developing a rating scale be sure that the scale measures the important dimensions of job performance, and that both scale dimensions and scale anchors are thoroughly defined.

Orient and Train Managers in Performance Rating and in the Use of the Firm's Performance Measures

Managers should be informed of the purposes and uses of performance measures in the firm. They should also be aware of various rater errors and biases than can compromise their ratings.

In addition to orienting managers to the rating scale dimensions and anchors, we recommend a technique known as **frame of reference training.**[15] This approach involves bringing together groups of managers who practice using the firm's rating scale, typically by observing videotaped examples or written case materials displaying employee performance. The managers compare their ratings and discuss their *use* of the organization's rating scale, including the meaning of each performance dimension, and how specific employee behaviors should be translated to a number on the scale. As a result of these discussions, the managers develop a common frame of reference, and the consistency of managers' use of the overall appraisal system is enhanced.

Instruct Managers in Keeping Records of Employee Performance

Specific examples of employee behavior are a valuable resource when managers fill out performance rating scales. Thus, managers should regularly record, across the entire performance appraisal period, key examples of both effective and ineffective behavior of their employees. The recorded examples in diaries or logs also provide an excellent framework for conducting performance feedback and counseling sessions.

PERFORMANCE MANAGEMENT AS A SYSTEM: AN OVERVIEW

In this chapter so far we have focused on key issues related to the appraisal of employee performance, the traditional core activity of performance management. But as we mentioned earlier, it is commonly recognized that performance management is more than the appraisal of performance. In the concluding section of the chapter we provide an overview of performance management as a *system*, connected to other parts of the organization.[16]

As a system, performance management includes a number of component parts, including

- Performance planning.
- Ongoing performance communication.
- Data gathering, observation, and documentation.
- Performance appraisal and feedback sessions.
- Performance diagnosis and coaching.

Performance Planning

Performance planning is the starting point for performance management. The manager and the employee work together to identify, at the beginning of the period being planned, the employee's work activities, standards of performance, criteria for measurement, and time frames. This planning might include the setting of concrete, measurable performance objectives, as in the management by objectives approach discussed earlier. The planning process might also include development planning—that is, planning for the employee to acquire new competencies needed to perform the upcoming work activities and goals.

Ongoing Performance Communication

Ongoing performance communication is a two-way process between the manager and the employee, designed to monitor progress, identify performance barriers, and share information. The two parties work together to ensure that job tasks stay on track and that problems are identified and solved before they get out of hand. Much of this ongoing communication will include interactions we could label as "coaching" or "mentoring" the employee.

Data Gathering, Observation, and Documentation

This important step involves the manager's regular collecting of information about the employee's performance, through regular observation and reviewing of the employee's work. Some of this data collection is informal and some is more formalized, such as the keeping of diaries or logs and use of performance rating scales.

Performance Appraisal and Feedback Sessions

We have asserted that in performance management managers and employees need to work together to assess the progress toward agreed-upon goals. They need to regularly communicate to identify and remove barriers to performance. In addition, formalized sessions for communicating performance evaluations, often annually, and providing additional performance feedback/counseling also provide a valuable component of performance management. Table 7–2 lists a recommended series of steps used in training managers for conducting one of these sessions. Embedded in these steps are the notions that (1) considerable *participation* by and input from the employee is important for the employee's perception that the process is fair; and (2) mutual problem solving and the setting of *specific goals* is important for achieving future performance improvement.[17]

1. Prepare thoroughly for the review. Be able to discuss specific incidents of effective and ineffective performance.

2. Schedule the review session at a convenient time and in an appropriate place. Arrange to be free from interruptions.

3. After establishing rapport with the employee, clearly communicate important strengths and weaknesses.

4. Encourage the employee to participate in the discussion and listen attentively to what is said.

5. Use problem-solving methods to improve areas of performance that significantly reduce work effectiveness.

6. Jointly set goals for improvement and communicate your confidence in the employee's ability to improve.

7. Conclude by summarizing your evaluation and the goals set during the session and by scheduling a follow-up meeting.

Source: M. S. Taylor and J. K. Harrison, *Personnel / Human Resources Management Skills Modules* (Cincinnati: South-Western, 1990).

Performance Diagnosis and Coaching

Performance diagnosis and coaching are an important part of a performance management system. These activities illustrate that performance management is not a "linear" process, in that diagnosis and coaching permeate every other part of the performance management system. When it is determined that an employee is falling short, it is important to determine *why* the problem occurred by identifying the underlying causes of performance problems. The manager and the employee can then work together to remove barriers to performance. This kind of coaching and mentoring activity can take place on a regular basis, in addition to being part of annual performance appraisal and feedback sessions. Managers should keep in mind that performance problems can be caused by a variety of factors, such as deficits in employee skills, motivational/reward system problems, and external constraints.

CONCLUSION

In this chapter we have provided an overview of key issues, options, and techniques general managers can choose in creating a performance management system. Performance appraisal and management is a complex and difficult undertaking, often accompanied by frustration and confusion on the part of managers and employees. But effective performance management is also crucial for enhancing organizational effectiveness.

There is no "one best way" to formulate a performance appraisal and performance management system. In constructing a system managers should consider the uses for performance data in their organizations, and identify the unique role and behavioral requirements for the relevant job classes. Managers also need to consider the options for measuring results versus measuring processes (or some combination) for these job classes, and select particular measures (e.g., output measures or particular rating scales) that suit their circumstances. The appropriate scope of performance appraisal should also be determined: Should the firm use a traditional unidirectional-hierarchical approach or adopt more multidirectional approaches such as 360 degree appraisal?

Managers should make every effort to improve the quality of appraisals through attention to choice of measures as well as training raters in observing employee behavior and using the firm's appraisal system. Finally, managers should recognize the importance of viewing performance management as a *system*, comprised of a number of components including communication, feedback, and employee development processes.

CONTINUOUS LEARNING: SOME NEXT STEPS

The performance management process continues to draw attention and generate concern among managers. New information and new services related to performance management are available from many sources. These next steps entail potentially useful activities that can take you further in your understanding of these types of systems.

- There is more to this process than simply assessing employee contribution and performance. Managers must provide feedback and counseling to employees in order to change behavior. Put yourself in the role of a general manager who wants to either develop or purchase a training intervention for first-line supervisors. This training intervention should be about helping supervisors become more skillful in providing performance feedback reviews. Go to the Internet and search for seminars, conferences, and products that focus on the performance appraisal and review process. Two useful places to begin might be the **Training and Development Resource Center** (www.tcm.com/trdev) and the **Training Forum** (www.trainingforum.com). These sites have links to bookshops, conferences and workshops, and CD-ROM training products. See what types of training experiences and products are available in the area of performance management, assessment, and feedback.
- Design a performance appraisal form for a position or targeted job for which you have some firsthand knowledge. First, be clear about the purpose of the assessment process: i.e., Will the assessment be used to allocate merit pay, assess training needs, or make layoff and promotion decisions? Next, specify and describe the key competencies or attributes that will be assessed. Finally, specify the rating format that will be used: Will employees, for example, be compared to some absolute external standard or will they be compared to their peers?

ENDNOTES

161

CHAPTER SEVEN
Performance
Management
Systems

1. T. D. Schellhardt, "Annual Agony: It's Time to Evaluate Your Work, and All Involved Are Groaning," *The Wall Street Journal*, November 19, 1996, pp. A1, A5.

2. C. Hymowitz and M. Murray, "Raises and Praise or Out the Door," *The Wall Street Journal*, June 22, 1999, pp. B1, B4.

3. S. J. Carroll and C. E. Schneier, *Performance Appraisal and Review Systems: The Identification, Measurement, and Development of Performance in Organizations* (Glenview, IL: Scott, Foresman, 1982).

4. H. J. Bernardin and R. W. Beatty, *Performance Appraisal: Assessing Human Behavior at Work* (Boston: Kent Publishing Co., 1984); R. L. Cardy and G. H. Dobbins, *Performance Appraisal: Alternative Perspectives* (Cincinnati: South-Western, 1994); and K. R. Murphy and J. N. Cleveland, *Performance Appraisal: An Organizational Perspective* (Boston: Allyn & Bacon, 1991).

5. A. M. Mohrman and S. A. Mohrman, "Performance Management Is 'Running the Business,'" *Compensation and Benefits Review*, July–August 1995, pp. 69–75.

6. C. O. Longenecker, H. P. Sims, and D. A. Gioia, "Behind the Mask: The Politics of Employee Appraisal," *Academy of Management Executive* 1 (1987), pp. 183–93.

7. J. M. Ivancevich and M. T. Matteson, *Stress and Work* (Glenview, IL: Scott, Foresman, 1980).

8. S. S. Masterson and M. S. Taylor, "Total Quality Management and Performance Appraisal: An Integrative Perspective," *Journal of Quality Management* 1 (1996), pp. 67–89.

9. P. Drucker, *The Practice of Management* (New York: Harper & Row, 1954).

10. G. P. Latham and K. N. Wexley, *Increasing Productivity through Performance Appraisal* (Reading, MA: Addison-Wesley, 1981).

11. L. R. Gomez-Mejia, D. B. Balkin, and R. L. Cardy, *Managing Human Resources,* 2nd ed. (Upper Saddle River, NJ: Prentice Hall, 1998).

12. D. A. Waldman, L. E. Atwater, and D. Antonioni, "Has 360 Degree Feedback Gone Amok?" *Academy of Management Executive* 12 (1998), pp. 86–94.

13. Gomez-Mejia et al., *Managing Human Resources.*

14. Waldman et al., "Has 360 Degree Feedback Gone Amok?" p. 91.

15. Bernardin and Beatty, *Performance Appraisal.*

16. Much of the material in this section is from R. Bacal, *Performance Management* (New York: McGraw-Hill, 1999). See this work for more detail and practical tips.

17. M. S. Taylor and J. K. Harrison, *Personnel/Human Resources Management Skills Modules* (Cincinnati: South-Western, 1990).

Aligning Human Resource Systems with Business Strategy

8

Human Resource Systems

THE LINK TO BUSINESS STRATEGY AND FIRM PERFORMANCE

Organizations pursue unique business strategies, which call for the use of unique HR systems. In this chapter you will see why this is important and you will

- Learn why designing the appropriate HR system for your firm can result in sustained competitive advantage.
- See how effective HR systems translate into organizational outcomes such as reduced costs and financial returns.
- Understand how to use a "marginal utility analysis" approach to determine if an investment in an HRM practice adds value to your firm.
- Become acquainted with the human resource management audit as a way to evaluate your firm's HR function.
- See why looking for a direct overall congruence between a firm's business strategy and "HRM strategy" makes *no* sense.

Consumers in the United States are likely to have a vastly different experience when shopping at a Target store than when shopping at Bloomingdale's. In turn, shopping at Bloomingdale's is likely to differ from shopping at a Nordstrom store. The experience differs because these three retailers pursue different business strategies. Each organization has its own strategic style—and each style requires a unique system for managing people.[1]

Edward Gubman convincingly argues that Target Stores is an **operations** company. Its core capability is the consistent application of procedures—that is, its focus is on efficiency and cost containment. The strategic style of Nordstrom, according to Gubman, is that of a **customer-oriented** organization. Its core competency is in-depth relationship building. Nordstrom's salespeople get to know the personal preferences of customers and go the extra distance to meet special customer needs. Finally, Bloomingdale's is categorized as a **products** company. Its core capability is constant innovation. Going to Bloomingdale's is about examining and experiencing innovative products and designer clothing.

166

*PART THREE
Aligning Human
Resource Systems
with Business
Strategy*

Each style, according to Gubman, requires unique employee types and employee behaviors. Salespeople at Bloomingdale's would be expected to be very knowledgeable about product features and design but not as knowledgeable about individual customers as salespeople at Nordstrom. Likewise, the salespeople at Target should behave differently from the salespeople at Bloomingdale's. At Target, customers need assistance in finding value-priced items on conveniently located and well-stocked shelves. Thus, HR systems need to differ across these strategic styles. With these, and other examples from a variety of industrial sectors, Gubman provides rich illustrations of the links between business strategy and the preferred characteristics of HR systems.

In this chapter we will build on Gubman's observations and introduce you to the area called *strategic human resource management* (SHRM). We want to emphasize, however, that this entire book is about *strategic* HRM, in the sense that different business strategies emphasize different role requirements and employee behaviors. But while a firm's business strategy sets the stage for selecting, designing, and implementing people-management systems, other contextual factors also are at work. This book is about selecting, designing, and implementing HR systems that fit the circumstances surrounding key job classifications within the firm. Business strategy, technology, attributes of labor markets, and the regulatory environment are all considered to be important contextual factors.

In Chapter 1 you were introduced to the decision-making process that we see as a useful tool when evaluating the quality of HRM practices and services. This framework is reproduced here to remind you of its component parts and to set the stage for a more detailed discussion of how HR systems relate to business strategy and ultimately to the performance of the firm.

Recall from Chapter 1 that sound HR system design must take into account the context surrounding any operating business. This context includes a concern for (1) how business strategy and technology influence the way work processes are designed and how these design issues specify the role/behavioral requirements for key classes of employees, and (2) designing HR systems that are appropriate given the realities of labor market and labor relations conditions. The goal of this chapter is to develop further ideas about how sound HRM practice can add value to the firm and serve as a source of sustained competitive advantage. The aim is to make you a better consumer of the services provided by in-house HR professionals and the growing number of HR-oriented consultants by providing you with more grounding in what you should demand from them.

Emerging academic research suggests that HRM practices are influenced by the contextual factors seen in Figure 1–1.[2] For example, based on data from 267 organizations, Jackson, Schuler, and Rivero provided evidence that HRM practices vary as a function of organizational characteristics.[3] Such factors as a focus on product innovation and the use of flexible manufacturing technologies were related to compensation and performance management practices. We emphasize, however, that the connection between strategic/technological context and HRM is a connection that passes through the behavioral/role requirements of targeted job classes. Work

FIGURE 1–1

167

CHAPTER EIGHT
Human
Resource
Systems

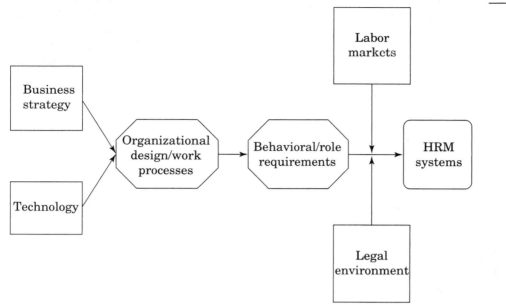

processes and their associated role requirements are directly influenced by strategy, technology, and other factors embedded in the business environment. Human resource systems can be designed (taking into account an extensive behavioral science literature) to maximize the likelihood that the right people accept job offers and that these employees contribute to meeting business objectives.

But the question of greatest importance to general managers is whether investing in HR system refinement—by creating integrated practices that are supported by available research evidence—will lead to improved organizational outcomes. To find the answer, one of the best starting points is the writing of Wright, McMahan, and McWilliams.[4] Using what is called a "resource-based" view of the firm,[5] these authors discuss how highly integrated HRM practices can help a firm achieve a "sustained competitive advantage" (SCA) in the marketplace. Human resource management practices influence the firm's "human capital" and the job-related behaviors of the firm's talent pool. According to the resource-based view of the firm, for something to lead to an SCA, certain conditions must hold. Wright and colleagues present the case that a firm's human resources, when properly managed and developed, meet the criteria for determining what can and cannot serve in this capacity. According to these authors the firm's talent pool and associated HRM practices are **valuable, rare, inimitable,** and **nonsubstitutable.** For HRM practices to make a sustained competitive difference they must, as a necessary first condition, be viewed as reaching SCA status.

In this chapter we review the criteria for SCA status and then move on to discuss how managers and researchers have assessed the value of HRM practices by considering the costs, behavioral impact, and marginal return associated with specific activities. Figure 8–1 presents the traditional way of

168

PART THREE
Aligning Human
Resource Systems
with Business
Strategy

FIGURE 8–1. HRM-business outcome linkages (the traditional view)

depicting strategy–HRM–outcome linkages. We see in the figure that HR systems that appropriately take into account business strategy and other contextual factors should affect firm performance by changing the composition of the firm's internal labor market and by influencing the behaviors of individuals making up this internal talent pool. However, we believe this traditional framework is overly simplistic because it moves directly from a typology of firm type to prescriptions about HRM strategy. The underlying theme of this book is that HRM practices must be specific to job class, because role requirements within a single company can vary across organizational levels and occupational specialties.

Figure 8–1 does not show that HR systems need to reflect the job-specific role requirements called for by a company's strategic and business context. Figure 8–2 presents a fuller picture of the relationships between business strategy, HRM systems, and business outcomes. Remember, however, that this way of representing HRM practices must be replicated across the different job types and levels that exist in a given firm. That is, the role/behavioral requirements shown in the figure are not at the organizationwide level; they are at the level of the job class (a level that typically is specific to organizational level and occupational specialty).

SUSTAINED COMPETITIVE ADVANTAGE

As noted previously, four conditions are required for a resource to qualify as a source of sustained competitive advantage.[6] We next discuss the four criteria that can qualify human resource management for SCA status.[7]

HRM Adds Value to the Firm

The knowledge and skills required to perform jobs at a high level of proficiency vary greatly within and across companies. Also, employees are not perfectly substitutable: Within any given labor market, individuals are likely to differ with respect to the possession of knowledge, skills, and other important job-related attributes.[8] Therefore, firms that are better than their competitors at selecting, developing, and motivating employees should have an advantage over their counterparts.

The research literature on what is termed *marginal utility analysis* has convincingly made the case that properly managed human resource systems

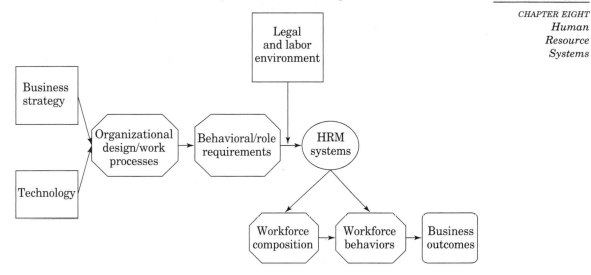

add value to the firm.[9] This work provides a methodology for estimating the financial value properly managed HR systems can contribute to the firm and uses this methodology to show that investing in HR systems often results in very high rates of return. In a subsequent section of this chapter we highlight the use of these techniques.

Human Resources as Rare Resources

For a resource to be a source of SCA it must be rare. Advancing technology is eliminating jobs at the bottom of the knowledge, skill, and ability hierarchy—jobs that sometime define human resources as a commodity[10]—while the remaining jobs are becoming increasingly complex and now require knowledge and skills often in short supply.

The notion of skills being in "short supply" (or rare) is supported by the evidence showing the growing wage inequality between high- and low-skill workers around the world in the last quarter of the twentieth century.[11] High-skill, high-wage jobs require knowledge and skills that are distributed normally throughout populations of workers. Workers at the upper end of these knowledge–skill distributions are rare, as indicated by escalating wages and salaries.

Human Resource Systems as Inimitable

If the advantages gained from using high-quality HR systems are easily imitated, then these practices cannot be a source of SCA. In Chapter 9 we argue in more depth that high-quality HRM practices should fit an organization's business goals and environmental circumstances and be

170

PART THREE
Aligning Human
Resource Systems
with Business
Strategy

interrelated and **internally consistent**. If HR systems are considered to be isolated practices, each separate piece could be copied by a competitor. Or a compensation system, benefit system, or management succession system "sold" by a consulting firm could be purchased and simply "installed." But it is the requirement that these systems work as an integrated unit that makes them difficult to copy. They arise as a function of a company's culture and traditions. They are simply too complex to be "dissected" and copied piece-by-piece.

When discussing this issue, Wright et al. correctly make a distinction between HRM practices and human resources.[12] If employees are highly mobile, companies could attempt to lure away top talent from competitors and take advantage of the HR systems developed by these other companies. But employees are not perfectly mobile; by moving from one employer to another they incur "transaction costs."[13] In addition, top talent from one employer may not thrive with a new employer because the reward system, culture, and other aspects of HR systems may not be compatible with the needs, interests, and skills of the mobile individual. Thus, even though some employees can be induced to move, the full package of the existing talent pool and the support systems that sustain its performance is not easily imitated.

Human Resources as Nonsubstitutable

If other firm resources have the potential to substitute for competent human resources, then the competitive advantage associated with HR will be minimized. It is certainly the case that machines are replacing human labor at an accelerating rate. In a rather chilling account of the future, Rifkin states that after "years of wishful forecasts and false starts, the new computer and communications technologies are finally making their long-anticipated impact on the workplace and the economy, throwing the world community into the grip of a third great industrial revolution."[14] While it is the case that the replacement of human labor with machine labor will diminish the productive value of many low-skill employees and the management systems used to hire, train, and motivate them, Rifkin is clear in stating that entrepreneurial, managerial, professional, and technical elites will be at the center of the formal economy of the future. Thus, these elites, and the systems required to support and sustain them, are simply not substitutable.

We conclude that a firm's talent pool, and the systems used to develop and motivate this resource, can serve as a source of sustained competitive advantage. This is because the individuals making up this talent pool and the associated HRM practices can be regarded as **valuable**, **rare**, **inimitable**, and **nonsubstitutable**. It then follows that cost-effective HRM practices have the potential to contribute to firm performance when they

1. Work to encourage people who possess the skill profiles needed to implement a firm's business strategy to join and stay with the firm.
2. Call out and reinforce needed role behaviors.

We next review the ways managers and researchers have attempted to show that improvements in HRM practices relate to firm performance.

LINKING HRM PRACTICES TO ORGANIZATIONAL OUTCOMES

171

CHAPTER EIGHT
Human
Resource
Systems

In reviewing how HRM practices translate into organizational outcomes, Napier classified what we know into three general categories:

1. Knowledge about reducing the costs of specific HRM activities.
2. Methods used to evaluate the behavioral impact associated with modifying HRM practices.
3. The literature devoted to "auditing" the strengths and weaknesses of HRM practices and departments.[15]

We now briefly comment on each, while developing in more detail another category—an integrative way of assessing value, the so-called "marginal utility" approach.

Assessing and Reducing Costs

Historically, many have viewed the HR function as a cost, paying little attention to the "return" side of the cost–benefit equation. Therefore, it is not surprising that one approach to managing HRM practices has been to focus on reducing costs and implementing HR systems in the most efficient manner possible. The automation of administrative transactions and the general "outsourcing" of many HR services have been at the forefront of this movement. The automation/computerization of basic administrative transactions is, of course, occurring across all business functions, as is the outsourcing phenomenon. The use of external vendors and consultants is based on the idea that a company should focus its energies on its "core" competencies. Specialized firms can then provide needed services using state-of-the-art practices and procedures.

One way that companies might attempt to control costs and provide their employees with exemplary service is through the use of a consulting firm. Hewitt Associates, for example, is a consulting firm well known for providing services to corporate clients in the area of benefits administration. Companies also can control fixed costs by outsourcing this administrative function. Hewitt currently operates a fully integrated **Total Benefit Administration System.**[16] Employees of corporate clients can call the Hewitt service center and discuss any aspect of their benefits package with Hewitt customer service representatives. The large facility and equipment costs associated with creating a computerized center of this type can be shared among the various corporate clients. A company like Hewitt also can devote its resources to its core competencies—the design of HR-oriented customer service centers and other compensation-oriented services.

Another developing method of cost control relates to procedures that are used to estimate the financial costs associated with employee behaviors that employers want to reduce in frequency. Cascio has provided detailed worksheets that are used to estimate the costs to the firm of such things as excessive employee absenteeism, smoking, and employee turnover.[17] (Turnover rates must be treated carefully, however, because some turnover is usually

172

PART THREE
Aligning Human
Resource Systems
with Business
Strategy

desirable.) Using this costing approach, HR practices can be judged in terms of their cost-saving consequences.

Behavioral Impact of HRM Practices

As noted in Chapter 1, much of what is currently known about sound HRM practice is based on behavioral science research—research designed to evaluate the effectiveness of specific practices through the analysis of "pre/post" and correlational data. For example, the training literature includes pre- and posttraining intervention studies.[18] Measures of job performance (or some other reasonable dependent variable, say, the amount of knowledge possessed about a particular topic) are collected among a target group of employees before the group is exposed to a training program. Then, posttraining performance data are gathered and compared to the pretraining measures.

When these studies are designed to control for competing reasons for a pre/post increase in performance, it is possible to estimate the degree to which the training program accounts for the change in performance. Often, this *effect size* is represented by a statistical index called a *z* score. In the training example just cited, a *z* score is merely the average posttraining performance score minus the average pretraining performance score divided by the standard deviation of performance observed among pretrained employees.

Another way to represent an effect size is to use another statistical index, the *correlation coefficient*. This index has traditionally been used in the literature devoted to selection and staffing systems.[19] Here, researchers gather preemployment information (e.g., cognitive ability test scores, work sample test scores, or interview ratings) about job candidates. These data are called predictor scores. Then, after an appropriate time interval, job-performance data are collected for the group of hired candidates. These data are called criterion scores. The correlation between predictor and criterion data then serves as an effect size indicator.

Marginal Utility Models

Each of the previously described approaches provides useful information, but taken alone each is incomplete. What is required is a way to simultaneously consider *both* the costs and the financial return associated with changes in HRM practices. The needed approach must take into account present and future HRM practice costs and future streams of revenue associated with improved levels of employee behavior that can be attributed to the change in HRM practice. For an investment in an HR system to add value to the firm it must generate a reasonable rate of return—that is, a rate of return that, at a minimum, exceeds the cost of capital. We will now illustrate how such an approach can be used in practice, drawing on the well-developed literature devoted to marginal utility analysis.[20]

For our discussion of this technique we use an example from the area of employee selection. Note that these same general concepts could be used to conduct a marginal utility study related to any HR system investment. This approach is very basic. It takes into account the money invested in system improvements, the relative level of improvement, the positive return (in dollars) associated with the hiring and retention of more productive employees, and the hiring context (the labor market associated with the targeted job class). The cost and revenue streams are then adjusted to take into account the time value of money and the cost of capital (costs and returns are put in present-value terms), variable costs associated with the improvements brought about by making better hiring decisions, and marginal taxes.

To illustrate how this approach works, let's assume that a clothing retailer will be hiring approximately 250 new sales personnel during the year. This is a company with 65 stores nationwide. The company sells mid- to upper-midrange men's and women's clothing and has built a reputation on high-quality customer service. In fact, this retailer was one of the first to put sales personnel on commissions, paying 10 percent of retail sales value to the salesperson. High-performing salespersons can make well above the industry pay average. High-performing sales associates (85th percentile national performers) average $41,000 per year in base pay and commissions. The average sales associate (the 50th percentile performer) earns $33,000 in base plus commission, and the average yearly pay level for a below-standard performer (the person performing at the 15th percentile) is $25,000. After taking into account that all sales personnel are paid a base rate of $7.50 per hour, this means that top performers are selling approximately $259,200 of merchandise per year, average performers are selling approximately $179,200 of merchandise, and below-standard performers only $99,200 per year.

The company currently uses a résumé review, a paper-and-pencil personality test, and an informal selection interview when hiring new salespersons. This current selection system costs the company approximately $100 per applicant in processing fees. A consulting firm wants to sell the company a much more costly selection system that it claims is more "valid" than the existing system. Statistical validity refers to the degree to which scores on a weighted average of predictor scores correlate with a measure of job performance. The consulting firm has provided evidence showing that in previous studies the correlation between applicant ratings (made with the use of their system) and job performance was typically in the 0.45 range. Past studies of the company's current system have shown that when résumé ratings, personality test scores, and interview ratings were used to predict job performance, the resulting multiple correlation was approximately 0.30. While the new selection system will more accurately predict the likely sales performance of job candidates (0.45 versus 0.30), before the company decides to purchase the consulting firm's product and related services, it must determine if the higher degree of selection system accuracy is worth the additional price. To answer this key question, the company must collect and/or estimate some additional information to be used in conjunction with the marginal utility model (discussed in a following section of this chapter). The new selection system will cost the company nearly $400 per applicant.

The return associated with improving a selection system depends on the degree of improved accuracy but also depends on a variety of other factors. For instance, it does not make much sense to invest in selection system

174

*PART THREE
Aligning Human
Resource Systems
with Business
Strategy*

improvements if the labor market is so tight that the company will have to hire virtually all applicants meeting just minimal hiring standards. The positive payoff comes from being better able to identify the best applicants and then selecting only the best of the best. Therefore, how selective the company can be and the overall "quality" of the labor market will affect this type of investment decision.

The decision-making model also must take into account the time value of money. Costs incurred to hire new applicants are spent in the present but the returns associated with having better employees will not be realized until some point in the future. To appropriately compare current expenditures with future revenues, all monetary values must be put in present-value terms.

Finally, gains associated with an improved selection system will not necessarily be realized; some of the enhanced revenue will be lost in the form of marginal taxes and increased variable costs brought about by the increased sales from the new, improved, group of employees. Assume that for this company, additional revenue will be taxed at a 30 percent rate and that approximately 65 percent of the additional revenue must be returned in the form of increased variable costs (these are costs that increase as a result of additional sales; e.g., larger commissions paid to this group of employees, the increased wholesale purchase price of additional garments sold, and other administrative costs associated with the higher performing sales group).

Should the company purchase the new selection system from the consulting firm if it plans to hire 250 new sales associates this year (assuming that the labor market will produce about five applicants for each position)? One basic framework for addressing this question is shown in Table 8–1, a utility model based on the adjustments to previous models made by Boudreau.[21]

The model can now be applied to the clothing retailer example. In light of the parameters considered previously, the values needed to operationalize the utility model are

$$N = 250$$

$$t = \text{the time period in which the benefit occurs}$$

$$i = \text{assume a current discount rate } 6\%$$

$$r_1 = 0.45$$

$$r_2 = 0.30$$

$$SD_y = \$80,000$$

$$\frac{\lambda}{p} = 1.40$$

$$T = \text{assume average tenure for this job class to be three years}$$

$$C_1, C_2 = \$400, \$100$$

$$V = -0.65$$

$$\text{TAX} = 0.30$$

$$P = 0.20$$

Staffing illustration

$$\Delta U = (N) \times \left\{ \sum_{t=1}^{T} \left[\frac{1}{(1 + i)^t} \right] (r_1 - r_2)(SD_y)\left(\frac{\lambda}{p}\right)(1 + V)(1 - \text{TAX}) \right\}$$

$$- \left[(N) \frac{(C_1 - C_2)}{p} \right] [1 - \text{TAX}]$$

where

ΔU = the increase in dollar payoff (realized over the tenure of the new employees) that results from selecting N employees using a new selection procedure instead of the existing procedure

N = the number of employees selected

t = the time period in which the benefit occurs

i = the current discount rate

r_1 = the validity of the new selection procedure

r_2 = the validity of the existing selection procedure

SD_y = the standard deviation of dollar-value payoff, what a one standard deviation difference in job performance is worth in annual revenue to the firm

$\dfrac{\lambda}{p}$ = the estimated average score on the predictor among the group hired (in standard score form)*

T = average tenure of new employees

C_1, C_2 = the cost per applicant of using the new (C_1) and old (C_2) procedure

V = the proportion of service value (attributable to improved selection) represented by variable costs (will take on a negative value when costs increase with increased revenue and a positive value when costs decrease with increased revenue)

TAX = the marginal tax rate

P = the selection ratio

*A table for estimating this value is shown as:

p (selection ratio)	λ/p (estimated mean z score)
0.05	2.05
0.10	1.75
0.20	1.40
0.30	1.16
0.40	0.96
0.50	0.80
0.60	0.65
0.70	0.50

Substituting these values in the marginal utility model leads to the following estimate of ΔU:

176

PART THREE
Aligning Human
Resource Systems
with Business
Strategy

$$\Delta U = (250) \times [(2.67)(0.15)(80,000)(1.40)(0.35)(0.70)] - \frac{[(250)(1,500)(0.70)]}{0.20}$$

$$= \$2,484,930$$

This positive return is realized over the full three years the 250 newly selected salespersons will work in this job class—a very good investment indeed!

Auditing HRM Practices and Departments

Finally, we bring to your attention a concept refined in the writing of Devanna, Fombrun, and Tichy: the evaluation of the HR function by way of the human resources management audit (HRMA).[22] Any "audit" is typically considered to be a first step in an improvement or change effort. To improve the overall effectiveness of the HR function, a diagnosis of the present state must be conducted. The audit represents the systematic collection and analysis of data that will lead to suggestions about areas needing improvement.

Devanna, Fombrun, and Tichy suggest that data be collected from multiple sources using available documents, interviews, observation, and questionnaires/surveys. Their approach is to structure the data collection and analysis around a set of basic issues or questions. For example, data need to be collected that address the following issues:

1. How well do the HR organization's mission and strategy match its environment, markets, and regulatory constraints?
2. How well do the structures of the HR organization fit its strategy?
3. How well do the characteristics of the people who conduct the human resources function match the way HR is organized and the task demands placed on them in such an environment?[23]

In many ways the HRMA is about determining if the HR function is properly designed (with properly thought-out work processes and reward systems) and staffed with individuals possessing needed skills and abilities.

As we discuss in a subsequent section of this chapter, we think it is difficult to directly address and answer questions of the "How well do the human resources organization's mission and strategy match its environment?" variety. Although the concept of the HRMA is appealing for a variety of reasons, we suggest that the audit be based on the framework established in Figure 8–2. Some issues to address include the following:

1. To what degree does the HR function contribute to designing work processes of the future (i.e., do HR processes exist and do HR professionals possess the skills needed to consider how business strategy and emerging technology will influence the future design of work)?
2. Do HR professionals possess information (e.g., about internal and external labor markets and organizational capability) that has the potential to inform decision makers who are formulating business strategy?
3. Are there mechanisms or structures in place that help ensure that HRM practices are internally congruent and focused on critical work roles?

4. Do HR systems reflect the unique role requirements associated with different business areas or are similar HRM solutions imposed on all business functions?
5. Is there evidence that cost-effective investments are being made to improve HR systems and practices (i.e., are HR professionals capable of estimating whether the returns on investments to improve HR systems are comparable to the rates of return associated with improving other aspects of the business)?

These are just illustrative questions, but they represent the issues informed consumers of internal HR services or external consulting services need to be asking.

LINKING STRATEGY TO HRM PRACTICES

We now have come full circle. Well-designed HR **systems** can influence business results because

1. The return on investing in the subsystems (staffing, training, etc.) can often exceed the return associated with investing in other areas of the business.
2. Highly motivated workers at the upper ends of certain knowledge–skill distributions are rare.
3. The **overall** HR system is very difficult to replicate in another company.
4. High-level managerial, entrepreneurial, professional, and technical employees are not easily replaced with machines and emerging information technology.

We see the need for congruence between a firm's behavioral/role requirements and HRM practices as self-evident. But the call for congruence between strategy and HRM should be viewed with caution and a demand for explanation. Be critical of the consultant or HR executive who continually talks about linking business strategy and **HRM strategy.** Is there such a thing as corporatewide HRM strategy? We think not, and we conclude this chapter with some reflections on why we hold this view.

Corporate HR Philosophy or Companywide HR Standards

It has become commonplace for a company's core values, or HR philosophy, to be presented in a written list of HR standards. Some may go so far as to label such a list as a statement of a firm's HRM strategy. A few elements from a well-known accounting firm's 10-item list of HR standards are used here to illustrate and critique the notion that lists of this type in some way provide strategic direction to a firm's HR practices.

The first element reads something like this:

Recruit people with superior character, talent, and the capacity for significant growth.

178

*PART THREE
Aligning Human
Resource Systems
with Business
Strategy*

This statement does provide some minimal direction for HR policy, but its generality reduces its usefulness. Few companies would base policy on a commitment to seek inferior employees not possessing the potential to learn and grow. This statement sounds good, but we don't think it is a very interesting or useful guideline.

Another example of a "standard" that does not offer much guidance reads as follows:

> Provide appropriate development opportunities that allow all employees to fully utilize their capacity for growth.

Once again, few companies would advocate the use of inappropriate assignments and developmental opportunities. While other elements in this company's list—such as sharing information and respecting the multiple commitments and interests of employees—do shape HR policy, this and other "statements of corporate HR philosophy" often fail to provide much guidance because many of the same elements repeatedly appear across firms and there are no meaningful alternatives to the elements as stated.

"Strategy," at least at the tactical level, can and should vary across organizational levels and occupational types within a particular firm. Yet, the notion of a corporate HRM strategy seems to fail to take this possibility into account. We agree with Napier, who repeatedly points out that the approach to selection or pay for many firms will vary as a function of whether the worker is a line worker, middle manager, or so on.[24] If it is appropriate to call this "role-contingent HRM" a type of corporate HRM strategy, we would advocate it over the practice of corporate HRM strategy that makes no or few allowances for intraorganizational work role differences.

Beware of the Direct Business Strategy–HRM Connection

Many strategy classification schemes have been described as starting points for the formulation of HRM strategy (Napier, 1996). Some of the more popular include:

Miles and Snow (1978)   defenders, prospectors, and analyzers

Rumelt (1974)   a product-diversity based scheme

Porter (1981)   cost leaders, focus firms, and differentiators

These typologies can serve many useful purposes—but we do not think it is useful or appropriate to move directly from a statement of firm type to a formulation of HR policy. Whereas general classification schemes may provide limited guidance when a general HRM orientation is planned, the notion of a direct link masks a complex reality: Role requirements vary across organizational levels and occupational types, even within the same organization. There simply is no substitute for the careful consideration of multiple role requirements when addressing issues related to HR practice and policy.

Perhaps a more useful approach to strategy formulation can be found at the level of business unit or tactical strategy. Although not all companies are attempting to grow (in declining or mature markets, for example, a divestment or liquidation strategy may be most appropriate), growth strategies are very commonplace. But companies attempt to grow market share in different ways. For example, Aaker distinguishes between firms that grow by (1) developing products for existing markets, (2) expanding markets for existing products, and (3) following vertical integration strategies.[25] These are all "growth" strategies, but they are likely to have different implications for the design and delivery of HR systems. If we use this framework and review the Compaq Computer discussion of Chapter 1, we might decide that Compaq, in the mid-1990s, was following a "product development for the existing market" tactical strategy.[26] This was accomplished through the use of product-feature or product-line expansion. Recall that in July 1996, the computer maker announced that it would target home computer users in all market segments, introducing five new computer lines, ranging from scaled-down models to full-option laptops and multimedia machines.

However, even when we are able to be reasonably specific about a company's specific or tactical strategy, we do not have enough information to move to very useful prescriptions about HR system design and delivery. The critical step required to link business strategy with HR system design is the careful review of role requirements. Human resource management practices that encourage team member cooperation, flexibility, and the continuous improvement of manufacturing processes (work roles required by Compaq's assembly cells) may not be called for in all areas of the business. Customer service employees, advertising and marketing specialists, and research scientists and engineers play unique roles that may call for unique HRM solutions.

HRM Leading Strategy Formulation

Finally, HRM can play a role in strategy formulation. But it is not so much that HR system characteristics inform the strategy formulation process as it is that knowledge about internal and external labor-market conditions informs this process. German auto manufacturers built assembly plants in the United States partly to have access to low-cost labor (relative to labor costs in Germany).

When Compaq aggressively followed its product-line expansion strategy, its earlier experiences and successes with flexible assembly-cell manufacturing techniques in all likelihood contributed to the decision to pursue such a strategic policy. By providing information about contextual factors (e.g., the costs and quality associated with local labor markets) and about the organizational capability to implement a strategic plan, HRM informs the strategy formulation process.

CONCLUSION

In this chapter we have developed further ideas about how sound HRM practice can add value to the firm and serve as a source of sustained

180

*PART THREE
Aligning Human
Resource Systems
with Business
Strategy*

competitive advantage. We frequently hear from HR executives and consultants that the HR function needs to be aligned with business strategy and that HR professionals need to become business partners at the strategic level. One important role for the general manager is that of informed consumer of HR-oriented practices and policies. The general manager as an informed consumer should demand a logical and systematic approach from those providing HR services. Competent HR professionals should be able to show that their prescribed investments in human capital will generate a reasonable rate of return, and that their prescribed changes will be compatible with other HR practices and with the technological and strategic changes taking place within and outside the firm.

We have attempted to provide a rationale for how business strategy and technology influence the design of HR systems and how HR professionals can contribute to and inform the process of strategic decision making. We see no simple rules or templates that can be used to formulate HR systems by considering a firm's strategic direction and core values. The connection comes by way of the behavioral/role requirements associated with job and occupational clusters.

CONTINUOUS LEARNING: SOME NEXT STEPS

The following two steps are designed to (1) give you some practice at defining and describing an organization's business strategy and organizational culture, and (2) provide some evidence that firms, even within a common industry, manage human talent in different ways.

- Select two industries that interest you and then select two companies within each industry. For example, consider Ford Motor Company (www.ford.com) and Toyota (www.toyota.com), or consider Eli Lilly (www.lilly.com) and Mylan Laboratories (www.mylan.com). Spend time reviewing the websites for these companies, looking particularly at their annual reports. What can you infer about each company's business strategy and organizational culture? How would you classify the dominant business strategy for Mylan Labs and how does it differ from the dominant business strategy for Eli Lilly? How are these differences in strategic type likely played out in how each company manages human resources? How might a company like Ford address the strategic differences that exist internally (i.e., consider the likely strategic differences between Ford and Jaguar)?
- Now go to the financial statements presented in the annual reports for each of your selected companies. Calculate some ratios that provide information about the value of people for each company. For example, divide the total number of employees by the total assets displayed for each company. How do these ratios compare and what meaning can you attach to any noted differences? What other meaningful ratios can be calculated from financial statements that provide information about how human resources are managed? What else can be learned about HRM by reviewing a company's annual report?

ENDNOTES

181

CHAPTER EIGHT
Human
Resource
Systems

1. This discussion is based on E. L. Gubman, *The Talent Solution: Aligning Strategy and People to Achieve Extraordinary Results* (New York: McGraw-Hill, 1998).

2. S. E. Jackson and R. S. Schuler, "Understanding Human Resource Management in the Context of Organizations and Their Environments," *Annual Review of Psychology* 46 (1995), pp. 237–64; and N. K. Napier, "Strategy, Human Resources Management, and Organizational Outcomes: Coming Out from Between the Cracks." In G. R. Ferris and M. R. Buckley (eds.), *Human Resources Management* (Englewood Cliffs, NJ: Prentice Hall, 1996).

3. S. E. Jackson, R. S. Schuler, and J. C. Rivero, "Organizational Characteristics as Predictors of Personnel Practices," *Personnel Psychology* 42 (1989), pp. 727–86.

4. P. M. Wright, G. C. McMahan, and A. McWilliams, "Human Resources and Sustained Competitive Advantage: A Resource-Based Perspective," *International Journal of Human Resource Management* 5 (1994), pp. 301–26.

5. J. Barney, "Firm Resources and Sustained Competitive Advantage," *Journal of Management* 17 (1991), pp. 99–120.

6. Ibid.

7. Wright et al., "Human Resources and Sustained Competitive Advantage."

8. B. D. Steffy and S. D. Maurer, "Conceptualizing and Measuring the Economic Effectiveness of Human Resource Activities," *Academy of Management Review* 13 (1988), pp. 271–86.

9. J. W. Boudreau, "Economic Considerations in Estimating the Utility of Human Resource Productivity Improvement Programs," *Personnel Psychology* 36 (1983), pp. 551–76; J. W. Boudreau and C. J. Berger, "Decision-Theoretic Utility Analysis Applied to Employee Separations and Acquisitions," *Journal of Applied Psychology* 70 (1985), pp. 581–612; and F. L. Schmidt, J. E. Hunter, R. C. McKenzie, and T. W. Muldrow, "Impact of Valid Selection Procedures on Workforce Productivity," *Journal of Applied Psychology* 64 (1979), pp. 609–26; and Steffy and Maurer, "Conceptualizing and Measuring."

10. J. Rifkin, *The End of Work: The Decline of the Global Labor Force and the Dawn of the Post-market Economy* (New York: Tarcher/Putnam, 1995).

11. "Work on the Workforce," *University of Chicago Magazine,* June 1997, pp. 8–9.

12. Wright et al., "Human Resources and Sustained Competitive Advantage."

13. M. Abelson and B. Baysinger, "Optimal and Dysfunctional Turnover: Toward an Organizational Level Model," *Academy of Management Review* 9 (1984), pp. 331–41.

14. Rifkin, *The End of Work,* p. xv.

15. Napier, "Strategy, Human Resources Management, and Organizational Outcomes."

16. Hewitt Associates, *Innovation: Our Story* (Lincolnshire, IL: Hewitt Associates LLC, 1996).

17. W. F. Cascio, *Costing Human Resources: The Financial Impact of Behavior in Organizations* (Boston: PWS-Kent Publishing Company, 1991).

18. I. L. Goldstein, *Training in Organizations* (Pacific Grove, CA: Brooks/Cole, 1993); and K. N. Wexley and G. P. Latham, *Developing and Training Human Resources in Organizations* (New York: HarperCollins Publishers, 1991).

182

PART THREE
Aligning Human
Resource Systems
with Business
Strategy

19. E. E. Ghiselli, "The Validity of Aptitude Tests in Personnel Selection," *Personnel Psychology* 26 (1973), pp. 461–77; and N. Schmitt and W. C. Borman, *Personnel Selection in Organizations* (San Francisco: Jossey-Bass, 1993).

20. Boudreau, "Economic Considerations"; H. E. Brogden, "When Testing Pays Off," *Personnel Psychology* 2 (1949), pp. 171–85; and Schmidt et al., "Impact of Valid Selection Procedures."

21. Boudreau, "Economic Considerations."

22. M. A. Devanna, C. J. Fombrun, and N. M. Tichy, "Human Resource Management: A Strategic Perspective," *Organizational Dynamics* 9 (1981), pp. 51–67.

23. Ibid.

24. Napier, "Strategy, Human Resources Management, and Organizational Outcomes."

25. D. A. Aaker, *Developing Business Strategies* (New York: John Wiley & Sons, 1995).

26. K. Blumenthal, "Compaq Is Segmenting the Home-Computer Market," *The Wall Street Journal*, July 16, 1996, p. A3.

9

Sustained Competitive Advantage through Inimitable Human Resource Practices

To promote critical role and behavioral requirements for a class of jobs, it is important to implement congruent HR systems. This key theme is developed in this chapter as you

- Learn how conflicting HR systems can sometimes have a negative effect on your firm.
- See that HRM practices must be targeted at "sticky" employee behaviors.
- Understand the role of individually oriented, group-oriented, and organizationally oriented "syndromes of action" for changing employee behavior.
- See how three key *principles of congruence* provide your organization with a distinct competitive advantage.
- Become acquainted with some examples of congruent HR systems in the literature of human resource management.

Suppose that as a forward-thinking manager you wish to put in place the most effective, cutting-edge HR practices for the shop floor employees in your division. Over a period of a few years you (1) implement detailed performance measurement and counseling for each employee, (2) offer financial bonuses to employees who reach their performance goals, (3) install a team system with training of employees in group interaction skills, and (4) empower teams to make key decisions affecting their work, including the hiring of new team members.

This set of state-of-the-art practices would be expected to add significant value for your firm, right? Maybe not. In this chapter we focus on the idea of enhancing *congruence*—the internal consistency and synergy among HR practices for promoting key employee behaviors—in HR systems. The shop floor example does reflect some progressive HR practices, but it also presents some potentially significant congruence problems related to "conflicting" HR practices, as you will see in this chapter.

In Chapter 1 we introduced the key themes of this book. These themes include the notion that HRM practices should fit an organization's business goals, culture, and environmental circumstances, and that HRM practices should be interrelated and internally consistent to affect key classes of employee behaviors. If HR systems are considered as separate, isolated practices, each separate piece could be copied by a competitor or "sold and installed" by a consulting firm. But the requirement that these systems work as an integrated unit makes HR systems very difficult to copy, and thus a source of sustained competitive advantage.

In Chapter 8 we clarified our views about the often-stated belief that HR systems should be congruent with the firm's strategy. This principle could be thought of as "external congruence" of HR systems with firm strategy. We discussed our belief that it does not make much sense to talk about an overall fit of HR systems with strategy. Instead, managers must take into account the **behaviors/role requirements** that are determined for **particular job classes** after considering the firm's strategy, its technology, and the resulting work processes. The determination of HR systems that are internally congruent should consider these key behaviors, along with the realities of the labor market and legal environment. Thus, we can agree that firm strategy should be matched to HR systems, but only through a number of intervening processes centered around key employee behaviors.

This chapter further develops our ideas about the use of interrelated and internally congruent HRM practices. More specifically, the purpose of this chapter is to develop our notion of congruence of HR systems and the essential components of congruent systems, to explain why congruence is an important and often overlooked aspect of HR management, and to provide examples of congruence and incongruence in HR systems that attempt to promote key employee behaviors. We argue that HR systems are often ineffective in supporting an organization's goals because of congruence problems. Perhaps the key idea in this chapter is that congruence problems in HR systems can stem from

1. A failure to direct enough forces—HRM activities—to promote targeted employee behaviors.
2. The application of HRM activities that are in conflict—that is, which support incompatible employee behaviors.
3. A failure to provide enough interrelatedness or mutually supportive HRM practices to affect target behaviors.

We find it interesting that until very recently neither scholarly nor popular writing about human resource management paid much attention to the idea that HRM activities should be integrated and mutually supportive. The authors of one scholarly review of theoretical models of strategic human resource management pointed out that human resource management activities have traditionally been grouped into the functional areas of selection, training, appraisal, and rewards. They also noted that "the importance of recognizing the functional differentiation within the HR field rests in the fact that the field has not evolved with great levels of integration across the various functions. Rather, each of the various HRM functions has evolved in relative isolation from one another, with little coordination across the disciplines. Thus, for example, researchers in the area of performance appraisal have become extremely adept at studying the various techniques that maximize the accuracy and effectiveness of the appraisal process, yet very little research attention has been devoted to understanding the relationship between appraisal systems and selection programs."[1]

185

CHAPTER NINE
*Sustained
Competitive
Advantage through
Inimitable Human
Resource Practices*

The need to consider the integration of and relationships among HR activities is central to this book's focus on developing integrated HR systems and is central to the notion of congruence discussed in this chapter.

THREE PERSPECTIVES ON ALTERNATIVE HR SYSTEMS

Recently several theorists of strategic human resource management have discussed the issue of congruence in HR systems. We briefly acknowledge some of their ideas as we introduce you to our own views about internally congruent HR practices.[2]

One perspective on HR systems is the **universalistic** perspective. This is the view that some HR practices are *always* better than others. In Chapter 1 we discussed the set of HR practices that Pfeffer observed as characteristic of effective firms.[3] This could be considered a universalistic perspective.

The **contingency** perspective, taken by other theorists, is the view that HR practices should be consistent with other aspects of the organization, especially its strategy. Some contingency theorists have also pointed out that an organization's strategy mandates certain employee behavioral requirements for success. Human resource practices can reward and control these employee behaviors.[4]

Finally, a third prevailing perspective, the **configurational,** takes a "holistic" approach, arguing that unique and often complex **patterns** of HR practices enable a firm to effectively achieve its goals. Human resource systems must achieve both a *horizontal fit* (internal congruence/consistency) and a *vertical fit* (congruence with firm strategy). As Delery and Doty put it in discussing the three perspectives, "An ideal configuration would be one with the highest degree of horizontal fit."[5] We term this horizontal fit "congruence," and it is the focus of this chapter. Our approach also includes elements of both the contingency and the configurational perspectives. Like the contingency perspective, we emphasize that HR systems must fit important aspects of the organization (e.g., the set of factors leading to a job class's behavioral requirements). But like the configurational perspective, we also emphasize that managers need to specify an entire set of internally consistent HR practices to promote key employee behaviors. We next develop the arguments for our particular definition of congruence in HR systems.

INTRANSIGENT EMPLOYEE BEHAVIORS

In recent years we have become aware that key employee behaviors may be much more "sticky" and difficult to change than was previously assumed. This stickiness has clear implications for the design of HR systems. Staw

186

*PART THREE
Aligning Human
Resource Systems
with Business
Strategy*

provided a valuable discussion of these issues, which is relevant for our arguments about the need for congruence in HR systems.[6] Staw cited several research studies which suggest that job satisfaction may be quite stable, determined as much by an employee's own disposition as by any changes in work environment or management practices. Some of Staw's own research found that an employee's job satisfaction was consistent over three- to five-year time periods, even across several different jobs. Another study found this same pattern of consistency even when people changed *both* their employers and their occupations. Thus, Staw concludes that people may not be as malleable as we tend to think they are, and employees tend to reach an "equilibrium" in their job attitudes.

Staw further argues that an employee's job **performance** may also be consistent: A person whose energy level is fairly constant over time may expend the same level of effort in different job situations. And even an employee who has a strong willingness to perform better may be severely constrained by lack of ability. Similarly, some employees' performance is constrained by the job itself or by the work cycle or technical procedures. Thus, doing one's job better may not result from increased willingness or effort, but only from increases in materials, financial support, or resources.

Although Staw's own research and the studies he cited focus on employee job satisfaction and performance, we believe that other key employee behaviors may also reflect these tendencies toward consistency. These behaviors might include job changes, attendance at work, and cooperation with others. What are the implications for HR systems? Staw pointed out that the tendency for consistency in key employee behaviors suggests that only **multiple** changes can provide the necessary impact to change these entrenched employee behaviors. Thus, an isolated change in one aspect of staffing, reward, or development activities is not likely to do the job. Instead, to change these key behaviors, managers must "throw the kitchen sink at the problem," to use Staw's phrase. As we will later discuss, for maintaining congruence it is also crucial that all of the HRM activities comprising a human resource system be **compatible** and **mutually reinforcing.**

HR SYSTEMS AND EMPLOYEE BEHAVIORS: INDIVIDUAL, GROUP, AND ORGANIZATIONAL SYSTEMS

Managers need to determine the appropriate system of congruent HR practices to support key employee behaviors for a job class. In these efforts, it is useful to think about HR systems at the individual, group, and organizational levels. In a sense all employee behaviors could be labeled as "individual" behaviors, but the **system** that affects these behaviors can be the individual, the group, or possibly even the overall organization. These different levels can be viewed as leverage points for changing behaviors or as "syndromes of action." Staw provided examples of practices promoting employee satisfaction and performance which reflect these three levels.[7]

First, an **individually oriented** system would emphasize features such as

187

CHAPTER NINE
Sustained
Competitive
Advantage through
Inimitable Human
Resource Practices

- Tying extrinsic rewards (such as pay) to performance.
- Setting realistic and challenging goals.
- Evaluating employee performance accurately and providing feedback.
- Promoting employees on the basis of skill and performance rather than personal characteristics, power, or connections.
- Building the skill level of the employees through development activities.
- Enlarging and enriching jobs through practices such as increases in responsibility and skill variety.

Next, a **group-oriented** system would emphasize features such as

- Organizing work around intact groups.
- Having groups themselves charged with selection, training, and rewarding of members.
- Using groups to enforce strong norms for behavior, with group involvement in off-the-job as well as on-the-job behavior.
- Distributing resources on a group rather than individual basis.
- Allowing and perhaps even promoting intergroup rivalry to build within-group solidarity.

Finally, an **organizationally oriented** system would emphasize features such as

- Socialization into the organization as a whole to foster identification with the entire business and not just a particular subunit.
- Job rotation around the company so that loyalty is not limited to one subunit.
- Long training periods with the development of skills that are specific to the company and not transferable to other firms in the industry or profession, thus committing people to the employing organization.
- Long-term or protected employment to gain organizational loyalty, with concern for survival and welfare of the firm.
- Decentralized operations, with few departments or subunits to compete for the allegiance of members.
- Few status distinctions between employees so that dissension and separatism are not fostered.
- Economic education and sharing of organizational information about the products, financial condition, and strategies of the firm.
- Use of various forms of profit sharing, stock options, and bonuses to tie individual rewards to organizational performance.

As a practical matter, just about all organizations, however they structure their employees' work, want to affect some employee behaviors at the individual level, some at the group level, and some at the organizational level. For example, a firm might structure work around groups using high-involvement work teams that engage in team-based hiring, firing, and work scheduling, thus promoting many group-oriented behaviors. However, the

188

*PART THREE
Aligning Human
Resource Systems
with Business
Strategy*

firm would almost always, in addition, want to promote certain **individual**-oriented behaviors such as attendance and skill acquisition.

Using the conceptualization just introduced, we could classify key employee behaviors as individual-, group-, or organization-oriented, as summarized in Table 9–1. Individual-oriented behaviors include such behaviors as attendance and punctuality, the decision to retire early, or acquisition of new high-tech skills. Group-oriented behaviors include cooperation in integrating one's individual work with others, working as a team to generate work innovations, or participative decision making as a team, including selection, work scheduling, performance evaluation, and reward decisions for a team. Organization-oriented behaviors which a firm might want to promote go beyond the employee's assigned role and include organizational citizenship behaviors, acquisition of knowledge of the firm's history and scope of operations, or commitment to the goal of furthering the overall organization rather than one's subunit or work group. Thus, it is likely that most organizations intend to simultaneously promote key behaviors at the individual, group, and organizational levels. We would also expect that the cultures of particular organizations often include tendencies to favor a particular level of HR systems.

AVOIDING CONFLICTING HR SYSTEMS

Staw points out that a case can be made for any of the three levels of systems for promoting employee behaviors and that the mixing of individual, group, or organizational systems may create a confused or conflicted environment for employees.[8] We believe that the concern about conflict is valid when the focus is on promoting a **particular behavior** such as task performance or cooperation with others. Thus, using Staw's examples, an individually oriented system may promote performance competition among individual employees, and so could not be easily combined with a group-oriented system, which promotes intragroup cooperation. Similarly, an

TABLE 9–1. Examples of Individual, Group, and Organizationally Oriented Behavior

Individual	Group	Organizational
Attendance	Cooperation	Organizational citizenship
Punctuality	Integrating work with others	Knowledge of firm history, operations
Early retirement	Teamwork for innovation	Commitment to overall organization goals
Acquiring new skills	Participative decision making	Enhancing firm's market share

organizationally oriented system emphasizing employees serving a common goal may not be compatible with a group-oriented system fostering intergroup competition.

189

CHAPTER NINE
Sustained
Competitive
Advantage through
Inimitable Human
Resource Practices

We agree that managers should ensure that the staffing, reward, and development practices comprising HR systems are not in conflict. If a particular behavior—say, cooperation with others—is considered to be important, then the practices comprising the HR system should not support conflicting or unwanted behavior—say, individual-based financial rewards for work output.

CONGRUENCE AND INTEGRATED HR SYSTEMS

The previous discussion set the stage for an explicit statement of our notion of congruence, or, similarly, the "horizontal fit" of HR systems.[9] We believe congruence in an organization's HR system provides a distinct competitive advantage, in that it is hard for competitors to copy an HR system that is integrated and comprehensive. Congruence essentially includes three key components:

1. **Managers must focus powerful forces on the target behaviors** they want to promote; they must use *all* the available HRM practices to influence employees' motivation, ability, and opportunity for important behaviors.
2. **Managers must make sure that staffing, reward, and development practices do not conflict;** that is, they must ensure that HR systems do not encourage employee behaviors which work against each other or are unwanted.
3. **Managers must ensure that interrelated HRM practices are sufficiently supportive of each other** since some HRM practices require the support of interrelated HRM practices in order to maintain targeted employee behaviors.

Another way of explaining the third component is that managers should recognize "complementarities, or synergies" among a firm's HRM practices.[10] Thus, the ultimate success of certain **reward** practices may depend on the use of certain interrelated **selection** practices. Likewise, the success of certain training initiatives may depend on the careful selection of employees most likely to benefit from training. Our notion of congruence is summarized in Table 9–2.

TABLE 9–2. Congruence in HR Systems

1. Focus many powerful forces on target behaviors
2. Ensure that staffing reward and development practices do not conflict
3. Ensure that HRM practices, if interrelated, are supportive of each other

190

PART THREE
Aligning Human
Resource Systems
with Business
Strategy

Lack of Congruence in an HR System

Let's look at a firm with a key target behavior of employee **teamwork** in task accomplishment. The firm's HR system consists of the following practices:

- Using individual employee performance measurement and feedback.
- Providing team training in group interaction skills.
- Having team members hire new team members.
- Having teams handle grievances and discipline problems.
- Providing individual employee bonuses for achieving quality goals.

This system of HRM practices lacks congruence because our key congruence principle 2 has been violated. Both the first and the last practices listed above support behaviors which conflict with the target behaviors of employee teamwork. Employees are being measured, coached, and financially rewarded for their **individual** accomplishments. This promotion of individual task performance would tend to result in competitive behavior, which of course is incompatible with the target behavior of cooperation.

Consider another example. A firm has decided that a key employee behavior is the generation of **innovative ideas,** and the firm

- Conducts employee training programs on creativity and innovation.
- Does not consider creative abilities in hiring new employees.
- Provides no financial incentives for employees who produce innovations.
- Does not consider creativity or innovations in assessing managers for promotions to more responsible positions.
- Does not include employees' innovation in the performance measurement or feedback system.
- Provides no broad development opportunities such as sabbaticals or support for attending special conferences.

This HR system also lacks congruence. Although there may be no problem with supporting conflicting behaviors, the firm is using only a fraction of the HRM practices potentially available to encourage and support innovative behavior. Thus, our principle 1 of congruence is violated. We could not be optimistic that this firm will see noticeable increases in the generation of innovations by employees.

Consider our principle 3 of congruence—that interrelated HRM practices must be mutually supportive. Suppose that an organization prices its pay hierarchy to be a pay leader. Management expects that providing high wages will lead to a large and unusually qualified pool of applicants, and they'll be able to hire the cream of the crop. But what if the organization does *not* also invest in a high-quality selection system? Without the support of an effective selection system for identifying the best applicants, the organization will never be able to take advantage of its high wages to bring the most outstanding people into the organization. Management has ignored the need for interrelated HRM practices to be **mutually supportive.**

Another example would be a firm that provides attractive **bonuses** for employees who reach their sales goals. These bonuses could have a strong

191

*CHAPTER NINE
Sustained
Competitive
Advantage through
Inimitable Human
Resource Practices*

impact on performance motivation (raising instrumentalities). However, if the firm does not also provide adequate *orientation* and *training* for sales staff, the bonus program's effectiveness may be hampered. Employees must have adequate information, skills, and strategies for sales (ability to perform), or their motivation will not translate into performance improvements. Similarly, these employees must be provided with an adequate opportunity to use their ability and their motivation to produce high sales in the form of *resource support*.

A final example of our third principle of congruence can be tied to some of our Chapter 1 discussion concerning HRM practices and a firm's competitiveness. Successful firms often put a strong emphasis on employee training: the acquisition of knowledge and skills relevant to job performance. Unfortunately, knowledge and skill adequacy will not necessarily lead to high performance. Employees must be allowed and encouraged to *use* these job-related capacities. In addition, the training must be complemented with selection procedures that hire new employees for their ability and willingness to learn, and by reward practices that reinforce employees for participating in training and development activities. Finally, if a firm invests in training but does *not* emphasize promotion from within or maintain workforce stability by controlling turnover, for example, the expected benefits of the investment in training may never materialize.

A Congruent HR System

Suppose that an organization decides that a critical target behavior for employees is effective **teamwork.** This organization

- Provides employee training in team interaction skills.
- Uses current team members to select new employees, emphasizing compatibility with the team and team skills as a key aspect of selection.
- Considers an employee's teamwork and cooperation with others in making promotion decisions.
- Provides financial incentives for team achievement of overall team performance quality and quantity goals.
- Measures overall team performance and provides performance feedback to the team as a whole.
- Authorizes the team to provide to its members peer feedback on team cooperativeness and to handle disciplinary problems on its own.
- Authorizes the team to schedule employees' work on its own.

This organization appears to have created an integrated and congruent HR system for promoting the target behavior of teamwork. First, the organization directs an **extensive** set of practices toward promoting the target behavior of teamwork. Second, these HR practices are **well-integrated** and aligned, so that the HR practices support each other and no conflicting or incompatible behaviors are being encouraged. Several detailed examples of how integrated HR systems in a variety of work settings could be designed to promote desired employee behaviors appear in Part IV.

192

PART THREE
Aligning Human
Resource Systems
with Business
Strategy

DESIGNING THE CONGRUENT SYSTEM
OF HR PRACTICES: TRADEOFFS

A theme of this book is that the system of HR practices should be designed to support key employee behaviors. These behaviors can be supported by enhancing employees' motivation, ability, and/or opportunity to perform the behaviors. However, elements of the system of HR practices which we summarize as staffing, reward, and development systems might sometimes overlap or duplicate each other. That is, they might provide alternative strategies for enhancing motivation, ability, or opportunity to perform the same behaviors. Cost-effectiveness considerations may require that managers carefully consider tradeoffs in picking the most appropriate HR practice. Thus, even though interrelated HR activities must support each other, managers can also take advantage of certain **tradeoffs** in the use of HR practices.

Consider the possibility that employees' capacity for creativity at work, the target behavior, could be greatly enhanced by a firm's employee selection practices. In hiring, the firm might screen employees based on scores on a valid **test** of creativity. The "cut score" for hiring using the creativity test could be set at a high level, thus ensuring a high probability that the new hires have the necessary capacity for creativity in their work.

Alternatively, the firm could enhance the level of employee capacity for creative behavior through the use of **training** programs. The firm could screen employees using whatever devices were already in place, but then provide employees with in-depth creativity training programs and other developmental experiences to develop their creative competencies—assuming that employees can be trained to be more creative.

Even though employee behaviors are often "sticky" and managers must try many HRM activities to encourage key employee behaviors, costs must also be taken into account. Should the firm in the example above emphasize selection, or training, or both, for acquiring a workforce with creative capacities? This is not an easy question to answer. Unfortunately, we currently have no body of research findings informing us of the relative impact of selection versus training for key employee behaviors. The important point here is that there probably are tradeoffs in the application of HRM practices such that one or the other practice (selection or training) could be given more emphasis.

Considering our example, the following factors could be assessed in contemplating the selection versus training tradeoffs:

1. The current availability of highly creative workers in the labor market, allowing for screening on creativity for new hires.
2. The relative availability, costs, and benefits of training versus selection to the particular firm. (Does the firm already have extensive training resources in place? Is there *not* a test available for assessing creativity?)
3. The firm's history, culture, and strategy. (Does this firm have a philosophy of "growing its own" managers and a historical commitment to employee training and development?)

The preceding example dealt with acquiring employees with an **ability** for a particular type of behavior—creativity. There are other kinds of tradeoffs which managers should also consider. For example, recall in Chapter 2 the discussion of employee **motivation** to engage in important behaviors. We pointed out that using the expectancy model, motivation for high task performance can be enhanced by HRM practices which enhance *expectancy* perceptions (e.g., selection, training, feedback), *instrumentality* perceptions (e.g., incentives, merit pay, supervisor reinforcement), or *valence* for task performance. Tradeoffs in enhancing employee motivation should also be considered.

193

CHAPTER NINE
Sustained
Competitive
Advantage through
Inimitable Human
Resource Practices

For example, for enhancing instrumentality perceptions (behavior–outcome linkage) management could consider distributing **merit salary increases** for creativity. In employees' performance appraisals, managers would assess employees' generation of creative ideas, and base salary would be adjusted upward based on this appraisal. Alternatively, the firm might choose to use a **lump-sum bonus** program. Employees would be given a one-time monetary bonus each time a significant creative idea or innovation is generated by the employee and adopted by the firm. Managers may even consider **gain-sharing** plans in which a portion of cost savings from innovative ideas generated by groups of employees is distributed back to the employees.[11]

Each of these HRM practices—merit increases, lump-sum bonuses, and gain-sharing programs—involves linking target behaviors with monetary rewards, and each could be used to enhance employee motivation to engage in creative behavior. Keep in mind that it would not typically be cost effective (and possibly not congruent) to use *all* of these money-based motivation programs simultaneously. Thus, to evaluate the tradeoffs managers would need to consider some of the same kinds of questions listed above in our example of enhancing employee ability to be creative.

HUMAN RESOURCE SYSTEMS IN THE MANAGEMENT LITERATURE

In Part IV of this book we present comprehensive examples of designing HR systems for particular situations. But as we mentioned earlier, a few management scholars have already begun to write of the need for integrated HR systems. Some of this writing has been a product of the recent attention to strategy and strategic HRM. We conclude this chapter by providing two examples taken from recent management writing of a focus on comprehensive **systems** of human resource practices. These authors describe entire systems of HR practices for achieving a firm's objectives, as opposed to the typical focus on separate human resource programs. The authors did not systematically define or illustrate the concept of congruence in these systems, although congruence was certainly implied.

194

*PART THREE
Aligning Human
Resource Systems
with Business
Strategy*

Competitive Strategies, Role Behaviors, and Typologies of HRM Practices

As noted in Chapter 8, Schuler and Jackson described the expected links among firms' competitive strategies, the employee role behaviors required under these strategies, and the typology or set of HRM practices for maintaining these role behaviors.[12] Their description of an entire *set* of HRM practices targeted toward desired employee behaviors illustrates our notion of congruence in HR systems. These authors first delineated three alternative competitive strategies firms might choose to adopt: an innovation strategy, a quality-enhancement strategy, and a cost-reduction strategy. As an example, firms adopting an innovation strategy strive to develop products different from those of competitors, with a primary focus on providing something new and different. Innovation-oriented firms would include such firms as Hewlett-Packard, the Raytheon Corporation, 3M, Johnson & Johnson, and PepsiCo.

Schuler and Jackson then explained the particular set of employee role behaviors required under each of the firm strategies. The innovative firms, for example, would require employee role behaviors such as a high degree of creative behavior, a high level of cooperative behavior, a moderate degree of concern for both quality and quantity, and a substantial degree of risk taking.

Next Schuler and Jackson delineated a potential set of HRM practices in the form of an HRM practice "menu," including choices for the areas of planning, staffing, appraising, compensating, and training and developing employees. As an illustration of one innovation-oriented firm's efforts to implement a set of HRM practices they cite Frost, Inc., a medium-sized manufacturer of overhead conveyor trolleys used in the auto industry. Frost decided to make a major change in automating the production process for enhanced flexibility. These efforts included HRM practices to support key employee behaviors needed for innovation.

Thus, Frost implemented HR practices that included

1. Installing a "celebration fund" for giving special rewards for individual employee innovations.
2. Offering a quarterly bonus based on companywide productivity for encouraging cooperative behavior.
3. Instituting a variety of incentives oriented toward a long-term focus, such as providing employees with stock in the firm and a corporate profit-sharing plan.
4. Eliminating special executive "perks" to encourage cooperation among all employees.
5. Paying for extensive training programs, both on-site and off-site, to encourage employees to broaden their skills and take risks.

Clearly, Schuler and Jackson's Frost, Inc., example illustrates the use of a congruent system of HRM practices to support key employee behaviors. It appears that this set of practices meets our conception of congruence—especially in targeting an impressive array of forces at the desired behaviors, and also in careful attention to supporting compatible rather than conflicting employee behaviors.

195

*CHAPTER NINE
Sustained
Competitive
Advantage through
Inimitable Human
Resource Practices*

Control and Commitment Human Resource Systems

As discussed in Chapter 1, Arthur empirically identified two types of human resource systems—*control* and *commitment* HR systems—in a sample of steel minimills.[13] This work is useful in our consideration here of congruent HR systems. Arthur pointed out that studying specific configurations, or systems of human resource activities, is a departure from the traditional approach of focusing on separate human resource practices or outcomes, a departure that is a key theme of this book. He developed and tested several hypotheses about the utility of these two alternative systems for manufacturing performance and for employee turnover in the minimills.

Control systems have a cost-reduction orientation, with a goal of reducing direct labor costs and improving efficiency. This goal is achieved by ensuring that employees comply with specific rules and procedures and by tying employee rewards to measurable output criteria. *Commitment* systems, in contrast, attempt to link the goals of employees to the goals of the firm. The objective is to create a workforce of committed employees who can be trusted to use their discretion to behave in a way which furthers the firm's goals.

Arthur expected these two systems to be represented by different types of HRM practices.[14] Commitment systems, for example, would be characterized by decentralized decision making, formal employee participation mechanisms, training in group problem solving, social activities, higher wage rates, and less attention to monitoring employee compliance with work rules. In contrast, the HRM practices of firms with control systems would include more centralized decision making, less employee participation, less general training (e.g., in people skills), lower wages, but more use of bonuses and incentives. Arthur's data tended to confirm these expectations about the differing HRM practices under the two systems. As noted in Chapter 1, the research also found that those minimills using commitment systems tended to have higher productivity, lower scrap rates, and lower employee turnover compared to the mills using control systems.

This work demonstrates *empirically* that firms can be described on the basis of a **system** of interrelated HRM practices. We emphasize that Arthur's study of control and commitment systems did not specifically examine the congruence (as defined in this book) of the HR systems used in the minimills. It is possible, for example, that the control systems were implemented with less congruence than the commitment systems, and this lack of congruence at least partially explains the control systems' lower firm performance. Arthur acknowledged that an unanswered question from his research relates to the performance implications of *mixed* systems and the possibility that deviations from the "ideal" system type weakens performance. This possibility is related to our contention that a careful analysis and implementation of congruence in HR systems is important for achieving the firm's goals.

196

PART THREE
Aligning Human
Resource Systems
with Business
Strategy

CONCLUSION

This chapter continued the discussion of how sound HRM practice can add value to the firm and serve as a source of competitive advantage. We believe that managers should not consider HR practices in isolation, but should instead promote the congruency, or internal consistency, of the entire set of HR practices for a job class. Competitors cannot easily imitate a set of congruent HRM practices, so they are a powerful source of sustained competitive advantage. Moreover, because employee behaviors can be quite "sticky," it is necessary for managers to target many HR practices at key employee behaviors. The set of HR practices may be focused at the individual, the group, or even the organizational levels. Managers should also be careful that HR practices do not conflict, or promote incompatible employee behaviors. Finally, managers should ensure that if interrelated, various HR practices (e.g., staffing, development, reward systems) should be supportive of each other and take advantage of whatever synergies are available.

CONTINUOUS LEARNING: SOME NEXT STEPS

In this chapter we focused on HR system congruence. This is an important notion because HR systems that are externally and internally congruent are difficult to copy—a critical attribute associated with a resource that fosters a **sustained competitive advantage.** Maintaining a sustained competitive advantage is central to the strategic planning process and is an idea worth learning more about. The first step below speaks to such an objective. The second step is more of an action learning step—a step that will require some data collection.

- Do a search of the following journals, with a focus on the key words "sustained competitive advantage":

  Harvard Business Review (www.hbsp.harvard.edu/home.html)

  McKinsey Quarterly (www.mckinseyquarterly.com)

  Strategic Management Journal (available online at (www.interscience.wiley. com)

  Look for articles that address the notion of a sustained competitive advantage and explore how this idea relates to other management systems (e.g., financial management systems, production and operations management systems, information systems).
- Identify an HR executive or HR-oriented consultant in a firm you have access to. The first thing to do is to meet with this individual and explain the concept of an internally congruent HR system. Then ask this individual for examples of HRM practices within the company, directed at a common job classification, that were clearly not internally congruent.

CHAPTER NINE
Sustained
Competitive
Advantage through
Inimitable Human
Resource Practices

1. P. M. Wright and G. C. McMahan, "Theoretical Perspectives for Strategic Human Resource Management," *Journal of Management* 18 (1992), p. 297.

2. J. E. Delery and D. H. Doty, "Modes of Theorizing in Strategic Human Resource Management: Tests of Universalistic, Contingency, and Configurational Performance Predictions," *Academy of Management Journal* 39 (1996), pp. 802–35.

3. J. Pfeffer, "Producing Sustainable Competitive Advantage through the Effective Management of People," *Academy of Management Executive* 9 (1995), pp. 55–69.

4. S. E. Jackson, R. S. Schuler, and J. C. Rivero, "Organizational Characteristics as Predictors of Personnel Practices," *Personnel Psychology* 42 (1989), pp. 727–86.

5. Delery and Doty, "Modes of Theorizing," p. 804.

6. B. M. Staw, "Organizational Psychology and the Pursuit of the Happy/Productive Worker," *California Management Review* 28 (1986), pp. 40–53.

7. Ibid.

8. Ibid.

9. As noted, this is the term used by Delery and Doty, "Modes of Theorizing."

10. J. T. Delaney and M. A. Huselid, "The Impact of Human Resource Management Practices on Perceptions of Organizational Performance," *Academy of Management Journal* 39 (1996), pp. 949–69.

11. G. T. Milkovich and J. M. Newman, *Compensation* (Burr Ridge, IL: Irwin, 1996).

12. R. S. Schuler and S. E. Jackson, "Linking Competitive Strategies with Human Resource Management Practices," *Academy of Management Executive* 1 (1987), pp. 207–19.

13. J. B. Arthur, "The Link between Business Strategy and Industrial Relations Systems in American Steel Minimills," *Industrial and Labor Relations Review* 45 (1992), pp. 488–506; and J. B. Arthur, "Effects of Human Resource Systems on Manufacturing Performance and Turnover," *Academy of Management Journal* 37 (1994), pp. 670–87.

14. Arthur, "Effects of Human Resource Systems."

10

Domestic and International Labor Markets

In designing HR systems for competitive advantage, a powerful contextual factor to consider is the market for labor. There is a market for labor that can be distinguished from product and financial markets. In this chapter you will

- See how both domestic and international labor markets can influence business decisions.
- Understand that trends in workforce diversity relating to age, sex, and ethnicity have direct consequences for designing effective HR systems.
- Become acquainted with a number of levels at which labor markets can be analyzed, including cultures, nations, regions, localities, and location inside and outside the firm.
- Learn how labor markets take into account differences in factors such as values, need for achievement, strength of work orientation, individualist versus collectivist orientation, and reward preferences.

The "market" for labor is a particularly powerful contextual factor that is related to the design, implementation, and evaluation of HRM practices. Knowledge of the changing characteristics of labor markets influences and informs the strategic decision-making process, providing a needed perspective on whether a business or tactical strategy can be implemented. For example, certain strategic options may be ruled out if sufficient talent in key job classes is not available either from within or outside of the firm. Consider the pharmaceutical company that wants to aggressively expand its research and development initiatives but can't find a sufficient number of Ph.D.-level chemists in certain specialties to make the strategy work. Also, an analysis of a firm's internal labor market—its reserve of talent and projected internal supply of employees across occupational specialties—may lead to the formulation of a particular strategic option. Comparative strengths in terms of the number and quality of employees available in various functional areas (e.g., marketing, operations, or R&D) can inform decisions to take businesses in new strategic directions. As noted in

Chapter 1, Compaq Computer's historical strength in the area of flexible manufacturing was an important factor when formulating and evaluating the decision to target new home computer users with the introduction of five new consumer lines in the summer of 1996.[1]

We begin this chapter by providing a few more illustrations showing how both domestic and international labor markets can influence business decisions. We then review some basic concepts from labor economics that define a market for labor. This is followed by a discussion of the multiple ways labor markets, and workforce attributes, in particular, can be described (with an emphasis on international comparisons). Finally, we offer some guidelines for learning, in a timely manner, about workforce attributes in targeted areas or regions.

This chapter is designed to increase your appreciation for the importance of taking information about labor markets into account when making and evaluating decisions that impact the behavior of employees. After completing this chapter you should be better prepared to initiate or direct the collection of labor-market information that will be relevant to reaching sound business decisions.

ON THE RELEVANCE OF LABOR MARKETS

We begin with brief illustrations of how labor-market characteristics influence business decisions related to people. In each instance, something about the supply of and demand for labor or some other characteristic of the workforce influenced the decision-making process. Often, worker shortages relate directly to labor costs because shortages in a particular labor market tend to drive up wages. But as you will see, this is not always the case.

Studying labor-market characteristics goes well beyond studying simple supply and demand. An analysis of a particular labor market also needs to include a look at such things as the knowledge, skill, ability, and interest profiles of its members. Thus, labor markets can differ with respect to quality, quantity, and diversity. Although what follows is just a brief sampling, variations on these themes are many and ignoring these issues can have severe negative consequences.

In 1997, General Motors Corporation (GM) initiated a "four-plant-international-expansion" strategy by breaking ground on four state-of-the-art assembly plants, one each in Argentina, Poland, China, and Thailand.[2] When building these new plants, GM's designs were influenced by attributes of local labors markets. In a very successful plant in Eisenach, Germany, the facility is 95 percent automated. In the new Rosario, Argentina, plant, the company will take advantage of lower labor costs by depending much more on workers, using a 45 percent automation ratio. This contributes to an estimated $350 million price tag for the new facility—one of the lowest ever for a new GM plant.

In order to hire a software developer away from a rival company, the Microsoft Corporation agreed to charter a plane to fly the engineer's two pet

200

*PART THREE
Aligning Human
Resource Systems
with Business
Strategy*

white-tailed deer from Texas to their new home in Washington State.[3] With the supply of high-tech workers much lower than the demand, other companies are behaving in similar ways. For instance, Sybase, Inc., is reported to have hired a biplane to fly over the Redwood Shores, California, headquarters of Oracle Corporation, pulling a banner reading "Sybase Wants You." This move was apparently in retaliation for Oracle's attempt, in a location in Bracknell, England, to lure away Sybase engineers by placing, on a flatbed truck in view of Sybase employees, a 40-foot placard reading "Make the Move to Oracle."

In Germany, as shown in Figure 10–1, companies have been faced with some of the highest hourly labor costs in the industrialized world. Germans also work fewer hours than their counterparts in Japan, the United States, France, and Britain, and are entitled to longer vacations (e.g., 30 paid vacation days in Germany versus 11 paid days in Japan and 12 paid days in the United States).[4] These factors, associated with labor costs and worker expectations, were undoubtedly related to BMW's decision to build a $400 million factory in Spartanburg, South Carolina. BMW estimated that labor costs in Spartanburg would be at least one-third lower than in Germany.[5] These same considerations were partly responsible for Mercedes-Benz officials selecting a site near Tuscaloosa, Alabama, to build a new $300 million assembly plant. Finally, in Germany, high wages and high unemployment have gone together—although, typically, an abundance of labor (resulting from high unemployment) would be associated with the lowering of wages. Political processes and social policies in Germany apparently account for this anomaly, but it is these very policies, along with the demographic profile of the country, that need to be taken into account when designing HRM systems.

FIGURE 10–1. Hours worked, wages, and vacation days in Germany—some comparisons

	BRITAIN	FRANCE	GERMANY	JAPAN	UNITED STATES
Average weekly hours worked in manufacturing	38.8	39.0	37.6	41.5	40.0
Average total hourly compensation for production workers	$14.24	$17.34	$26.23	$18.75	$15.49
Average annual vacation days	27	25	30	11	12

Source: Benjamin, D. (1993, May 6). "Losing its edge: Germany is troubled by how little its workers are doing." *Wall Street Journal*, B1. Cowell, A. (1997, July 30). "German workers fear miracle is over." *The New York Times,* A1.

In the United States, as competition for skilled workers mounted, less-skilled workers were losing their jobs. On November 3, 1997, Levi Strauss & Company announced that it would close 11 U.S. plants and lay off 6,400 workers.[6] The company, along with other clothing makers, has had a history of moving operations offshore to take advantage of lower labor costs. Another typical example comes from Bloomington, Indiana. Over a one-year period, the local newspaper provided a detailed commentary on the decision by Thomson Consumer Electronics (a French company) to close the largest television assembly plant in the world and move operations to a site in Mexico.[7] All articles in the series began with a graphic similar to the one shown in Figure 10–2. Apparently, labor-market conditions in Mexico allowed for the hiring of qualified television assemblers for a fraction of the labor costs required to continue operations in Bloomington.

Our final illustration relates directly to the increasingly tight labor markets confronted by trucking companies in the United States during the last half of the 1990s.[8] During this five-year period, the trucking industry was booming due to the vibrant U.S. economy, with the number of heavy trucks increasing 25 percent to 1.5 million. Because industry profit margins were so thin, companies were not able to dramatically raise wages in an attempt to attract new drivers. So they began to use a variety of perks to attract drivers from rival companies. For example, popular inducements included more-comfortable trucks as well as free Internet access and subsidized telephone calling cards for staying in touch with home.

The foregoing illustrations focused on how supply, demand, and other basic attributes of a labor market influence decision making. Other aspects of the composition of the workforce also can dramatically influence business decisions and the legal liability faced by companies. As the level of diversity in labor markets around the world increases, major workforce trends that relate to age, sex, and ethnic diversity have direct consequences for the way work gets done within a given firm. Understanding the nature of these

FIGURE 10–2. Thomson's move to Mexico

202

*PART THREE
Aligning Human
Resource Systems
with Business
Strategy*

labor-market characteristics is now central to designing sound management practices. The degree of change is profound. For example, in the United States, over 45 percent of all net additions to the labor force between 1992 and 2005 will likely be nonwhite (many of these will be first-generation immigrants from Asian and Latin American countries), and almost two-thirds will be women.[9]

An appreciation for the need to properly manage and take advantage of increasing diversity within labor markets is not unique to the United States. Ethnic minorities in the Netherlands now exceed 5 percent of the population,[10] and in France the figure exceeds 8 percent.[11] It also should be noted that increases in the representation of women in the workforce will accelerate more rapidly in the developing world and in Europe than in the United States in the early twenty-first century.[12]

Concern for the increased level of diversity is played out in many different ways. At one level, age, sex, and ethnic differences can lead to tensions regarding perceived value and temperament differences.[13] Or consider the HRM implications of the changes in the United States represented by the data seen in Figure 10–3. But at another level, many see the successful management of diversity as being a key dimension of leadership effectiveness.[14] Taking full advantage of all available talent in a firm must certainly be linked to higher levels of firm performance.

To summarize, these and other illustrations easily show how powerful labor-market considerations are in the current international business environment. Labor costs (which often reflect the supply and demand for labor), worker interests and values, and worker knowledge and skill profiles represent attributes of labor markets that influence decisions ranging from the

FIGURE 10–3. Women, children, and work in the United States

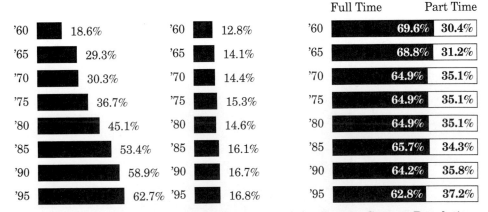

Of all women with children under 6 and living with their husbands, how many work?

Year	Percent
'60	18.6%
'65	29.3%
'70	30.3%
'75	36.7%
'80	45.1%
'85	53.4%
'90	58.9%
'95	62.7%

Of all women who work, how many have children under 6 years old?

Year	Percent
'60	12.8%
'65	14.1%
'70	14.4%
'75	15.3%
'80	14.6%
'85	16.1%
'90	16.7%
'95	16.8%

Of all working women with children under 6 and living with their husbands, how many work . . .

Year	Full Time	Part Time
'60	69.6%	30.4%
'65	68.8%	31.2%
'70	64.9%	35.1%
'75	64.9%	35.1%
'80	64.9%	35.1%
'85	65.7%	34.3%
'90	64.2%	35.8%
'95	62.8%	37.2%

Source: Bureau of Labor Statistics, U.S. Bureau of the Census, Current Population Reports. U.S. Government Printing Office, Washington, DC, 1996.

selection of plant sites to the design of compensation plans. The abundance versus lack of talent available in relevant labor markets also helps to determine when a selection system improvement or a training system improvement is called for. In Part IV we will revisit some of these issues when we prescribe HR systems for five very different business environments—environments comprised of very different labor-market characteristics.

Labor Markets and the Return on Investments

For an investment in an HR system to add value to the firm it must generate a reasonable rate of return. Recall from Chapter 8 that the marginal return associated with such an investment can be estimated by the utility model developed by Boudreau.[15] Within this model, there was explicit consideration of the selection ratio—the number hired divided by the number of applicants—for a particular selection problem. The selection ratio provides information about the supply and demand characteristics of a local labor market. Remember, it does not make much sense to invest in selection system improvements if the labor market is so tight that the company will have to hire virtually all applicants meeting "just-minimum" hiring standards. The positive payoff comes from being better able to identify the best of the best. Likewise, the overall quality of applicants making up the local labor market will affect the rate of return associated with these types of investments.

Overall quality is captured in these marginal utility models by taking into account a *base rate:* the proportion of applicants of an applicant pool who, if given the chance, would be able to perform the target job and meet minimum performance standards. The probability of making one type of costly selection error—selecting someone who then fails—increases as the base rate decreases. The probability of making the other type of selection error—failing to select a candidate who would have been an excellent employee—decreases as the base rate decreases. The point is, labor market characteristics influence investment decisions.

Labor Markets and Equal Employment Opportunity Laws

In the United States, the Civil Rights Act of 1964 banned race, sex, ethnic background, and religious discrimination in staffing and pay practices. As will be developed in further detail in Chapter 11, there are various ways an employer can be found to be in violation of Title VII (the employment title) of the Civil Rights Act. The essence of one definition of discrimination, the disparate or adverse **impact** definition, goes something like this:

> If a management practice that is used to allocate something scarce to employees (e.g., a job, promotion, pay increase, or opportunity to be trained) adversely impacts members of a protected group, the practice (if challenged) will be illegal unless the employer can show that the practice is job-related.

204

*PART THREE
Aligning Human
Resource Systems
with Business
Strategy*

Determining whether a management practice adversely impacts[16] members of a protected group can be somewhat complex and almost always depends on the nature of a local labor market. In fact, a practice applied in one region of the United States may entail no legal liability for a company, whereas the same practice applied in another region may be successfully challenged. The reason for this is that the regional labor markets may differ in terms of the number and quality of available minority job candidates as measured by the possession of specified knowledge, skills, and abilities. For instance, a selection procedure—say, a standardized ability test—may adversely impact minority applicants in a labor market where public schools are predominantly attended by minority students while majority students more likely attend expensive private schools. If the employer in this labor market is challenged in a Title VII case and is not able to show that the employment test is job-related, the employer could lose the case. This same employment practice, when used in a labor market with high-quality public schools available for all students, may pose absolutely no legal liability. This objectively scored test never adversely impacts minority-group applicants in this other labor market.

GENERAL CHARACTERISTICS
OF THE MARKET FOR LABOR

Decision makers need information about the characteristics of labor markets. Much of the remainder of this chapter is intended to help you see the various ways these attributes can be organized into useful categories and where you can find needed information. Before proceeding, however, we provide a little background about whether there really is a market for labor in addition to product and financial markets.

Labor markets are somewhat unique, but do operate much like product and financial markets. The uniqueness comes from two sources:

- The inputs to labor markets—people—cannot be bought and sold; they can only be rented for specific periods of time.[17]
- Labor markets tend to be more heavily regulated than their product or financial counterparts.

In the United States regulations on labor markets range from the Civil Rights Act to minimum wage legislation to the National Labor Relations Act. These regulations place major restrictions on how employers can price labor and how they can allocate other scarce resources (promotions to higher level jobs, training opportunities, etc.).

Labor markets operate much like other markets because two primary conditions have been met. First, a price is determined for labor services. This price is determined either through standard market mechanisms (an equilibrium wage rate reflects the supply of and demand for labor) or through the collective bargaining process (the economic and political strength of unions and management determine how much should be allocated to workers and how much should go to shareholders).[18] Second, renters and sellers of labor services use formal institutions that help make transactions more efficient. For example, union hiring halls, help wanted ads in traditional and electronic media, and government-sponsored and private employment agencies all provide for the flow of information needed for exchanges of this type.

An excellent example of how labor markets operate is the recent escalation of salaries at the top (CEO pay). As discussed in Chaper 4, CEO pay has escalated at a very high rate in comparison to the rate for the average worker. The growing use of stock options (during a bull market), changes to proxy-disclosure rules, and new tax laws have contributed to this phenomenon. In addition, however, mounting evidence indicates that there is a shortage of talent at the top. Demand for senior-executive talent is growing. In 1996, searches for CEOs climbed 28 percent from the previous year, and searches for senior managers in marketing, operations, and research and development were up 20 percent to 36 percent. This has been coupled with what many executives describe as a dearth of senior-management-ready talent. Many reasons are cited to explain this low level of supply at the top, but most agree that the dearth is primarily the result of (1) the new level of complexity associated with running a company, brought about by the move to compete in international markets, and (2) the long-term impact of corporate downsizing, leading to a loss of career-development opportunities.[19]

WAYS OF CHARACTERIZING LABOR MARKETS

Levels of Analysis

When considering how labor markets differ, one is confronted with variation both between and within some defined boundary. The notion of a boundary is somewhat abstract and therefore difficult to define. One starting point is to consider levels of analysis, or some type of clustering approach useful for making informed business decisions.

A first boundary may be at the level of **culture.** Values, attitudes, and interests that affect employee behavior can vary across cultures. The term "culture" is used to describe the norms of behavior that are reflected in the attitudes, values, and beliefs that people within a common culture subscribe to. One standard way to begin categorizing cultures is to use **national** boundary as a first clustering step. This, of course, has its limitations because not everyone in a country is alike, and certain common values and beliefs may closely link people from different countries. Nevertheless, empirical studies of some countries have shown that it is possible to form meaningful clusters.[20] Clustering on attitudinal dimensions, Ronen and Shenkar provided the framework shown in Table 10–1.

The problem with these types of clustering schemes is that, for many of the variables of interest to managers, extensive variation may exist within a country. Thus, there often is the need to consider a labor market at a **regional** or **local** level. Even if we hold values and beliefs somewhat constant, knowledge, skill, and ability profiles can differ dramatically from one region to another.

Finally, clustering on the basis of geography (no matter how narrow the boundaries) does not go far enough. This is because a distinction can be drawn between **external** and **internal** labor markets.[21] An internal labor market is characterized by the supply of and demand for talent within one firm. Attraction, selection, and retention cycles create within-firm commonalities. Often, similarity of attributes within a firm, brought about through firm-specific hiring, training, and reward practices, is described as **company culture** or **organizational climate.** While we think terms such as organizational "culture" and "climate" are often misused and carelessly defined by managers and theorists, they do convey the importance of drawing boundaries around a unit of analysis that does not need to be specific to a particular geographic region.

Attribute Types

Demography

Attributes like race, age, and level of educational attainment are distributed in unique ways across and within labor markets. The number of people in various groups that have potential relevance to employers make up the demographic landscape confronted by an employer. Two new examples (now we focus on age and educational attainment, whereas earlier in this chapter, sex and ethnicity were highlighted), each at two levels of aggregation, illustrate how labor markets can vary on common but important demographic factors. We leave it up to the reader to consider how these demographic profiles are likely to prompt managerial reaction and planning for the future.

At the level of nations, consider Figure 10–4. Projections to the year 2020 show that the elderly are becoming an increasingly large share of the populations of many industrialized countries. Japan's profile differs rather dramatically from that of the United States. The consequences that flow from these demographic trends will affect public policy decisions as well as aspects of firms' HR systems.

At a more micro level, a review of United States census data reveals that age can be distributed very differently among even geographically adjacent counties within one state. For example, in Monroe County, Indiana, about 50 miles south of Indianapolis, 9.2 percent of the population is over 65 years of age. However, in adjacent Jackson County, 13.2 percent of the population is over 65.[22]

At a macro level of analysis, data presented by the Geneva-based International Labour Organization provide an interesting comparative summary of adult literacy rates across the nations of Africa, the Americas, Asia and Oceania, and Europe.[23] Table 10–2 lists adult literacy rates (percentage of population 15 years of age and older exceeding minimum literacy standards) for 10 nations of Asia and Oceania.

Finally, moving back to a more micro level of analysis, U.S. census data again reveal that even among counties located within one small region of the United States, large differences on an important dimension can exist.

TABLE 10–1. Attitudinal Similarity and Employee Behaviors Clustered by Country*

Anglo	Latin America	Germanic	Nordic	Latin European	Near Eastern	Arab	Far Eastern
Australia	Argentina	Austria	Denmark	Belgium	Greece	Abu Dhabi	Hong Kong
Canada	Chile	Germany	Finland	France	Iran	Bahrain	Indonesia
Ireland	Colombia	Switzerland	Norway	Italy	Turkey	Kuwait	Malaysia
New Zealand	Mexico		Sweden	Portugal		Oman	Philippines
United Kingdom	Peru			Spain		Saudi Arabia	Singapore
United States	Venezuela					United Arab Emirates	Taiwan
							Thailand
							Vietnam

Source: S. Ronen and O. Shenkar, "Clustering Countries on Attitudinal Dimensions: A Review and Synthesis," *Academy of Management Review* 10 (1985), pp. 435–54.

*Among the dimensions used to form these clusters were (1) individualism, (2) power distance (a measure of interpersonal power or influence between a boss and a subordinate), and (3) uncertainty avoidance. One interesting example provided by the authors, regarding the implications of their analysis, related to a hypothetical case involving the selection of managers to be sent to Switzerland for the purpose of running a joint venture. Managers could be sent from France, Germany, or Italy (all three languages are spoken in Switzerland, albeit in different areas). The country clustering suggested that German managers would be expected to be closer to and more familiar with the attitudes of workers in Switzerland—thus the more likely choice for the assignment.

208

PART THREE
Aligning Human
Resource Systems
with Business
Strategy

Again, consider the Monroe versus Jackson County comparison. In Monroe County, 32.9 percent of the population possesses college degrees, whereas in Jackson County, only 8.7 percent hold college degrees. If we move to another part of the United States, in Marin County, an affluent county just north of San Francisco, 44 percent are college graduates.

Ascribed Characteristics

Factors such as age, sex, and family of birth are ascribed and often characterized as dimensions of demography, but country-by-country attitudes about them often vary greatly, and these attitudes directly impact employment decisions.[24] For instance, in cultures that assume that age and wisdom are correlated, seniority-based systems for advancement are the norm.

There are clear country-specific differences in attitudes toward male and female work roles. In the United States, over 40 percent of administrative and managerial positions are filled by women; in Japan, less than 10 percent of these jobs are filled by women.[25] At the extreme, consider the situation in Afghanistan. Since the 1996 takeover by religious fundamentalists, women have been prohibited to attend school and to work and also have been required to be shrouded from head to toe when outside the home.[26] These prohibitions mean that the labor market for managerial talent in Afghanistan has been greatly constrained.

Finally, in some societies, family membership takes precedence over attributes such as an individual's level of past achievement when securing jobs or attaining promotions. Daniels and Radebaugh suggest that in societies where family ties are very strong, and "where there is a low trust outside the family, such as in China and southern Italy, family-run companies are more successful than large business organizations, where people are from many different families."[27]

Values/Valence Perceptions

Values, valence perceptions, interests, and a sense of what is important in life are attributes that are acquired. While there can be large within-

FIGURE 10–4 Aging societies

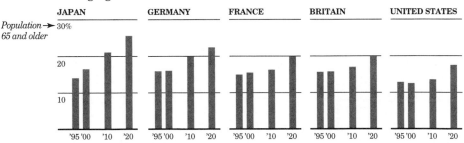

Source: International Labour Organization, World Labour Report 1995 (Geneva, Switzerland: Author, 1995). S. Shellenbarger and C. Hymowitz "Over the Hill: As Population Ages, Older Workers Clash with Younger Bosses," *The Wall Street Journal,* June 13, 1994, pp. A1, B1, B2.

TABLE 10–2. Adult Literacy Rates* for Selected Countries from Asia and Oceania

Country	Male	Female
Afghanistan	44	14
Bangladesh	47	22
China	87	68
Republic of Korea	99	94
Iraq	70	49
Jordan	89	70
Kuwait	77	67
Pakistan	47	21
Singapore	92	74
Vietnam	92	84

*Percentage of 15+ age group meeting minimum literacy standards.

culture variability, general differences have been observed between cultures and nations. For example, Daniels and Radebaugh argue that in some countries (Malaysia, Mexico, Panama, Guatemala, and Venezuela) an autocratic style of leadership is preferred, whereas in others (Austria, Israel, New Zealand, and Scandinavian countries) a consultative style is strongly preferred.[28] A few other value- or need-oriented attributes that can be used to characterize labor markets are briefly illustrated next.

McClelland's Learned Needs. McClelland proposed a theory of motivation that focuses on learned needs.[29] Three of these are the *need for achievement* (*n* Ach), the *need for affiliation* (*n* Aff), and the *need for power* (*n* Pow). High *n* Ach is characterized by people who desire accomplishment. These individuals seek situations in which it is possible to take personal responsibility and get credit for a successful outcome. They attempt to achieve success through their own efforts and abilities, prefer tasks characterized by intermediate levels of difficulty and risk, and seek situations that provide knowledge of results within a reasonable time. Individuals with high *n* Pow seek to control their environment and influence the behavior of others, while *n* Aff is associated with a need to develop friendships and to be sociable and caring of others.

Work Orientation. A variety of attributes relate to what has been termed *work orientation*.[30] Work orientation is characterized by high personal work standards. Regardless of task type, highly work-oriented people are described as industrious, conscientious, responsible, and persevering. The concept resembles what has historically been termed the "Protestant work ethic."

210

PART THREE
Aligning Human
Resource Systems
with Business
Strategy

Individualism versus Collectivism. Here, labor markets can differ on the degree to which members value the submergence of individual concerns to those of the group. This often is seen at the level of the nation. For example, loyalty to a work group is likely to be much higher in Japan than it is in the United States.[31] However, this is a complex concept. While both Japan and Mexico may be characterized as collectivist cultures, the link to work groups is not as strong in Mexico as it is in Japan.[32] Collectivism in Mexico is more heavily based on kinship, not the workplace. This focus on kinship means that geographical mobility on average is less common in Mexico than in other, more individualistic cultures—or in cultures where the collectivism is played out in the workplace. This dimension also has clear implications for the likely effectiveness of individual versus group rewards and benefits.

Reward Preferences. Recall that an expectancy theory perspective on what motivates employees is based on three perceptions. Highly motivated employees will believe that effort leads to accomplishment (expectancy perceptions), that accomplishment leads to various organizational outcomes (instrumentality perceptions), and that the accomplishment-contingent outcomes are highly valued (valence perceptions). Understanding what people value (what outcomes are associated with high valence perceptions) is central to being an effective leader and to creating a highly motivated workforce.

Labor markets can vary with respect to reward preferences or the valence perceptions associated with work-related outcomes. These outcome-specific valence perceptions can address such things as direct forms of cash compensation and benefit options (preferences for health insurance, life insurance, number of holidays, child care assistance or vouchers, dental care, retirement counseling, legal counseling, exercise and fitness facilities, investment and brokerage services, etc.).

Wages and Unemployment Rates

As presented in Figure 10–1, wage rates and unemployment rates can vary greatly across national boundaries. These indexes, of course, can be important factors for companies when making decisions about where to locate new plants and when evaluating the likely financial returns associated with investing in HR system improvements. These rates also can vary greatly within countries and over time—at the level of the local market for labor. For example, the unemployment rate in the area surrounding Grand Rapids, Michigan, peaked at 8.8 percent in 1992, then dropped and stayed at the 4 percent level for 1995 and 1996, then plunged to 3.1 percent in April 1997.[33] With unemployment rates well below the national average, more than 60 temporary-help firms were reported to be competing to find office and factory workers for area employers. Wages for entry-level jobs in the Grand Rapids region also were reported to be increasing at a 4 percent to 5 percent annual rate.

Labor-market information needs to be current and accessible if it is to be of use to decision makers. Information about U.S. labor markets is readily available from the U.S. Census Bureau and the Bureau of Labor Statistics, a branch of the U.S. Department of Labor. Regular publications and bulletins from both of these organizations contain summaries relevant to labor-market analysis. At the international level, the International Labour Organization, the United Nations Development Programme, the Organization for Economic Cooperation and Development, and other organizations, provide relevant information in this area. For example, the International Labour Organization's report titled *World Employment 1996/97: National Policies in a Global Context* includes detailed summaries of such things as labor force growth, employment growth, and unemployment rates for countries in Latin America and the Caribbean, Asia, sub-Saharan Africa, and North Africa and the Middle East.[34]

Of course, as you might expect, high-quality information is available and expensive from individuals providing international trade and investment consulting services and through full-service consulting firms such as Coopers & Lybrand. Very often the advice from seasoned HR executives, who have experienced start-ups in emerging markets, is that consultants are generally the first in and the best source of needed labor-market and regulatory information.

Finally, we turn to the contemporary approach to data collection. As you might expect, vast amounts of information are available on the Internet. At the time this chapter was prepared a variety of websites provided very useful labor-market information. These sites are listed below. Of course, a little browsing will quickly introduce you to new and more and more sophisticated sites. We encourage you to take a look and to complete the continuous learning exercises for this chapter.

Fedstats: www.fedstats.gov

Census Bureau: www.census.gov

Business Cycle Indicators: www.globalexposure.com

Exchange Rate Data from Olsen & Associates: www.oanda.com/cgi-bin/ncc

CONCLUSION

As discussed throughout this chapter, labor-market conditions can affect a wide range of HRM-related decisions. These conditions also can vary greatly both within and across nations and regions of the world. Labor shortages can affect the wage levels that must be paid to attract and retain talented individuals in all types of jobs and positions—from television assemblers to CEOs. KSA and work value differences across and within national and regional boundaries can affect the design and implementation of training and

212

PART THREE
Aligning Human
Resource Systems
with Business
Strategy

reward systems. Labor-market conditions can even influence decisions about where to build new manufacturing and administrative centers. It also is the case that high-quality and up-to-date labor-market data is now available as never before because of Internet-based services and information. This means that as general managers you need to demand that internal HR professionals and consultants from HR-oriented consulting firms be well prepared to address these complex issues.

CONTINUOUS LEARNING: SOME NEXT STEPS

Knowledge about the attributes of regional labor markets is invaluable when making a variety of HRM decisions. For example, decisions about where to locate manufacturing plants in other countries must, in part, take into account regional and local labor-market conditions. Put yourself in the place of the two HR executives described below who have been asked to assist in the selection of a "greenfield" manufacturing site (a new facility built from scratch on a new site) in the United States. Use information that can be found at the U.S. Bureau of Labor Statistics' web page (www. stats.bls.gov) and the page for the Social Statistics Briefing Room (www. whitehouse.gov/fsbr/ssbr.html) to assist you in making your decisions.

- As the ranking HR executive for BMW you are participating in a series of meetings to decide where in the United States to locate a new manufacturing facility to be used to assemble the company's newly designed sports car. The process to date has narrowed the decision down to two sites: Spartanburg, South Carolina, and Omaha, Nebraska. What labor-market-oriented factors should be used to help make an informed decision and how useful are the two websites listed above in gathering this information? What other websites can you find to provide useful information about these two U.S. metropolitan areas? Which area would you select?
- Go to Companies Online Search (www.companiesonline.com), the company's actual web page, and the free *New York Times* subscription service (www.nyt.com) to learn about the clothing manufacturer Levi Strauss. Why has this privately held company closed many of its U.S.–based manufacturing plants and moved production to offshore sites? What labor market factors have contributed to these decisions? If you could locate a clothing manufacturing plant for the high-volume production of men's casual clothing anywhere in the world, where would it be and why did you select this location?

ENDNOTES

1. K. Blumenthal, "Compaq Is Segmenting Home-Computer Market," *The Wall Street Journal*, July 16, 1996, p. A3; and K. Blumenthal, "Compaq to Unveil Three New Lines at Lower Prices for the Business Market," *The Wall Street Journal*, July 22, 1996, p. B2.
2. R. Blumenstein, "Global Strategy: GM Is Building Plants in Developing Nations to Woo New Markets," *The Wall Street Journal*, August 4, 1997, pp. A1, A4.

3. S. Chan, "In Frenzy to Recruit, High-Tech Concerns Try Gimmicks, Songs," *The Wall Street Journal*, August 9, 1996, p. B1.

4. D. Benjamin, "Losing Its Edge: Germany Is Troubled by How Little Work Its Workers Are Doing," *The Wall Street Journal*, May 6, 1993, p. B1; and A. Cowell, "German Workers Fear the Miracle Is Over," *The New York Times*, July 30, 1997, pp. A1, A4.

5. Benjamin, "Losing Its Edge."

6. "Levi Strauss Plans Closings, Layoffs," *Bloomington Herald-Times*, November 4, 1997, p. B1.

7. B. Werth, "Thomson Adds $800,000 to Exit Deal," *Bloomington Herald-Times*, September 30, 1997, p. A1.

8. "Trucking Companies Use Perks to Haul in Rivals' Drivers," *The Wall Street Journal,* January 4, 2000.

9. T. C. Cox, *Cultural Diversity in Organizations: Theory, Research and Practice* (San Francisco: Berrett-Koehler Publishers, 1994).

10. S. de Vries, *Working in Multi-ethnic Groups: The Performance and Well Being of Minority and Majority Workers* (Amsterdam: Gouda Quint bu-Arnhem, 1992).

11. T. Horwitz and C. Forman, "Clashing Cultures," *The Wall Street Journal*, August 14, 1990, p. A1.

12. Cox, *Cultural Diversity in Organizations.*

13. For an interesting discussion of age-related clashes in the workplace, see S. Shellenbarger and C. Hymowitz, "Over the Hill: As Population Ages, Older Workers Clash with Younger Bosses," *The Wall Street Journal*, June 13, 1994, pp. A1, B1, B2.

14. Cox, *Cultural Diversity in Organizations.*

15. J. W. Boudreau, "Economic Considerations in Estimating the Utility of Human Resource Productivity Improvement Programs," *Personnel Psychology* 36 (1983), pp. 551–76.

16. Typically, adverse impact can be defined in one of two ways. The first focuses on differences that may exist between an employer's internal labor market and the external market for labor for a specified job class. For instance, if only two women hold accounting professorships in a graduate school of business (out of a total of 20 full-time professors) and women make up 50 percent of the external labor market for Ph.D.-level accounting professors, it could be inferred that the school's hiring and promotion practices adversely impact female candidates. The other way directly addresses selection ratios. If a staffing practice results in hiring a smaller proportion of female applicants (e.g., 20 percent of all females applicants are offered jobs, but 50 percent of all male applicants are offered jobs), the practice could be judged to adversely impact women.

17. R. Ehrenberg and R. S. Smith, *Modern Labor Economics: Theory and Public Policy* (Glenview, IL: Scott, Foresman, 1985).

18. R. B. Freeman and J. L. Medoff, *What Do Unions Do?* (New York: Basic Books, 1984).

19. T. D. Shellhardt, "Star Search: Talent Pool Is Shallow as Corporations Seek Executives for Top Jobs," *The Wall Street Journal*, June 26, 1997, pp. A1, A10.

20. J. D. Daniels and L. H. Radebaugh, *International Business: Environments and Operations* (Reading, MA: Addison-Wesley, 1998); and S. Ronen and O. Shenkar, "Clustering Countries on Attitudinal Dimensions: A Review and Synthesis," *Academy of Management Review* 10 (1985), pp. 435–54.

21. Peter Doeringer and Michael Piore provide the standard definition of an internal labor market: "The internal labor market, governed by administrative rule, is to be distinguished from the external labor market of conventional economic theory

214

PART THREE
Aligning Human
Resource Systems
with Business
Strategy

where pricing, allocating, and training decisions are controlled directly by economic variables. These two markets are interconnected, however, and movement between them occurs at certain job classifications which constitute ports of entry and exit from the internal labor market." P. B. Doeringer and M. J. Piore, *Internal Labor Markets and Manpower Analysis* (Lexington, MA: D. C. Heath, 1971).

22. All U.S. data come from the U.S. Bureau of the Census.

23. International Labour Organization, *World Labour Report 1995* (Geneva, Switzerland: Author, 1995).

24. Daniels and Radebaugh, *International Business.*

25. "Comparing Women Around the World," *The Wall Street Journal*, July 26, 1995, p. B1.

26. B. Crossette, "Afghans Draw U.N. Warning over Sex Bias," *The New York Times*, October 8, 1996, p. A1.

27. Daniels and Radebaugh, *International Business,* pp. 69–70.

28. Ibid.

29. D. C. McClelland, *The Achievement Motive* (New York: Appleton-Century-Crofts, 1953).

30. H. G. Gough, "A Work Orientation Scale for the California Psychological Inventory," *Journal of Applied Psychology* 70 (1985), pp. 505–13.

31. R. M. Kanter, "Transcending Business Boundaries: 12,000 World Managers View Change," *Harvard Business Review*, May–June 1991, pp. 151–64.

32. J. J. Lawrence and R. Yeh, "The Influence of Mexican Culture on the Use of Japanese Manufacturing Techniques in Mexico," *Management International Review* 34 (1994), pp. 49–66.

33. D. Wessel, "Up the Ladder: Low Unemployment Brings Lasting Gains to Town in Michigan," *The Wall Street Journal*, June 24, 1997, pp. A1, A13.

34. International Labour Organization, *World Employment 1996/97: National Policies in a Global Context* (Geneva, Switzerland: Author, 1996).

11

The Equal Employment and Labor Relations Environment

All managers need to be aware that equal employment opportunity (EEO) and labor relations laws, guidelines, and country-specific customs affect the choice and implementation of HRM practices. In this chapter you will

- Be introduced to key EEO laws and government guidelines in the United States.
- Acquire a feel for how employment regulations vary across countries.
- See how managers in multinational firms must deal with a unique set of EEO issues.
- Become acquainted with some key labor relations issues that vary across countries.

A jury awarded a former cafeteria manager at the Smithsonian Institution's National Museum of American History $10,000 as compensation for pain and suffering and $390,000 in punitive damages in an age discrimination suit. The manager, who was 54 years old, had been regularly referred to by his apparently younger boss as an "old fart" and had been greeted with "How you doing, old man?" and "Here comes the old man, let's get out the wheelchair."

A prospective lawyer passed the bar exam only to have the state examining committee refuse him admission to the bar, holding that his psychological depression made him unfit to practice law. He filed an Americans with Disability Act (ADA) suit and submitted a psychiatric opinion that he could, in fact, adequately represent clients.

In late 1999 the press reported that some firms were purchasing special computer-monitoring devices to stop the flow of sexually offensive e-mail messages within the firms. One study reported that 85 percent of employers have policies to avert sexual harassment via e-mail.

A jury awarded $120 million in punitive damages to 17 black former employees of a San Francisco bakery that produces Wonder Bread, Twinkies, and Hostess Cupcakes. The plaintiffs claimed they were forced to endure racial epithets, were denied promotions, and were given the worst shifts.

216

PART THREE
Aligning Human
Resource Systems
with Business
Strategy

And in February 2000, Honda Motor Company, along with 17 major Japanese electronics makers, complied for the first time with union requests to extend employment for workers beyond the traditional retirement age in Japan of 60; major steelmakers refused to grant this extension.

Examples such as these appear in the media on a daily basis. They illustrate issues of equal employment opportunity—another contextual factor important for managers to consider in the design, implementation, and evaluation of HRM practices. Knowledge of equal employment opportunity (EEO) and labor relations laws, government guidelines, and country-specific practices affects the strategic decision-making process and the implementation of strategies. All aspects of a firm's human resources activities, such as hiring, promotions, discipline, termination, transfers, training, and compensation, are to some extent influenced and constrained by the equal employment and labor relations environment. In this chapter we do not attempt to provide detailed information on all the important issues and concepts of equal employment opportunity and labor relations. Instead, we wish to instill in the reader an appreciation of key issues, perspectives, and differences managers can expect to see in EEO and labor matters when taking a global perspective.

A firm that operates in more than one country must comply with the legal constraints imposed in the area of EEO and labor relations in each country of operation. Thus, global managers must grapple with a complex web of laws, regulations, and levels of enforcement in formulating and implementing human resource strategies. Managers must not only be knowledgeable of the EEO and labor laws and regulations in the countries in which they operate, but they must also maintain a consistent—or at least coherent—set of practices within the firm. Thus, issues of employee equity perceptions throughout the firm's locations are often a key consideration in global HR management.

In this chapter we provide an overview of the major types of EEO and labor relations laws, guidelines, and issues that managers must consider in managing human resources. After examining key EEO laws and guidelines in the United States, we look at general approaches to EEO and how specific practices might vary across countries. As an example, we consider differences in the regulation of employee termination in various countries across Europe. We then briefly look at some key issues involved in equal employment opportunity in multinational firms, including the effects of U.S. employment law on foreign operations in the United States, the "extraterritorial" application of U.S. labor laws in foreign countries, the existence of *international* equal employment opportunity standards and their implications for global operations, and the existence of host country laws in foreign operations. The final section of the chapter focuses on some key labor relations issues, including levels of unionization across countries, organizing, representation and bargaining, forms of union–management cooperation, and government regulation of labor relations.

AN OVERVIEW OF U.S. EQUAL EMPLOYMENT OPPORTUNITY LAWS AND REGULATIONS

217

CHAPTER ELEVEN
The Equal
Employment and
Labor Relations
Environment

Managers in the United States are constrained in their human resource management strategies, decisions, and practices by a large number of laws, executive orders, and guidelines. We cannot discuss all of these laws and regulations in the present chapter, but we provide an overview of some key laws and EEO issues for managers. We focus most of our attention in this chapter on Title VII of the Civil Rights Act of 1964. Table 11–1 summarizes some additional U.S. laws related to employment.

TABLE 11–1.   Some Additional U.S. Employment Laws

Law	Key Provisions
Norris-LaGuardia Act (1932)	Established a legal right of union membership for employees.
Wagner Act (1935)	Requires employers to collectively bargain over wages, hours, conditions of work if a majority of employees desire representation. Established the National Labor Relations Board (NLRB).
Fair Labor Standards Act (1938)	Set minimum wage, overtime pay, child labor restrictions.
Taft-Hartley Act (1947)	Forbids employers from establishing labor organizations; includes provisions for a union to represent all employees in a bargaining unit when majority of employees vote for it.
Equal Pay Act (1963)	Requires equal pay for men and women doing substantially equal work; exceptions include seniority or merit-based differences.
Vietnam-Era Veterans Readjustment Act (1974)	Forbids discrimination against Vietnam-era veterans, and requires affirmative action; applies to federal contractors and agencies.
Pregnancy Discrimination Act (1978)	Requires policies and benefits for pregnancy and related conditions to be the same as for disabilities.
Family and Medical Leave Act (1993)	Requires employers to provide up to 12 weeks of unpaid leave for family and medical emergencies.

Title VII of the Civil Rights Act of 1964

Arguably the most important EEO law for U.S. managers is Title VII of the Civil Rights Act of 1964, passed by the U.S. Congress as part of President Lyndon Johnson's wide-ranging program designed to promote social justice. Title VII, the section that deals with employment discrimination, applies to most firms employing at least 15 people; it forbids treating employees differently on the basis of race, color, creed, sex, or national origin. Employers must not discriminate in **any** aspect of employment, including such activities as hiring, promotion, pay, termination, benefits, and training. This law has transformed the workplace by opening employment opportunities previously unavailable to many people, including women and African-Americans, in the United States. We now provide an overview of some key components of Title VII and its enforcement.

Potentially illegal discrimination can occur two ways under Title VII.[1] First, employers may engage in **disparate treatment** if they overtly treat people differently or restrict employment opportunities on the basis of race, color, creed, sex, or national origin. For example, a firm placing a newspaper recruitment ad that sought "aggressive, outgoing, self-starting men" for sales work would be engaging in disparate treatment against women. Second, employers create a **disparate impact** on a protected group of people if the firm engages in a practice which, although apparently neutral, **differentially affects** the employment of those in a protected group. For example, if a firm screens out applicants for jobs on the basis of a test "cutoff score," and that cutoff score screens out significantly more blacks than whites, this screening process might have a disparate impact on blacks' employment opportunities. The rule of thumb for computing disparate impact has been the "80 percent rule." For example, if 70 of 100 white applicants for employment (70 percent) are hired by a firm, then *if fewer than* 56 percent (80×70) of the black applicants are hired, the firm's hiring procedures have a disparate impact on black applicants.

It is important to note that the existence of disparate impact does not necessarily constitute an *illegal* activity under Title VII. A finding of disparate impact does **shift the burden of proof** to the employer to defend its practices as "job-related." That is, the employer may be required to provide evidence that the employment practices in question (e.g., the screening test) is in fact **related to successful job performance.** This principle of job-relatedness is an important one for all managers to keep in mind. All policies or techniques used for human resource decisions—including hiring, termination, promotion, and pay—should be in some fashion related to employees' performing of their jobs. To ensure fair treatment of employees and avoid illegal practices, decisions should not be made on the basis of irrelevant factors such as race and sex.

Table 11–2 illustrates the employer's responsibilities in defending itself if charged with disparate treatment or disparate impact. It shows, for example, that after a plaintiff in a discrimination case establishes the prima facie case for disparate impact (e.g., by statistical analysis of applicant

TABLE 11–2. Shifting Burden of Proof in Title VII Cases

219

CHAPTER ELEVEN
The Equal
Employment and
Labor Relations
Environment

Phase I	Phase II
Plaintiff establishes:	Defendant required to:
1. Disparate treatment $\longrightarrow$	1. Explain the nondiscriminatory reason for the disparate treatment
2. Disparate impact $\longrightarrow$	2. Demonstrate the job-relatedness or business necessity of the practice

flows), the burden of proof shifts to the employer. The employer then has the burden of justifying the job-relatedness of the practices or policies involved in the disparate impact.

Employers in certain cases may be legally allowed to discriminate against some groups of people if the screening requirement is a "bona fide occupational qualification," or **BFOQ,** necessary for performing the job. Sex might be a BFOQ for hiring for some jobs, for example, if necessary for purposes of authenticity; consider jobs modeling women's clothing or men's restroom attendants. But both the Title VII enforcement agency (Equal Employment Opportunity Commission) and the courts have tended to interpret the BFOQ provision narrowly, allowing these kinds of BFOQ exceptions only in rare cases. For example, in no cases would race or color be acceptable as a BFOQ for a job. And considerations such as "customer preferences" (e.g., for male employees) or co-worker preferences have been specifically ruled out as constituting valid reasons for a BFOQ. Employers may also defend an apparently discriminatory practice using a **business necessity** argument, arguing that a particular employment practice is necessary for the operation of the business and its survival.

An additional feature of discrimination enforcement under Title VII involves the concept of **reasonable accommodation.** Employers are expected to make "reasonable" efforts to accommodate employees in matters related to their religion, and also related to their disability status under the Americans with Disabilities Act, as we will discuss later. A typical example would be an expectation that employers accommodate in a reasonable fashion Jewish employees' desire for Saturday worship by making schedule adjustments.

Title VII is enforced by the Equal Employment Opportunity Commission (EEOC), which (1) processes discrimination complaints, and (2) issues written regulations relevant to employment practices.[2] The EEOC issues written regulations which are interpretations of Title VII and other statutes, telling employers what the EEOC believes the law requires. Managers often must have at least some familiarity with these guidelines. They typically rely on HR specialists to have knowledge of the details of these guidelines and to provide expert advice. Table 11–3 illustrates the scope and variety of EEOC regulations.

TABLE 11–3. Principal EEOC Regulations

Sex discrimination guidelines

Questions and answers on pregnancy disability and reproductive hazards

Religious discrimination guidelines

National origin discrimination guidelines

Interpretations of the Age Discrimination in Employment Act

Employee selection guidelines

Questions and answers on employee selection guidelines

Sexual harassment guidelines

Recordkeeping and reports

Affirmative action guidelines

EEO in the federal government

Equal Pay Act

Policy statement on maternity benefits

Policy statement on relationship of Title VII to 1986 Immigration Reform and Control Act

Policy statement on reproductive and fetal hazards

Policy statement on religious accommodation under Title VII

Policy guidance on sexual harassment

Source: J. Ledvinka and V. G. Scarpello, *Federal Regulation of Personnel and Human Resource Management,* 2nd ed. (Boston: PWS-Kent, 1991), p. 38. Reprinted with permission of South-Western College Publishing, a division of Thomson Learning. Fax 800-730-2215.

Sexual Harassment under Title VII

Sexual harassment, a pervasive problem in the workplace, is forbidden under Title VII as a type of sex discrimination. The EEOC defines sexual harassment as follows:

> Unwelcome sexual advances, requests for sexual favors and other verbal or physical conduct of a sexual nature constitutes sexual harassment when:
>
> 1. Submission to such conduct is made either explicitly or implicitly a term or condition of an individual's employment,
> 2. Submission to or rejection of such conduct by an individual is used as the basis for employment decisions affecting such individual, or
> 3. Such conduct has the purpose or effect of substantially interfering with an individual's work performance or creating an intimidating, hostile, or offensive working environment.[3]

There are basically two types of sexual harassment, both of which are illegal. First, what is commonly termed **quid pro quo harassment** refers to situations in which sexual behavior is required of an employee as part of getting or keeping some kind of "tangible job benefit" such as being hired, promoted, or given a pay increase. The first two points above relate to quid pro quo harassment. The second type of sexual harassment is commonly referred to as **hostile work environment sexual harassment.** This is a situation in which a hostile or offensive work environment is created and interferes with the victim's performance. This hostile environment may be created by repeated offensive verbal comments, sexual jokes, or even pinup photos in the work setting. The third point above relates to hostile work environment sexual harassment.

221

CHAPTER ELEVEN
The Equal
Employment and
Labor Relations
Environment

There no doubt is considerable ambiguity in particular work situations, as to whether or not illegal sexual harassment is occurring. For assessing the existence of a hostile work environment the courts typically examine questions such as

- How frequent and severe is the behavior?
- Is the behavior threatening or humiliating?
- Is there interference with an employee's work performance?

Managers must be aware of sexual harassment and what they can do to reduce potential liability for it.[4] Typically, managers should

- Establish a written policy forbidding harassment.
- Communicate the policy and train employees.
- Establish an effective complaint procedure.
- Investigate all claims in a timely manner.
- Take remedial action to correct past harassment.

Executive Order 11246 and Revisions

Concurrently with the passage of the Civil Rights Act of 1964, President Lyndon Johnson issued Executive Order (EO) 11246, which forbade discrimination on the part of federal contractors, subcontractors, and federal agencies. Thus, this executive order is similar to Title VII, and it applies to a large number of U.S. employers.

One major difference was that E.O. 11246 also required **affirmative action,** in which covered employers (e.g., contracts of at least $50,000 and at least 50 employees) were required to prepare an annual Affirmative Action Plan.[5] This plan reflected a more aggressive effort to rectify the "underutilization" of various minority groups, including women, within organizations. In effect, affirmative action was designed to "play catch-up"— to achieve accelerated progress in employment opportunities for minorities, in order to make up for many years of past discrimination. In preparing the Affirmative Action Plan, the employer's key activities include

1. Performing an **underutilization analysis,** by determining the discrepancy between the availability of various minorities in the area labor pool compared to the current percentages within the firm.
2. Setting **goals** and **timetables** for increasing the utilization of these minorities within the firm.
3. Implementing **policies** and **programs** to achieve the goals.

222

*PART THREE
Aligning Human
Resource Systems
with Business
Strategy*

The potential sanction for inadequate progress in attaining a firm's goals is cancellation of government contracts. Note that under affirmative action the use of goals and timetables is *not* the same as "quota-hiring." Affirmative action does *not require* a particular percentage of hires or rigid hiring restrictions in order to produce the "correct number of minorities." Nevertheless, some employers may choose to resort to more rigid or quotalike practices in their efforts to reach their hiring goals. This approach could be unfair and legally risky if it results in discrimination (under Title VII) against those in the majority groups.

Clearly, affirmative action has become increasingly controversial, and some firms' attention to required goals and timetables has diminished. But at the same time, many firms in recent years have voluntarily implemented various kinds of **diversity programs,** designed to encourage and support a more diverse, multicultural workforce. Much of the impetus for these programs has come from managers' recognition of the demographic changes in the workforce toward more females and minorities. Diversity programs often include various types of training programs and workshops to increase employees' and managers' sensitivity to diverse cultures, values, and lifestyles. These programs are expected to enhance firms' ability to attract, retain, and maintain the morale of a more diverse population of employees.

Civil Rights Act of 1991

This more recent law is an amendment to Title VII. Some notable features include the opportunity for victims of intentional discrimination to ask for compensatory and punitive damages in jury trials, and the application of Title VII to employees of American firms in foreign countries if they are U.S. citizens.

Age Discrimination in Employment Act (1967)

This law, known as ADEA, forbids discrimination against employees who are 40 years old and older. Its implementation is similar to that for Title VII, including concepts of BFOQ, disparate treatment, and disparate impact. A typical employment issue involving ADEA would be a firm's deliberate "plateauing" of older managers in the company hierarchy. For example, if a 55-year-old manager's upward career progress was halted by the firm, the firm may be required to provide a job-related reason for this decision—a reason **other than** age. In recent years there has been an increase in age discrimination problems and lawsuits in the United States. Because the large cohort of "baby boomers" (born between 1946 and 1964) is aging, a rapidly increasing portion of the working population is over 40 years of age, and thus protected from age discrimination (see Chapter 10).

As we point out throughout this chapter, discrimination and labor laws and practices can vary dramatically in various countries around the world. As an example in the area of age discrimination, in the 1990s one Japanese auto manufacturer, Toyota, specified that its deputy general managers must be 53 years of age or younger; similarly, section chiefs cannot be over the age of 50.[6] As just reported, these practices would be illegal in the United States.

Americans with Disabilities Act (1990)

223

*CHAPTER ELEVEN
The Equal
Employment and
Labor Relations
Environment*

This recent and far-reaching law, known as ADA, protects people with "disabilities" from employment discrimination. Determining who is classified as having a disability can be a complicated issue, and an issue fraught with ambiguity.[7] "Disability" is essentially defined as *a substantial physical or mental impairment that limits a major life activity (e.g., walking, talking).* A person is also protected—considered as having a disability—if he or she has a *past record* of impairment (e.g., past treatment in a mental institution) or is *"regarded" as having* an impairment by others—even if there is no actual impairment. Thus, employees with many different kinds of physical and mental impairments are now protected from discrimination and must be accommodated.

As long as a person with a disability can fulfill the **essential duties** of a job, that person cannot be discriminated against in employment. Employers are also expected to make reasonable accommodations—up to the point where the firm would experience **undue hardship**—for employees with disabilities. As with all the discrimination laws, these reasonable accommodations have to be determined on a case-by-case basis.

To illustrate the actions managers need to consider to comply with ADA, here are a few examples of reasonable accommodations:[8]

1. **Making facilities accessible and usable.** This might include installing ramps at building entrances, making restrooms accessible, or rearranging office furniture and equipment.
2. **Job restructuring.** An employer may be expected to change when or how essential job functions are performed, say, by shifting duties from morning to afternoon or by providing a person who is mentally challenged with a task checklist for remembering the order of job functions.
3. **Modifying work schedules.** This may be appropriate for people who need special medical treatment or who have special transportation schedules.
4. **Acquiring or modifying equipment and devices.** Many devices can allow people to overcome barriers to performing job functions (e.g., an elastic band allowing a person with cerebral palsy to hold a pencil). The applicant is the best source of information about these devices.
5. **Modifying exams, training materials, or policies.** Applicants with learning disabilities may be given extra time to finish a test, or hearing-impaired trainees may be provided with interpreters or note takers.

The Complexity of EEO Regulation

Now that we have surveyed major U.S. EEO laws and guidelines, we want to point out that a broader view of equal employment opportunity encompasses a complex regulatory model. This model includes

1. Laws, government agencies, and regulatory activities related to EEO.
2. The social and political problems which led to this regulatory structure.
3. Management activities implemented to respond to that structure.[9]

Figure 11–1 illustrates the complexity of this regulatory model.

FIGURE 11–1. The regulatory model applied to EEO.

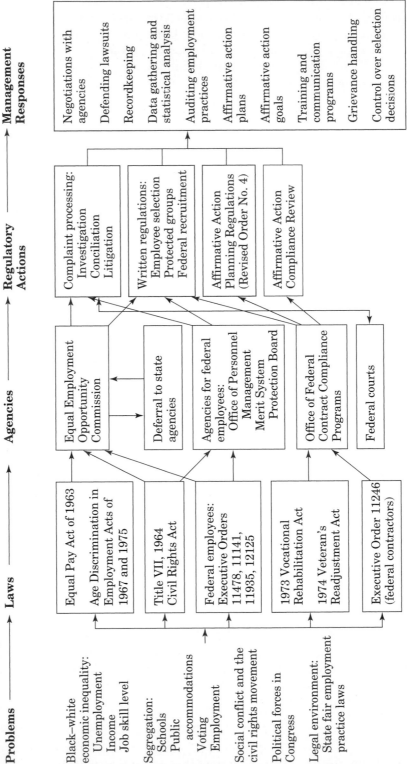

Problems ⟶ **Laws** ⟶ **Agencies** ⟶ **Regulatory Actions** ⟶ **Management Responses**

Source: J. Ledvinka and V. G. Scarpello (1991), *Federal Regulation of Personnel and Human Resource Management,* 2nd ed. Reprinted with permission of South-Western College Publishing, a division of Thomson Learning. Fax 800-730-2215.

INTERNATIONAL EMPLOYMENT REGULATION: VARIABILITY ACROSS COUNTRIES

225

CHAPTER ELEVEN
The Equal
Employment and
Labor Relations
Environment

One of the examples that introduced this chapter reported the decision by certain Japanese firms in early 2000 to extend employment beyond the normal retirement age of 60. This is a stark contrast to the ADEA in the United States, which has removed all mandatory retirement age requirements for most employees. Managers must be aware that basic approaches, values, and philosophies about employment regulation vary widely from country to country around the world. There is no universal model or philosophy of human resource management. These differences can reflect historical and cultural phenomena.[10] In the United States, for example, employment regulation reflects the free enterprise–capitalistic values of the nation.[11] There are no European-style laws about "worker councils" and few worker demands for other group- or class-oriented rights in the United States. Similarly, employers in the United States have had almost complete freedom to employ workers "at will," with few constraints on terminating workers for any reason, although this right has been somewhat eroded in recent years.

Employment law in the United States tends to be most rigorous in requiring employers to deal with employees in a fair and somewhat "objective" fashion, using rational, clearly specified criteria, such as validated tests for hiring and clear performance standards.[12] The U.S. approach also focuses much attention on ridding the workplace of "discrimination" against certain groups in all aspects of employment, as spelled out earlier in this chapter.

Thus, the U.S. approach to employment regulation could be called an individualistic approach, with much autonomy, and with little of the emphasis on class-based rights or paternalism seen in other countries, especially in Europe. Instead, the emphasis is on economic and market criteria for management decisions about employment, and also on the requirement of fairness and objectivity for all employees.

In Japan, as in the United States, the role of culture is apparent in the approach to employment regulation. The Japanese are less legalistic than are Westerners, seeing laws as state-imposed constraints that present a kind of pain or penalty to organizations.[13] Given that Japanese laws were often adapted wholesale from other countries (especially after World War II), there is often a large disparity between the laws as *written* and as *practiced*. Thus, antidiscrimination laws would be likely to fail if not compatible with the realities of Japanese life and employment practices. Japanese managers also have a strong preference for conciliation and mediation as opposed to legal resolution of disputes.

European countries take a different approach to regulation of employment. While U.S. antidiscrimination legislation protects the rights of women, ethnic minorities, religious groups, and others, Europe has directed its legislation mostly toward women.[14] Although there are many countries with significant numbers of ethnic minorities, only Britain extends equal opportunity to race. European countries also tend to forbid preference programs, in contrast to the affirmative action programs of the United States.

Instead of preferences, European nations provide government-financed training programs and encouragement of special recruiting efforts for

226

PART THREE
Aligning Human
Resource Systems
with Business
Strategy

women. But most European countries, while employing significant percentages of women in the overall workforce, experience very low representation of women outside traditional female occupations (e.g., secretary, nurse). For example, it has been reported that Marks & Spencer, the leading British retailer, recently had no women among its top executives, even though 85 percent of its employees are women.[15] Similarly, in Sweden, the labor force of 4.4 million is equally split between men and women, but few women work in traditionally male jobs.

Managers in Europe have much less autonomy than U.S. managers in employment matters. For example, Belgium recently passed a law forbidding all new forms of pay beyond that set by nationally negotiated labor agreements, in order to control inflation and promote egalitarian values. In Europe, managers often must comply with HR decisions made at the national level through industrywide agreements or employers and union associations. Governments also tend to dictate funds to be spent on training—and even which employees are to receive the training.[16]

It is important to recognize, however, that very substantial differences can exist in both the nature and the application of employment laws even within a region such as the European Union. Managers doing business anywhere in Europe must have a clear idea of the country-by-country differences.[17] Consider the issue of employee termination. As mentioned earlier, the right of employers to terminate employees is much more restricted in most European countries than in the United States. This type of constraint emanates both from laws and from broad collective bargaining agreements. Employers must typically provide substantial justification of the reasons for termination of employment. These reasons, which are sometimes specifically codified, include worker "redundancy," financial or economic considerations, and various kinds of employee performance problems or rule transgressions. Employers must usually provide some form of written notice in advance of the termination. Employees have substantial opportunities for due process in making charges of unfair termination. In general, there is little of the free-ranging "employment at will" which still characterizes most employment in the United States.

Table 11–4 lists some key features of termination constraints in selected European countries. Of course, this illustration cannot be considered a precise comparison of the termination laws and guidelines in these countries. Our purpose here is to provide a sense of both the flavor and the variability of laws related to this particular human resource issue.

EQUAL EMPLOYMENT ISSUES IN MULTINATIONAL FIRMS[18]

Many managers nowadays are faced with the challenge of doing business overseas and managing human resources globally. Earlier in this chapter we provided an overview of U.S. equal employment opportunity laws and

227

CHAPTER ELEVEN
The Equal
Employment and
Labor Relations
Environment

TABLE 11–4. Key Aspects of Restrictions on Termination of Employment in Various European Countries

Country	Policy
Belgium	Employer and employee free to terminate employment unilaterally, with a reasonable notice period.
Czech Republic	Employer can terminate employees only for specific reasons stated by law. These include plant closing, restructuring, employee health problem, performance deficiency (if 12 months advance, written notice of need for improvement).
Denmark	Determined by collective bargaining. Dismissal of salaried employees and those with over nine months service usually requires good reason—typically based on economic considerations.
Finland	Employers cannot terminate for employee conduct unless grounds are serious; can terminate for financial reasons, if no relocation is possible.
France	Employee must have a "real and substantial" reason, which is often decided by certain tribunals.
Germany	Employer's notice of termination must be "socially justified," that is, based on conduct (e.g., alcohol abuse), personal factors (e.g., lack of qualifications), or business factors (e.g., redundancy).
Ireland	Employees who have one year of continuous service protected from "unfair dismissal," meaning reasons other than job competence, employee conduct, or redundancy.
Switzerland	Employers and employees can terminate employment unilaterally, as long as notice is given. Dismissal may be considered "wrongful" in certain specified cases (e.g., race, gender-based, tied to union activity).

Source: The information for preparing this table was obtained from Trowers and Hamlins (ed.), *European Employment Law: A Country by Country Guide* (Burr Ridge, IL: Financial Times/Irwin, 1995).

guidelines. These laws and guidelines may or may not be relevant for global HRM. If the firm is based in the United States, the manager may need to deal with

1. U.S. labor and employment laws and regulations that apply to U.S. businesses.
2. U.S. labor laws as applied to foreign direct investors.
3. The "extraterritorial" application of U.S. laws applied to U.S. companies doing business in another country.
4. International employment law as it affects global operations.
5. The role of host country laws in foreign operations.

U.S. Employment Law and Global Operations

Employment laws of the United States may have a bearing on overseas operations, especially in parity or "equity" issues involving group and individual benefits for employees in host and foreign locations and whether or not disparities in these benefits meet legal requirements. For example, pay or training disparities between managers in U.S. and foreign operations may need to be justified under EEO laws.

The "form" of business can be very important in determining whether U.S. laws apply to *foreign direct investors* in the United States. One recent U.S. Supreme Court case held that a foreign wholly owned subsidiary incorporated in the United States was subject to U.S. labor laws. However, many questions remain in other situations, such as *unincorporated* divisions or branches of foreign companies.

Extraterritorial Application of U.S. Employment Laws

Although there are exceptions, most U.S. labor and employment laws do not extend to global operations and employees operating in foreign locations. Most U.S. laws regulate only the U.S. operations of the U.S.–based parent company. Of course, because of the importance of equity perceptions (see Chapter 2), there may be good reason to create parallel and consistent HRM practices for employees at home and abroad, especially if the firm tends to rotate employees back into the parent company's operations.

An exception to this general lack of extraterritoriality is U.S. nondiscrimination legislation, which forbids discrimination on the basis of race, color, creed, sex, national origin, age, and disability. The Age Discrimination in Employment Act (ADEA) in 1984 defined "employee" to include citizens of the United States employed by an employer in a workplace in a foreign country, while "employer" was defined to include a U.S. firm, or a foreign branch of a U.S. firm, or a foreign corporation controlled by a U.S. firm. More recent laws extended beyond U.S. boundaries are the Civil Rights Act of 1991 (CRA) and the Americans with Disabilities Act of 1990 (ADA), both discussed earlier in this chapter. The CRA explicitly applies the law (forbidding discrimination on the basis of race, color, creed, sex, and national origin) to citizen-employees who work outside the United States for the covered employer, including foreign companies controlled by the U.S. company.

Managers of human resources should also be aware that extraterritorial application of U.S. discrimination laws can have an impact on U.S. operations. They will likely need to be able to document key decisions (e.g., selection and promotion decisions) for employees sent to foreign locations, just as they do within the United States. Compensation disparities for U.S. versus foreign employees may also need to be justified. There are still many complicated legal issues involved in global HRM, such as the potential rights of U.S. citizen-employees to sue firms under foreign laws, and the possibility that a U.S. law may be "excused" when there is compliance with the foreign law. Clearly, global HR managers must carefully consider how business decisions and human resource policies affect or are affected by U.S. equal employment laws, including both domestic and overseas operations.

229

CHAPTER ELEVEN
The Equal
Employment and
Labor Relations
Environment

International Equal Employment Law and Global Operations

Global HR managers must also consider how laws outside U.S. boundaries may affect global operations. Local laws within foreign countries may be influenced by historic periods (e.g., U.S. labor law in Japan), traditions of civil versus common law, and secular versus religious laws. But along with local influences on foreign employment law, there are international and regional employment laws. In addition to treaties, international employment law standards primarily have grown out of the International Labor Organization (ILO), an agency of the United Nations, and the UN's own human rights covenants, which apply to all member nations. The ILO has adopted more than 170 conventions establishing labor standards dealing with numerous issues including unemployment and employment of women and children. These are not binding obligations, however, until they are ratified by member states and then enacted into local law.

Some employment standards may also be enforced by trading companies, indirectly, under international agreements like the General Agreement on Tariffs and Trade (GATT). Global managers may also need to pay attention to the laws and regulations of *regional organizations*, such as the European Economic Community (EEC) and the Organizations for Economic Cooperation and Development (OECD), which provide important voluntary guidelines for multinationals in areas including employment standards.

Managers should also be aware that some *U.S. trade laws* enforce internationally recognized employment standards. The major law in this area is the U.S. Generalized System of Preferences (GSP), designed to promote increased exports from foreign countries via favorable tariff and custom rates to qualifying countries. Thus, international employment standards must be considered by HR managers operating in foreign countries. Foreign investments can be affected by local laws, but local business conditions may also be used as a reason for U.S. laws to come into play to cut off investment services, loans, or guarantees.

When operating in foreign countries, in addition to laws and regulations, managers must consider whether local governments actually *enforce* these laws in a meaningful way. It is not unusual for developing countries to adopt international standards for prestige and trading advantages, only to underfund and fail to enforce these laws and standards.

Host Country Laws

Laws of the host country also have a significant effect on managing human resources, and they are especially important in deciding whether to locate operations overseas. These laws might include legal requirements placing financial obligations on employers for employee hiring, layoffs, or plant

230

PART THREE
Aligning Human
Resource Systems
with Business
Strategy

closings. Host countries may also impose restrictions on management decisions concerning hiring, disciplining, and terminating staff (as noted earlier in this chapter). Moreover, immigration laws in host countries may restrict expatriates from the home country from work on foreign soil. Before beginning operations in a host country, managers should carefully evaluate legal constraints on the major human resource decisions and activities.

A GLOBAL PERSPECTIVE ON LABOR RELATIONS

In this section we focus on several labor relations issues that are particularly relevant to the work of global managers of human resources: variations in unionization "density" across countries, union organizing and representation issues across countries, bargaining issues, some forms of union–management cooperation, and the extent of government regulation of labor relations.

Some General Points about International Labor Relations

As we reported at the beginning of this chapter, our purpose in the chapter is to instill an appreciation of key issues, perspectives, and differences across countries that managers of human resources can expect to see. Thus, we take the advice of Dowling, Schuler, and Welch in considering some general points about labor relations from an international perspective.[19]

We begin by acknowledging the difficulty of comparing labor relations systems and behavior across national boundaries, particularly because the meaning of key concepts change considerably from one context—one country—to another. Even a basic concept such as "collective bargaining" may mean different things in different countries. In the United States it means negotiations between a labor union local and management, whereas in Sweden and Germany the term refers to negotiations between an employers' organization and a trade union at the industry level.[20] Collective bargaining also is often viewed by European unions as a kind of ideological class struggle between labor and management, whereas U.S. unions take a more pragmatic economic view of collective bargaining.

Another difficulty arises because no industrial relations system can be understood without an appreciation of its historical origin. Historical differences, for example, are reflected in the structures of trade unions, which differ considerably among countries. They include industrial unions, representing all employees in an industry; craft unions, based on skilled occupational groups across industries; conglomerate unions, which represent workers in several different industries; and general unions, open to almost all employees in a country. If multinational managers of human resources are unfamiliar with local industry and its history and political conditions, they may have difficulty resolving conflicts that local firms would be able to resolve. It is also important that industrial relations policies be flexible enough to adapt to local requirements.

As an example of historical trends, the United States is characterized by an "adversarial" relationship between labor and management. Labor unions and management meet for direct negotiations on contracts and labor issues (as contrasted with European "employer associations"). The concerns of U.S. labor unions are typically monetary or directly work-related, reflecting the U.S. tradition of business unionism.[21] American labor unions for a long time have accepted "free market economy" values and the rights of ownership, and the government rarely involves itself in labor negotiations.

231

CHAPTER ELEVEN
The Equal
Employment and
Labor Relations
Environment

Variation in Unionization across Countries

"Union density" rates—the percentage of employees who are union members—vary greatly across countries. Table 11–5 displays union density rates from 1970 to 1988 in selected countries. The United States has one of the lowest rates of union density, at least partially reflecting deeply rooted managerial values of union avoidance. Union members are found mostly in traditional industries such as steel and auto manufacturing.[22] Thus, U.S. managers are likely to have less experience with unions than managers in other Western countries.

However, a significant development in global HRM is the overall diminished power of trade unions, including shrinking membership for most trade unions in western Europe and the United States in the decade of the 1980s. Industrial areas of western Europe that are traditional bastions of union membership have seen a strong trend toward individualism.[23] The number of blue-collar workers who formerly comprised the vast majority of union

TABLE 11–5. Aggregate Union-Density Rates for Selected Countries, 1970–1988

	Union Density					Change in Density		OECD Rank Order*	
	1970	1975	1980	1985	1988	1970–80	1980–88	1970	1988
Australia	52[h]	51[a]	49[b]	46[c]	42	NA	−14[f]	NA	11
Canada[d]	31[e]	34	35	36	35	13	−1.4	16	14
France	22	23	19	16	12	−15	−37	19	24
Germany	33	37	37	37	34	12	−8.6	15	15
Italy	36	47	49	42	40	36	−20	13	13
Japan[d]	35	34	31	30	27	−11	−14	14	17
Sweden	68	74	80	84	85	18	6.6	1	1
UK	45	48	51	46	42	13	−18	11	12
USA	NA	23	23	18	16[g]	NA	−29	NA	22

*Rank order of 20 OECD countries in 1970, but 24 in 1988.

Notes: a. 1976; b. 1982; c. 1986; d. recorded membership; e. 1971; f. 1982–88; g. 1989; h. BLS unpublished series January 1991.

Source: P. J. Dowling, R. S. Schuler, and D. E. Welch, *International Dimensions of Human Resource Management* (2nd ed.). Belmont, CA: Wadsworth, 1994, p. 189. Reprinted with permission.

232

PART THREE
Aligning Human
Resource Systems
with Business
Strategy

members is shrinking, while the number of nonunionized white-collar workers in the service sector is growing. Although this trend might appear to be an advantage for HR managers, it can cause problems in countries where managers are accustomed to centralized collective bargaining. Bargaining partners who no longer represent the majority of labor cannot guarantee that bargaining results will be accepted by all or most employees.[24]

Union organizing and representation in the other industrialized nations of the world is quite different from the United States. For example, except for Great Britain, the European Economic Community (EEC) countries do not have mechanisms for workers to vote on representation. Instead, in these countries there is national-level recognition. Workers outside the United States also tend not to have "exclusive" representation by a union.[25] In a number of European countries, managers may need to deal with several unions in the workplace, each with somewhat different agendas. Some unions in Europe even have religious affiliations.

Bargaining is an area in which the United States is also unique. Thousands of local U.S. unions bargain over the details of contracts setting members' wages, while managers determine the wages for nonunion workers. In most of the rest of the world, however, bargaining tends to be **centralized**, with nationwide or industrywide agreements that have the force of law. For example, French and German unions negotiate industrywide or regional agreements; the ministries of labor can extend these agreements to nonunion workers.[26] In Italy, unions sometimes bargain with the government on social concerns, with employer associations at the industry level on economic concerns, and at the plant level for working conditions.[27]

Various countries around the world have developed different approaches to enhance union–management cooperation. It is common in western European countries to require employee involvement in a firm's strategic decisions.[28] One notable example is the implementation of **works councils** in Germany. Similarly, in the Japanese steel and auto industries there are a number of enterprise-level labor councils.[29] Industrial democracy has developed to a much higher degree in industrialized countries other than the United States. This might also include worker-owned cooperatives, worker input into management selection, and other types of union consultation.

Government Regulation

Government regulations usually play a strong role in a country's labor relations. Government regulations in the United States have been described as "intensive, detailed and controlling" when the government is involved—but the areas of involvement are not extensive at all.[30] For example, the National Labor Relations Board (NLRB) establishes precisely which workers can be part of a bargaining unit. But government involvement is not extensive to the point that management cannot keep control over key strategic decisions, such as plant location or investments. In contrast, the German government's intervention is much more extensive. The government sets up a broad framework with interlocking webs of influence. Company ownership may be concentrated in the hands of a few banks, other social legislation limits managerial options, and centralized bargaining structures set wages for an entire industry or region. Any single firm would have great difficulty adopting its own strategy to manage its workforce.[31]

233

CHAPTER ELEVEN
*The Equal
Employment and
Labor Relations
Environment*

CONCLUSION

Knowledge of equal employment opportunity and labor relations laws and practices is important for managers' strategic decisions and the implementation of these decisions. In this chapter we provided an overview of key equal employment opportunity and labor relations issues from an international perspective. We emphasized differing constraints, philosophies, and practices managers could expect to see in various parts of the world. Because of this variability across countries, managers of human resources will likely be required to develop specific knowledge and skill sets for operating in particular geographic regions.

CONTINUOUS LEARNING: SOME NEXT STEPS

Monitoring and managing within the context of a company's regulatory environment creates real challenges for the general manager. These challenges come about because legal concepts and principles can vary greatly across countries, are subject to legislative and case law changes, and at times are so complex that only full-time legal professionals can stay current and properly briefed. The following next steps can serve to update the material presented in this chapter and help managers prepare for the legal challenges they will confront when allocating scarce resources and opportunities to employees. We hope this will help you know when you don't know enough—and when to decide to seek legal counsel.

- Take a look at www.lawcrawler.com. This site lets you search the Internet for court case summaries and articles about legal issues. Use this site to remind yourself about the international scope of employment and labor law. Searches at this site can be focused on a specific country. Go to two or three countries that interest you and search for information about topics such as age discrimination and sexual harassment.
- Consider a few companies that interest you as potential employers. Go to Wall Street Research Net (www.wsrn.com) and research each in terms of any recent publicity over employment discrimination complaints or related court decisions.
- The U.S. Department of Labor provides a great deal of statutory and regulatory information. Go to www.dol.gov and explore the home pages and associated links of Department of Labor agencies. Where is it most likely that information useful to the middle manager or executive will be located? What types of summaries or "briefing" might an executive request from HR staff professionals that could be produced from U.S. Department of Labor data?
- Perform an Internet search to learn about a labor union that is likely to affect the management of people in a company you have an interest in joining. For example, go to www.aflcio.org to learn about the policies and current issues of concern for this union. For assistance in finding related sites, go to the Union Resource Network (www.unions.org) and review the index of union websites.

1. R. D. Arvey and R. H. Faley, *Fairness in Selecting Employees* (Reading, MA: Addison-Wesley, 1988).
2. J. Ledvinka and V. G. Scarpello, *Federal Regulation of Personnel and Human Resource Management,* 2nd ed. (Boston: PWS-Kent, 1991).
3. *Sexual Harassment Manual for Managers and Supervisors* (Chicago: Commerce Clearing House, 1991).
4. Ibid.
5. *Equal Employment Opportunity Manual for Managers and Supervisors,* 2nd ed. (Chicago: Commerce Clearing House, 1991).
6. A. Pollack, "Toyota Has Decided to Set Age Limits on Its Managers," *The New York Times*, October 25, 1994, p. D16.
7. *ADA Training Manual for Managers and Supervisors* (Chicago: Commerce Clearing House, 1992).
8. Ibid.
9. Ledvinka and Scarpello, *Federal Regulation of Personnel.*
10. R. Pieper, "Human Resource Management as a Strategic Factor." In R. Pieper (ed.), *Human Resource Management: An International Comparison* (Berlin: Walter de Gruyter, 1990), pp. 1–26.
11. B. Springer and S. Springer, "Human Resource Management in the U.S.-Celebration of Its Centenary." In R. Pieper (ed.), *Human Resource Management: An International Comparison* (Berlin: Walter de Gruyter, 1990), pp. 41–60.
12. Ibid.
13. J. M. Bergeson and Y. Oba, "Japan's New Equal Employment Opportunity Law: Real Weapon or Heirloom Sword?" In P. Burstein (ed.), *Equal Employment Opportunity: Labor Market Discrimination and Public Policy* (New York: Aldine de Gruyter, 1994), pp. 357–65.
14. G. T. Milkovich and J. W. Boudreau, *Human Resource Management,* 8th ed. (Burr Ridge, IL: Irwin, 1997).
15. Ibid.
16. Ibid.
17. Trowers and Hamlins (ed.), *European Employment Law: A Country by Country Guide* (Burr Ridge, IL: Financial Times/Irwin, 1995).
18. Much of the material in this section is drawn from R. C. Brown, "Employment and Labor Law Considerations in International Human Resource Management." In O. Shenkar (ed.), *Global Perspectives of Human Resource Management* (Englewood Cliffs, NJ: Prentice Hall, 1995), pp. 37–59.
19. P. J. Dowling, R. S. Schuler, and D. E. Welch, *International Dimensions of Human Resource Management,* 2nd ed. (Belmont, CA: Wadsworth, 1994).
20. Ibid.
21. Springer and Springer, "Human Resource Management."
22. Ibid.
23. Pieper, "Human Resource Management."
24. Ibid.
25. J. A. Fossum, *Labor Relations: Development, Structure, Process,* 5th ed. (Burr Ridge, IL: Irwin, 1992).
26. Milkovich and Boudreau, *Human Resource Management.*
27. Fossum, *Labor Relations.*
28. Milkovich and Boudreau, *Human Resource Management.*
29. Fossum, *Labor Relations.*
30. Milkovich and Boudreau, *Human Resource Management,* p. 591.
31. Ibid.

Part IV

Designing Human Resource Systems for Specific Business Situations

As we noted in the preface, in Part IV we describe five unique business settings and we then prescribe a set of interrelated HRM practices that fit each setting. We selected the five settings to provide a wide range of examples, calling for very different IIRM prescriptions. As explained in Chapter 1 and illustrated in Figure 1–1, the proper mix of HRM practices depends on how work processes are organized and the unique environmental circumstances surrounding a given firm. We emphasize that the illustrations in Part IV demonstrate a **process** managers should follow when making judgments about the quality of existing HR systems or proposed improvements that come from internal HR staff or consultants. Given that we illustrate a process, we acknowledge that our particular choices of practices in the five illustrations are not "set in stone" but instead are matters for discussion.

In each illustration we will prescribe integrated HR systems that fit targeted job classes for companies with particular business strategies that are operating in particular business environments. Rather than identifying a company by name and describing its characteristics and circumstances, we will use multiple sources to create company composites. We will draw from the popular press, the research literature, and our consulting and executive education experiences to create very realistic but hypothetical situations.

As you consider our five illustrations, we encourage you to take up the issue of congruence of the recommended HR systems, as presented in Chapter 9: Have *enough forces* been focused on this firm's target behaviors? Is there any potential *conflict* among the recommended staffing, reward, and development practices? Are interrelated HRM practices sufficiently *supportive* of each other? Remember that it is this interrelated set of HR practices that is difficult for other firms to copy which makes HRM a source of sustained competitive advantage.

ILLUSTRATION 1

Human Resource Systems for the Customer Contact Tier

Two things will happen in each illustration in this final section of the book: First, we will stress HR system integration. By focusing on a particular company, a targeted set of jobs, and associated environmental and strategic factors, it will be possible to simultaneously consider a complementary set of staffing, development, reward, and performance-management practices that **together** will likely accomplish the desired objectives. Second, we will use the decision-making process presented in Figure 1–1 as a conceptual map. Each illustration will consider how business strategy and technology lead to a prescribed way to organize work processes. Based on the way work is organized for a targeted set of jobs, we will then derive the key employee behaviors and the associated KSAs that will be required in such a situation. The relevant labor market and legal context will then be taken into account as we move to develop the appropriate HR system.

THE TARGETED JOB CLASS: CUSTOMER SERVICE REPRESENTATIVE

The job class we examine in this illustration is a class that exists within many types of service organizations. It is a class that is expanding rapidly because of available technology and the realization that service quality may make the difference between success and failure in today's competitive business environment. Following the terminology of Schneider and Bowen,[1] it is a class at the "boundary tier" of the service organization. This tier is shown as having permeable boundaries, susceptible to influence from the coordination tier above and the customer tier below.[2] The people in the boundary tier spend much of their time interacting with customers while responding to a system devised by managers to deliver service quality.

To illustrate the types of positions we have in mind, and to point out the speed with which the business environment is changing, consider the following examples. First consider a British bank, First Direct, a bank with a million customers and no branch offices. In the mid-1990s it was the world's largest telephone-only bank and the fastest growing bank in Britain.[3] At this bank, customers do not interact face-to-face with employees—they pay bills, buy stock, and arrange and pay mortgages by calling customer service representatives (CSRs, or "bankers"). The phone lines are open 24 hours a day, seven days a week. This approach represents a very inexpensive way to grow by eliminating the high cost of opening and operating branch offices while relying on the low-tech telephone and an existing network of automated teller machines. The workplace for the CSRs, technicians, and

238

*PART FOUR
Designing Human
Resource Systems
for Specific
Business
Situations*

officers of the bank is a large, almost warehouselike structure, where more than 24,000 calls a day are handled at peak times by 150 bankers. The CSRs work alone at work stations that, in addition to the telephone, are very much high-tech. The CSRs have access to instant customer account and credit records. This is the environment for customer service representatives that is being replicated over and over again in industry after industry.

Another illustration is a U.S.–based company familiar to readers who have joined a music or video club with Columbia House. Part of this company's strategic business plan is to provide exceptional customer service. Columbia House distributes music videos, tapes, and similar products to customers who make purchasing decisions from their homes or offices. The company has no retail stores, only large distribution and customer service centers. Just like the First Direct example, Columbia House employs large numbers of customer service representatives. These individuals respond to written customer orders and inquiries, inquiries directed to the company's website, and they also work directly with customers who call toll-free service lines. These CSRs, like their banking counterparts, have instant access to customer accounts via state-of-the-art information systems.

Positions very much like the positions of First Direct and Columbia House exist in many organizations, across almost all industries. As another example, consider that the manuscript of this book is being prepared on a Sony notebook computer. Sony, like virtually all of its competitors, provides customers around the world with 24-hour-a-day, seven-day-a-week access to what is often termed a "Customer Response Center." Supporting material from Sony points out that the purpose of the center is to put the customer in touch with the right person—the person who can answer the customer's question or solve the customer's problem *at the time* the question arises.

For the remainder of this illustration we will be focusing on the CSR job class—the customer-oriented positions so often found in contemporary organizations. We will describe a hypothetical company and its environmental circumstances. This company, of course, employs a large number of CSRs. This class of employees is the target for our prescribed HR system. After describing the company's corporate and business strategy, the technology that drives the design of work processes for CSRs, the company's immediate labor market, and the legal context that relates to HRM practice, we will prescribe the HR system that should promote the display of behaviors required of high-performing CSRs. This same approach is used, with different targeted job classes, for all of the remaining illustrations in the book.

BUSINESS STRATEGY AND TECHNOLOGY: HOME ENTERTAINMENT SERVICES

Our illustrative company, Home Entertainment Services (HES), looks very much like Columbia House. It is a company that sees excellent customer service as being central to its long-term survival and growth. The very nature of the business—providing customers with video and audio entertainment products through the convenience of home shopping—requires special attention to individualized customer service. The company believes that, in addition to the use of state-of-the-art technology, the continuous improvement of customer service depends on a highly skilled and committed workforce. Thus, the processes and procedures used to select, reward, and train individuals who have direct contact with customers must be of very high quality.

It is interesting to attempt to classify this type of company from a business strategy perspective. For example, using the Gubman (1998) framework described in Chapter 8 (i.e., **operations-, customer-,** or **product-oriented** companies), we might be tempted to classify this as a "customer-oriented" organization. Customer service is certainly central to this company's business model. However, this company is primarily about providing consistent, high-quality service, at a very competitive price. This company competes by providing customers with very competitive prices on music and video products. They also provide customers with the convenience of being able to shop at home, using mail order, phone, or web-based ordering options along with the home delivery of products. In many ways, this resembles the operations-oriented company described by Gubman. The core competency for HES is probably not in-depth relationship building.

One way to help resolve this classification issue is to consider another key point developed by Gubman. He argues that while one strategic focus will typically become the lead focus, all high-performing companies must be very good at all three areas represented by his framework. That is, high-performing operations companies must execute their lead strategy with exceptional skill. However, these firms must also be very good at meeting customer needs and demonstrating appropriate levels of innovation. For example, being innovative is very important to HES because this type of business model is now spreading rapidly to web-based ordering and distribution systems for a wide variety of products and services (e.g., Amazon.com)—thus HES will need to carefully consider what new directions to take the business. The company already is moving to become a web-based distributor of computer software products and services. Thus, we would classify HES to be an operations company—but an operations company that relies on technology and well-trained CSRs to provide very good customer service. The ability to provide individualized customer service comes from the use of technology and information system sophistication—not from the building of one-on-one personal relationships. Even though this is an operations company, the HRM practices for the customer-service area of this business will need to take on characteristics that may be appropriate in some customer-oriented companies. These practices may not apply to the company's highly automated distribution centers or to the staff responsible for taking the business into new product and service realms. The point here is the point we have made throughout this book—HRM practices must be designed to take into account the unique circumstances surrounding a particular set of job classes. In fact, it is technology that is the prime driver of job design in the customer-service sector of this company. It is to this technology that we now turn our attention.

240

*PART FOUR
Designing Human
Resource Systems
for Specific
Business
Situations*

The work of the CSR is organized around existing technology. To handle millions of calls and incoming requests via the Internet, high-tech information systems are utilized. These systems allow CSRs to pull up complete records on customers within seconds of initiating the telephone or Internet-based exchange. The technology is centralized so that approximately 250 CSRs can be on line at peak custom-demand times. The CSRs work alone at well-appointed work stations, using telephone headsets and the typical keyboard and computer monitor. The CSRs talk with customers and have access to software that allows for semiautomated written correspondence. For example, if the work with the customer requires the preparation of a reply letter, the CSR can access prewritten paragraphs and very rapidly construct an appropriate written reply. A few keystrokes will initiate the printing and mailing of the completed document—a process that is carried out in the printing/mailing center, located in a building separate from the customer service center. The important point to note here is that the organization of work is largely determined by available technology, software, and the design principles used in constructing work stations.

KEY EMPLOYEE BEHAVIORS AND CRITICAL EMPLOYEE ATTRIBUTES

A job analysis has revealed that the work of the CSR can be characterized by a common sequence of duties and activities. First, CSRs process incoming calls and correspondence. While working "live" with HES customers, CSRs access and review relevant information about the customer's account. This requires the review and updating of files and the occasional review of the customer's complaint or correspondence history. Once the nature of the inquiry has been determined, CSRs then gather other relevant information required to process the customer's request. Finally, CSRs perform specified transactions to meet customer needs or, in some instances, to provide unique services to address unusual or infrequently occurring customer concerns.

The results of the job analysis also demonstrate that certain knowledge, skills, and abilities are central to being an effective CSR. Some of the most critical KSAs are listed and described as follows:

1. **Reading ability:** The ability to read, comprehend, and follow complex written instructions.
2. **Customer sensitivity:** Skill in perceiving and reacting sensitively to the needs of customers.
3. **Mathematical/computational skills:** Skill at using basic arithmetic to add, subtract, divide, and multiply monetary figures; skill at translating verbal or written statements into mathematical expressions for the purpose of solving customer problems related to billing or account statements (e.g., discount questions or tax rate questions).
4. **Stress tolerance:** The ability to perform under pressure and when facing opposition—that is, to communicate with angry and/or confused customers while remaining calm.

241

*ILLUSTRATION ONE
Human Resource
Systems for
the Customer
Contact Tier*

5. **Written communication skills:** Aptitude for writing—using proper punctuation, syntax, and spelling to express ideas clearly in writing using proper grammatical form.

6. **Oral communication skills:** Facility for verbally expressing ideas with clarity, while using appropriate tone, grammar, and level of professionalism; being able to listen and ask probing questions while not offending or criticizing the customer; conveying a friendly and concerned manner during conversations with customers.

7. **Problem analysis skills:** Ability to seek out pertinent data and information and to determine the source of a problem or complaint.

8. **Judgment:** Ability to reach logical conclusions based on available information and procedural standards.

In addition to these KSAs, a great deal of company-specific knowledge must be learned after joining the company. Rules, codes, and much technical information about HES procedures and practices must be acquired through extensive company-provided training. Along with the capacity to work as an effective CSR, employees must have the motivation to accept job assignments, attend work regularly and on time, undertake additional training, and exert effort to provide the highest quality customer service.

Before we say more about motivation, however, we need to develop our ideas about a prescribed reward system for HES. Understanding motivation requires an understanding of the rewards and outcomes associated with a particular situation and organizational culture. After considering the relevant labor market and legal context facing HES, we will begin our review of the appropriate HR system for HES by considering prescribed reward and compensation practices.

LABOR-MARKET ATTRIBUTES

The primary distribution and customer service facilities for HES are located in a midwestern city of the United States with a population of approximately 300,000. This community is served by a state university (with a student body of over 15,000), a community/technical college, and a private college which focuses on engineering and technology at both the undergraduate and graduate levels. Graduates of the public high schools vary greatly in terms of academic achievement.

This community also is approximately a one-hour drive from a large metropolitan area. While there is a manufacturing base in this region of the United States, many high-paying manufacturing jobs have been replaced with lower paying service sector jobs. High-paying positions (with benefits) are in very short supply for individuals possessing only a high school education. It is interesting to note that a large proportion of the area's high school graduates do not go on to college.

For a variety of reasons related to the unique realities of this community and its surrounding labor market, many applicants respond each time a customer service position becomes available. Relative to entry-level positions in other companies (requiring similar skill and experience), the HES

242

*PART FOUR
Designing Human
Resource Systems
for Specific
Business
Situations*

customer service jobs provide an attractive mix of pay and benefits. They also can provide both full- and part-time opportunities for college students who need to work evening and night shifts. This pool of talent is very diverse with respect to age, race, ethnicity, and gender.

THE LEGAL ENVIRONMENT

Because of its location, this company must abide by a number of state as well as national labor and employment laws. In addition, some workers are represented by unions, although the customer service area has not yet been unionized. Thus, HR systems are regulated by federal and state laws that relate to employment (e.g., Title VII of the Civil Rights Act, Age Discrimination in Employment Act, Americans with Disabilities Act), compensation (e.g., Fair Labor Standards Act, Equal Pay Act), and labor relations (e.g., National Labor Relations Act). For full reviews of these employment and labor laws we suggest that you read the comprehensive text of Witney and Taylor.[4]

THE PRESCRIBED HR SYSTEM

In presenting our prescribed HR system we purposefully consider the components in a particular order. First, the reward/compensation system is described. This component follows naturally from the way work is designed—the work processes that are congruent with the company's business strategy and associated production technologies. Reward system design must be addressed first because we need this information before we can make informed decisions about other HR system components. For example, as discussed in Chapter 2, the performance-related work outcomes provided to workers by a company must be taken into account when explaining or predicting employee motivation to engage in various activities. Making informed staffing decisions (e.g., identifying job candidates who will accept job offers, be motivated to participate in continuous training experiences, and focus on satisfying the customer) requires that we compare the reward properties associated with jobs with the value/interest profiles (valence perceptions) of job candidates. Following from Chapter 2, the staffing system will need to identify candidates who have high valence perceptions for available performance-related work outcomes.

The way the reward system is designed will have implications for the form and structure of training programs (e.g., will there be sufficient incentives to encourage employees to be motivated learners?). Training program prerequisites and demands will, in turn, relate to staffing practices. Therefore, before the company hires someone, there needs to be relevant information about the work and training settings to which the new employee will be assigned.

Considering the choices outlined in Chapter 3 and the standard framework provided by compensation theorists and scholars,[5] we will develop the pay system by considering how this company should price jobs and how it should pay individual employees.

Pay Level. As noted in Chapters 3 and 4, pay-level decisions are related to external competitiveness—that is, the pay rates of the organization's jobs in relation to its competitors' pay rates. Thus, it differs from the concept of internal equity or consistency, which is concerned with relative pay rates within organizations.[6] If the lower bound of a job-specific pay rate is defined as the point below which it is not possible to attract newcomers to the organization and the upper bound as the point beyond which payroll costs translate into noncompetitive product or service prices, reflecting product market competition, management must use its discretion to set the appropriate base pay for the entry-level CSR position.

As you can see from this statement, we will be developing a **job-based pay** system for HES. The pay system will be organized around the concept of an **internal labor market.** We do this for HES because the entry-level CSR must acquire a great deal of company-specific knowledge and information, and we will hire only at the entry level. Our prescription will be to price the entry-level position to be very competitive—to **lead** the market—in relation to the external "market" wage, with a goal of attracting a large and talented group of job applicants. However, to control costs, other positions within the CSR job hierarchy will be priced at or below the market wage. This is possible because as CSRs move up the hierarchy they will be acquiring primarily company-specific KSAs. These KSAs are not highly transferable in the external labor market, making the at- or below-market wage sufficient for retaining experienced CSRs. The nature of this internal labor market is summarized in Figure I1–1. Note that this is a four-level hierarchy (CSR I through telephone CSR [level IV]). All hiring is done at the CSR I level and progression through the hierarchy requires completing a structured training experience, described in a subsequent section of this illustration.

As CSRs move through this progression of positions they become increasingly autonomous and deal with a progressively more complex set of customer issues. At the CSR I level, the primary task is to handle basic customer correspondence. The CSR I answers basic and straightforward customer questions by providing reply letters (and scripted e-mail replies) that require only putting together a sequence of prewritten reply paragraphs. Level II and III CSRs work on progressively more complex correspondence, requiring the composition of an original letter or e-mail reply. Finally, at level IV, the CSR must be able to deal with any form of inquiry and react instantly to any request from a telephone caller. Level IV work incorporates the KSAs from the first three levels and requires the development of KSAs needed to behave interactively with the customer.

244

PART FOUR
Designing Human
Resource Systems
for Specific
Business
Situations

FIGURE I1–1. The internal labor market for customer service representatives (CSRs) at HES

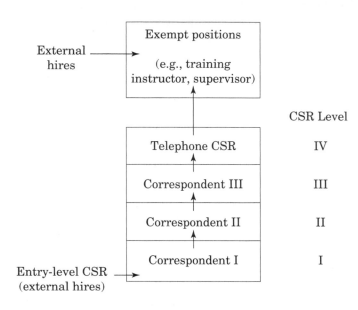

Returning to the issue of external competitiveness, refer to Figure I1–2, a graph of the suggested pay hierarchy for HES. The four job levels are plotted in relation to what is often called a pay line. The pay line shows the relationship between a job's internal standing and the midpoint of what the market (other firms competing for similar workers) tends to pay for positions of this type. Note that only the entry-level position (CSR I) is positioned well above the market midpoint. It is here that the company needs to attract the top talent from the relevant labor market. As employees move up the pay hierarchy, pay rates can be controlled because of the company-specific nature of training. However, these training costs are relatively high and HES needs to find a variety of ways to retain high-performing CSRs. We will return to this issue when we address pay practices at the level of individual employees (employee equity/contribution) and practices that relate to indirect forms of compensation (benefits).

To determine the market midpoints displayed in Figure I1–2, HES will need to conduct a **wage and salary survey.** Such a survey is a systematic way to collect information about the pay rates of other employers.[7] This information can be collected using a variety of means, ranging from telephone interviews to mail surveys. Often, HRM-oriented consulting firms provide services of this type. Thus, HES might be able to purchase the results of such a survey and use this information to price the pay hierarchy shown in Figure I1–2. Key decisions that need to be made by HES include defining the geographic location of the relevant labor market (e.g, other employers within a 50-mile radius of HES facilities) and the industries across which HES competes for entry-level CSR talent.[8]

245

ILLUSTRATION ONE
Human Resource
Systems for
the Customer
Contact Tier

FIGURE I1–2. Suggested pay hierarchy for HES

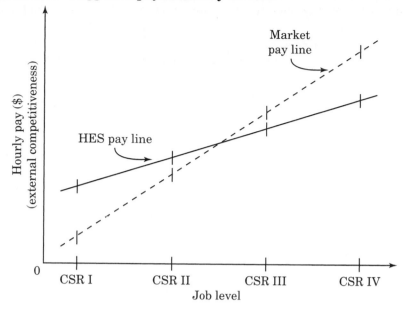

Job Pricing. As suggested by Figure I1–2, external competitiveness will be stressed only for the entry-level position (CSR I). The pricing hierarchy for the CSR II through CSR IV positions will strive for internal equity. The concept of internal equity relates to the relative pay differences between jobs (in this case, between jobs in the CSR pay progression). Because the company typically cannot make external hiring decisions above the entry-level position (outsiders would have no way to learn all the company-specific information required of HES employees), the pay differences between levels must be established to achieve a set of very important objectives. The differences must be large enough to encourage new employees to engage in the training required to move up the hierarchy and the differences must be perceived as fair and equitable. Perceptions of equity and fairness will contribute to the company's ability to retain top-performing CSRs.[9]

One way to establish the relative worth of jobs within a given firm is through the application of a **job evaluation** (see Chapter 4 for discussion of this measurement technique). Here, through the use of a structured rating procedure,[10] relative pay differences can be established. HES could devise its own job evaluation method or could buy such a system from a consulting firm. It is likely, however, that HES will simply determine the appropriate differences by making adjustments over time based on employee reaction and behavior.

Pay at Risk and Performance-Contingent Pay. Even though the prescribed pay system is job-based, it will still be useful to vary pay, that is, put some pay at risk, within each CSR level, to accomplish other objectives. The circumstances that make the use of an **individually oriented** incentive system most appropriate[11] are present for CSRs at HES. First, CSRs

246

*PART FOUR
Designing Human
Resource Systems
for Specific
Business
Situations*

work alone. They are not part of work teams. Thus, work tasks are performed independently of others. Also, motivation, or effort expended, makes a real difference in terms of the quantity and quality of performance. Pay based on individual performance should clearly link performance-related behavior and valued outcomes, such as a meaningful bonus. Also, by linking pay to job performance, top-performing CSRs will receive more of what they want from the job, assuming we are selecting people who value bonus pay. This, following the framework provided by Dreher,[12] should help HES retain top-performing CSRs. Finally, another situational requirement for the use of individually oriented incentive pay is in place: It is possible to objectively measure the key aspects of task performance—and do so at a reasonable cost.

Performance measurement at a reasonable cost is possible because HES is able to use low-cost computer monitoring of CSR performance. First, computer software is available that allows the company to count the number of letters sent and the number of calls handled per work shift. These counts are made and regularly fed back to CSRs. But simply counting, or focusing on quantity, can have negative consequences for performance quality.[13] To ensure that the performance measurement system is not deficient, a layer of measurement that addresses quality will be required. Here, the company can use a system that systematically samples calls, letters, and e-mail replies. These sampled outcomes can be "graded" or rated by a "quality control" staff who use objective standards to rate the quality of the exchange with the customer. This incurs a cost, but it is a cost more than balanced by the effect on employee attention to quality service.

We suggest, then, that in addition to base pay, HES should use a bonus system that provides quarterly cash bonuses for high levels of performance quantity and quality. These bonuses should increase the belief that high levels of task performance are related to valued outcomes (i.e., they should increase instrumentality perceptions associated with the link between performance and pay).

Benefit Flexibility and Benefit Level. Finally, even though indirect forms of compensation were not part of the external versus internal employee-equity framework, they serve an important function for HES. To encourage high levels of employee commitment and loyalty it will be worthwhile to build a highly competitive, and yet cost-effective, benefit plan for CSRs. This links staying with the company with valued outcomes: increasing instrumentality perceptions associated with tenure or decisions not to resign.

Valued benefit options need to be offered to those who continue on as employees. What is valued needs to be determined by surveying current employees and individuals who present themselves for employment. Another way to ensure that offered benefits are valued by employees is to provide some level of choice (i.e., a flexible or cafeteria benefit plan). We suggest that CSRs be provided with medical insurance that is at the midpoint of plans provided by other firms competing with HES for CSR talent. Also, a retirement plan and vacation and holiday benefits need to be provided in such a way that the benefit increases with length of service (e.g., pension benefits that vest after an appropriate length of employment with HES and vacation benefits that increase with years of employment). This all should be designed to increase instrumentality perceptions associated with the link between continued employment with HES and valued job outcomes (outcomes for which there are high valence perceptions).

247

ILLUSTRATION ONE
Human Resource
Systems for
the Customer
Contact Tier

Training and Development

Skill Orientation. The prescribed training and development practices need to take into account the internal job hierarchy. There is a structure and logic associated with HES training requirements because CSRs must progress up a well-defined hierarchy of pay levels. HES has created specific procedures and practices for many of the possible exchanges with customers. A high degree of CSR discretion takes place only among level IV CSRs. Most of the work, therefore, requires the CSR to learn a great deal about these HES-specific rules and guidelines. This represents a form of skill-based pay in that progression up the hierarchy requires the CSR to pass a series of training hurdles, demonstrating competence at each successive level of work. This is not, however, a true form of the skill-based pay concept. For this to be truly skill based, base pay would be a function of employee skill level only, not of what the employee may be working on during a particular period of time. That is, a person skilled to work at any level would receive the highest level of base pay, even when doing only level I work on a particular day. At HES, incoming work requiring only written correspondence with the customer is sorted and categorized by skill level. Level I work is performed only by level I CSRs, level II work only by level II CSRs, and so on. Level IV work can be at any level of complexity, but it is all performed on the telephone, live with customers.

Four conditions exist at HES that make it most appropriate for a training solution:[14]

1. The knowledge, skills, and abilities to be acquired are, by definition, job-related. The CSRs simply cannot perform their jobs without possessing these KSAs.
2. Most or all of these KSAs are not possessed by incoming employees. There are no ways to acquire these KSAs without going through HES training because the training (for the most part) is about procedures and guidelines established by HES. Therefore, job-related KSA deficiencies exist among newly hired employees.
3. Employees should be motivated and ready to be trained. The motivation is a function of the reward system (CSRs receive more base pay as they pass the various training hurdles) and trainee ability to learn should be in place if the staffing system is working properly.
4. The transferability of training content from the training setting back to the job setting can easily be built into the training process. Given the job-related nature of the training, the behaviors requiring the new KSAs also should be rewarded (positively reinforced) when the trainee returns to work or moves to a higher level.

248

*PART FOUR
Designing Human
Resource Systems
for Specific
Business
Situations*

Given the overall nature of this training environment, the primary focus of training should be on helping newcomers acquire all the company-specific knowledge and skill required to be effective in CSR roles. As will be developed in a subsequent section of this illustration, certain selection standards will help guarantee that at the time of hire these newcomers will possess the more general skills related to mathematical reasoning and interpersonal behavior.

Training Method Orientation. The proposed training for the CSR job class will follow some traditional recommendations from the training literature. The CSRs must acquire specific, and often company-specific, knowledge and skills. Some of this can be acquired through standard information presentation techniques such as reading or listening to lectures and tapes. However, training content in this case lends itself to the use of a very powerful technology—a technology based on well-established learning principles. This technology builds on the notion that people learn new skills by (1) observing the correct way of addressing an issue, (2) practicing the behavior or skill, (3) receiving feedback about how close the practiced behavior matches the standard, and (4) continuing the practice–feedback cycle until an acceptable level of proficiency has been achieved. A great deal of research in industry has demonstrated that the use of **behavior modeling** concepts[15] and other standard learning principles can lead to enhanced training performance.[16] Our prescribed training practices for HES will be based on these simple yet powerful ideas.

The training programs for CSRs at HES should consist of formal, structured sets of experiences that provide trainees with information and knowledge, role models characterizing effective performance, simulated practice and extensive feedback, carefully monitored exposure to actual customer correspondence and telephone inquiries, and, finally, on-the-job, experience-based learning. These programs need to be thorough and integrated, requiring qualification or skill-checks at each transition point as the CSR moves from level I to level II to level III to level IV. Thus, we are proposing a hybrid approach, consisting of both formal and on-the-job training.

The general training process could begin by promoting company loyalty through a general orientation and discussion of the history of the company. This would be followed by information about the nature of the required work activities and the level of performance expected of the fully functioning CSR. Trainees would learn about the information and data systems they will be expected to use at their designated work stations. They also would review the various reference materials to be used in their work.

The training process next turns to practice, feedback, and more practice. For example, level I trainees would work with sample customer letters under the direction and guidance of their training instructor. Then the training would progress to the processing of actual customer correspondence, although no actual transactions would be finalized until the work had been reviewed for correctness. Trainee output would be carefully monitored and extensive feedback received until the trainee was working at a predetermined standard. Note that as the training progresses, individuals are making the transition from trainee to operational level I CSR. The skills acquired during training should generalize to the actual work setting because formal off-site training becomes something very much like on-site (on-the-job) training.

Level II and III training would be structured much like that of level I, with progressively more complex issues and types of customer complaints being processed. Finally, in addition to becoming proficient at dealing with the most complex forms of correspondence, level IV training would prepare the CSR to work with customers who have reached the CSR via the telephone. Here trainees would be shown films and videos that prepare them for situations likely to be encountered on the job by demonstrating the correct way to handle a particular situation. Trainees also would observe experienced CSRs and training instructors processing actual customer calls. After observing these role models, trainees would role play a series of simulated customer calls, receive systematic feedback regarding their performance, and repeat this cycle until proficiency had been achieved.

Finally, we propose that a systematic posttraining experience be put in place. After completing formal training for each level, CSRs would be paired with a "job coach." This experienced CSR would provide posttraining feedback and assistance for two to three weeks after the individual has been "released" from the formal training program.

Career Pathing. This is a highly structured internal job hierarchy. Movement up the hierarchy is totally dependent on taking and completing the required training for each step. Therefore, this particular career path should be clear to new employees. However, in addition to this type of career pathing, new employees should know that other opportunities may become available to high-performing CSRs. For example, as seen in Figure I1–1, movement into certain exempt positions (training instructors, first-line supervisors, etc.) is possible for internal CSRs.

Formal Succession Planning and Skill Inventories. Although elaborate planning systems are not needed for this general class of jobs, a systematic way to help determine which internal candidates are appropriate, interested, and ready for promotion into an exempt position will be needed. A skill inventory would provide readily available information.

The Staffing System

Finally, we are ready to consider the procedures to use in identifying, from among the many applicants, those who will likely be successful in the role of a CSR. Recall that the labor market provides a plentiful supply of interested candidates. This results from (1) a lack of high-paying manufacturing jobs in this region of the United States, (2) the large supply of job seekers who possess only a high school diploma, (3) many part-time college students in this area who need full-time employment for the evening and night shift, and (4) hiring standards for the CSR position that do not include specialized technical skills.

249

ILLUSTRATION ONE
Human Resource
Systems for
the Customer
Contact Tier

250

*PART FOUR
Designing Human
Resource Systems
for Specific
Business
Situations*

In fact, the labor market is so plentiful that it is not uncommon to receive more than 200 applications for every 10 to 20 openings. Given the company's growth strategy and success in introducing new products (e.g., audio books), the number of openings for entry-level CSRs has been averaging nearly 20 per month for the last two years. But these opening are only at the entry level. Because external hires cannot move directly into levels II through IV, the **career system** is decidedly internal.

Candidate Preference and Organizational Fit. Assume HES received a large number of applicants, many of whom are unlikely to have a clear sense of what work as a CSR entails. Our first staffing prescription then is to produce a realistic video that depicts the work and the work environment at HES. All potential applicants will be asked to view the videotape before actually submitting an application. This prescription is based on the notion of a "realistic job preview."[17] We think there is sufficient evidence to suggest that such a preview will help certain applicants realize that they would not be able to cope with the demands of this job; thus, they would self-select out of the screening process.

The remaining components of the selection system will be comprised of a two-staged process. The selection procedures will explicitly address the eight KSAs described earlier. As seen in Figure I1–3, each selection procedure addresses a particular set of KSAs (some representing the **potential** to acquire company-specific knowledge and skills, and others representing current skill or **achievement** levels). The first stage will use relatively low-cost work/training samples to assess KSAs 1, 3, 5, 7, and 8. The content of the selection test must represent the tasks actually performed on the job. However, since much of what CSRs do on the job requires knowledge and skills acquired during training, the use of pure work sample tests is not

FIGURE I1–3. Predictors and selection system phases for HES

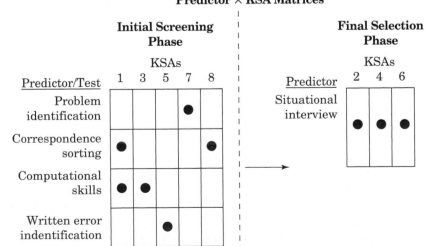

Predictor × KSA Matrices

appropriate in this situation. Instead of work samples we will use "training samples,"[18] which contain representative material from training program content. Job candidates review sampled rules, procedures, and other "instructional" materials and then must demonstrate that they have been able to master or learn the work-related concepts. This phase of the selection process consists of four paper-and-pencil training samples, or trainability tests (see Figure I1–3). Each must be "passed" for the trainee to progress to stage two of the selection process and each is briefly described next.

251

*ILLUSTRATION ONE
Human Resource
Systems for
the Customer
Contact Tier*

Problem Identification Test. This test requires the applicant to search for and identify the essence of a customer's concern, problem, or request. Hypothetical letters, representative of the letters actually sent by HES customers, are read by the applicant. Applicants are instructed to identify the central set of customer concerns after being informed about the types of problems or issues to search for. As seen in Figure I1–3, this test is designed to measure **problem analysis skills** (KSA 7).

Correspondence Sorting Test. This test is designed to measure KSA 1 (the ability to read, comprehend, and follow written instructions) and KSA 8 (the ability to reach logical conclusions based on available information and procedural standards). Instructions for sorting correspondence into categories are presented to the applicant. These categories represent the level of sensitivity, complexity, or risk associated with an incoming customer inquiry. The test requires the applicant to read and classify 15 hypothetical letters using these classification guidelines.

Computational Skills Test. This test measures **mathematical/computational skills** (KSA 3) and the ability to read, comprehend, and follow written instructions (KSA 1). The test is divided into two parts. The first part presents 25 arithmetic problems that directly measure computational skills. The second part includes 10 problems that require the applicant to read and follow an HES policy and then answer a hypothetical customer question about an account. These questions require the calculation of such things as the total charges associated with a discounted order or the balance due on a customer's account.

Written Error Identification Test. This test measures KSA 5 (ability to write using proper punctuation, syntax, and spelling). The test presents the applicant with a series of hypothetical letters (drafts of letters to be sent to customers) and asks for the identification of misspellings, comma errors, instances of subject–verb disagreement, incorrect words, sentence fragments, and run-on sentences.

The second phase of the selection process will use a *situational interview*[19] to assess KSAs 2, 4, and 6. The interview also will be used to make an assessment about "organizational fit"—the degree to which the work-related outcomes associated with being a CSR match the values, interests, and **valence** perceptions held by the job candidate.

To construct a situational interview, individuals very familiar with the work of the CSR (subject matter experts, who may be current CSRs or supervisors of CSRs) are asked to describe situations they have observed in the past in which a CSR displayed particularly effective or ineffective behavior. These "critical incidents" are then organized around the KSAs of interest (2, 4, and 6). These incidents will then be used to construct situational interview questions (e.g., "What would you do if, while working with a customer on the telephone, the customer accused you and other HES employees

252

PART FOUR
Designing Human
Resource Systems
for Specific
Business
Situations

of gross incompetence and threatened to pursue the issue in court?"). Usually, two to three interview questions will be constructed for each KSA. Also, note that because the interview requires a verbal, interactive reply from the candidate, all questions can be used to assess oral communication skills. As discussed in Chapter 5, this form of interviewing, when properly developed, can be shown to be job-related because of the connection to the KSAs identified in the job analysis. Also, this type of interview has been shown (empirically) to lead to relatively accurate predictions about future behavior.[20]

When this technique is used to assess organizational fit, the other components of the HR system must already be in place (this is why we addressed the staffing system last). To see what we have in mind, recall that CSRs will be paid a base wage (depending on the level of training completed and the type of work they are qualified to perform) and will participate in an individual-incentive plan (based on work quantity and quality). The interview should elicit the importance of bonus pay to the applicant and whether the applicant will be willing to put a portion of his or her pay at risk. It also will be important to learn about the applicant's interest in and past record as a trainee. We must explore with the applicants how interested they are in being part of continuous and extensive training experiences. Finally, the applicant's need to be part of a work team should be assessed. Although there is constant contact with customers (particularly at level IV), the CSR at HES works alone, at an individualized work station. An individual's need to work face-to-face with other employees should be explored during the interview. Because of the highly structured nature of CSR work, **right types** should be the focus of the selection system.

Exit Orientation. Although turnover costs are high among employees in this job class because of the high training costs, we recommend a focus on **managed turnover.** Providing a high degree of job security makes good sense when employees are asked to improve productivity. Employees are not likely to make productivity improvement suggestions if proposed changes can lead to layoffs. The CSRs are not being asked to modify work processes. In fact, given the need for highly reliable and consistent customer service, CSRs must comply with a variety of company procedures and rules. The work procedures of the CSR also are largely determined by available information technology. Anyone not able to provide the level of service demanded of CSRs simply cannot be allowed to stay in this critical position. That is why CSR job performance is continuously monitored and a number of training hurdles are in place; inability to successfully complete training would be grounds for dismissal.

The Performance Measurement System

Measurement Scope and Type. Earlier, when discussing the need for individually oriented performance-contingent pay, the needed performance measurement approach was discussed. Recall that low-cost computer monitoring of CSR performance is possible through the use of sophisticated technology and that this allows for the measurement of **both** the number of calls (or letters and e-mail replies) processed and the quality of each customer exchange. Thus, a focus on both **process** and **quality** is needed in this situation.

253

ILLUSTRATION ONE
Human Resource
Systems for
the Customer
Contact Tier

Finally, to expand this discussion beyond the CSR job class, Table I1–1 summarizes two relevant articles. These illustrate how employee monitoring can take many forms in the customer contact tier.

CONCLUSION

This illustration has looked at a prescribed HR system for the CSR job class within a company like HES. Our prescriptions are presented in Table I1–2, which describes the total HR system in terms of the 19 dimensions first developed in Chapter 3.

Now that the HR system has been designed and described it is interesting to look back at the final product and consider its systemslike attributes. While we were not thinking of a taxonomy of HR system types when considering the HR system components for HES, it now seems apparent that what we have designed looks very much like the "Individually Oriented System" characterized by Barry Staw (as discussed in Chapter 9) in his important

TABLE I1-1. Employee Monitoring Takes Many Forms in the Customer Contact Tier

BROKERAGE COPS WARY OF CYBERSPACE	THAT CRANKY SHOPPER MAY BE A STORE SPY
Brokerage and securities firms monitor broker-client relationships electronically.	Feedback Plus dispatches professional shoppers, posing as amateurs, to monitor retail sales employees (and to rate employees on the following questions):
• Pamela Cavness, director of compliance at Edward Jones, states: "If a broker chooses to use e-mail to communicate with his or her customer, we ask that they have those e-mails reviewed before they are delivered."	• Was the sales associate knowledgeable about products in stock?
• Brokers are monitored to make sure they are not breaking securities laws and stock exchange rules.	• How long before a sales associate greeted you?
• Edward Jones also was evaluating new software that could "identify communication that might be inappropriate" in e-mail, said Ms. Cavness. For example, the software might flag the words "my mother," because the broker might be suggesting that the stock is so safe he would recommend it to his mother.	• Did the sales associate act as if he wanted your business?
	Neiman Marcus Group, Inc., has found that, of its 26 stores nationwide, "those stores that consistently score high on the shopping service not so coincidentally have the best sales," says a senior vice president.

Source: column 1: E. Hubler, "Brokerage Cops Wary of Cyberspace: E-Mail Brings Compliance Headaches," *The New York Times,* April 12, 1998, p. BU4; *column 2:* K. Helliker, "Smile: That Cranky Shopper May Be a Store Spy," *The Wall Street Journal,* November 30, 1994, pp. B1, B6.

254

PART FOUR
Designing Human
Resource Systems
for Specific
Business
Situations

TABLE I1–2. A Recommended HR System for Customer Service Representative at HES

PAY LEVEL
Lag
Meet   Lead for CSR I, meet or lag for levels II–IV
Lead

PAY-AT-RISK
None
Moderate   Moderate
Extensive

PERFORMANCE-CONTINGENT PAY
Individual
Team   Individually oriented
Organization

JOB PRICING
Internal equity   Internal equity
External equity

SKILL-BASED PAY
Yes   No
No

SENIORITY-BASED PAY
Yes   No
No

BENEFIT FLEXIBILITY
Yes   Yes
No

BENEFIT LEVEL
Lag
Meet   Meet
Lead

CAREER SYSTEM
Internal   Internal
External

(Continued)

article in the *California Management Review*.[21] Recall that Staw characterized this system using six central features:

1. Extrinsic rewards (pay, bonuses, etc.) are tied to job performance (performance attributable to individual, not team, contribution).
2. Performance standards are realistic and challenging.
3. Systems are employed to measure and monitor employee performance and provide timely feedback about the quantity and quality of work.

CANDIDATE PREFERENCE
Potential
Achievement

"Potential" to learn is the primary focus—with some concern for "achievement" as related to basic skills in math and in written and interpersonal communication

ORGANIZATIONAL FIT
Right types
Diversity

Right types

EXIT ORIENTATION
Security
Managed turnover

Managed turnover

SKILL ORIENTATION
Technical
General

Technical/company-specific KSAs

TRAINING METHOD
Informal/on-the-job
Formal/classroom

Hybrid (moving from formal to informal as skills improve)

CAREER PATHING
Yes
No

Yes

FORMAL SUCCESSION PLANNING
Yes
No

Yes (in abbreviated form)

SKILL INVENTORIES
Yes
No

Yes—some relevance as it relates to the limited opportunity to move into supervision or other specialty roles

MEASUREMENT TYPE
Results
Process

Results and process

MEASUREMENT SCOPE
Traditional
360 degree

Traditional

4. Promotions are based on skill, performance, and demonstrated readiness, not on such things as power and connections.
5. Well-developed training and development systems are used to build the skill level of the workforce.
6. Jobs are enriched through increases in task variety, responsibility, and significance.

256

PART FOUR
Designing Human
Resource Systems
for Specific
Business
Situations

A comparison of the key components of our HR system for HES with the attributes of Staw's individually oriented management system shows almost complete agreement. The only factor that did not receive explicit attention in our prescribed system was the factor concerned with enlarging and enriching job tasks. We suspect that job design issues were not central to our prescriptions because job design for CSRs is largely determined by available technology. There is little room for modifying tasks when work station design and computer software design set powerful constraints on how tasks can be organized and sequenced.

In summary, the individually oriented system seems to fit this unique set of circumstances. Not only does it fit the circumstances surrounding the CSR job class at HES—it represents an internally consistent mix of HR practices that, taken together, should prove useful in directing employee behavior in ways that will add value to HES.

ENDNOTES

1. B. Schneider and D. E. Bowen, *Winning the Service Game* (Boston: Harvard Business School Press, 1995).
2. Ibid., p. 7.
3. S. Hansell, "5,000 Clients, No Branches: Phone Banking Is Catching On," *The New York Times,* September 3, 1995, Sec. 3, pp. 1, 10.
4. F. Witney and B. J. Taylor, *Labor Relations Law* (Englewood Cliffs, NJ: Prentice Hall, 1996).
5. G. T. Milkovich and J. M. Newman, *Compensation* (Burr Ridge, IL: Richard D. Irwin, 1996), pp. 11–16.
6. Ibid., p. 207.
7. Ibid., p. 245.
8. S. L. Rynes and G. Y. Milkovich, "Wage Surveys: Dispelling Some Myths about the 'Market Wage'," *Personnel Psychology* 39 (1986), pp. 571–95.
9. G. F. Dreher, "The Role of Performance in the Turnover Process," *Academy of Management Journal* 25 (1982), pp. 137–47; and W. H. Mobley, H. H. Griffeth, H. H. Hand, and B. M. Meglino, "Review and Conceptual Analysis of the Employee Turnover Process," *Psychological Bulletin* 86 (1979), pp. 493–522.
10. For a discussion of how to consider this issue, see T. A. Mahoney, "Organizational Hierarchy and Position Worth," *Academy of Management Journal* 22 (1979), pp. 726–37.
11. G. P. Latham and D. L. Dossett, "Designing Incentive Plans for Unionized Employees: A Comparison of Continuous and Variable Ratio Reinforcement Schedules," *Personnel Psychology* 31 (1978), pp. 47–62.
12. Dreher, "The Role of Performance in the Turnover Process."
13. T. L. Griffith, "Teaching Big Brother to Be a Team Player: Computer Monitoring and Quality," *Academy of Management Executive* 7 (1993), pp. 73–80.
14. K. N. Wexley and G. P. Latham, *Developing and Training Human Resources in Organizations* (New York: HarperCollins Publishers, 1991), pp. 36–107.
15. A. Bandura, *Social Foundations of Thought and Action* (Englewood Cliffs, NJ: Prentice Hall, 1986); and A. Bandura, *Social Learning Theory* (Englewood Cliffs, NJ: Prentice-Hall, 1977).
16. For representative reviews, see G. P. Latham and L. M. Saari, "Application of Social-Learning Theory to Training Supervisors through Behavior Modeling," *Journal of Applied Psychology* 64 (1979), pp. 239–46; and H. H. Meyer and M. S.

Raich, "An Objective Evaluation of a Behavior Modeling Training Program," *Personnel Psychology* 36 (1983), pp. 755–61.

17. J. P. Wanous, *Organizational Entry: Recruitment, Selection and Socialization of Newcomers* (Reading, MA: Addison-Wesley, 1980).

18. I. Robertson and S. Downs, "Learning and the Prediction of Performance: Development of Trainability Testing in the United Kingdom," *Journal of Applied Psychology* 64 (1979), pp. 42–50; and A. D. Siegel, "Miniature Job Training and Evaluation as a Selection/Classification Device," *Human Factors* 20 (1978), pp. 189–200.

19. G. P. Latham, L. M. Saari, E. D. Pursell, and M. A. Campion, "The Situational Interview," *Journal of Applied Psychology* 65 (1980), pp. 422–27.

20. M. A. McDaniel, D. L. Whetzel, F. L. Schmidt, and S. D. Maurer, "The Validity of Employment Interviews: A Comprehensive Review and Meta-Analysis," *Journal of Applied Psychology* 79 (1994), pp. 599–616.

21. B. M. Staw, "Organizational Psychology and the Pursuit of the Happy/Productive Worker," *California Management Review* 27 (1986), pp. 40–53.

ILLUSTRATION 2

Human Resource Systems for Total Quality Management–Oriented Manufacturing Teams

This illustration, like the last, is organized around three guiding principles. First, we will stress HR system integration by focusing on multiple HRM practices for a targeted set of positions within one company. The company will be described within the context of its strategic and environmental circumstances. Second, we will structure the chapter around the decision-making process presented in Figure 1–1. Finally, after addressing the key employee behaviors required to meet company objectives and the relevant legal and labor-market context, we will prescribe an HR system. Our prescription will be presented after considering and selecting from the 19 dimensions contained in the HRM practices domain statement developed in Chapter 3.

THE TARGETED JOB CLASS: MANUFACTURING ASSOCIATE

The job class for this illustration is "manufacturing associate," a class frequently seen in manufacturing companies. The company considered here assembles midsize diesel engines for sale to truck manufacturers; for example, some models of Dodge pickup trucks are equipped with diesel engines designed and manufactured by Cummins Engine Company. In fact, we will base our company composite around a set of circumstances that existed for the Cummins Engine Company, as described in considerable detail in *The Wall Street Journal*.[1] Imagine that the circumstances for our composite company, a company we will call Columbus Engine Works (CEW), were very much as they were for a specific Cummins manufacturing facility.

Three years ago CEW's midrange engine plant, located in Columbus, Indiana, was closed as a result of a major cost-cutting and reorganization initiative. At the time of the closing the plant made engine components (compressors, piston and rod assemblies, etc.) for the main engine assembly plant and employed approximately 2,100 workers. Based on a combination of factors—state and local tax breaks, demand for high-quality engines that could be modified to include various options, an agreement with the Diesel Workers Union, and so on—CEW decided to reopen the plant. In its new form the plant would employ no more than 1,500 manufacturing associates and would set a target of 200 engines per day. The goal was to create a very flexible manufacturing system, which could quickly change from one engine configuration to another and would meet very high quality standards.

Although the plant would be "reopened," the process was to be very much like that associated with designing, building, and opening a new facility. The assembly process and degree of automation would be unique to the needs of this facility. Even the staffing process resembled that of opening a new facility. Here, although CEW would have to first consider formerly laid-off workers, particularly members of the Diesel Workers Union (DWU), there was no requirement to consider seniority in previous CEW jobs as a selection criterion. CEW would be able to devise its own selection standards. After considering DWU applicants, the company would be free to go to the external labor market to fill remaining openings.

We will now begin the analysis of CEW by following the framework set forth in Figure 1–1. After further analysis of the company and its environment, the objective will be to design the ideal HR system for the midrange engine plant in Columbus, Indiana. The focus will be on the dominant job class at the facility, the job of manufacturing associate.

259

ILLUSTRATION TWO
Human Resource
Systems for
Total Quality
Management–
Oriented
Manufacturing
Teams

BUSINESS STRATEGY AND TECHNOLOGY: COLUMBUS ENGINE WORKS

CEW's primary strategic orientation is to differentiate along the quality dimension, thus its stated goal is to be "the best diesel-engine producer in the world." The company links product innovation and manufacturing flexibility to its quality orientation. By being the first to market new-generation technologies (e.g., engine features that lengthen engine maintenance schedules and improve fuel efficiency), producing high-quality engines that meet and often exceed truck manufacturers specifications, and meeting production schedules, the company hopes to gain a sustainable competitive advantage. In addition to the standard advantages associated with being perceived as the top quality producer of diesel engines,[2] CEW sees the quality-oriented strategy leading to reduced defects and lowered manufacturing costs.

While at the corporate level, CEW focuses on innovative engine design and product quality (the company is an industry leader in terms of research and development expenditures), at the level of the midrange engine plant the focus is on a different type of innovation. Here it is innovation to improve the manufacturing process. The mission of this manufacturing plant is to provide a flexible and high-quality manufacturing process that also enables the company to compete in a competitive product market. Thus, flexibility, quality, and cost targets must simultaneously be met. HRM practices for CEW's research and development product teams will need to differ from the HRM practices that will be implemented at the midrange engine plant. Here again is an example of the need to decentralize and create unique HRM solutions within one corporate entity. At the manufacturing level the tactical strategy is most like what Gubman (1998) described as an operations orientation. At the research and development level the orientation is

260

*PART FOUR
Designing Human
Resource Systems
for Specific
Business
Situations*

more like that of a products company. We also note that it is possible to prescribe HRM practices at one operations company that differ from the practices prescribed for another operations company. This is because technology, product or service type, and business strategy all must be taken into account when designing appropriate work processes. It is to this CEW manufacturing plant that we now turn our attention.

To implement what the company calls a total quality management (TQM) strategy, a number of steps have been taken, including:

1. The focused use of robotics and other forms of automation has been stressed throughout the plant. For example, a highly automated engine painting process was installed.
2. Assembly teams, charged with finding ways to streamline their jobs and reduce defects, are utilized throughout the plant. These teams assemble engine components such as head and valve-train assemblies and meet as problem-solving units; team members are expected to learn all the jobs associated with their area of the assembly process.
3. A set of systems—suggestion systems, measurement systems, recognition systems, and the like—was installed to address quality and cost-control issues.
4. Throughout the plant, there is a focus on process, in addition to quantity. Teams use problem-solving tools and methods to improve production processes. For example, teams gather and track information about quality variation and work to identify and remove the causes of any observed problems. Data collection, summarization, and feedback systems are emphasized throughout the facility.
5. To further break down barriers, production workers (manufacturing associates) and managers alike wear company-issue khaki pants and dress shirts with no neckties.
6. Suppliers are thoroughly involved when changes are made in the manufacturing process.
7. There is constant engagement with customers.
8. The physical setting has been dramatically altered. Where there once were dirty brick floors, there now are freshly painted concrete floors. Natural light enters through large windows and skylights. The entire facility is very clean. Special conference/breakout rooms, used by teams gathered to work on improvement projects, overlook the assembly floor.

Finally, while the quality dimension might be considered the lead strategy, the need for flexibility and the ability to respond to rapidly changing market conditions cannot be overestimated. What if one of CEW's primary customers were to decide to purchase engines from another supplier? For example, in early 2000, DaimlerChrysler was reported to be considering using Mercedes-Benz diesel engines in the future production of Dodge Ram pickup trucks.[3] If CEW were to lose a large-scale customer like DaimlerChrysler, the company would need to seek other markets for this class of engines—with customers who would undoubtedly require engine modifications and unique accessory and power configurations.

KEY EMPLOYEE BEHAVIORS AND
CRITICAL EMPLOYEE ATTRIBUTES

261

ILLUSTRATION TWO
Human Resource
Systems for
Total Quality
Management–
Oriented
Manufacturing
Teams

A primary role of manufacturing associates is to work as members of an assembly team. Teams are formed to work on specific engine components. For example, some teams are valve-train specialists, others focus on peripheral component assemblies (e.g., the installation of oil pumps, water pumps, compressors, and exhaust systems), and some teams specialize in such things as paint system setup and maintenance and engine testing. All teams are charged with maintaining a safe and clean work environment, inventory control, and (of course) quality and process improvement.

The quality and process improvement work requires that team members meet regularly to review information about the number of engines produced, the number and types of defects observed, and the results of prior improvement initiatives.[4] Team members regularly apply the principles of statistical process control to this aspect of their work. An example is the use of the Pareto chart, a bar graph that summarizes and ranks the causes of process variation by the effect on product quality.[5]

One illustration of how a team improved a work process comes from the team assigned the task of testing all completed engines. The original process required that each engine be connected to a cooling system before being fired and checked. The process of connecting the engine to the cooling system and then draining the engine block was very time-consuming. Team members observed that the tests being conducted required only a few minutes of engine run time—thus the engines never reached operating temperatures. Because the engines never reached temperatures requiring block cooling, the team correctly reasoned that the cooling step could be completely eliminated—leading to an improvement in process cycle time.

The results of a job analysis revealed that certain knowledge, skills, and abilities (KSAs) are central to being an effective manufacturing associate. Some of the most critical KSAs are listed and described as follows:

1. **Physical stamina and agility:** The work can be physically demanding because of its rapid pace and repetitive assembly processes, but it does not require heavy lifting or other strenuous physical activity. Stamina—being able to stand and move about the work space for long periods of time—is more important than strength. Also, the eye–hand coordination and manual dexterity required to assemble engine components is essential, since associates must be able to use a wide variety of hand tools.

2. **Reading comprehension:** Associates must be able to read, comprehend, and follow complex written instructions. As production processes are improved or new equipment is installed, the ability to stay informed is essential.

3. **Mathematical and statistical reasoning:** The ability to understand and use mathematical concepts at the level of basic statistics is essential to being effective in a TQM-oriented manufacturing center. This

262

PART FOUR
Designing Human
Resource Systems
for Specific
Business
Situations

includes the ability to collect and statistically summarize data (basic descriptive statistics) about work processes and the ability to formulate and use basic forecasting and prediction tools.

4. **Oral communication skills:** Associates must be able to listen and verbally express ideas with clarity. They must be able to exchange ideas with individuals and team members.

5. **Presentation skills:** Associates must be able to make oral presentations to teams and other audiences (e.g., general managers) using appropriate audio and visual support materials.

6. **Problem analysis skills:** Being able to seek out pertinent data and information and being able to determine the root causes of a problem or excessive quality variation are core competencies for workers at CEW's midrange engine plant.

7. **Learning ability:** Associates must be able to learn, follow, and apply new and changing operating procedures. Also, the successful manufacturing associate must be able to learn about diesel engine design and functioning, and about the application of computer-assisted manufacturing technology. The position requires the ability to take on and master continuous training opportunities.

8. **Team-oriented interests:** Associates must be willing to work to improve team effectiveness by helping and training other team members.

9. **Dependability:** Associates must display an exemplary attendance and punctuality record and must be very dependable in adhering to work schedules.

LABOR-MARKET ATTRIBUTES

The labor market in this region of the United States is characterized by a great deal of diversity in skills. Even among high school and college graduates, literacy levels vary widely. Such variability is common to other regions of the United States as well. For example, the results of the 1992 National Adult Literacy Study showed that about 50 percent of four-year college graduates and 60 percent of two-year graduates would not be successful at reading a bus schedule or at using an instructional pamphlet to calculate the yearly amount a couple would receive for supplemental social security income.[6]

In addition to vast differences in the possession of critical skills, workers in this labor market experienced dramatic changes in their circumstances over the last 10 to 15 years. Manufacturing jobs had been plentiful, even for less-skilled workers. These jobs, supported by unions like the United Auto Workers or the DWU, paid wages in the $15 to $17 hourly range and also provided liberal benefit packages. Today, while the overall unemployment rate in the area surrounding the midrange engine plant is a low 3.9 percent, many workers feel underpaid and often take multiple part-time assignments through temporary employment agencies.[7] These jobs rarely pay above $8 or $9 hourly and offer few benefits. Therefore, even with what appears to be a low unemployment rate, job announcements will generate large numbers of applicants if the advertised wage is above $9 or $10 an hour. Although there still are higher paying jobs among some unionized employees, this segment of the workforce is continuing to shrink. For example, one local cost-conscious cereal mill now makes 20 percent more cereal with 20 percent fewer workers.[8] This has resulted in the loss of nearly 300 jobs paying $15.50 an hour (even though those who remain still make the higher wage).

This region of the United States also is becoming popular to foreign companies choosing to open manufacturing plants in North America. For example, Onkyo Corporation of Japan employs 400 workers to make car stereo speakers for export to Japan, and Toyota Industrial Equipment Manufacturing makes forklifts for the United States, Canada, and Mexico. Thus, competition for the most skilled workers is becoming more and more intense.

THE LEGAL ENVIRONMENT

As with any U.S. company manufacturing products in the United States, there is a need to comply with both federal and state laws and regulations that apply to equal employment opportunity; wage, hour, and safety rules; and labor relations. Whereas this particular labor market is very homogeneous with respect to race, many women have begun to apply for manufacturing-associate positions. The labor-relations environment also is complicated by the existence of other unionized CEW plants that work under very different collective bargaining agreements.

THE PRESCRIBED HR SYSTEM

In developing our idealized HR system for CEW we again follow the structure provided in Chapter 3. Each of the 19 dimensions associated with the HRM domain statement is considered and then summarized in tabular form. In Chapter 3 we illustrated this approach by discussing a few HRM choices that seemed to fit a TQM-oriented manufacturing environment. Now, because additional information has been provided, we can move deeper into the process initiated in Chapter 3 and develop further the arguments supporting our prescriptions. We also can now provide more detail about the prescriptions themselves. Let's begin our review with a look at attributes of the reward system.

Reward and Compensation Practices

Pay Level. Deciding about whether to pay at (meet), below (lag), or above (lead) the market is a complex question for CEW. The company is faced with the conflicting objectives of controlling costs and at the same time

264

*PART FOUR
Designing Human
Resource Systems
for Specific
Business
Situations*

attracting high-quality applicants able to meet the facility's TQM standards. Moreover, it faces a labor market that now includes a growing number of competing manufacturing companies. Setting a pay level slightly above the average pay level offered by companies competing for employees with similar skill profiles is likely to be the most appropriate approach. By offering a base-pay rate slightly above the market level, CEW will attract many workers in this labor market who feel underpaid and who will also be attracted by CEW's long-term community presence and reputation as an excellent employer. Being only slightly above market will help control costs.

Ideally, CEW's quality requirements suggest a base pay clearly above the market in order to convince the most talented individuals to apply. To balance the decision to only slightly beat the market, other components of the HR system must compensate for the need to control costs. Many of CEW's subsequent decisions represent attempts to be the **employer of choice** in this labor market.

Pay at Risk. CEW needs to hire manufacturing associates who will (1) train and assist each other, (2) focus on ways to improve the manufacturing process, (3) learn multiple skills so that each associate can be utilized in a flexible manner, and (4) work diligently to meet difficult production targets. The company also must find a way to retain employees who fit the required skill profile. Putting some pay at risk makes good sense in this case. We believe the real issue is not whether or not to put some pay at risk, but to determine what form the pay practice needs to take.

Performance-Contingent Pay. This environment seems most appropriate for a team-oriented performance-contingent plan. The manufacturing associates are organized into assembly or test teams; thus, naturally occurring work units create considerable task interdependence among team members. The payoff rule needs to be at some aggregate level rather than the individual level because

1. It is not possible to measure output at the individual level.
2. A primary goal is to promote cooperation, cross-training, and teamwork.

If an associate helps, trains, or cooperates with a team member, he or she needs to perceive that this behavior will be instrumental in receiving something of value.

Given these circumstances, we recommend a type of **gain sharing.** Originally called Scanlon plans, after their originator, Joseph Scanlon, these plans were popular in the 1930s and are experiencing a resurgence in the team-based companies of the 1990s.[9] The key to a Scanlon plan is to share the benefits that come from process improvements with the work groups responsible for the savings. Teams are assigned the tasks of monitoring their work processes and devising ways to save costs. A portion of these cost savings are then returned to the team, to be distributed equally among team members.

A team-based payoff rule makes conceptual sense, but the situation at this particular CEW plant is complex. While it is true that associates are

265

*ILLUSTRATION TWO
Human Resource
Systems for
Total Quality
Management–
Oriented
Manufacturing
Teams*

organized into production teams, the teams interact and interface throughout the assembly process. In fact, the boundary between teams can change as improvements are devised. It is not that team members change; it is that the tasks assigned to teams may change at transition zones between teams. The point is, teams must interact, cooperate, and assist one another. A purely team-based payoff rule would interfere with the needed level of interteam cooperation. Therefore, a level of aggregation above the team level is called for in this engine plant. Because of team interdependence, the appropriate aggregation level for the gain-sharing plan must include all manufacturing associates.

Following the tradition of a Scanlon-like gain-sharing plan, the sales value of production (SVOP) for a base period must be compared to the variable costs of production (VCOP) associated with this same time period. Unlike fixed costs, which must be paid regardless of how much output is produced, variable costs depend on how much of a good is produced. At this CEW engine plant, variable costs include such things as the plant's payroll expenditures, costs associated with transporting and storing supplies and equipment, maintenance costs, costs associated with injuries and equipment repairs, and costs associated with training and other staff support roles. If a more favorable VCOP/SVOP ratio can be achieved, part of the savings will be distributed to manufacturing associates.

As summarized in Table I2–1, a VCOP/SVOP ratio is computed for a representative base period. Teams are then charged with seeking ways to reduce variable costs. As teams find ways to improve assembly efficiency (perhaps reducing the need for part-time temporary employees), reduce the number of engines that require rework, reduce maintenance costs, reduce the number of on-the-job injuries, and reduce the costs associated with absenteeism, the VCOP/SVOP ratio in a subsequent time period is reduced

---

**TABLE I2–1. Hypothetical Scanlon Plan
Bonus Calculation for CEW**

1998 Data (base year) for CEW midrange engine plant:

SVOP	= $216,000,000
VCOP	= $54,000,000
VCOP/SVOP	= 54,000,000 ÷ 216,000,000 = 0.25

Operating month, October 1999:

SVOP	= $18,500,000
Allowable VCOP	= .25(18,500,000) = $4,625,000
Actual VCOP (October)	= $4,350,000
Savings	= $275,000*

---

*Some percentage (e.g., 65%) of the $275,000 is available for bonus distribution to manufacturing associates.

266

*PART FOUR
Designing Human
Resource Systems
for Specific
Business
Situations*

and a portion of the benefit is shared with manufacturing associates. The remainder of the cost savings can be shared with shareholders, saved in a reserve fund to address unforeseen price changes, or used in capital improvement projects.

Internal versus External Job Pricing. This CEW manufacturing facility is characterized by a very flat organizational structure. Among production employees, there is only one job class—the **manufacturing associate.** Issues about pay differences between different types of associates do not need to be addressed. Assignments to any team are considered equal with respect to base pay, and bonus pay is determined at the plant level. Thus, the traditional issues that must be addressed when valuing jobs in a career ladder or hierarchy do not exist in this case.

Skill-Based Pay. While all associates enter with the same base pay and equally share in any gain-sharing bonuses, we do advocate a form of skill-based pay. New employees must acquire a great deal of company-specific knowledge. In fact, much of this knowledge is specific to this particular manufacturing facility. For example, knowledge about the factory's physical layout and databases can be learned only after being hired. Base pay should be increased as newcomers pass required training courses, demonstrate competence to perform all the tasks assigned to a team, and master new roles as safety officers and project-improvement team leaders. The amount of pay associated with skill acquisition should be small, but it seems appropriate given the need to motivate on-the-job learning. We think the official skill-based component of pay should be small because

1. The gain-sharing plan should encourage everyone to develop the skills needed to improve efficiency and assist newcomers in their attempts to master assignments.
2. A great deal of the knowledge that resides within a plant of this type is likely to be of the "tacit" variety—the informal, lorelike knowledge that team members share with each other.

Seniority-Based Pay. Seniority-based pay plans make sense when there is a need to promote company loyalty and commitment—so that employees can acquire company- or plant-specific knowledge and skills—and when there is a need to encourage cooperative and team-oriented behavior. These conditions are present at this CEW facility, but here other components of the pay system serve some of the same functions served by seniority-based rules. The gain-sharing plan promotes cooperative behavior; indeed, gain-sharing plans can lead to high levels of peer pressure to learn and contribute to team performance. The skill-based component provides a pay premium for acquiring plant-specific knowledge; this premium is not easily transferable to better job opportunities in the external labor market and therefore should not encourage turnover. Thus, a clear case for a seniority component cannot be made.

We also note that this is the exact situation that requires some degree of job security, which is what seniority offers to those who stay with a particular firm. If CEW is going to expect manufacturing associates to generate cost-saving ideas (the primary reason for using the Scanlon-like gain-sharing plan), these associates must all experience some level of security. Without this belief that their jobs are relatively secure, ideas that could eliminate the need for workers will not be forthcoming.

Benefit Flexibility and Benefit Level. While the local labor market for this CEW manufacturing plant is homogeneous with respect to race, the labor market is very heterogeneous with respect to other attributes. In fact, given the competition for qualified workers, CEW has formulated a recruiting plan that attempts to encourage women who have no previous experience in manufacturing and individuals who have retired early from other employers to consider employment as a manufacturing associate. In this regard, benefit plan characteristics are being used to influence applicant behaviors (in addition to attempting to promote loyalty among current employees).

The key to using benefit options in a cost-effective way, while still addressing critical behavioral objectives, is to maximize the fit between what is provided and the unique needs and preferences of employees. The benefit system required for this situation is a highly flexible, or "cafeteria," plan.[10] These plans provide flexibility by giving employees choices. One such plan gives employees what amounts to a benefits spending account, an account they use to "purchase" benefits that meet their needs at a particular time in their lives. For instance, a 55 year old with grown children and no mortgage payments may no longer need extensive life insurance coverage but may find high-quality medical insurance much more important. This individual could allocate proportionally more of a benefits spending account to medical coverage and less or even none of it to life insurance. On the other hand, a 20 year old with a young child may be willing to forgo extended vacation and holiday time for more substantial life insurance coverage. The interesting point of all of this is that, for a constant payroll expenditure, the employer is able to maximize the return associated with benefit options by maximizing the overall level of valence perceptions employees hold for their benefits package.

This approach also is useful because it represents a way to continually inform employees of the value associated with company-provided benefits. Because employees are regularly asked to reconsider the allocation of their benefits spending account, the benefit value becomes more salient.

Because of the need to control costs, it is not reasonable for CEW to be a benefit-level leader. Overall benefit expenditures should meet the market while being competitive because of how well the flexible system is administered. A high level of flexibility and delivery quality should be the focus. This system will be part of how CEW distinguishes itself from the competition and strives be become the employer of choice in this labor market. Benefits will be a prime recruiting and retention tool for CEW's midrange engine plant.

268

PART FOUR
Designing Human
Resource Systems
for Specific
Business
Situations

The Staffing System

Career System Orientation. The career system for manufacturing associates is straightforward in its internal focus. However, it is also rather limited. Associates are hired only into the entry-level position and have little opportunity to be promoted into other job classes. While it is true that skill sets develop and associates take on new roles, they are still part of this single and dominant job class. Associates are nonexempt (they are covered by the Fair Labor Standards Act), hourly employees. It is possible to move into exempt positions requiring specialized training and education, but typically people are hired directly into positions such as accountants, HR specialists, and industrial engineers.

Potential versus Achievement Orientation. This is an interesting dimension for a variety of reasons, but particularly because it offers a look at the concept of within-system congruence (see Chapter 9). For example, the reward system encourages cross-training and the acquisition of new knowledge and skills. As noted earlier, a central qualification for employment is the ability to learn and master continuous training opportunities. Competitiveness in the labor market also means that a search only for people with considerable previous manufacturing experience will not result in the needed number of applicants. To staff this facility, the key will be to identify people who have the potential to become effective manufacturing associates but who already possess certain key attributes; thus, the focus is on potential, but certain attributes are taken as givens.

Although the potential to learn is the key, other attributes are required of applicants at the time of hiring. These are attributes that are difficult to acquire or to change through training. The attributes we will consider to be least trainable and therefore the focus of early screening and selection procedures are

1. Physical stamina and agility
2. Reading comprehension
3. Mathematical reasoning
4. Oral communication skills
7. Learning ability
8. Team-oriented interests

Note that from our original list of nine critical attributes, only two, **presentation skills** and **problem analysis skills,** are considered to be trainable; the third attribute not shown above, **dependability,** is considered to be a behavior that can be controlled via the reward system. We think that peer pressure from team members and clear rules about terminating employees who do not display a high degree of dependability will be sufficient to address dependability.

To screen and select for the six at-time-of-hiring attributes we propose the following approach. To address costs, we suggest a two-stage process. The first stage, considered the screening stage, consists of a series of commercially available paper-and-pencil tests. These are low-cost, yet highly

ILLUSTRATION TWO
Human Resource
Systems for
Total Quality
Management–
Oriented
Manufacturing
Teams

sophisticated ways to identify applicants who clearly do not have the basic knowledge or skills to handle the work of a manufacturing associate in this facility. Reading comprehension, mathematical reasoning, and learning ability are addressed at this stage.

For applicants who are successful at this stage of the process, we suggest a second stage, which requires more costly techniques. The selection system approach is shown graphically in Figure I2–1. Note that because of its importance, learning ability is considered in second-stage selection even though it was addressed in the screening stage. This stage also focuses on oral communication, team-oriented interests, and physical stamina and agility. A brief review of the selection techniques to be used is presented next:

Test of Learning Ability. A general paper-and-pencil mental abilities test would be appropriately used in this context. We suggest the use of a test battery like the Differential Aptitude Tests for Personnel and Career Assessment. You can learn about this test battery by going to the web page for the Psychological Corporation (www.psychcorp.com/catalogs/hra) and reviewing the Human Resource Assessments catalog. The test publisher states that this battery measures multiple dimensions of cognitive ability. We recommend the use of three subtests— these are the tests for Verbal Reasoning, Abstract Reasoning, and Mechanical Reasoning.

Test of Reading Comprehension. Here we recommend a basic reading comprehension test like the Industrial Reading Test. This test is also sold by the Psychological Corporation and can be reviewed at this company's web page.

Test of Mathematical Reasoning. Here we suggest that a test be developed in house by sampling from technical and training materials to create a test that replicates the types of mathematical problems employees are likely to face early after being hired. This method of test development, based on the concept of **content validity,** is used to show that a test is job-related by creating a realistic sample of the problems to be encountered in training or on the actual job.[11]

Team Discussion Exercise. Following the Japanese tradition of using simulation exercises when staffing auto assembly plants in North America, we suggest using

FIGURE I2–1.   Predictors and selection system phases for CEW's midrange engine plant.

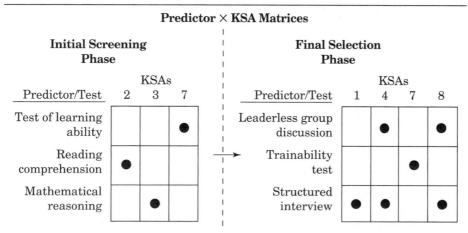

Predictor × KSA Matrices

Initial Screening Phase					Final Selection Phase				
	KSAs					KSAs			
Predictor/Test	2	3	7		Predictor/Test	1	4	7	8
Test of learning ability			●		Leaderless group discussion		●		●
Reading comprehension	●				Trainability test			●	
Mathematical reasoning		●			Structured interview	●	●		●

270

PART FOUR
Designing Human
Resource Systems
for Specific
Business
Situations

a form of work sample testing called a **leaderless-group discussion exercise** to assess oral communication skills—skills that are central to being an effective member of a TQM-oriented team. Well-developed work sample tests have a long history of being useful for this purpose and are considered to be job-related techniques for assessing skills of this type.[12] This procedure puts a group (usually about six applicants) together to solve a realistic problem they might face as members of a manufacturing team. Each member of the simulated team is of equal rank or status—thus the name **leaderless group.** The group interaction is videotaped and each participant's behavior is observed by two trained assessors who will rate each candidate on the target dimension (oral communication skills). For this exercise we will use an actual valve-train assembly and ask the team to devise a way to organize a three-person assembly cell for the purpose of assembling the cylinder head and valves. The team will be supplied with a model of a fully assembled cylinder head and all the actual component parts required for assembly. The team will be charged with organizing the assembly process to maximize production speed and quality. The team will be given one hour to develop its assembly process. The real issue for grading participants does not involve the quality of the solution but how team members communicate with each other when formulating their plan. For example, assessors will be watching for instances when participants clearly listen to another participant's ideas and summarize the ideas for other group members. Or assessors will look for instances when participants are able to help the team understand that it is using faulty logic or making assumptions that will not hold in a real work setting. The objective is to assess oral communication skills and not knowledge of valve-train assembly procedures.

Statistical Reasoning Trainability Test. The ability to use basic statistical process control techniques is essential to being an effective associate at the midrange engine plant. This knowledge/skill is, however, something that new employees will learn after being hired; indeed, mastering this skill set is a core training objective. Therefore, it would not be appropriate to assess this knowledge/skill at the time of hiring. However, there is an innovative way to measure **learning ability** using what is called a *trainability test.*[13] Trainability tests are like work sample tests, but they sample from training content, not actual work content. The idea here is to construct a representative sample of a training experience and determine whether the applicant will be able to master the training material if given the chance. For the purposes of this exercise, applicants read segments from training manuals and view a representative segment of a training video. These training materials focus on a basic statistical process control concept. Each candidate is given one hour to review the training materials and then is given an objective test covering these concepts. The score on the test measures learning ability.

Structured Interview. The final selection tool is a structured interview.[14] This tool also serves as a work sample, allowing reassessment of the oral communication dimension. The primary reason for using an interview, however, is to make an assessment of organizational fit: The manufacturing associate must be willing to work to improve team effectiveness by helping and training others—thus, team-oriented interests and values will enhance the degree to which the associate will find work at the midrange engine plant satisfying. We propose using a structured interview to assess work-related interests.

Expectancy theory (see Chapter 2) can serve as a guide in developing this interview. First, outcomes that typically follow exceptional team effort need to be identified. The interview then becomes a search for information about how valent each of these outcomes is to the applicant. For example, the interviewer might review with the applicant how satisfying it has been in the past to participate in successful team efforts rather than seeking opportunities to excel on an individual basis. Another outcome (some may call this an intrinsic outcome) associated with the CEW midrange engine plant is the opportunity to modify and improve a work process. Applicants should be assessed in terms of how interested they are in problem-solving tasks and how much satisfaction they feel when they are able to improve something at work. A final example of an outcome that should be highly important to CEW employees is the opportunity to learn new work procedures and acquire new skills. A sense of curiosity and a desire to improve oneself are attributes that will be sought in successful candidates.

These and other valence perceptions can be assessed by using two interview question formats. First, the interview can include a set of questions that review with applicants when and where in the past they experienced satisfaction when encountering specified work outcomes. The other approach can be more futuristic, describing hypothetical situations to the candidates and asking for judgments about which situation would be preferred. This approach represents a modified "situational interview," a form of interviewing that has received a great deal of support in the research literature.[15] Situational interviews describe to job applicants situations they are likely to encounter if they take a position with the interviewing company and ask the applicant to state how they would address such a situation if given the chance.

Finally, the interview is used to preview for the candidate the reality that this work is repetitious and requires physical stamina and agility. The candidate's previous exposure to situations of this type and likely ability to cope need to be thoroughly explored.

Organizational Fit. While it is important to find job candidates who will bring new ideas and approaches to solving problems at the CEW midrange engine plant, the value–interest profile (valence perceptions) discussed in the previous section of this illustration needs to be present in each successful job candidate. A reasonably high degree of organizational fit needs to be an objective of this selection system because of the unique way work is organized at the CEW midrange engine plant.[16]

Exit Orientation. Because manufacturing associates will be asked to improve work processes and find ways to reduce costs, this company clearly needs to establish stability and loyalty by creating a reasonably high degree of job security. If employees believe they run the risk of eliminating their own jobs, they are unlikely to engage in innovative thinking and behavior.[17] This does not, however, ensure continued employment for team members who do not contribute to team improvement and who fail to comply with production and attendance standards. Teams will be assigned the role of disciplining and terminating below-standard team members.

Before leaving the discussion of the staffing system, we would like to point out that the approach we have taken is very much like the approach being taken by other manufacturing companies. For an illustration, take a look at Table I2–2, which summarizes a *Wall Street Journal* article about new methods for hiring workers in the auto industry.

271

*ILLUSTRATION TWO
Human Resource
Systems for
Total Quality
Management–
Oriented
Manufacturing
Teams*

272

PART FOUR
Designing Human
Resource Systems
for Specific
Business
Situations

TABLE I2-2. Viewing Workers as
Major Capital-Equipment Investments

U.S. automakers (behaving more like their Japanese counterparts) are beginning to view new workers as if they were capital-equipment investments.

The lean manufacturing techniques of the Japanese (techniques now being imitated by U.S. firms) require a different type of worker from the traditional assembly-plant worker of the past.

Ford and Chrysler are now imitating the more selective employee-screening techniques used by the Japanese when they staff new U.S. and European assembly plants.

Ford uses a 3½-hour applicant testing procedure:

- *Arithmetic test*—candidates are assessed on the use of fractions and percentages
- *Technical material reading test*—candidates read segments of a technical manual and then answer a series of related questions (this would likely measure reading ability and "trainability")
- *Dexterity test*—candidates complete one of several manual dexterity tests, such as quickly placing washers, in the correct order, on a pole
- *Group exercise*—in a simulation exercise, candidates are assessed on their ability to work in teams
- *Peer interview*—candidates are interviewed by two current employees

Source: N. Templin, "Dr. Goodwrench: Auto Plants, Hiring Again, Are Demanding Higher-Skilled Labor," *The Wall Street Journal,* March 11, 1994, pp. A1, A4.

Training and Development

Skill Orientation. Should training focus on narrow functional and technical skills or on broad, general skills such as problem solving and group-process facilitation? The prescription here depends on different phases of the manufacturing associate's career. In the first few months after being hired, the associate needs to be exposed to broad, general skill acquisition. The need early will be to help associates learn about how to be effective in their TQM-oriented teams. Team facilitation and problem-solving skills must be acquired, along with other basic knowledge and skills (knowledge of statistical process control, presentation skills, etc.).

Later, very narrow skills and technical issues associated with assembling engines or operating special equipment such as automated painting machines will require considerable training attention. Thus, this dimension, unlike the others addressed so far, takes on different characteristics over time.

Training Method Orientation. As was the case with the previous dimension, this dimension varies as a function of the training phase. Early after being hired, general skill acquisition requires formal "classroom" training and orientation. The actual engine assembly processes (processes specific to each team) will need to be acquired through on-the-job experience and coaching from team members. For certain training tasks we also recommend what might be termed "just-in-time" training methods. For example, for certain assembly or testing tasks, teams should be responsible for creating training manuals or videos that can be used when a new team member requires the information.

273

*ILLUSTRATION TWO
Human Resource
Systems for
Total Quality
Management–
Oriented
Manufacturing
Teams*

In fact, this situation illustrates well the general blurring that is taking place between on-site training methods and more formal off-site methods.[18] While the general part of the curriculum can be addressed in a classroom-like setting, more individualized training methods can be used by employees within their work areas. Computer-based training (CBT), interactive/multimedia CBT, and other forms of self-paced instruction can be used in this facility.[19] For example, new employees could work with interactive/multimedia instructional systems to learn about the basic responsibilities associated with being part of a problem-solving team. Once the team actually begins its work, team members could take a more active role in coaching and informing newcomers about their roles and responsibilities.

Perhaps the most interesting development in the training and development area relates to providing just-in-time training. Very technical information about how to operate or maintain a piece of equipment can be provided at the time the information is needed. Computer programs can provide information about operating and maintenance sequences in a timely, graphic manner. Because the information is provided just before it will be applied in the real work setting, trainees will see the obvious connection to actual job performance and therefore should experience a high degree of motivation to learn.

Career Pathing. Because this manufacturing facility recognizes only one operating job class—the manufacturing associate—the concept of a career path is virtually irrelevant. But there are other opportunities that may be of interest to associates, so we recommend a system for **posting** all available jobs within and across all CEW manufacturing plants. A job-posting system is an official way to explicitly let current employees know of other positions as they become open within the company, thus affording current employees the first opportunity to become job candidates.

Formal Succession Planning. Whereas a formal succession planning system is likely to be necessary in other areas of CEW, a succession planning process, as it relates to manufacturing associates, is not particularly relevant (see career pathing and skills inventory discussions).

Skills Inventories. A computerized skills inventory that characterizes employees in terms of career interests, training and development experiences, and other facts about job capability is potentially useful. Although career opportunities beyond the **associate** classification are limited, there is some possibility for promotion to certain supervisory positions and for movement to other CEW assembly plants. A system that takes advantage of internal talent encourages company loyalty and commitment.

274

PART FOUR
Designing Human
Resource Systems
for Specific
Business
Situations

The Performance Measurement System

Measurement Type. It is important to monitor a variety of results (e.g., maintenance costs, number of engines that need reworking, number of engines produced per shift, number of days with perfect delivery records), but performance measurement at the individual level needs to be process-oriented. The results-oriented measurement occurs at the group or plant level (this is necessary for calculating such things as the Scanlon plan bonus ratios). But TQM programs and principles require that individuals receive feedback (for the purpose of improving performance and contribution) at the level of the skills and abilities required to perform well in teams.[20] Other aspects related to the manufacturing process also will need to be monitored so that the factors accounting for any quality variation can be identified.

Measurement Scope. At the level of performance feedback, peers should participate in the appraisal process. This is a form of **360 degree performance review,** a process that typically gathers information from multiple perspectives (peers, managers, and even customers) to help employees improve their performance levels. In fact, given that this manufacturing plant is organized around problem-solving, self-managed teams, turning team-management responsibilities over to team members makes perfect sense.[21]

CONCLUSION

This concludes our overview of a prescribed HRM system for the job class of manufacturing associate at the CEW midrange engine plant. This system resembles the management processes other writers have prescribed for TQM-oriented organizations.[22] In many ways our prescribed system takes on the properties of Staw's[23] **group-oriented** management system, discussed in Chapter 9:

1. Work is organized around intact groups.
2. Group members play a role in selecting, training, disciplining, and providing performance feedback to other group members.
3. Groups are used to enforce strong norms for behavior.

However, our prescribed system also incorporates many features of Staw's **organizationally oriented** management system. For example,

1. Rewards are tied to saving costs at the organizational level.
2. Some degree of security is offered to promote organizational loyalty.
3. Status distinctions between employees are minimized to reduce dissension and separatism.
4. Manufacturing teams engage in cross-training and cooperation.

This unique HR system is summarized in Table I2–3.

ILLUSTRATION TWO
Human Resource
Systems for
Total Quality
Management–
Oriented
Manufacturing
Teams

PAY LEVEL
Lag
Meet   Slightly above market midpoint
Lead

PAY AT RISK
None
Moderate   Moderate
Extensive

PERFORMANCE-CONTINGENT PAY
Individual
Team   Team-oriented; Scanlon plan
Organization

JOB PRICING
Internal equity   Not highly relevant dimension for this job
External equity   class

SKILL-BASED PAY
Yes   Yes
No

SENIORITY-BASED PAY
Yes   No
No

BENEFIT FLEXIBILITY
Yes   Yes
No

BENEFIT LEVEL
Lag
Meet   Meet
Lead

CAREER SYSTEM
Internal   Internal
External

CANDIDATE PREFERENCE
Potential   Potential
Achievement

ORGANIZATIONAL FIT
Right types   Right types emphasized for certain work
Diversity   values, but some background diversity for
                                  the generation of new ideas

EXIT ORIENTATION
Security   Security (level 2)
Managaged turnover

(Continued)

276

PART FOUR
Designing Human
Resource Systems
for Specific
Business
Situations

TABLE I2–3. *(Concluded)*

SKILL ORIENTATION
Technical   Hybrid (depends on career stage)
General

TRAINING METHOD
Informal/on-the-job   Hybrid (with a focus on "just-in-time")
Formal/classroom

CAREER PATHING
Yes   Not highly relevant for this job class
No

FORMAL SUCCESSION PLANNING
Yes   No
No

SKILL INVENTORIES
Yes   Yes; some relevance as it relates to the
No   limited opportunity to move into supervision
                                             or other specialty roles

MEASUREMENT TYPE
Results   Results and process
Process

MEASUREMENT SCOPE
Traditional   360 degree
360 degree

ENDNOTES

1. R. L. Rose, "Humming Mills: Once the 'Rust Belt,' Midwest Now Boasts Revitalized Factories," *The Wall Street Journal,* January 3, 1994, p. A1.

2. D. A. Aaker, *Developing Business Strategies* (New York: John Wiley & Sons, 1995), pp. 204–5.

3. T. P. Wyman, "Mercedes Engines Eyed for Dodges: DaimlerChrysler May Switch from Cummins Diesel Engines for Its Line of Ram Pickups," *Indianapolis Star,* March 7, 2000, pp. C1, C2.

4. W. E. Deming, *The New Economics* (Cambridge, MA: MIT Center for Advanced Engineering Study, 1994); and A. Rao, L. P. Carr, I. Dambolena, R. J. Kopp, J. Martin, F. Rafii, and P. F. Schlesinger, *Total Quality Management: A Cross Functional Perspective* (New York: John Wiley & Sons, 1996).

5. H. R. Roberts and B. F. Sergesketter, *Quality Is Personal: A Foundation for Total Quality Management* (New York: Free Press, 1993).

6. "Literacy Study Results 'Alarming'—Researchers Find Some Graduates Unable to Do Simple Reading, Math Problems," *Bloomington Herald-Times,* December 10, 1994, p. A7.

7. P. T. Kilborn, "Even in Good Times, It's Hard Times for Workers," *The New York Times,* July 3, 1995, pp. C1–C3.

8. D. Wessel, "Wage-Gap Blues: Strong Growth Brings Jobs to Cedar Rapids, but Many Pay Poorly," *The Wall Street Journal,* June 24, 1994. p. A1.

9. W. N. Cooke, "Employee Participation Programs, Group Based Incentives and Company Performance," *Industrial and Labor Relations Review* 47 (1994), pp. 594–610; A. J. Geare, "Productivity from Scanlon Type Plans," *Academy of Management Review* 1 (1976), pp. 99–108; and S. E. Gross, *Compensation for Teams* (New York: American Management Association, 1995).

10. B. Heshizer, "The Impact of Flexible Benefit Plans on Job Satisfaction, Organizational Commitment and Turnover Intentions," *Benefits Quarterly* 4 (1994), pp. 84–90; Hewitt Associates, *Fundamentals of Flexible Compensation* (New York: John Wiley & Sons, 1998); and R. M. McCaffery, *Employee Benefit Programs: A Total Compensation Perspective* (Boston: PWS-Kent Publishing Company, 1992).

11. G. F. Dreher and P. R. Sackett, *Perspectives on Employee Staffing and Selection* (Burr Ridge, IL: Richard D. Irwin, 1983), pp. 3–38.

12. Ibid.

13. I. Robertson and S. Downs, "Learning and the Prediction of Performers: Development of Trainability Testing in the United Kingdom," *Journal of Applied Psychology* 64 (1979), pp. 42–50; and A. D. Siegel, "Miniature Job Training and Evaluation as a Selection/Classification Device," *Human Factors* 20 (1978), pp. 189–200.

14. M. M. Harris, "Reconsidering the Employment Interview: A Review of Recent Literature and Suggestions for the Future," *Personnel Psychology* 42 (1989), pp. 691–726; and G. P. Latham, L. M. Saari, E. D. Pursell, and M. A. Campion, "The Situational Interview," *Journal of Applied Psychology* 65 (1980), pp. 422–27.

15. G. F. Dreher and S. D. Maurer, "Assessing the Employment Interview: Deficiencies Associated with the Existing Domain of Validity Coefficients." In R. W. Eder and G. R. Ferris (eds.), *The Employment Interview: Theory, Research, and Practice* (Newbury Park, CA: Sage Publications, 1989), pp. 249–68; and Latham et al., "The Situational Interview."

16. D. E. Bowen, G. E. Ledford, and B. R. Nathan, "Hiring for the Organization, Not the Job," *Academy of Management Executive* 4 (1991), pp. 35–51.

17. W. F. Cascio, "Downsizing: What Do We Know? What Have We Learned?" *Academy of Management Executive* 7 (1993), pp. 95–104.

18. K. N. Wexley and G. P. Latham, *Developing and Training Human Resources in Organizations* (New York: HarperCollins Publishers, 1991).

19. D. Shandler, *Reengineering the Training Function* (Delray Beach, FL: St. Lucie Press, 1996).

20. D. E. Bowen and E. E. Lawler, "Total Quality-Oriented Human Resources Management," *Organizational Dynamics,* Spring 1992, pp. 29–41.

21. J. W. Dean and J. R. Evans, *Total Quality: Management, Organization, and Strategy* (Minneapolis: West Publishing, 1994).

22. Bowen and Lawler, "Total Quality-Oriented Human Resources Management"; and Rao et al., *Total Quality Management.*

23. B. M. Staw, "Organizational Psychology and the Pursuit of the Happy/Productive Worker," *California Management Review* 28 (1986), pp. 40–53.

ILLUSTRATION TWO
Human Resource Systems for Total Quality Management–Oriented Manufacturing Teams

ILLUSTRATION 3

Human Resource Systems for Financial Services Sales

In this illustration we again focus on a company composite, a targeted class of jobs, and associated environmental and strategic factors. We will simultaneously consider an integrated set of staffing, development, and reward practices that together should accomplish the company's objectives. Again, Figure 1–1 is used as a conceptual map. We describe how business strategy and technology lead to the organization of work processes. Based on the way work is organized for a targeted job class, we derive the key employee behaviors and KSAs required. The relevant labor market and the legal context are then considered in developing the appropriate HR system.

THE TARGETED JOB CLASS: INSURANCE SALES AGENT

The job class we examine here is a class that is well-known to most people: financial services sales. We focus particular attention on salespersons who sell insurance, including such products as auto, homeowner, life, small business, disability, property/casualty, and hospital indemnity insurance. This is another job class which is at the "boundary tier" of an organization, susceptible to influence from above (coordination tier) and below (customer tier).[1] Boundary tier employees spend much time interacting with customers while also responding to expectations from management.

These types of positions involve working in individual office locations (agencies) to provide service to existing insurance customers and also to generate new contacts and customers in the community. The sales agents, whose locations may be scattered across a wide spectrum of large and small communities, perform work which has components both inside and outside the office. They work autonomously, often putting in long hours. They must be highly independent, motivated, self-starting individuals. Although this illustration focuses on a company that deals primarily with insurance sales, many of the work requirements bear a close resemblance to the work of professionals who provide sales and service for other types of financial services.

The company in our example employs a large sales force—the target of our prescribed HR system. After describing the company's strategy, the relevant technology, the immediate labor market, and the legal context for HRM practices, we prescribe the HR system that should promote the key behaviors required of high-performing salespersons.

Midwest Insurance Company is a medium-sized insurance company located in 13 midwestern states. Midwest's headquarters is in a medium-sized university city located 120 miles equidistant between two major metropolitan areas. Midwest employs 1,250 agents (85 percent white males) in its sales force, placed in individual agencies dispersed across both large and small communities in the 13-state area. *The company believes that continuous growth in both premiums and the number of policies is essential to its long-term survival and growth.* Thus, Midwest's strategic plan includes decisions about where to locate agencies in the future; some communities are targeted as sites for additional agencies while other communities are slated for removal of agencies (e.g., the firm recently decided to remove agencies from a region considered to be highly susceptible to earthquakes).

The nature of the business and its strategic objectives are such that it is crucial to maintain a sales force with outstanding skills in generating new customers. Salespersons also need outstanding customer service skills to maintain a positive image and retain customers. Thus, Midwest needs an effective HR system for rewarding, selecting, and developing a high-quality sales force.

The work of Midwest's sales force is performed in individual agencies dispersed across the many communities in which the company operates. Each agent typically has a small office support staff. Agents are connected to Midwest's home office electronically, by a recently introduced technology which is convenient for completing new customer insurance applications. All application information is electronically submitted by agents and is completely processed at the home office by the end of the next day. In the past, agents mailed their applications to the home office, which maintained a large pool of data entry operators—jobs now eliminated. Midwest's agents also have ready access to all of their customers' data by computer. Thus, they can use laptops for sharing information with customers, which serves as a handy "point-of-sale" tool.

KEY EMPLOYEE BEHAVIORS AND CRITICAL EMPLOYEE ATTRIBUTES

Midwest's sales force, as previously mentioned, performs both inside- and outside-the-office work. Inside, the sales force primarily serves current customers who telephone or visit the agency. This work might be expanding a customer's coverage, adding a family member to coverage (e.g., auto insurance), and administrative work involving auto accidents and claims adjustment. Agents also deal with potential customers who call in for quotes of Midwest's insurance rates.

280

PART FOUR
Designing Human
Resource Systems
for Specific
Business
Situations

The outside work, especially for a new agent, centers around prospecting for new customers. This might include, for example, making contacts with small-business owners in the community and providing them with brochures and information about Midwest's business owner policies. Agents also call potential customers to inquire about "ex-dates," which are the expiration dates of a potential customer's current policies with another company. The agents then typically mail letters to these potential customers, following up with phone calls to provide information about Midwest's products and services. These ongoing prospecting activities require agents to engage in energetic "networking" in the community via a variety of local activities, organizations, and other community involvement.

Based on the nature of the sales force's work as just described, Midwest has determined that successful agents must have both extensive **product knowledge** and well-honed **sales skills.** Because few of the new hires already possess such knowledge and skill, the company must provide extensive training. For product knowledge, agents first acquire "prelicensing" training, a state licensing requirement, on their own before they are hired by Midwest. The company subsequently provides new agents with thorough training for product knowledge. Extensive sales training is also necessary, as discussed later in this chapter. A great deal of this training is not particularly company-specific, so that an agent's knowledge, skills, and abilities could be transferred fairly easily to other companies.

In addition to product knowledge and sales skills, key behaviors which the HR system would need to support include **motivation to receive training** to develop one's knowledge, skills, and abilities; applicant **attraction** to the company and its sales positions; and **retention** of sales agents with the company. High-quality **customer service** and high levels of **individual sales productivity** as well as **dollar volume of sales** are also crucial for successful salespersons.

In addition, a systematic job analysis has identified key skills, abilities, and personal attributes required at Midwest for success in the agent's job. The dimensions which emerged make sense in light of the critical sales agent behaviors we discussed in the preceding paragraphs:

1. **Integrity:** Maintaining social, ethical, and organizational norms in job-related activities.
2. **Job motivation:** Deriving personal satisfaction from activities and responsibilities available in the job.
3. **Sales ability/persuasiveness:** Utilizing appropriate interpersonal strategies and methods of communication to gain agreement or acceptance of activities, ideas, plans, or products.
4. **Initiative:** Actively attempting to influence events to achieve goals; self-starting rather than passive acceptance. Taking action to achieve goals beyond what is necessarily called for; originating action.
5. **Practical learning:** Assimilating and applying new, job-related information, taking into consideration rate and complexity.
6. **Oral communication skill:** Effectively expressing oneself in individual or group situations.
7. **Behavioral flexibility:** Modifying behavior to reach a goal.

8. **Judgment:** Making rational and realistic decisions which are based on logical assumptions and which reflect factual information and consideration of organizational resources.
9. **Planning and organization:** Establishing a course of action for self and others to accomplish a specific goal.
10. **Sensitivity:** Acting in a manner that indicates a consideration for the feelings and needs of others.
11. **Analysis:** Identifying problems, securing relevant information, relating data from different sources, and identifying possible causes of problems.

Thus, Midwest's agents must have the **ability, motivation,** and **opportunity** to perform a number of key behaviors. We will next consider the relevant labor market and legal context facing Midwest, and then begin a review of the appropriate HR system for sales agents by considering reward and compensation practices.

LABOR-MARKET ATTRIBUTES

As mentioned previously, Midwest Insurance employs a sales force of 1,250 agents working in agencies in 13 states. These agencies are divided into 92 districts, each with a district manager. In addition there are 14 state sales managers (two in the home office state), two directors of sales, and one vice-president of marketing, all in the home office. The headquarters (home office) is a university city with a population of 75,000. However, agencies are located in both urban and rural areas. In fact, a large portion of the agencies are located in small communities. Midwest makes every effort to identify potential agents from within the communities in which the company has agencies or plans to start new agencies. This is important because of the need for agents to prospect for new customers via networking, personal contacts, and community involvement.

Developing applicant pools for new sales agent openings is a significant challenge for Midwest Insurance. Sales of financial services, especially insurance, carries a stigma in the minds of many potential applicants. Potential recruits not only see the work as less than prestigious; they also quite accurately perceive the work as demanding, stressful, and requiring high levels of initiative, persistence, and tolerance for rejection. Moreover, many of the geographic regions in which Midwest's agencies are located have very low unemployment rates.

Thus, for a variety of reasons, Midwest cannot easily generate sufficient pools of high-quality applicants. Applicants are found by the "nominator" method: Current agents, managers, or other company employees make referrals to the district managers, who supervise the recruiting process. Although the overall size of the sales force has not grown in recent years, significant recruiting is still necessary. The four-year retention rate for Midwest's new agents is extremely favorable (60 percent) compared to the norm in the industry (approximately 15–17 percent). Nevertheless, the turnover of recent hires, along with some losses through retirement, death, and disability, fuels a constant need for new hires.

282

*PART FOUR
Designing Human
Resource Systems
for Specific
Business
Situations*

In attempting to compete for quality applicants, Midwest benefits from a strong company reputation in its agency communities. The company also has a special "subsidy plan," which guarantees income security for new agent hires during the training period. Additionally, the management committee monitors industry pay and benefit levels to keep Midwest's entry-level compensation package competitive.

THE LEGAL ENVIRONMENT

The company must, of course, abide by a large number of federal and state labor and employment laws. Thus, the company's HR systems are also affected by these federal and state laws. These laws include Title VII of the Civil Rights Act of 1964, the Age Discrimination in Employment Act, the Americans with Disabilities Act, and the Fair Labor Standards Act.[2] The legal environment for Midwest Insurance and its sales force, then, is comparable to that of a large number of U.S. industries and organizations employing managers and professionals.

THE PRESCRIBED HR SYSTEM

As in previous illustrations in Part IV of the book, we consider the components of the prescribed HR system in a particular order. We begin with the reward/compensation system, which follows from the way the work is designed. Again, we need the reward system information before we can decide about the other HR system components. We must take into account, for example, the performance–reward links provided to agents if we want to explain agents' motivation for performance. Making effective staffing decisions also requires us to identify applicants who will value (perceive high valence for) the rewards provided by the company for key employee behaviors, as discussed in Chapter 2. In addition, the design of the reward system has implications for the design of training programs in order to, for example, motivate Midwest's agents to continue to attend new training programs offered by the company over the span of their careers. Training program requirements will also likely be affected by staffing practices, as discussed in Chapter 9 on maintaining congruence in HR systems.

Reward and Compensation Practices

We will develop our system of pay and rewards using the HRM practices framework introduced in Chapter 3, which includes a number of reward system attributes. For purposes of this chapter and the situation at Midwest Insurance, we will discuss the issues of pay level, pay at risk, performance-contingent pay, job pricing (internal versus external equity), skill-based pay, seniority-based pay, benefit flexibility, and benefit level.

Pay Level. Pay level refers to the pay rates of the company's jobs compared to the pay of competing organizations, or the "going rate" in the labor market.[3] If the company offers salaries too low compared to the market, recruits will not be attracted. On the other hand, pay outlays cannot be so high that the firm cannot compete in the product market.

Midwest can choose to meet, lag, or lead the external market in its pay levels. Lagging the market could minimize compensation costs, but given the recruiting challenges discussed earlier, this strategy would not allow Midwest to attract sufficient applicants. It is also important that the company's salespersons receive highly competitive levels of overall compensation throughout their careers. Not only is there a scarcity of quality applicants in the labor market, but the knowledge and skills acquired at Midwest Insurance are readily transferable to other firms.

We also note that the sales force at Midwest has very little career progression, which could serve as a source of rewards and motivation in the company. New agents are hired as **salaried agents** while they are learning the business and being trained. At this entry level they receive a guaranteed amount of take-home pay per month, plus new policy and renewal policy commissions (the guaranteed monthly pay is deducted from commission earnings). After an average of three years, successful agents are shifted to **contract agent** status, in which they are essentially self-employed agents with great autonomy. In summary, a salesperson's career progression at Midwest consists of only two levels—in a hierarchical sense one could label it a "no-career-ladder" system.

Thus, for maintaining sales force attraction and retention, competitive compensation is a necessity. However, it appears that the company could meet its goals for attraction and retention of agents by **meeting** the market in entry-level base pay for new agents—and in addition making extensive use of pay at risk. For attracting new agents to the firm **wage and salary survey data** would be highly desirable, to ensure that the total compensation package of new hires is competitive and is achieving the compensation objective of meeting the external market.

Pay at Risk. As introduced in Chapter 3, pay at risk involves some rule for linking performance to supplementary financial rewards, such as a lump-sum cash payment. More pay is at risk as the supplementary, performance-based component comprises a higher proportion of total pay compared to a base level of pay. As discussed earlier, for the sales force at Midwest a high level of motivation for performance is extremely important, as is the opportunity to receive highly competitive amounts of pay. Thus, the situation calls for a very high proportion of at-risk pay. In order to accomplish the difficult goal of attracting and supporting new agents, some guarantee of a market-competitive base salary for new agents appears to be a sound practice, with a shift to virtually total at-risk pay for those who have become contract agents.

Performance-Contingent Pay. Making pay contingent on performance should enhance instrumentality perceptions and thus enhance

284

PART FOUR
Designing Human
Resource Systems
for Specific
Business
Situations

performance motivation for Midwest's sales force (see Chapter 2 on expectancy theory). Remember that the performance–reward connection can be at the individual, group, or organizational level. Given the autonomy with which Midwest's insurance agents perform their work, individual pay at risk is the recommended approach. As explained in Chapter 3, individual-based pay for performance is appropriate when (1) individuals perform independent tasks (performance does not depend on the performance of others), (2) job performance can be measured in a complete and objective way, and (3) performance can be measured at a reasonable cost.[4] All of these requirements are met at Midwest.

An effective approach would be the use of **commissions,** which are directly tied to sales. Employers share the risk with employees because pay levels rise and fall in line with revenues. These plans can be quite elaborate and specific to unique situations.[5] Midwest Insurance might, for example, provide a percentage commission both for generation of new customer policies and for renewals of existing customers' policies. The commission structure might vary somewhat for different types of insurance products. New policies would produce higher percentage commissions than renewals. As another example, there tends to be a customer "procrastination factor" for some types of insurance, such as homeowner's and life insurance (versus auto insurance). Customers are not as interested in or motivated to purchase or upgrade these types of insurance. Thus, higher sales force commissions for sales of these products would be a recommended practice. In addition, the company could use **lump-sum bonuses,** distributed each year, based on a percentage of individual agency profits. Other special rewards for high levels of sales performance are often used in the industry and could also be useful at Midwest, including **sales contests** and **incentive trips** for outstanding levels of performance.

Internal versus External Job Pricing. External job pricing focuses on setting pay rates to reflect what the competition is paying. In contrast, internal pricing focuses on internal equity—fairness of a job's pay relative to other jobs in the organization. The situation at Midwest clearly calls for a focus primarily on *external* pricing. First, it is necessary to compete aggressively for new hires in the labor market; thus, pay must be competitive. Second, the sales force performs only one "job," so that internal equity among jobs is not much of a concern for agents.

Skill-Based Pay. Some organizations choose to pay employees based on their acquisition of additional job-relevant skills—a practice considered to be new and innovative (see Chapter 4). Certainly, Midwest's agents should be motivated to enhance their skills in order to enhance their performance. However, there is no particular need for cross-training for flexibility in rotating employees among jobs. Acquiring both a depth and breadth of skills is important in enhancing sales agents' bottom-line performance, which should be amply rewarded. But we do not see a movement toward skill-based pay as providing any particular advantage for Midwest's agents.

Seniority-Based Pay. Seniority, defined as length of service in an employment unit, can be used as a basis for allocating many organizational outcomes, including financial rewards. Some objectives can be achieved with seniority-based rewards, primarily the maintaining of employee stability and perceptions of fairness.

However, seniority-based pay would be the wrong prescription for the sales force at Midwest Insurance. As we explained in Chapter 3, seniority makes sense when (1) the goal is to promote a high degree of company loyalty and commitment, (2) there is a need to encourage cooperative and team-oriented behavior, and (3) the situation requires extensive learning of company-specific knowledge and skills. Effective job performance at Midwest clearly does not involve a focus on cooperative and team-oriented behavior. In addition, the knowledge and skills which the sales force acquires are *not* company-specific but highly transferable. Although the company wants contract agents to maintain a long-term association with the firm, even the traditional concept of "seniority" does not make much sense in that Midwest Insurance's contract agents are essentially self-employed.

Benefit Flexibility and Benefit Level. Indirect forms of compensation can also be important in Midwest's HR system. Attractive benefits comprise part of a total compensation package that must be competitive, especially for the objectives of attracting and retaining a high-quality sales force. Which benefits are most valued can be determined by surveying both current employees and prospective applicants. Benefit flexibility (e.g., a cafeteria plan) could also ensure that the sales force values the benefit package.

We suggest that entry-level salaried agents be provided with a total package of benefits comparable to those provided by other firms with which Midwest competes for talent. Some of the benefits might increase with length of association with the company, such as pension benefits that vest after an appropriate length of time. Benefits which increase in value over the years would increase retention by increasing the instrumentality perceptions (strength of connection) between staying with Midwest and receiving valuable financial outcomes.

The Staffing System

Midwest Insurance needs systematic staffing strategies for acquiring a highly qualified sales force. We will describe a recommended staffing system, including approaches for providing a realistic job preview to applicants and for selecting new agents from the pool of applicants, as summarized in Figure I3–1. Then we will discuss the following attributes of the staffing system which were introduced in the framework provided in Chapter 3: career system orientation, potential versus achievement orientation, organizational fit, and exit orientation.

Recall that the labor market does not offer up a plentiful supply of qualified candidates for sales positions at Midwest Insurance. In spite of a few "walk-in" applicants, management must exert considerable effort to find

286

PART FOUR
Designing Human
Resource Systems
for Specific
Business
Situations

FIGURE I3–1. The staffing sequence for Midwest's agents.

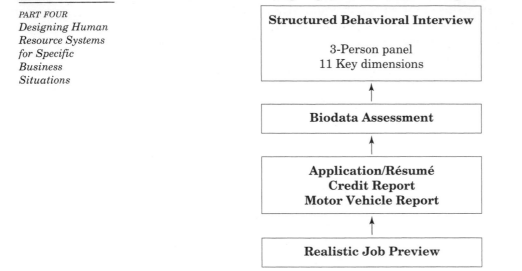

candidates. The firm uses what Midwest's managers refer to as the "nominator" method, with district managers relying on referrals from current agents, employees, and citizens in the communities which are sites for Midwest's agencies. As discussed earlier in this chapter, successful agents must possess a number of skills, abilities, and personal attributes, but specialized skills or experience is not required of applicants, who need only a bachelor's degree and prelicensing training, regulated by individual states. Fortunately, vigorous efforts to attract potential recruits has paid off, and Midwest has adequate pools of applicants who can be put through a selection process.

One of our first staffing prescriptions is to provide a **realistic job preview** of the work of a salesperson.[6] Since most of the applicants have no previous experience with insurance sales, they are unlikely to have a clear, complete picture of the work of an agent. Thus, a realistic preview is important both for applicants and for the company's investment in the staffing process. We endorse a practice sometimes used in the industry called "practice prospecting." At the time of recruits' initial application they are asked to go out into the community and to fill out 100 "insurance reviews," consisting of basic information on prospective customers. This experience provides a realistic albeit somewhat less demanding preview of the actual efforts required of the sales force in making contacts with possible customers. If completing these insurance reviews does not match the skills and interests of a recruit, he or she can withdraw from the staffing process at an early stage. We also consider this activity part of the recruit's self-assessment of "fit" with the culture of insurance sales organizations.

The remaining components of our recommended staffing system comprise a three-staged process. Once an **application** blank and **résumé** have been filed, the first step includes obtaining a **credit report** and **motor** vehicle report on applicants. Admittedly, one's credit worthiness and driving record are not always related to the requirements of performing a job. These kinds of hiring requirements may also have a "disparate impact" on the hiring prospects of various groups protected by discrimination laws (see Chapter 11). Nevertheless, given the personal and work requirements placed on insurance sales agents, credit and motor vehicle reports are appropriate and job-related, and in fact are widely used in the industry.

The second stage is a systematic assessment of **biographical history,** using a "biodata instrument." Applicants respond to objectively scored items of a demographic, life-style, experience, and preference nature. Biodata measurement follows the selection principle that "past behavior is the best predictor of future behavior." These instruments have an impressive track record of predictive validity: Scores on the instrument have a statistical relationship with important criteria of employee success. Biodata research has been conducted with a variety of populations and settings.[7]

Fortunately, a particular instrument has been carefully developed, validated via extensive research, and widely used in the insurance industry: the **LIMRA Career Profile.** This biodata instrument includes 162 items and measures an applicant's

1. Work history.
2. Commitment to present situation.
3. Belief in the value of insurance.
4. Personal financial situation.
5. Income expectations.
6. Career expectations.

This instrument has been demonstrated to predict sales agents' level of production and also retention, both important success criteria for Midwest's agents.[8] We could also consider this biodata instrument a measure of **organizational fit** in that applicants with particular patterns of beliefs, preferences, and expectations have been found to function more effectively in the environment of an insurance sales organization. Based on industry averages, we expect approximately 10 percent of the applicants to score high enough on this instrument to continue in the staffing process.

The third stage of hiring in our recommended staffing system focuses more directly on the particular skills, abilities, and personal attributes derived from the job analysis described earlier in this chapter. For focusing on these attributes we recommend using a **structured behavioral interview.** Remember that Midwest's job analysis identified the following key sales force attributes: **integrity, job motivation, sales ability/ persuasiveness, initiative, practical learning, oral communication skill, behavioral flexibility, judgment, planning and organization, sensitivity,** and **analysis.** The structured interview process would follow the recommendations of Campion, Pursell, and Brown[9] for an effective interview process:

1. Use job analysis as the source of interview questions.
2. Ask the same questions of each candidate.

288

*PART FOUR
Designing Human
Resource Systems
for Specific
Business
Situations*

3. Anchor the rating scales for scoring answers with examples and illustrations.
4. Use an interview panel to record and rate answers, to reduce idiosyncrasies of individual interviewers.
5. Administer the process consistently to all candidates.

As an example of behavioral interview questions, consider the dimension "initiative," identified as one of the required abilities for Midwest's sales force. The interview guide used by each interviewer might include the following questions:

What changes have you tried to implement in your area of responsibility?

Tell me about some projects you generated on your own.

Give me some examples of your doing more than required in your past job at _____.

Thus, our recommended procedure would involve developing a standard set of questions for each of the 11 dimensions to solicit behavioral information and examples from each applicant. A standard scoring procedure for each dimension and for a total interview score would be developed and used by the panel of interviewers. The panel would likely include the district sales manager, state sales manager, and a third panelist who is familiar with the work (e.g., state claims manager).

We now discuss several staffing system attributes introduced in our Chapter 3 framework, and how these staffing attributes apply to the situation at Midwest Insurance.

Career System Orientation. This attribute of the staffing system pertains to the emphasis on "promotion from within" versus hiring from the external labor market.[10] Midwest does not have much of a career hierarchy for salespersons, but there is an emphasis on promotion from within. Employees are hired from the external labor market only for the entry-level salaried agent positions; if successful, they progress to contract agent status. In addition, Midwest fills openings for district sales managers, state sales managers, directors of sales, and vice-president of marketing from within the ranks of its sales agents. This practice ensures that those promoted to managerial positions are fully socialized members of the company culture, and also helps to maintain the sense of stability and integrity which is important for the company's image with customers and the public.

Potential versus Achievement Orientation. This staffing system attribute focuses on the use of sponsored versus contest mobility norms for the career system. The **sponsored** approach involves the early identification of talent, along with specialized training and socialization for high-potential candidates.[11] The **contest** approach emphasizes identifying those with proven achievement records and current possession of the knowledge, skills, and abilities for higher level positions. As previously discussed, Midwest Insurance does not have much of a career hierarchy for the sales force. However, for choosing those agents who will fill district or state sales manager positions, for example, the company clearly (and we believe, appropriately) uses the **contest** mobility approach. There is no systematic effort for early identification of agents for managerial positions, and there is no special socialization or grooming for management slots.

289

*ILLUSTRATION
THREE
Human
Resource
Systems for
Financial
Services
Sales*

Organizational Fit. Some companies, as explained in Chapter 3, seek "right types," or candidates who fit the company's culture and who are similar to current employees. Our recommended staffing system for Midwest includes components of cultural fit—especially the use of the biodata instrument which measures values, preferences, and expectations predicting sales productivity and retention. However, given the lack of diversity of the sales force at Midwest (85 percent white males), some efforts to seek "non–right types" could also be useful. A more diverse sales force, which included more females and racial/ethnic minorities, might be better matched to the gender and ethnic distribution of Midwest's customer base, especially in the urban areas. As an example, attempts to diversify could take the form of explicit efforts to recruit for agents on minority college campuses and to develop more contacts and relationships with minorities in the communities in which Midwest operates.

Exit Orientation. This attribute pertains to the level of job security the company attempts to provide employees. Midwest Insurance's image with customers in terms of integrity, stability, and reliability is extremely important for the company's success. This leads to a strong preference for a loyal and stable workforce. In this vein, note that Midwest's four-year retention rate for agents (60 percent) is much higher than industry averages. The company would like the retention rate to be even higher. However, the sales force performs a challenging and stressful job, and a certain amount of attrition is unavoidable. We should also note that since all pay is at risk for contract agents, these agents must maintain some minimum level of performance or they would not survive in the business. Nevertheless, Midwest has never shown any strategic preference for downsizing or restructuring.

Training and Development

Again following the HRM practices framework provided in Chapter 3, we will develop a recommended system of training and development for Midwest Insurance's sales force. We will pay particular attention to skill orientation, training method orientation, career pathing, formal succession planning, and use of skill inventories.

Skill Orientation. As discussed in Chapter 3, we should decide if the company's orientation to training should focus on functional and technical skills or, alternatively, on the development of skills that generalize to a variety of situations (conflict resolution, problem-solving skills, etc.). The more general training is often valuable for firms that desire cross-functionally trained employees, who are able to rotate to a variety of jobs, thus providing staffing flexibility. For the job of sales agent at Midwest the **technical skills orientation** is clearly most appropriate.

290

PART FOUR
Designing Human
Resource Systems
for Specific
Business
Situations

Midwest's new agents typically have no experience in the sales of financial services. The overriding purpose of training should be to develop as quickly as possible the necessary knowledge, skills, and abilities for high-quality sales and customer service. Midwest wants to place new agents in individual agencies soon after hiring. Management hopes these agents will "hit the ground running," with rapid development of KSAs for sales performance. The company provides some initial support with a subsidy plan and salaried agent status, hoping that an agent's productivity and profitability will be acceptable for transition to contract agent status within about three years. In addition to the initial development of KSAs for sales performance, Midwest needs to provide periodic training to established contract agents. This training would include both updating agents' product knowledge and providing more advanced knowledge. Experienced agents can also benefit from periodic training for improving sales skills—a set of skills which is complex and difficult to master.

The situation at Midwest necessitates training for new hires, if we consider the four conditions which call for training interventions.[12] First, the knowledge, skills, and abilities to be acquired are clearly needed for performing one's job—true for Midwest's agents. Second, most or all of these KSAs are not possessed by incoming hires, which is also true at Midwest. Third, employees should be motivated and ready to be trained. This should not be a problem at Midwest. The sales agents' early sales productivity determines their initial survival in the company and progression to contract agent status. In addition to their survival, the agents' opportunity to receive powerful financial incentives hinges on developing these critical KSAs. The fourth condition necessary for a training intervention is the training's transferability to the actual job performance setting (i.e., back in one's agency). This transfer of training can easily be built into the training system, as we will see in the next section.

Training Method Orientation. Here we are concerned with the traditional distinction between emphasizing on-site or off-site training methods.[13] An organization can decide to use a coaching, on-the-job, apprenticeship, job rotation, or project team assignment basis for training. Alternatively, an organization can emphasize formal training centers and programs, including a corporate campus, classroom training, correspondence courses, or computer-assisted instruction.

Midwest could use a variety of both on-site and off-site training methods for achieving its training goals. Since training is so important for Midwest's agents, we will illustrate in some detail a sequence of training activities. First, an initial two-week **classroom training** program at the home office training center can provide (1) general and company information, (2) product and policy knowledge, and (3) introductory sales skills necessary for getting agents started in their careers. For developing introductory sales skills the **behavior modeling** approach could be quite effective. This learning technology includes the components of (1) communication of key "learning points," (2) observing the correct way to perform each behavior, (3) practicing the behaviors or skills, (4) receiving feedback about how well the behavior has been performed, and (5) practicing the behavior and receiving feedback for additional improvements in proficiency.[14]

Second, after being assigned to an agency an **on-the-job coaching** approach can be used, in which a new agent makes sales calls accompanied for two to three weeks by the district manager. The district manager can assist the new agent in developing sales skills by providing some additional modeling, feedback, and encouragement. Third, Midwest's new agents need to continue to develop their product knowledge, which could be accomplished through the use of **correspondence courses,** with the agent's work submitted to and evaluated by the district manager. Fourth, after six months new agents could be provided with a week of classroom training back at the home office, for additional development of both product knowledge and sales/customer service skills. Fifth, after another six months, Midwest can provide an "advanced school" for agents, with more information on the firm's products and special emphasis on sales skills. At this phase of an agent's progression, agents have become aware of some of the frustrations of not only identifying new customers but locating desirable, high-quality customers. At this advanced school Midwest could provide examples, panel discussions by experienced agents, and other information related to the "art" of finding the most desirable customers. Finally, Midwest could periodically offer special workshops for all agents for a variety of purposes, such as imparting information about changes in policies or procedures and new product information. Figure I3–2 illustrates a sequence of training activities for the sales force at Midwest Insurance.

Career Pathing. Career development in many organizations involves clearly defined career paths and formal advice on career planning and development. Alternatively, career management processes can be informal and depend on self-initiated mentoring relationships. We pointed out in Chapter 3 that a heavy emphasis on career development and career pathing often includes the use of HR information systems that assess employees in terms of career interests, training and development experiences, and measures of current and future capability.

At Midwest Insurance formal career pathing does *not* seem very relevant for salespersons. The members of the sales force start as salaried agents and then progress within a few years to become self-employed agents in a contractual relationship with the company. However, some *informal* career processes certainly do deserve attention for new hires, in that these agents need mentoring, coaching, and informal developmental relationships to develop their knowledge and skills for career success. We described earlier, for example, the one-on-one coaching to be provided on the job by district managers, who accompany new agents on sales calls.

Formal Succession Planning. Since Midwest's sales agents become what is essentially self-employed contractors, formal succession planning would not seem relevant. However, at Midwest there periodically are managerial positions available. The company employs 92 district managers, 14 state sales managers, 2 sales directors, and a vice-president of marketing.

291

ILLUSTRATION
THREE
Human
Resource
Systems for
Financial
Services
Sales

292

PART FOUR
Designing Human
Resource Systems
for Specific
Business
Situations

FIGURE I3–2. The sequence of training experiences for Midwest's agents.

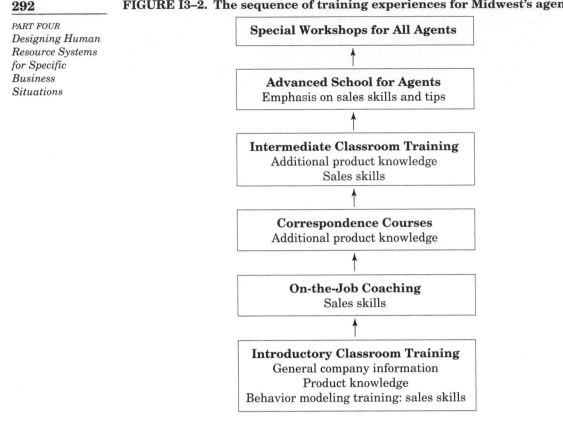

These positions are filled from the ranks of the sales force. At a minimum, the company would want to inform its new hires about these positions. Any agent who would like to consider an administrative position could develop a career plan for acquiring the requisite skills and knowledge. The company would also want to alert the sales force about these positions as they become available. An open **job posting** system would be a useful technique for advertising these positions to the sales force.

Skills Inventories. We have argued that it does not make sense for Midwest's agents to have formal career paths and formal succession planning. Similarly, systematic maintenance of skills inventories would not be particularly useful.

The Performance Measurement System

The final attribute we will consider in designing the HR system for salespersons is performance measurement. In Chapters 3 and 7 we acknowledged the astonishing array of types, forms, and purposes of performance measurement systems.[15] Instead of focusing on all the possibilities, we chose to address a fundamental way of distinguishing among firms.

Measurement Type. Some firms follow a "process" orientation while others choose to focus on a "results" orientation in performance measurement. Results-oriented measurement systems count the outcomes at work (e.g., dollar sales value per month) or the time taken to complete assignments. Process-oriented systems rate the *way* work is completed (e.g., salesperson greets the customer within the first three minutes the customer is in the office). The type of feedback provided to employees also differs under the two approaches. A process-oriented system would provide information about process improvements the employee can implement, whereas the results-oriented system tends to be used to allocate scarce resources such as money.

A **results-oriented** performance measurement system, which appears to be best suited to the nature of the agents' work, is the industry norm. Midwest's managers set goals for the entire company and have available clear measures of important outcomes. For example, Midwest expects to see 7–8 percent overall growth in sales per year. Thus, it is relatively easy to translate these company goals into objectives for individual sales agents, in terms of standards reflecting both monthly productivity (number of sales) and dollars of sales. The setting and acceptance of concrete and challenging goals, along with feedback (knowledge of results) serves as a powerful tool for increasing employee performance levels.[16]

Measurement Scope. As discussed in Chapter 7, many organizations have recently experimented with multidirectional performance assessment, such as 360 degree feedback. Given the highly individualized nature of the work of Midwest's agents, and their relative physical isolation from colleagues and managers, it would not seem to be easy to implement multidirectional performance assessment.

CONCLUSION

We have now completed our overview of a prescribed HR system for the job class of financial services sales, as illustrated by the insurance sales force at Midwest Insurance. Using Staw's terminology, as introduced in Chapter 9, this system is highly **individually oriented,** given the nature of the work performed by these agents and the unique set of circumstances at Midwest.[17] Based on the key sales force behaviors at Midwest, when we consider the entire system of 19 HRM attributes we see that the HR system can be characterized as displayed in Table I3–1.

294

PART FOUR
Designing Human
Resource Systems
for Specific
Business
Situations

TABLE I3–1. Midwest's Agents: Recommended HR System

Pay Level

Lag	Meet
Meet	
Lead	

Pay at Risk

None	Extensive
Moderate	
Extensive	

Performance-Contingent Pay

Individual	Individual
Team	
Organization	

Job Pricing

Internal equity	External equity
External equity	

Skill-Based Pay

Yes	No
No	

Seniority-Based Pay

Yes	No
No	

Benefit Flexibility

Yes	Yes
No	

Benefit Level

Lag	Meet
Meet	
Lead	

Career System

Internal	Internal
External	

Candidate Preference

Potential	Achievement
Achievement	

Organizational Fit

Right types	Right types emphasized
Diversity	

(Continued)

ILLUSTRATION
THREE
Human
Resource
Systems for
Financial
Services
Sales

Exit Orientation

Security	Security
Managed turnover	

Skill Orientation

Technical	Technical
General	

Training Method

Informal/on-the-job	Hybrid
Formal/classroom	

Career Pathing

Yes	No
No	

Formal Succession Planning

Yes	No; some open job posting
No	

Skill Inventories

Yes	No
No	

Measurement Type

Results	Results
Process	

Measurement Scope

Traditional	Traditional
360 degree	

ENDNOTES

1. B. Schneider and D. E. Bowen, *Winning the Service Game* (Boston: Harvard Business School Press, 1995), p. 7.
2. As we mentioned in earlier chapters, comprehensive reviews of these employment laws can be found in human resource management texts such as J. Ledvinka and V. G. Scarpello, *Federal Regulation of Personnel and Human Resource Management* (Boston: PWS-Kent Publishing Company, 1991).
3. G. T. Milkovich and J. M. Newman, *Compensation* (Burr Ridge, IL: Richard D. Irwin, 1996).
4. G. P. Latham and D. L. Dossett, "Designing Incentive Plans for Unionized Employees: A Comparison of Continuous and Variable Ratio Reinforcement Schedules," *Personnel Psychology* 31 (1978), pp. 47–62.

296

PART FOUR
Designing Human
Resource Systems
for Specific
Business
Situations

5. J. K. Moynahan, *The Sales Compensation Handbook* (New York: Amacom, 1991); and J. Tallitsch and J. K. Moynahan, "Fine Tuning Sales Compensation Programs," *Compensation and Benefits Review,* March–April 1994, pp. 34–37.

6. J. P. Wanous, *Organizational Entry: Recruitment, Selection, and Socialization of Newcomers* (Reading, MA: Addison-Wesley, 1980).

7. For example, see J. E. Hunter and R. F. Hunter, "Validity and Utility of Alternative Predictors of Job Performance," *Psychological Bulletin* 83 (1984), pp. 1053–71; and W. A. Owens, "Background Data." In M. D. Dunnette (ed.), *Handbook of Industrial and Organizational Psychology* (Chicago: Rand McNally, 1976).

8. S. H. Brown, "Long-Term Validity of a Personal History Item Scoring Procedure," *Journal of Applied Psychology* 63 (1978), pp. 673–76.

9. M. A. Campion, E. D. Pursell, and B. K. Brown, "Structured Interviewing: Raising the Psychometric Properties of the Employment Interview," *Personnel Psychology* 41 (1988), pp. 25–42.

10. J. A. Sonnenfeld and M. A. Peiperl, "Staffing Policy as a Strategic Response: A Typology of Career Systems," *Academy of Management Review* 13 (1988), pp. 588–600.

11. J. E. Rosenbaum, *Career Mobility in a Corporate Hierarchy* (New York: Academic Press, 1984).

12. K. N. Wexley and G. P. Latham, *Developing and Training Human Resources in Organizations* (New York: HarperCollins Publishers, 1991), pp. 36–107.

13. Ibid.

14. A. P. Goldstein and M. Sorcher, *Changing Supervisor Behavior* (New York: Pergamon, 1974); F. P. Latham and L. M. Saari, "Application of Social-Learning Theory to Training Supervisors through Behavior Modeling," *Journal of Applied Psychology* 64 (1979), pp. 239–46; and H. H. Meyer and M. S. Raich, "An Objective Evaluation of a Behavior Modeling Training Program," *Personnel Psychology* 36 (1983), pp. 755–61.

15. H. J. Bernardin and R. W. Beatty, *Performance Appraisal: Assessing Human Behavior at Work* (Belmont, CA: Wadsworth, 1984).

16. E. A. Locke, K. N. Shaw, L. M. Saari, and G. P. Latham, "Goal Setting and Task Performance: 1969–1980," *Psychological Bulletin* 90 (1981), pp. 125–52.

17. B. M. Staw, "Organizational Psychology and the Pursuit of the Happy/Productive Worker," *California Management Review* 28 (1986), pp. 40–53.

ILLUSTRATION 4

Human Resource Systems for Project Development Teams

In this illustration we again discuss a company composite, described within the context of its strategy and environmental circumstances. We emphasize maintaining an integrated HR system, focusing on multiple HRM practices for a targeted class of jobs. We structure the chapter around the model presented in Figure 1–1, using it as a conceptual map. After discussing the key employee behaviors required to meet company objectives and the legal and labor-market context, we prescribe an HR system, selecting from the 19 dimensions of an HR system presented in Chapter 3.

THE TARGETED JOB CLASS: TELEVISION SITCOM WRITER

The job class we examine here is television "sitcom" writer. Many people are familiar with the 30-minute situation comedies which are a staple of prime-time television fare in the United States and, increasingly, around the world. Sitcom writers are highly paid creative professionals who work in teams to produce the script for an entertaining 22 minutes of television comedy. These writers must, of course, be skilled at writing comedy scripts. They must also be capable of working long hours "in the room" with a team of fellow sitcom writers to generate story ideas and refine written scripts, often under intense time pressure. In addition to generating and revising scripts, the writers provide key input to the acting, editing, and direction of each television comedy episode produced. Thus, they must also be able to collaborate, communicate, and negotiate with a variety of others, including actors, directors, production crews, executives, and support staff.

We now turn to the analysis of XYZ Productions, following the framework set forth in Figure 1–1. After describing the company and its environment, we consider how business strategy and technology lead to the organization of work processes. Next, based on the way work is organized for the targeted job class, we derive the key employee behaviors and KSAs required, consider the labor market and legal context, and then design the appropriate HR system for television sitcom writer at XYZ Productions.

BUSINESS STRATEGY, TECHNOLOGY, AND WORK PROCESSES: XYZ PRODUCTIONS

XYZ Productions creates new television comedies on a contract basis for sale to the three major U.S. broadcast television networks, and for syndication

298

*PART FOUR
Designing Human
Resource Systems
for Specific
Business
Situations*

(reruns) on independent and cable networks. The company employs writers, directors, producers, production crews, actors, editors, support staff, and a small corporate staff of executives. XYZ maintains a single location in Los Angeles, California, including offices, studios, and sound stages, although it sometimes leases these facilities in other locations in the area. XYZ was formed 20 years ago by two television producers and became one of the most successful television production companies.

XYZ typically produces from one to four "first-run" network television shows per television season. Generally, a network commissions the writing of a script for a television comedy, then, if the network likes the script, it may "shoot" it—that is, commission the taping of the "pilot" episode. If the network still sees promise in the show, network executives may then order a minimum of 6, up to 22 episodes from XYZ Productions, to air on prime-time television. The preproduction and production seasons, a time of intense activity for most XYZ employees, begins in June (June–July is preproduction) and extends to February or March each year. For each show, XYZ employs a team of approximately 6 to 10 sitcom writers. Most of the writers are hired on a two-year contract basis, with an option to cancel after the first year; the contract is usually void if the specific show is canceled by the network. Not surprisingly, the turnover of XYZ's sitcom writers is high from year to year, as is customary in this industry. Writers build their careers across time by working for numerous companies on numerous different shows. The writers, who hold a variety of job titles, play a pivotal role at all phases of the process of creating and producing television comedies.

The key aspects of business strategy at XYZ Productions are easy to understand and to communicate. First, the company seeks to produce television comedies that are attractive to mass viewing audiences and therefore viable for sale to the major U.S. television networks. Second, the key to the business success of XYZ is to keep its major network shows on the air for approximately five years; the shows can then be sold into **syndication** and rerun in major markets throughout the world. XYZ receives payment for each airing of a show in syndication—the most important source of revenue for the company. The vast majority of the "pilot" scripts commissioned by the major networks are never actually produced and aired to the public. Similarly, only a fraction of the comedies that air on the networks last for the five years, which is necessary for syndication. Nevertheless, getting shows into syndication is the crucial strategic goal for XYZ's business success. The company currently has a number of shows in syndication, airing to audiences around the world, especially Europe. Employment of talented teams of sitcom writers plays a crucial role in XYZ's ability to fulfill its business strategy.

The preproduction and production season for XYZ shows extends from June through February–March of each year. The working year for an XYZ sitcom writer corresponds to this season—approximately 40 weeks per year. The **preproduction process** begins in June, with the writers working 8 to 10 hours per day. The writers, under the direction of a head writer (usually called executive producer), generate story lines as a team for the individual episodes to be produced during the season. Individual team members are then assigned to flesh out the basic story lines into outlines for specific episodes, and then to write the first rough draft scripts. The writers then again work in a collaborative fashion as a team to rewrite each of these scripts, offering "notes" for revisions, sharing new ideas, and providing feedback and suggestions on written scripts. When necessary, the head writer makes the final decisions about the composition of a script. The team of writers continues this work throughout the summer in preparation for production, which begins in August. During the preproduction process the team of writers can typically complete six scripts for the upcoming season. The remaining scripts are written and revised during the production season.

The **production process** extends from August through February. The production season brings together the work of all XYZ employees, including writers, producers, actors, directors, production crews, editors, and support staff. During this process, one television show per week is produced at XYZ, following a schedule of three weeks of shooting (shows taped on Friday evenings), followed by one week off, followed by another three weeks of shooting. During a week of production at XYZ, a consistent daily schedule is followed on all XYZ comedy shows—a systematic production process. In fact, a very similar schedule is followed throughout the industry. We will now describe the day-by-day schedule to communicate the essential flavor of work processes at XYZ Productions.

Monday could be characterized as "read-through and rewrite" day. At around noon, the actors, attended by the writers, XYZ executives, and network executives, read aloud, word-for-word, the script for the week's show. The actors then exit to begin rehearsals, while the network and XYZ executives, along with "star" actors on the show, discuss the script and recommend changes. The 22-minute time span for the show is also assessed, including time allowances for the "laugh spread," "blocking spread" (movements on stage), and an extra 2 to 3 minutes for editing out undesirable moments. On Monday afternoon after the reading, the team of writers begins an intensive process of revision of the script. If *major* structural changes are required in the script, the team may be divided into task subgroups, each led by a highly experienced writer. This rewriting is usually completed late at night. The latest iteration of the script is then delivered to the homes of the actors, in advance of Tuesday's morning rehearsal.

On Tuesday morning the actors and director rehearse in preparation for the afternoon "producers' run-through." This is a rehearsal on the set without interruption. The team of writers attends, observing and making notes about what works and what does not. They may place checkmarks in parts of the script that appear to produce laughs from those present, and circles to indicate parts of the script which do not work. After the run-through, the actors also provide input to the director and/or the head writer about the script. The team of writers returns to "the room," where they compile notes on the script generated by the director, XYZ executives, and the writers. The team then revises the script on a page-by-page basis, often not completing the new script revision until 3 A.M. on Wednesday.

Wednesday is a critical day in the weekly production cycle: Network executives join the group of actors, director, executives, producers, and writers

299

ILLUSTRATION FOUR
Human Resource
Systems for Project
Development
Teams

300

*PART FOUR
Designing Human
Resource Systems
for Specific
Business
Situations*

in attending what is called the "network run-through." After the run-through on stage, the writers may offer notes with suggestions for the actors and in turn receive notes on the script from the actors. The writers return to the room for the most important rewrite of the week, because the actors begin to "lock-in" their lines for the show starting on Thursday. Again, the team of writers typically works into the early morning hours.

Thursday is the day of the "camera run-through." The actors wear their costumes and the director finalizes the shots to be used in the show. On this day the writers will also give notes with suggestions to the director. Rewriting continues on this day also.

Friday is the day of the actual taping of the week's show. As on every day of the work week, the writers arrive at work midmorning (around 10 A.M.) and continue to revise the script. They may also oversee activities such as the editing of a previous week's show or the hiring of guest actors for a future show. Two performances of the current week's show are taped before a live audience on Friday in the late afternoon and evening, with a dinner for the staff (and exchange of more notes among actors, writers, and director) between the two tapings. The writing team observes the tapings on stage and performs last-minute rewriting of failed jokes or lines. The show which airs on the network several weeks later is created from a blending of the "best takes" from the two Friday tapings.

Our discussion of the summer preproduction phase and the work cycle during the production phase sets the stage for our discussion of key behaviors and attributes for XYZ's sitcom writers.

KEY EMPLOYEE BEHAVIORS
AND CRITICAL EMPLOYEE ATTRIBUTES

XYZ's sitcom writers play an important role in the company's producing of competitive products—television comedies which will be purchased and shown on a major TV network, and which will air for enough years to be sold into syndication. In addition to possessing strong comedic creativity and strong writing skills, the writers must be amenable to spending many hours (often from midmorning to past midnight) working in close quarters in the room with their fellow writers, generating story ideas, accepting feedback, critiquing their colleagues' work, and suggesting revisions. This kind of intense teamwork requires that each writer possess a number of additional skills. The writer's job also involves important and often sensitive interactions with other key XYZ professionals, including the director, actors, and editors.

The television and movie industries are notable (or notorious) for their informality and lack of systematic processes for managing human resources. Not surprisingly, XYZ Productions has developed neither systematic job analyses nor objective measurement of knowledge, skills, and abilities for sitcom writers. Nevertheless, those who work in or are knowledgeable about these jobs appear to recognize and agree on critical sitcom writer behaviors, and some important kinds of knowledge, skill, and ability. These behaviors and KSAs are also consistent with the discussion earlier in this chapter of the work processes for sitcom writers:

301

ILLUSTRATION FOUR
Human Resource
Systems for Project
Development
Teams

1. **Creativity:** We would expect sitcom writers to have a good sense of humor; a more precise statement of the required ability is that they must be creative to be effective in their work. For example, creativity is required for generating humorous story lines and scripts, "punching up" (improving on the humor in) scripts, and making useful suggestions for the acting and directing of a comedy.
2. **Scriptwriting skills:** Sitcom writers must be able to produce well-written scripts which meet a number of criteria, including appropriate structure, plot development, character development, and plenty of funny lines.
3. **Oral communication skills:** Sitcom writers must be able to verbally express ideas with clarity. They must be able to exchange ideas with individuals and with team members.
4. **Team orientation:** Sitcom writers must be willing to work toward the interests of the team as a whole and promote the overall team's work.
5. **Sensitivity:** Displaying a consideration for the feelings and needs of others is important both in the room with the team of writers and also in providing feedback and suggestions to directors, actors, and other colleagues.
6. **Behavioral flexibility and openness to feedback:** Sitcom writers must be able to modify their behavior to fit the situation and they must be receptive to feedback from others, especially the writers with whom they work in the room.
7. **Stamina and energy:** Sitcom writers must have the stamina to work extremely long hours, including late-night hours, while continuing to focus with a high level of intensity on their work.
8. **Stress tolerance:** Sitcom writers must be able to think well on their feet and to work under intense deadline pressure and in situations with the potential for interpersonal conflict.

Thus, XYZ's sitcom writers must have the ability, motivation, and opportunity to perform a number of key behaviors. We next consider the labor market and legal context in which XYZ Productions operates, and we specify the appropriate HR system for sitcom writers at XYZ.

LABOR-MARKET ATTRIBUTES

The job of sitcom writer is highly paid and highly prestigious work. Salaries of more than $400,000 per year are not unusual; a number of successful veteran writers earn well over a million dollars a year.[1] As a result, large numbers of writers (or would-be writers) seek positions as staff writers for television production companies. The Writers Guild of America, west, to which XYZ's writers belong, has 8,500 members (television and film

302

PART FOUR
Designing Human
Resource Systems
for Specific
Business
Situations

writers); approximately half are not employed in a given year. There is a widespread perception among industry executives, however, that most in the labor market who seek positions do not possess the necessary critical skills for the work, especially scriptwriting skills (the same perception holds for the labor pool of actors).

The typical mechanism a writer seeking employment uses is an **agent,** who forwards a "spec script"—sent on speculation—to executives of the production company. The spec script is a sample script, written by the applicant for a specific show, although not usually the show for which the applicant is applying. The agent and applicant hope that an XYZ executive will be impressed by the talent displayed in the spec script and set up an interview (a "meeting") with the writer. Agents in the entertainment industry often specialize; thus, there are a number of agents who specialize in placement of sitcom writers. For writers in the labor market, being accepted as a client by a well-connected agent is the most important step in gaining employment by a television production company.

XYZ Productions draws from a labor market which could be termed "bicoastal," in that applicants tend to reside in either New York City or Los Angeles. The "model" successful applicant at XYZ (and similar companies) tends to be a young—twenties to early thirties—white, male, college graduate, often from a prestigious university. The other major source of applicants for entry-level sitcom writer jobs is the pool of in-house **writers' assistants.** These assistants, who tend to share the demographic characteristics of the writers, are employed at low wages at XYZ to assist the sitcom writers in a number of tasks, especially taking and compiling notes from various parties for the continual process of generating revisions of television scripts. Many of these assistants aspire to careers as sitcom writers.

In summary, there is a vast supply of people in the labor market who aspire to positions as sitcom writers for firms such as XYZ Productions. However, it appears that only a fraction of those in the pool possess the requisite skills. For applicants, receiving serious consideration for one of these highly paid positions is difficult. Although the labor market contains huge numbers of applicants, XYZ executives perceive that competition among employers for highly skilled sitcom writers is actually quite intense in the industry.

THE LEGAL ENVIRONMENT

Of course, XYZ Productions must comply with federal and state laws and regulations that apply to equal employment opportunity, wages and hours, safety, and labor relations. Even as we acknowledge the necessity to comply with these laws and guidelines, we should also acknowledge that the television industry does not have an impressive record of hiring diverse groups of people. The Writers Guild has a Department of Employment Access which administers programs, primarily with television producers, to enhance the training and employment opportunities for writers who are women, minority, over 40, and/or disabled.

303

ILLUSTRATION FOUR
Human Resource
Systems for Project
Development
Teams

The industry is also not known to have received much scrutiny from federal or state enforcement agencies in the area of equal employment opportunity. This may be partly because of the unique nature of the business and staffing processes used, and partly because of the small numbers of staff hired for particular positions in particular companies. As we reported earlier, XYZ's sitcom writers continue to be predominantly white, male, and relatively young.

The Writers Guild *does* play a significant role in employment of sitcom writers. All of XYZ's writers belong to the Writers Guild of America, west. Members pay a $2,500 initiation fee and dues are 1.5 percent of gross income, paid on a quarterly basis. The Writers Guild's "Minimum Basic Agreement" determines (a myriad of types of) minimum pay for various writing assignments. The Guild also oversees and administers the employers' contribution to writers' benefit funds, provides a legal staff to handle arbitration or lawsuits relating to contracts, determines all TV credits according to guild rules, monitors re-airings, and collects and distributes all residuals worldwide on behalf of writers, among other activities.

THE PRESCRIBED HR SYSTEM

Our discussion of a prescribed HR system again considers the 19 dimensions associated with the HRM domain statement, summarized in tabular form in Chapter 3. We begin this discussion with the attributes of the reward system.

Reward and Compensation Practices

Pay Level. Pay level refers to the company's decision about whether to pay at (meet), below (lag), or above (lead) the market.[2] A company may wish to control labor costs, but it must pay well enough to attract qualified applicants. For XYZ Productions, it is essential to hire the best creative talent from the labor market. Thus, highly competitive compensation is a must. As discussed earlier, although there are many willing applicants in the labor market for sitcom writers, only a fraction of these writers possess the high levels of skill required to produce a successful network television show. One way for XYZ to continue its success in this highly competitive business is to be a pay **leader** relative to competing employers. Leading the market can also allow XYZ to attract writers with more specialized writing skills, such as writers who are particularly skilled at contributing jokes or skilled at punching up scripts.

Pay at Risk. Putting some pay at risk involves linking performance to some source of direct supplemental income, such as lump-sum bonuses. More pay is at risk when the job-based component of total pay is reduced and the supplementary component is increased.[3] Although conventional types of pay at risk may be difficult to implement for sitcom writers, the

304

PART FOUR
Designing Human
Resource Systems
for Specific
Business
Situations

system of royalty payments, or residuals, for shows in syndication could be considered a type of long-term pay at risk. Remember that the primary strategy of XYZ Productions is to maintain a sitcom on a network for five years, thus allowing the show to be sold into syndication. *If* XYZ's writers have produced a successful show which meets this criterion, their income will be supplemented in the future by royalties. Each writer will receive a royalty payment for every episode shown in reruns around the world. This is potentially a significant stream of supplemental income—directly related to the success of XYZ's television show in its first run on the network.

Performance-Contingent Pay. Linking pay increases to level of performance enhances employees' instrumentality perceptions and thus raises their performance motivation (see Chapter 2). The pay–performance link can be at the individual, group, or organizational levels. As discussed earlier, individual sitcom writers at XYZ produce the first rough drafts of scripts; however, an intensive team process is used to produce the final product. Thus, for motivation, any pay–performance contingencies would need to be at the group level. This practice would encourage the critical behaviors of group cooperation and teamwork. Note, however, that writers' pay increases from year to year are negotiated with the writers' agents. In addition, measures of performance for the output produced by the writing team (i.e., individual scripts) are not available. Even if these measures were available, it would be difficult to attribute the quality of the product completely to the writing team, given that so many different parties provide input into the final script and the television show. Thus, a standard pay-for-performance system for XYZ Productions does not seem feasible.

Nevertheless, in the *long run* there is a kind of performance–reward connection for writers in that (1) they are likely to continue to be employed on a show by XYZ Productions if the show is a success (renewed by the network); and (2) royalties per show will be paid to the writers in future years if the show makes it into syndication.

Internal versus External Job Pricing. A focus on external job pricing is a focus on what other companies pay employees in similar jobs—a focus on relative pay rates among (not within) organizations.[4] In contrast, internal pricing focuses on internal fairness relative to other jobs within the company. The situation at XYZ Productions clearly calls for a focus on **external** pricing for sitcom writers. First, an important objective is to hire the most talented writers available from the labor market. Second, writers do not expect to remain with a particular production company such as XYZ for a career. In addition, sitcom writers all perform essentially the same "job," so a hierarchy of jobs and their relative worth is not an issue. As we will explain next, there *is* a hierarchy of job titles and pay levels, but this reflects what is essentially a system of paying higher salaries for more skills and role mastery within the same job class.

Skill-Based Pay. This dimension deals with the issue of an organization's paying employees for acquiring additional job-relevant skills as opposed to paying strictly for the job performed. As we explained in Chapters 3 and 4, skill-based pay is considered to be a new and innovative approach to compensation. However, these plans have been around for a long time.[5] For example, the crafts have long made the distinction between the apprentice, journeyman, and master. This recognizes differences in skill level, even though the journeyman and master may perform essentially the same tasks over long periods of time. Similarly, teachers have traditionally been paid on the basis of educational level achieved.

At XYZ Productions, writers are paid higher salaries and also provided with new job titles for each year they work on an XYZ show. These salaries and titles are negotiated with XYZ executives by the writers' agents. This system essentially involves paying higher wages for a writer's developing more effective skills as a writer and team member, similar to the apprentice-to-journeyman progression in the crafts. When a writer moves to a different production company and television show, he or she typically continues this upward progress in title and salary. Given the competitive nature of the business, writers who do not maintain and enhance their skills will not continue to be employed in the industry.

As shown in Figure I4–1, XYZ's writers might hold seven different job titles, depending on where they are in their careers, beginning with the term writers and progressing to the executive producers, who are typically the head writers. Progression through these job titles and higher pay levels reflects writers' increased mastery of their roles as comedy writers, writing team members, and all-around contributors to the production of successful television comedies. This salary progression contributes to XYZ's ability to retain talented sitcom writers on its successful shows.

FIGURE I4–1. Hierarchy of job titles for sitcom writers.

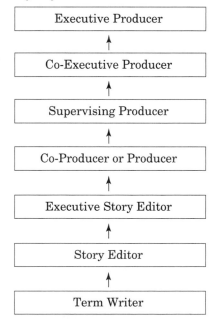

305

*ILLUSTRATION FOUR
Human Resource
Systems for Project
Development
Teams*

306

PART FOUR
Designing Human
Resource Systems
for Specific
Business
Situations

Seniority-Based Pay. As we explained in Chapter 3, seniority-based pay plans make sense when there is a need to promote company loyalty and commitment. Long-term employment also allows employees to acquire company-specific knowledge and skills.

Seniority-based pay does not make sense for sitcom writers. At XYZ Productions, as elsewhere in the television industry, writers are not expected to maintain an entire career within the company; thus, company loyalty and commitment are not important. Writers' skills are also not particularly company-specific. Writers are paid handsomely for their skills in contributing to a successful show, usually on a relatively short-term basis. These writers move regularly from show to show and to different production companies as they progress in their careers. As reported earlier, writers do negotiate for higher salaries for each year they work in the industry. However, these increases reflect payment for enhanced skills as writers and for overall mastery of their role, not as payment simply for seniority.

Benefit Flexibility and Benefit Level. Given that attracting talented sitcom writers is a crucial HRM objective for XYZ Productions, the use of benefit flexibility to assist in employee attraction seems sensible. However, the Writers Guild plays a key role in benefits, and in fact administers television writers' benefits. Employers contribute 6.5 percent of gross income to the health fund and 6.5 percent to the pension plan for writers. Members may choose various benefit options to fit their needs. This approach is appropriate in that company loyalty is not important for sitcom writers, whose careers typically involve movement from firm to firm at a rapid rate.

Benefit level for sitcom writers is an example of labor relations constraints in HR systems. Because the benefits provided to XYZ's sitcom writers are determined by the Writers Guild, the only option possible for the competitive level of benefits for XYZ and every other company in the industry is to meet the market.

The Staffing System

In this section we first describe a recommended staffing system for hiring sitcom writers at XYZ Productions. Then we will proceed to discuss the key attributes of the staffing system.

In describing a recommended staffing system for television sitcom writers, as in describing a total HR system for these professionals, we must acknowledge a dilemma. Although our intent is to recommend a set of HRM practices that promote key employee behaviors—an "ideal" set of practices—we must also be realistic in recognizing the constraints imposed by the culture of the organization and that of the industry in which the organization is embedded. The people who manage and work for a television production company typically work in an extremely informal culture. This informality pervades the workplace, including everything from dress styles to time schedules to styles of workplace interaction. As mentioned previously in this illustration, HRM practices are also much more informal than in most other industries. One might observe that compared to other industries, the television industry "has a long way to go" in the use of systematic HRM practices, especially staffing practices. Thus, in our attempt to be **realistic,** we will recommend a somewhat more modest set of staffing practices for XYZ Productions than for other illustrations in this part of the book. Nevertheless, these recommended practices would be a notable step beyond the informal processes used today by firms such as XYZ.

307

ILLUSTRATION FOUR
Human Resource
Systems for Project
Development
Teams

Recall that the labor market includes large numbers of professionals who are interested in positions as sitcom writers for television production companies. To secure work on a particular show, these writers' agents submit the writers' spec scripts to XYZ executives. The first step in the recommended hiring process for sitcom writers would be a thorough **assessment of the spec script.** The assessment of a spec script would be conducted by at least two evaluators, including an XYZ executive and the show's executive producer, or head writer, in order to produce a more reliable overall decision. This assessment is a type of work sample of a writer's **scriptwriting skills** and a partial assessment of **creativity,** which are two of eight key KSAs for sitcom writers. An actual sample of the work can be contrasted with a predictor, such as a measure of one's *aptitude* to be trained for the work.[6] XYZ strives to hire directly from the labor market writers who already possess the skills to construct a high-quality comedy script. By far the largest number of applicant rejections would be expected to occur at this step in the staffing system. We must also acknowledge that getting a spec script into the hands of an XYZ executive and then having the script evaluated is a formidable hurdle for the applicant. We could describe this as a major barrier to one's **opportunity** to display one's knowledge, skills, and abilities (see Chapter 2). Writers must be well "networked" in the industry, including association with agents who know the executives at major production companies.

The second step in the process would be a procedure commonly used in the industry: telephone contact with **references.** Most of these references would be executives or executive producers for companies that employed the applicant as a sitcom writer previously. Because the television industry is widely known to be characterized by close-knit networks of personal relationships, the XYZ executive would, in many cases, be contacting a reference who is a personal friend (and very likely a former colleague). Although reference checks are informal procedures, we recommend that a standard set of open-ended questions be asked of each reference, for purposes of consistency.

The third step in the recommended staffing system would be applied to a small number of remaining applicants and is the most systematic from the standpoint of measurement: a **structured behavioral interview.** This interview can serve as a work sample for the oral communication skills dimensions and would also tap into the remaining key attributes of effective sitcom writers reported earlier in this chapter: team orientation, sensitivity, behavioral flexibility/openness to feedback, stamina and energy, and stress tolerance. The structured interview process would serve as a key method for assessing what is commonly seen as crucial for XYZ's sitcom writers: the fit

308

*PART FOUR
Designing Human
Resource Systems
for Specific
Business
Situations*

of the applicant with the XYZ culture. The structured interview process would follow the recommendations of Campion, Pursell, and Brown:[7]

1. Use job analysis to generate interview questions.
2. Ask the same questions of each applicant.
3. Anchor the rating scales using examples.
4. Use several interviewers as a panel to record and rate answers.
5. Use a consistent procedure for all applicants.

As an example of behavioral interview questions for sitcom writers, consider the dimension "team orientation." For this dimension, the panel might ask questions such as the following:

What have you found satisfying and dissatisfying about your previous work in teams?

Could you give examples of when your ideas and preferences have differed from those of your work group, and how you handled it?

Our recommended procedure would involve a standard set of questions for each of the five dimensions, generating behavioral information and examples from each applicant. A standard scoring procedure for each dimension and for a total interview score would be developed and used by the panel of interviewers. The panel would likely include an XYZ executive, the executive producer (head writer), and a supervising producer (also a writer). Figure I4–2 summarizes this recommendation.

We now turn to discussion of staffing system attributes and the application of these attributes to sitcom writers at XYZ Productions.

Career System Orientation. This component of the staffing system focuses on the extent of use of "promotion from within" versus openness to hiring from the external labor market at all levels.[8] For sitcom writers, XYZ Productions is clearly **external**-labor-market oriented. The most talented writers for a show must be hired from the labor market for positions ranging from term writer (entry level) up to and including executive producer. As

FIGURE I4–2. The staffing sequence for XYZ's sitcom writers.

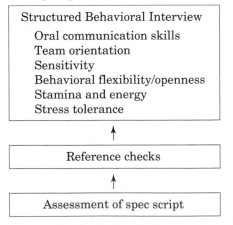

discussed earlier, the television industry is characterized by frequent job-hopping of writers from company to company. Writers' contracts for specific XYZ shows rarely exceed a two-year term.

309

ILLUSTRATION FOUR
Human Resource
Systems for Project
Development
Teams

This career system, under which writers have operated for many years, represents what has recently been labeled the "protean" career.[9] The protean career is shaped by the individual rather than the organization and is characterized by movement through a number of different organizations and roles. The protean career is now becoming the norm for employees in many industries.

Potential versus Achievement Orientation. This attribute pertains to the use of sponsored versus contest mobility for the company's career system. The **sponsored** approach includes early identification of talent, accompanied by specialized training and socialization for high-potential candidates.[10] The **contest** approach involves identifying those with proven achievement records and current possession of the knowledge, skills, and abilities for higher level positions. Given that sitcom writers do not expect to maintain their careers within one organization, an **achievement** orientation (contest mobility) is clearly the appropriate approach. Writers take responsibility for their own skills improvement and socialization within the industry, developing these attributes across a number of different production companies and television shows.

Organizational Fit. In hiring sitcom writers should XYZ Productions seek right types, who fit the company culture and who share common values with current writers on the team? Alternatively, should XYZ seek to purposely hire some non–right types to create a more diverse team of professionals?[11] XYZ's writers work long hours under intense pressures; effective teamwork and a good fit in the room with fellow writers are mandatory. It follows that one could argue for the hiring of right types at XYZ.

On the other hand, we believe that a more compelling argument can be made for the hiring of **non–right types** at XYZ. More attention to diversity and the hiring of non–right types would not only provide equal employment opportunities but could also enhance the creative output of XYZ's teams of writers. In this vein, we would point out that Cox has cited several streams of research that confirm the notion that deliberate establishment of heterogeneous teams can promote creativity and innovation.[12] We also note that the television industry is notorious for a lack of gender, ethnic, and racial diversity in the employment of writers and other professionals. This lack of diversity is likely to constrain the creativity of the product as well as the product's acceptability to diverse viewing audiences. In addition, we recommend that the company enthusiastically work with the Writers Guild's Department of Employment Access, which, as noted earlier, administers programs to enhance the employment opportunities for women, minority, over-40, and disabled writers.

Exit Orientation. This attribute of the staffing system pertains to the level of job security the company attempts to provide to employees. The

310

*PART FOUR
Designing Human
Resource Systems
for Specific
Business
Situations*

company might attempt to promote stability and loyalty by providing job security. Conversely, a company might emphasize turnover and restructuring, in order to retain only those employees with a critical set of skills. Clearly, XYZ Productions falls into the latter category in the employment of sitcom writers. As discussed throughout this illustration, sitcom writers are frequent jobhoppers who develop their careers across firms. No loyalty to the company is expected by the firms or the writers. The company is looking for writers with a particular set of skills to work on a short-term contract for a show; in a sense, XYZ creates a new organization (or subunit) for each new show which goes into production.

Training and Development

Skill Orientation. Skill orientation relates to whether employee training should focus on fairly narrow functional and technical skills or instead on acquisition of broad general skills such as communication, problem-solving, or conflict resolution skills. Remember that XYZ expects to be able to select highly skilled scriptwriters from the large pool of writers in the labor market; thus, training is not a key human resource activity for the company. Training for writers in the television industry tends to be self-directed, informal, on-the-job training—if it exists at all. Certainly writers, over time, should become more effective in communicating and interacting with team members. However, opportunities for the most *systematic* skill development pertains to the writers' regular receipt of feedback on scripts (from fellow writers, directors, actors, and executives) and the resulting sharpening of their scriptwriting skills over time. Thus, for sitcom writers at XYZ Productions, the **technical skills orientation** is most appropriate. These scriptwriting skills are developed by what could be labeled an intensive process of feedback, coaching, and peer mentoring.

Training Method Orientation. This dimension pertains to the distinction between formal, on-the-job, classroom-style training and off-the-job training methods. Clearly, everything about the work of sitcom writers and the work environment at XYZ points to the use of informal, on-the-job training and coaching.

Career Pathing. Should a company offer clearly defined career paths and formal career planning programs, or is the career management process informal and dependent on self-initiated mentoring and networking relationships? Because sitcom writers develop their careers by rapidly changing jobs across production companies, there is little value in a company such as XYZ Productions developing formal career pathing. Writers (and their agents) take personal responsibility for mentoring, networking activities, and receiving career opportunities.

Formal Succession Planning. Given the short-term nature of a comedy writer's employment with a particular production company, formal succession planning for writers would not appear to make sense for XYZ Productions.

311

*ILLUSTRATION FOUR
Human Resource
Systems for Project
Development
Teams*

Skills Inventories. The informal nature of the work environment and the short-term tenure of comedy writers in a particular company create a situation in which maintaining systematic skills inventories makes little sense for XYZ.

The Performance Measurement System

Measurement Type. Some organizations choose to follow a "process" orientation to performance measurement, whereas others focus on bottom-line "results." In addition, measurement can be at the individual, work team, or organizational level. In a sense, XYZ can and does use process-oriented feedback to sitcom writers (on both an individual and a group basis) about the way a script and a television show are completed. This detailed feedback, provided on a day-to-day basis, is quite informal, as opposed to systematic and formalized. Given the constraints of the work and the culture, a systematic performance measurement system would likely not be feasible. The most objective measurement and the most important measures for XYZ are clearly **results-oriented** measures, including ratings of XYZ's shows on the network and success at selling shows into syndication. These measures, of course, are organization-level measures of performance.

Measurement Scope. The issue here is whether XYZ should measure performance in a unidirectional and hierarchical fashion or in a multi-directional fashion, such as 360 degree feedback. As discussed in this illustration, XYZ's comedy writers do receive input on their scripts from multiple sources, including fellow writers, producers, actors, and network executives. We would not go so far as to label this a 360 degree feedback system, but we believe that a somewhat more formal multidirectional feedback process would be a good idea for XYZ.

CONCLUSION

We have now completed our discussion of a recommended HR system for the job class of television sitcom writer, as illustrated by the writers at XYZ Productions. Using Staw's terminology as explained in Chapter 9,[13] our system could be considered a **group-oriented** system in that much of the work is organized around the team of writers working together "in the room." Activities such as the hiring of a writer who is appropriate for the writing team and the culture, the skill development of the writers, and the feedback and mentoring processes have a strong group-oriented nature. However, some aspects of the HR system are **organizationally oriented.** For example, the overall success of XYZ's show is the product of many types of professional employees—the entire organization. The show's being sold into syndication generates royalties for XYZ's writers. We summarize our prescribed HR system for XYZ Productions in Table I4–1.

312

PART FOUR
Designing Human
Resource Systems
for Specific
Business
Situations

TABLE I4–1. Sitcom Writers at XYZ Productions:
Recommended HR System

Pay Level

Lag	Lead the market
Meet	
Lead	

Pay at Risk

None	Moderate; long-term basis (royalties)
Moderate	
Extensive	

Performance-Contingent Pay

Individual	No
Team	
Organization	

Job Pricing

Internal equity	External equity
External equity	

Skill-Based Pay

Yes	Yes
No	

Seniority-Based Pay

Yes	No
No	

Benefit Flexibility

Yes	Yes; administered by Writers Guild
No	

Benefit Level

Lag	Meet
Meet	
Lead	

Career System

Internal	External
External	

Candidate Preference

Potential	Achievement
Achievement	

(Continued)

TABLE I4–1. *(Concluded)*

313

ILLUSTRATION FOUR
Human Resource
Systems for Project
Development
Teams

Organizational Fit

Right types	Diversity
Diversity	

Exit Orientation

Security	Managed turnover
Managed turnover	

Skill Orientation

Technical	Technical
General	

Training Method

Informal/on-the-job	Informal/on-the-job
Formal/classroom	

Career Pathing

Yes	No
No	

Formal Succession Planning

Yes	No
No	

Skill Inventories

Yes	No
No	

Measurement Type

Results	Results
Process	

Measurement Scope

Traditional	360 degree
360 degree	

ENDNOTES

1. All data concerning the Writers Guild provided by Cheryl Rhoden, Assistant Executive Director, Writers Guild, personal communications, April 4 and 7, 1997.
2. G. T. Milkovich and J. M. Newman, *Compensation* (Burr Ridge, IL: Richard D. Irwin, 1996).

314

PART FOUR
Designing Human
Resource Systems
for Specific
Business
Situations

3. T. A. Mahoney, "Multiple Pay Contingencies: Strategic Design of Compensation," *Human Resource Management* 28 (1989), pp. 337–47.

4. Milkovich and Newman, *Compensation,* p. 207.

5. Mahoney, "Multiple Pay Contingencies."

6. P. F. Wernimont and J. P. Campbell, "Signs, Samples, and Criteria," *Journal of Applied Psychology* 52 (1968), pp. 372–76.

7. M. A. Campion, E. D. Pursell, and B. K. Brown, "Structured Interviewing: Raising the Psychometric Properties of the Employment Interview," *Personnel Psychology* 41 (1988), pp. 25–42.

8. J. A. Sonnenfeld and M. A. Peiperl, "Staffing Policy as a Strategic Response: A Typology of Career Systems," *Academy of Management Review* 13 (1988), pp. 588–600.

9. D. T. Hall and P. H. Mirvis, "The New Protean Career: Psychological Success and the Path with a Heart." In D. T. Hall & Associates (eds.), *The Career Is Dead— Long Live the Career* (San Francisco: Jossey-Bass, 1996), pp. 15–45.

10. J. E. Rosenbaum, *Career Mobility in a Corporate Hierarchy* (New York: Academic Press, 1984).

11. T. Cox, *Cultural Diversity in Organizations: Theory, Research and Practice* (San Francisco: Berret-Koehler, 1994).

12. Ibid.

13. B. M. Staw, "Organizational Psychology and the Pursuit of the Happy/Productive Worker," *California Management Review* 28 (1986), pp. 40–53.

ILLUSTRATION 5

Human Resource Systems for Marketing Managers in Asia

We continue in this illustration our focus on a company composite, a targeted class of jobs, and relevant environmental and strategic factors. Again, we start with an overview of the factors presented in Figure 1–1 of Chapter 1, using it as a conceptual map. We discuss business strategy, technology, and the organization of work processes, and then we discuss the key employee behaviors and KSAs required for the targeted job class. We then discuss the relevant labor market and the legal context. Finally we prescribe a set of HRM practices, consisting of choices from the 19 dimensions of an HR system presented in Chapter 3.

THE TARGETED JOB CLASS: COUNTRY BRAND DIRECTOR

The job class we focus on in this illustration is "country brand director" for a global company producing footwear, apparel, and equipment for sports. This global firm markets "the brand"—meaning all the company's products sold—around the world. The country brand directors play a crucial role in enacting the firm's vision, strategies, and objectives in marketing the firm's products on a global basis. A country brand director is responsible for the brand in a particular country. These managers must understand the company's global vision and business plan and develop a unique way to implement this vision in the particular country of operation, including the allocation of marketing dollars and resources. Country brand directors must maintain a keen awareness of consumer attitudes and preferences for sports products in the particular country, and they must define consumer opportunities for sales growth. They must build and maintain networks of contacts around their countries, including retailers, athletes, and others in the world of sports. The country brand director must also perform "people management" functions, including building a marketing team and creating a brand vision for the country with the team.

In the remainder of this illustration we focus on the job class of country brand director, describing a hypothetical company we will call Fleet Sports, Inc. We first describe the company's basic strategy and technology, the relevant labor market for country brand directors in the firm's Asia Pacific region, and the legal context for HRM practices. We then prescribe an HR system that would be expected to promote the key behaviors required of high-performing country brand directors.

316

PART FOUR
Designing Human
Resource Systems
for Specific
Business
Situations

BUSINESS STRATEGY, TECHNOLOGY,
AND WORK PROCESSES: FLEET SPORTS, INC.

Fleet Sports, Inc., is one of the world's major sports companies; its distinctive logo is familiar to people of many nations. Fleet produces and markets sports footwear, apparel, and equipment. The firm's headquarters is in a major city in the United States; its four marketing regions include the United States, European, Latin American, and Asia Pacific regions. The company produces and markets a wide variety of sports products in 20 different countries and a diversity of cultures. The Asia Pacific region consists of operations in the People's Republic of China (including Hong Kong), Taiwan, Japan, South Korea, New Zealand, Australia, Singapore, and Malaysia. Each of these countries has its own favorite sports, and thus provides a unique set of consumer preferences for sports products.

Fleet sees its mission as striving to be "the world's best" sports company. Its overall business strategy includes having the strongest possible brand positioning in *every* market in which it operates, with a minimum of a 50 percent market share per country. Fleet aspires to grow its market every year by finding market opportunities in every country. The firm also wishes to keep the brand "strong," aligned with its unique identity and global brand definition, on a long-term basis. The country brand directors, the majority of whom are nationals from the country in which they work, are key players in Fleet's implementation of this vision and strategy.

For the country brand directors, a key aspect of implementing Fleet's strategy is participation in the **annual planning cycle** for each fiscal year. This planning cycle is begun one and one-half years in advance of implementation. It involves a series of steps, all of which require coordination of the global (companywide) vision/plans with the vision/plans for a particular country. Groups of managers at the global, regional, and country levels get together several times each year to discuss, formulate, and monitor the components of this planning cycle. The country brand director has primary responsibility for the planning components at the level of the individual country. The components of the overall planning cycle (see Figure I5–1) include

1. Determining which aspects of Fleet's **global vision** are being fulfilled or not fulfilled in the country.
2. Formulating the **country marketing plan** in coordination with the global and regional plans.
3. Formulating for the country a **brand business plan,** aligned with the global and regional plans.
4. Formulating a **human resource plan** for the country twice each year, taking into account the need to relocate people into or out of the country in fulfilling the business plan.
5. Formulating **budgets** for the country.

As mentioned earlier, this planning cycle is initiated one and one-half years in advance of implementation. Additional discussions are held at the end of

FIGURE I5–1. Annual planning cycle for country brand directors.

317

ILLUSTRATION FIVE
Human Resource
Systems for
Marketing
Managers
in Asia

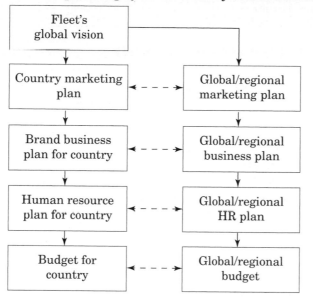

a fiscal year and just before implementation of the new plan, to monitor progress and see if the new year's plan is "ready to go." The annual planning cycle is a key component of the work of the country brand director, establishing a set of goals for the director and his or her team for the year.

Another responsibility of the country brand director is building an effective marketing team, including activities such as recruiting, hiring, developing, and rewarding team members. These team-building activities for the director go on constantly, as team members regularly enter and leave assignments in the particular country. Each team ranges from 5 to 20 members, depending on the country, and includes those holding the positions of product line manager, retail manager, category (e.g., soccer) marketing manager, and communication manager (e.g., advertising, public relations). The director and the team make considerable efforts to evaluate the Fleet brand's strengths and weaknesses in the minds of local consumers, define consumer opportunities for growth, create a brand vision for their country, direct the allocation of marketing dollars and resources, and constantly observe changes in the marketplace.

The country brand director must also be able to achieve these goals while coping with the sometimes volatile economic environment in Asia, as was the case with the severe economic downturn experienced in a number of Asian countries in the late 1990s (see Figure I5–2).

The country brand director spends much time in travel, both within and outside the country. Inside the country the director keeps in touch with consumers, especially by talking with retailers, athletes, attendees at sports events, and other parties involved in the sports world. The director also attends numerous meetings with other Fleet managers at the global, regional, and country levels, for a variety of purposes, such as completing next year's planning cycle.

318

PART FOUR
Designing Human
Resource Systems
for Specific
Business
Situations

FIGURE I5–2. The volatile economic environment faced by Fleet's Asian country brand directors.

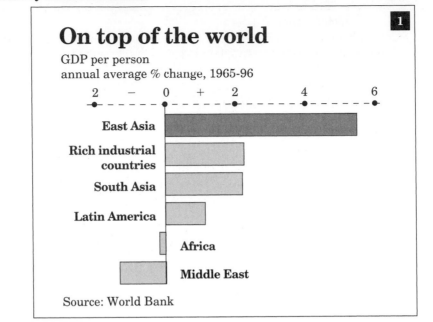

On top of the world

GDP per person
annual average % change, 1965-96

Source: World Bank

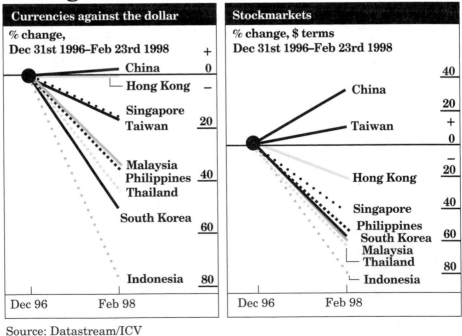

Falling stars

Source: Datastream/ICV

Source: "A Survey of East Asian Economies," *The Economist,* March 7, 1998, p. 4.

KEY EMPLOYEE BEHAVIORS AND CRITICAL EMPLOYEE ATTRIBUTES

319

ILLUSTRATION FIVE
Human Resource
Systems for
Marketing
Managers
in Asia

Country brand directors play a critical role at Fleet Sports in fulfilling the firm's global vision, strategies, and marketing objectives. The extremely challenging work requires a diverse set of knowledge, skills, and abilities. Managers at Fleet have recently invested considerable effort to determine the most critical employee attributes separating the successful from the unsuccessful country brand directors. As part of this process, for example, managers carefully observed the "top performers" among directors in an attempt to discover their special attributes. Similarly, the company looked at those directors who appeared to be poorly matched to their work. As a result of this process of observation and discussion, the company recently identified eight key qualities for country brand directors:

1. **Brand builder:** Successful country brand directors must understand the foundation of the Fleet brand and possess a firm vision of what the brand can be. They must be able to think of creative strategies to achieve the goals set for the brand in their country.

2. **Inspired by consumers:** Directors must have a strong curiosity about consumers, be able to pick up on consumer trends, and see opportunities to expand the market.

3. **Sports foundation:** Country brand directors must derive personal excitement from sports. They must have a strong feel for the "authenticity" of the brand—that is, an understanding that the brand adds value to the sport, and is not about "fashion."

4. **Understands product innovation:** Directors must know how to create new product concepts from a thorough understanding of the consumer. They must understand how the brand can enhance the performance of athletes, what new products to make to drive business, and what to add to products to add value, not superficial bells and whistles.

5. **Visionary and risk-taker:** Country brand directors must be creative and innovative as well as willing to develop and maintain a unique point of view.

6. **Communicator:** These managers must be skilled in all aspects of communication, including listening, writing, and speaking, whether in large groups, small teams, or one-to-one.

7. **Action orientation:** Country brand directors need to have drive and energy, to be assertive, to have a strong impulse to "follow through," to be persistent, and to be excited by change.

8. **Leadership orientation:** These managers must be able to lead local teams and global teams—to "lead across an ocean" in terms of relationships with other groups and managers around the world.

Thus, Fleet Sports, Inc., has determined that country brand directors must have the ability, motivation, and opportunity to perform a number of key behaviors. Next, we discuss the labor market and legal context in which Fleet

320

PART FOUR
Designing Human
Resource Systems
for Specific
Business
Situations

operates in the Asia Pacific region, and we specify a recommended HR system for country brand directors.

LABOR-MARKET ATTRIBUTES

As mentioned previously, in the Asia Pacific region Fleet employs country brand directors in eight different countries. The majority of these managers are nationals from the countries in which they work. This approach provides a number of advantages to the firm, such as fulfilling the need for a thorough knowledge of the preferences of local consumers of sport products. The firm strives to provide, whenever possible, opportunities for nationals in its eight Asia Pacific countries. But in general, Fleet finds it quite a challenge to identify managers who possess the necessary competencies for the country brand director positions.

The size and quality of the pools of applicants vary widely across the countries in which Fleet operates (see Chapter 10 for a discussion of global labor-market issues). The size of the labor pool appears to be linked to the popularity of the Fleet brand among the population in the particular country. In some countries (including the United States) the Fleet brand is well known, the firm has a stellar reputation, it is seen as a high-prestige employer, and the name generates large pools of applicants. In other countries the firm's brand is not as well known and recruiting is more difficult. Not surprisingly, the firm tends to rely heavily on referrals and networking for finding quality applicants.

In addition, given the scarcity of suitable applicants and the requirement of many different kinds of KSAs for success, Fleet wishes to retain and develop on a long-term basis the people it hires. Compatible with this philosophy, some of the new country brand directors are promoted into the positions from other marketing positions within the company.

THE LEGAL ENVIRONMENT

This global company must, of course, abide by a large number of labor and employment laws and regulations. For each of the 20 countries in which it operates, Fleet has a country human resource manager who must stay informed of the labor and employment laws in that country, whether these requirements involve discrimination issues, vacations and other benefits, constraints on termination, or collective bargaining regulations. As discussed in Chapter 11, legal constraints on human resource policies and practices vary from country to country. This variability extends even to such practices as more, less, or no employee testing for selection, according to legal restrictions in a particular country. Overall, the legal environment for Fleet Sports, Inc., presents a complex challenge because of the global nature of the firm.

ILLUSTRATION FIVE
Human Resource
Systems for
Marketing
Managers
in Asia

As in the previous illustrations in Part IV of the book, we develop our idealized HR system for Fleet Sport's Asia Pacific country brand directors following the structure provided in Chapter 3. Each of the 19 dimensions associated with the HRM domain statement is considered and then summarized in a table. We begin by considering attributes of the reward system.

Reward and Compensation Practices

Pay Level. The decision of whether to lead, lag, or match the market for country brand directors is an important question for Fleet Sports. Remember that the size and quality of applicant pools vary considerably across countries in the Asia Pacific region. Thus, one might suggest that Fleet should lead the global going rate in the market in some countries, match in others, and even lag in some countries. This policy would probably be inadvisable, however, because of Fleet's tendency to rotate managers from country to country. Serious pay equity problems within the company could result. As discussed earlier, in general, Fleet finds it a challenge to identify managers who possess the necessary competencies for the country brand manager position. Thus, setting a pay level slightly above the average pay offered by companies competing for similar kinds of marketing managers is likely to be the most appropriate approach.

Pay at Risk. Should performance of country brand directors be linked to a source of direct supplemental income? We believe this would be a powerful incentive for managers at Fleet Sports. These managers must be highly motivated as the key players in strengthening the brand in their respective countries and finding ways to grow Fleet's market every year. We suggest that as much as 20 percent of a country brand director's pay might be at risk each year.

Performance-Contingent Pay. As we have discussed numerous times in this book, linking pay increases to level of performance enhances an employee's motivation to perform, by raising instrumentality perceptions (see Chapter 2). The issue here is whether the pay–performance link should be at the individual, group, or organizational level.

For Fleet's Asia Pacific country brand directors, the appropriate level for the pay–performance link would appear to be the **organizational** level. This is because these managers must work closely with their own country's marketing team to evaluate the brand's strengths and weaknesses in the minds of consumers, define opportunities for growth, create and maintain a brand vision for their country, and perform other critical activities. Moreover, the country brand directors must coordinate with other managers at the country, regional, and global levels to successfully create and maintain the Fleet brand's unique identity and global brand definition. They must

322

PART FOUR
Designing Human
Resource Systems
for Specific
Business
Situations

also coordinate with these other levels to formulate and monitor the components of the planning cycle. Thus, considering the amount and level of coordination and teamwork required, it makes sense to link at least some of the supplemental rewards for country brand directors to organization-level indexes such as country, region, and global profitability and market share.

Recall that Fleet Sports strives to hire country brand directors who are nationals from the Asian countries in which Fleet operates. Managers from these countries are likely to hold group-oriented, "collective" values as opposed to "individualistic" values, and thus to prefer group or organization-oriented rewards (see Chapter 10).

Internal versus External Job Pricing. A focus on external job pricing is a focus on paying what other companies pay employees performing similar jobs, as explained in Chapters 3 and 4. In contrast, an internal job pricing focus emphasizes within-company fairness in the relative pay of jobs, often referred to as "internal equity." External job pricing and equity are certainly crucial for country brand directors, in maintaining Fleet's efforts to attract outstanding managers who possess critical competencies for the work. However, internal equity would also be somewhat important, in that country brand directors work closely with staff in a variety of other distinct positions, such as product line managers, retail managers, and category managers. To maintain the ability to attract and retain quality managers, and to maintain employee morale and good working relations on teams, base pay differentials among these positions must be systematically determined and carefully monitored. But considering everything, we believe that for country brand directors external job pricing would be the most important consideration.

Skill-Based Pay. As we have discussed in previous chapters, skill-based pay is considered to be a new and innovative approach to rewarding employees in which pay increases correspond to increases in either the depth or breadth of skills acquired by employees.[1] Skill-based pay increases make sense for country brand directors at Fleet Sports. As we reported earlier, these managers must possess and constantly work to enhance their knowledge about the culture, customers, and changing consumer preferences in their country of operation. In addition, they must develop their skills in planning, and also in staffing, motivating, and developing a country marketing team. These managers must be in a state of constant learning, and Fleet Sports wants to be a "learning organization."[2]

Given the importance of these managerial competencies, or skills, it makes sense to systematically reward managers who acquire or improve on their competencies. This approach might involve each country brand director's selecting a few key competencies annually (e. g., conflict resolution, delegation) and generating an **individual development plan** for enhancing each competency. A team of fellow managers could provide periodic coaching and feedback throughout the subsequent year. At the end of the evaluation period, the director would be evaluated as to his or her success in enhancing the particular competency. This level of success would be a key input into the country brand director's salary increase.

Seniority-Based Pay. Seniority-based pay plans make sense when there is a need to promote company loyalty and long-term commitment and when there is a need to encourage cooperative and team-oriented behavior. These conditions are present for Fleet's country brand directors. However, other components of the pay system and the overall HR system should serve as substitutes for seniority-based pay in achieving these goals. For example, these managers are rewarded for their success in building and maintaining their country marketing teams, both in terms of the variable pay system and the rewards for developing their managerial competencies. Other aspects of the recommended HR system related to the career system (to be discussed later) are also designed to enhance loyalty and tenure with Fleet Sports. Thus, Fleet Sports should be able to instill loyalty and commitment, while also targeting pay and pay increases toward enhancing profits, market share, and the development of enhanced managerial competencies.

Benefit Flexibility and Benefit Level. Fleet Sports attempts to obtain its country brand directors for the Asia Pacific region from the pool of nationals in the eight countries in the region. The overall labor market in the region is quite heterogeneous in terms of benefit preferences. Thus, a highly flexible, or cafeteria, benefit plan would fit the unique needs of managers from diverse cultures.[3] The ability to provide benefits that managers from the various countries most desire should enhance the overall attractiveness (valence) of this form of compensation. An attractive benefit package can enhance Fleet's ability to attract and retain country brand directors.

Given Fleet Sports' desire to attract outstanding people with a diverse set of qualities, it makes sense to offer a total package of benefits which is at least as high as competitors in the labor markets. It may even make sense to offer benefits slightly **above** the market, given the firm's unique vision and values, which reflect a strong orientation toward health and fitness. This orientation is an important value in the Fleet culture, and it is strongly held by employees.

The Staffing System

In this section we first specify a recommended staffing system for hiring country brand directors for the Asia Pacific region at Fleet Sports. We will then discuss the key attributes of the staffing system.

As we reported earlier, Fleet Sports finds it a challenge to identify in the relevant labor markets outstanding candidates who possess the key qualities required of country brand directors. Fleet also finds that the number and quality of applicants vary from country to country in the Asia Pacific region, based largely on the popularity of the brand in the particular country.

The first step in the recommended staffing process, along with the assessment of **résumés** and applications, would be the assessment of written and telephone **references.** In this process, some preliminary information could be gathered relevant to a number of the eight key qualities for country brand directors, such as the candidate's sports foundation, leadership orientation, and action orientation. It is important that the information gained be

323

ILLUSTRATION FIVE
Human Resource
Systems for
Marketing
Managers
in Asia

324

*PART FOUR
Designing Human
Resource Systems
for Specific
Business
Situations*

candid and provided by a knowledgeable source. References appear to have a moderate level of validity in predicting job success.[4]

The next step in the recommended staffing system would be a **structured behavioral interview.** The interview could serve as a type of work sample for assessing the applicant as a communicator, and would also tap into the remaining key attributes for country brand directors, as identified by Fleet Sports: brand builder, inspired by consumers, sports foundation, understands product innovation, visionary and risk-taker, action orientation, and leadership orientation.

As we have suggested in other illustrations in this section of the book, the structured interview process can have strong predictive validity and would follow the recommendations of Campion, Pursell, and Brown,[5] including

1. Using job analysis to generate interview questions.
2. Asking the same questions of each applicant.
3. Anchoring the rating scales using examples.
4. Using several interviewers in a panel to record and rate answers.
5. Using a consistent procedure for all applicants.

As an illustration of behavioral interview questions for country brand directors, consider the attribute leadership orientation. For this dimension, the panel might ask the following questions:

Could you provide examples of when you have introduced new ideas to a team and influenced them to accept the ideas?

What have you found to be most rewarding and most frustrating in your work with teammates?

It is clear from considering the eight key qualities for country brand directors that these managers' innovation and creativity are crucial to their overall success. See, for example, the definitions of the brand builder, understands product innovation, and visionary and risk-taker qualities. Thus, the final step in our recommended staffing process is a direct **assessment of the creativity** of the applicants for country brand director positions.

Yale psychologist Robert Sternberg recently developed a conceptualization of creativity that seems especially relevant for the success of country brand directors at Fleet Sports.[6] In this conceptualization, **creativity** is defined as the ability to come up with new ideas. Creativity includes three aspects of intelligence: creative, analytical, and practical intelligence. **Creative intelligence** is one's ability to go beyond what is given to generate new and interesting ideas. It is related to seeing connections other people might not see. **Analytical intelligence** is the ability to analyze ideas, solve problems, and make decisions. Creative people must have a special ability to evaluate their own ideas, to consider their implications, and even to test them. Finally, **practical intelligence** is the ability to translate theory into practice and to take abstract ideas and turn them into practical accomplishments.[7] The highly creative person has a balance of these three skills.

We recommend that Fleet Sports, working with a qualified consultant, develop a **test of creativity** for country brand directors. (The test would likely be valuable for other marketing positions also.) The test might include some of the components reported in the work discussed above. Sternberg has reported the development of tests of creativity in the domains of writing, drawing, advertising, and science. Subjects are asked to be imaginative and are given as much time as needed to produce their work. The creativity test in the advertising domain, for example, asks people to generate television commercials for two products for which they are not likely to have seen a commercial. A panel of judges then rates the creativity of the resulting products. Sternberg has also demonstrated that these panels show high inter-rater agreement—that is, raters tend to agree on what is creative or not creative.

325

ILLUSTRATION FIVE
Human Resource
Systems for
Marketing
Managers
in Asia

We believe that a test of creativity could be developed in-house at Fleet, and that it could provide significant gains in the hiring of country brand directors possessing the kinds of creative and innovative qualities believed to be crucial for success. This test of creativity would be the final step in the staffing process for country brand directors in the Asia Pacific region (see Figure I5–3).

We now discuss the staffing system attributes introduced in Chapter 3 and the application of these attributes to country brand directors at Fleet Sports, Inc.

Career System Orientation. The career system for country brand director would tend to be internally focused. Although these managers are typically hired directly from the outside, it is also likely that they would be groomed over time to move into higher level marketing positions at Fleet. Fleet Sports would want to strive to identify people who have the potential for positions of higher responsibility and to promote from within. This approach would be an important part of its IIRM philosophy of inspiring loyalty and commitment from marketing managers. However, Fleet might

FIGURE I5–3. The staffing sequence for Fleet Sports's country brand directors.

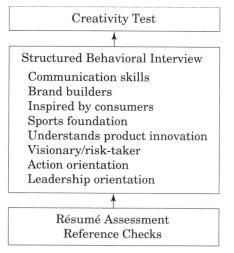

326

PART FOUR
Designing Human
Resource Systems
for Specific
Business
Situations

occasionally want to bring in outsiders for higher level marketing positions, in order to promote fresh ideas, creativity, and innovation in its marketing operations.

Potential versus Achievement Orientation. As we have discussed previously, the sponsored mobility approach (versus contest mobility) involves early identification of talent, accompanied by specialized training and socialization for high-potential candidates. Fleet Sports might benefit most from a sponsored mobility strategy, which would reflect the efficiencies of specialized socialization and training for these challenging positions. A program of succession planning would be part of this process, in which Fleet managers identify those who may be five to seven years away from readiness to assume a country brand director position as well as positions at higher levels.

Organizational Fit. Should Fleet Sports seek right types, who will fit the company culture and who are similar to current managers? Should the company follow the opposite approach and explicitly seek non–right types to take advantage of workforce diversity and enhance creativity and innovation?[8] Although some level of organizational fit is necessary for country brand directors, we would recommend efforts to hire non–right types. A diversity of managers' backgrounds, approaches, and styles should enhance the critical activities of sensing changes and trends in consumer preferences and introducing necessary innovations to keep the brand strong. The hiring of country brand directors who are nationals from the eight countries of the Asia Pacific region ties in with these efforts for obtaining a diverse workforce.

Exit Orientation. To be consistent with Fleet Sports's desire to develop a loyal and committed cadre of managers, Fleet should provide a reasonable level of job security. The literature of downsizing suggests that too much job insecurity stands in the way of innovative thinking and behavior.[9]

Of course, changes in the economic environment, such as the serious economic crises experienced by some countries in the Asia Pacific region in the late 1990s, might be expected to have an effect on Fleet's security-oriented exit strategy. The effect, however, could be complex. We might expect a decline in sales to consumers in these countries. But currency devaluation could also result in lowered labor costs for Fleet Sports. We would expect Fleet to be able to maintain its strategy regarding employee exit.

Training and Development

Skill Orientation. Skill orientation is the issue of whether to focus training on narrow functional and technical skills or on broader skills. Our previous description of the work and skill requirements for country brand directors suggests that the training of these managers would tend toward an emphasis on fairly broad, general skills, such as communication and presentation skills, conflict resolution, team building, delegation, and problem analysis and solution.

Training Method Orientation. This dimension pertains to the relative emphasis in training on-site or off-site. Although Fleet's country brand directors would probably receive some training in both settings, the majority of the training would be on-site. An important part of the role of country brand director is the developing and implementing (annually) of an **individual development plan,** pursued in the context of one's work, and including on-the-job coaching and feedback.

327

ILLUSTRATION FIVE
Human Resource
Systems for
Marketing
Managers
in Asia

Career Pathing. Fleet Sports makes at least some effort to define paths and provide developmental experiences for the position of country brand director and beyond. These career paths help employees to identify the knowledge, skill, and ability requirements for positions at higher levels. This information assists aspiring country brand directors as they formulate their individual development plans to help achieve their career goals.

Formal Succession Planning. Fleet Sports does conduct succession planning. Managers meet on a regular basis to identify early career managers as replacements for current managers in key positions, including country brand director. As part of this planning, managers discuss their junior colleagues on an individual basis, including skills, experiences, strengths, weaknesses, and developmental needs. This practice appears to be appropriate given Fleet's emphasis on maintaining an internal career system and on encouragement of employee loyalty and commitment.

Skills Inventories. Computerized skills inventories would be highly recommended for Fleet's marketing managers, including country brand directors, and would provide an effective source of support for Fleet's career pathing and succession planning programs. Such an inventory would list education level and type, information about past work experiences and assignments, performance appraisal data, and information about career objectives and preferences.

The Performance Measurement System

Measurement Type. For country brand directors monitoring both bottom-line results outcomes and also the processes for individual managers is important. The results outcomes would focus on market share in the particular country and an overall assessment of the strength of the brand in the country. The process-oriented measures would consist of performance rating scales tapping into behaviors reflecting the eight key dimensions of performance. These dimensions were identified by the firm as separating the outstanding from the poor performers in the country brand director positions. These eight dimensions were discussed earlier in this illustration.

Measurement Scope. As discussed in Chapters 3 and 7, the traditional approach to performance measurement is unidirectional and hierarchical, consisting solely of supervisors evaluating their employees. In contrast, many organizations have recently begun to experiment with "multidirectional" performance measurement, one form being 360 degree

328

*PART FOUR
Designing Human
Resource Systems
for Specific
Business
Situations*

appraisal. This multidirectional approach would be recommended for Fleet's country brand directors. First, these managers could be evaluated and receive valuable feedback from their peers and higher level managers with whom they work at the country, regional, and global levels. They could also receive feedback from their subordinates on the country marketing team, and even from customers. This approach should work quite well, given the many interactions and relationships that are part of the role of the country brand director. Multidirectional feedback would also be compatible with the use of individual development plans and competency-based salary increments, which we discussed earlier in this illustration.

CONCLUSION

We have now completed our overview of a recommended HR system for country brand directors at Fleet Sports, Inc. The prescribed system illustrates the use of Staw's individual, group, and organizational management systems in a way that makes sense for an integrated HR system for this particular job class.[10] The prescribed system for country brand directors and others on the marketing team reflects a distinct **group-oriented** flavor, in that, for example, much of the work is organized around the country marketing team, and group members provide performance feedback to each other. The prescribed system also reflects something of an **organizational** orientation. Country brand directors must coordinate with managers at the country, regional, and global levels for much of the important decision making relevant to marketing at Fleet Sports. We have advocated linking some of these managers' supplemental rewards to organization-level indexes such as country, region, and global profitability and market share. Our prescribed HR system is summarized in Table I5–1.

TABLE I5–1. Country Brand Directors at Fleet Sports: Recommended HR System

Pay Level

Lag	Slightly above market midpoint
Meet	
Lead	

Pay at Risk

None	Moderate
Moderate	
Extensive	

Performance-Contingent Pay

Individual	Organization
Team	
Organization	

(Continued)

TABLE I5–1. *(Continued)*

329

ILLUSTRATION FIVE
Human Resource
Systems for
Marketing
Managers
in Asia

Job Pricing

Internal equity	Both internal and external equity
External equity	

Skill-Based Pay

Yes	Yes
No	

Seniority-Based Pay

Yes	No
No	

Benefit Flexibility

Yes	Yes
No	

Benefit Level

Lag	Meet or lead
Meet	
Lead	

Career System

Internal	Internal
External	

Candidate Preference

Potential	Potential
Achievement	

Organizational Fit

Right types	Diversity
Diversity	

Exit Orientation

Security	Security
Managed turnover	

Skill Orientation

Technical	General
General	

Training Method

Informal/on-the-job	Emphasis on informal
Formal/classroom	

Career Pathing

Yes	Yes
No	

(Continued)

330

PART FOUR
*Designing Human
Resource Systems
for Specific
Business
Situations*

TABLE I5–1. *(Concluded)*

Formal Succession Planning	
Yes No	Yes

Skill Inventories	
Yes No	Yes

Measurement Type	
Results Process	Results and process

Measurement Scope	
Traditional 360 degree	360 degree

ENDNOTES

1. E. E. Lawler and G. E. Ledford, "Skill-Based Pay: A Concept That's Catching On," *Personnel,* September 1985, pp. 30–37; G. T. Milkovich and J. M. Newman, *Compensation* (Burr Ridge, IL: Richard D. Irwin, 1996); and J. R. Schuster and P. K. Zingheim, *The New Pay: Linking Employee and Organizational Performance* (New York: Lexington Books, 1992).

2. P. M. Senge, *The Fifth Discipline: The Art and Practice of the Learning Organization* (New York: Currency/Doubleday, 1990).

3. R. M. McCaffery, *Employee Benefit Programs: A Total Compensation Perspective* (Boston: PWS-Kent Publishing Company, 1992).

4. G. T. Milkovich and J. W. Boudreau, *Human Resource Management,* 8th ed. (Burr Ridge, IL: Richard D. Irwin, 1997).

5. M. A. Campion, E. D. Pursell, and B. K. Brown, "Structured Interviewing: Raising the Psychometric Properties of the Employment Interview," *Personnel Psychology* 41 (1988), pp. 25–42.

6. R. J. Sternberg, *Successful Intelligence: How Practical and Creative Intelligence Determine Success in Life* (New York: Simon & Schuster, 1996).

7. Ibid., pp. 191–92.

8. T. Cox, *Cultural Diversity in Organizations: Theory, Research and Practice* (San Francisco: Berret-Koehler, 1994).

9. W. F. Cascio, "Downsizing: What Do We Know? What Have We Learned?" *Academy of Management Executive* 4 (1993), pp. 35–51.

10. B. M. Staw, "Organizational Psychology and the Pursuit of the Happy/Productive Worker," *California Management Review* 28 (1986), pp. 40–53.

Index